Addictions

Concepts and Strategies for Treatment

Edited by

Judith A. Lewis, PhD

Professor and Director of Curriculum and Instruction
Illinois Addiction Training Center
Governors State University
University Park, Illinois

An Aspen Publication®
Aspen Publishers, Inc.
Gaithersburg, Maryland
1994

Library of Congress Cataloging-in-Publication Data

Addictions: concepts and strategies for treatment/edited by Judith A. Lewis
p. cm.
Includes bibliographical references and index.
ISBN 0-8342-0563-7
1. Substance abuse—Treatment. 2 . Compulsive behavior—Treatment.
I. Lewis, Judith A., 1939- .
[DNLM: 1. Behavior, Addictive—Therapy. 2. Substance abuse—therapy. WM 176 A2243 1994]
RC564.A2916 1994
616.86'06—dc20
DNLM/DLC
for Library of Congress
94-9159
CIP

The editors have made every effort to ensure the accuracy of the information herein, particularly with regard to product selection, drug selection and dose. However, appropriate information sources should be consulted, especially for new or unfamiliar procedures or drugs. It is the responsibility of every practitioner to evaluate the appropriateness of a particular opinion in the context of actual clinical situations and with due consideration to new developments. The editors and the publisher cannot be held responsible for any typographical or other errors found in this book.

Editorial Resources: Ruth Bloom
Jill A. Berry

Library of Congress Catalog Card Number: 94-9159
ISBN: 0-8342–0563-7

Printed in the United States of America

1 2 3 4 5

Table of Contents

Contributors

Andrea G. Barthwell, MD
Medical Director
Interventions
Chicago, Illinois

Linda J. Beckman, PhD
Professor
California School of Professional
    Psychology—Los Angeles
Alhambra, California

Peter Bishop
Department of Psychology
DePaul University
Chicago, Illinois

Gregory A. Blevins, PhD
Alcohol and Drug Abuse
    Science Program
Governors State University
University Park, Illinois

Peter J. Bokos, PhD
President and Chief Executive Officer
Interventions
Chicago, Illinois

Blake S. Bowden
Department of Psychology
DePaul University
Chicago, Illinois

Linda Paulk Buchanan, PhD
Licensed Psychologist
Clinical Director
Atlanta Center for Eating Disorders
Atlanta, Georgia

Jon Carlson, PsyD, EdD, ABPP
Distinguished Professor
Psychology and Counseling Division
Governors State University
University Park, Illinois
Director and Psychologist
Wellness Clinic
Lake Geneva, Wisconsin

Robert K. Conyne, PhD
Professor of Counseling
University of Cincinnati
Cincinnati, Ohio

Michael D'Andrea, EdD
Associate Professor
Department of Counselor Education
University of Hawaii
Honolulu, Hawaii

Judy Daniels, EdD
Assistant Professor
Department of Counselor Education
University of Hawaii
Honolulu, Hawaii

James H. Fisher, PhD
Assistant Professor and
    Research Director
Substance Abuse Intervention
    Programs
School of Medicine
Wright State University
Dayton, Ohio

Virginia Gil, MA
Senior Case Manager
UCLA/Matrix Institute on Addictions
UCLA Drug Abuse Research Center
University of California at
    Los Angeles
Los Angeles, California

H. L. "Lee" Gillis, PhD
Associate Professor of Psychology
Coordinator, Adventure Therapy
    Masters Program
Department of Psychology
Georgia College
Milledgeville, Georgia
Coordinator, Therapeutic
    Programming Team
Project Adventure, Inc.
Covington, Georgia

Gwen Grams
Department of Psychology
DePaul University
Chicago, Illinois

Charles F. Gressard, PhD
Associate Professor, Counselor
    Education
School of Education
The College of William & Mary
Williamsburg, Virginia

Albert L. Hasson, MSW
Administrative Director
UCLA/Matrix Institute on Addictions
UCLA Drug Abuse Research Center
University of California at
    Los Angeles
Los Angeles, California

F. James Hoffmann, PhD
Associate Professor
Counselor Education Program
School of Education
Augusta College
Augusta, Georgia

Lawrence K. Horberg, PhD
Horberg, Schlesinger and Associates
Department of Psychiatry and
    Behavioral Sciences
Northwestern University
    Medical School
Chicago, Illinois

James A. Inciardi, PhD
Professor and Director
Center for Drug and Alcohol Studies
University of Delaware
Newark, Delaware

Howard Isenberg, MA
Project Director
NorthEast Treatment Centers
Wilmington, Delaware

Leonard A. Jason, PhD
Professor
Department of Psychology
DePaul University
Chicago, Illinois

Karen A. Koch, MHS
Certified D.A.R.E. Instructor
Mentor Officer Instructor
Oak Forest Police Department
Oak Forest, Illinois

Katherine Kohner
Department of Psychology
DePaul University
Chicago, Illinois

Ann W. Lawson, PhD
Associate Professor, Marriage and
    Family Therapy
United States International University
Private Practice
Center for Family and
    Psychological Studies
San Diego, California

Gail S. Lederer, MSW
Family Institute of Westchester, Inc.
Mount Vernon, New York
Private Practice
Greenwich, Connecticut

Linda Lesondak
Department of Psychology
DePaul University
Chicago, Illinois

Robert A. Lewis, PhD
The Norma Compton Distinguished
    Professor of Family Studies
Department of Child Development
    and Family Studies
Family Research Institute
Purdue University
West Lafayette, Indiana

Jill Littrell, PhD, MSSW
Clinical Psychologist,
    Clinical Social Worker
Georgia State University
Atlanta, Georgia

Dorothy Lockwood, PhD
Associate Scientist
Center for Drug and Alcohol Studies
University of Delware
Newark, Delaware

Steven S. Martin, MA
Associate Scientist
Center for Drug and Alcohol Studies
University of Delaware
Newark, Delaware

**E. Michael Maslar, MA, PhD
    Candidate**
Case Management Supervisor
Interventions
Chicago, Illinois

Eric E. McCollum, PhD
Assistant Professor and
    Clinical Director
Marriage and Family Therapy
    Program
Department of Family and
    Child Development
Virginia Tech University–
    Northern Virginia
Falls Church, Virginia

Martin C. McGurrin, PhD (Dec.)
Assistant Professor of Psychology
Center for Mental Health Policy and
    Services Research
Departrnent of Psychiatry
University of Pennsylvania
Philadelphia, Pennsylvania

Cheryl L. Mejta, PhD
Director
Illinois Addiction Training Center
Professor and Department Chair
Governors State University
University Park, Illinois
Research Consultant,
  Case Management
Interventions
Chicago, Illinois

Judith H. Mickenberg, MSW, ACSW
Study Supervisor, Case Management
  Study
Interventions
Chicago, Illinois

Lynn D. Miller, MA
Doctoral Candidate
Program of Educational Leadership
  and Integrated Services
Honorarium Professor
Division of Counseling Psychology
  and Counselor Education
University of Colorado at Denver
Denver, Colorado

Carol L. Naylor, MHS
Adjunct Faculty/Therapist
Governors State University
University Park, Illinois

Thorana S. Nelson, PhD
Associate Professor and Director
Marriage and Family Therapy
  Program
Department of Family and Human
  Development
Utah State University
Logan, Utah

Zane O'Keefe
Case Manager
UCLA/Matrix Institute on Addictions
UCLA Drug Abuse Research Center
University of California at
  Los Angeles
Los Angeles, California

David A. O'Donnell, MHS
Unit Manager
Aunt Martha's Youth Service Center
Treatment/Prevention Programs
Park Forest, Illinois

Margaret E. Pechota
Department of Psychology
DePaul University
Chicago, Illinois

Steven B. Porkorny
Department of Psychology
DePaul University
Chicago, Illinois

Elena Quintana
Department of Psychology
DePaul University
Chicago, Illinois

Richard C. Rapp, MSW
Instructor and Project Director
Substance Abuse Intervention
  Programs
School of Medicine
Wright State University
Dayton, Ohio

Doreen Salina, PhD
Department of Psychiatry and
   Behavioral Sciences
Northwestern University
   Medical School
Chicago, Illinois

Cindy Sangerman
Department of Psychology
DePaul University
Chicago, Illinois

Stephen E. Schlesinger, PhD
Horberg, Schlesinger and Associates
Department of Psychiatry and
   Behavioral Sciences
Northwestern University
   Medical School
Chicago, Illinois

Harvey A. Siegal, PhD
Professor and Director
Substance Abuse Intervention
   Programs
School of Medicine
Wright State University
Dayton, Ohio

Cindy A. Simpson, EdS
Director
Project Adventure, Inc.
Covington, Georgia

Len Sperry, MD, PhD
Professor of Psychiatry and
   Preventive Medicine
Medical College of Wisconsin
Milwaukee, Wisconsin

Patricia Stevens-Smith, PhD
Director, Marriage and Family
   Training Program
University of Colorado at Denver
Denver, Colorado

Stephanie Taylor
Department of Psychology
DePaul University
Chicago, Illinois

Terry S. Trepper, PhD
Professor of Psychology
Director, Family Studies Center
Marriage and Family Therapy
   Program
Department of Behavioral Sciences
Purdue University Calumet
Hammond, Indiana

Joseph H. Wagner, MPH
Instructor and Research Associate
Substance Abuse Intervention
   Programs
School of Medicine
Wright State University
Dayton, Ohio

Joseph L. Wetchler, PhD
Associate Professor and Director
Marriage and Family Therapy
   Program
Family Studies Center
Department of Behavioral Sciences
Purdue University Calumet
Hammond, Indiana

Introduction

This book has been designed to bridge the gap between theory and practice in the addictions field. It includes both general, state of the art reviews of current treatment practices and brief descriptions of innovative concepts and strategies.

Part I, **Conceptualizing Addictions**, provides an overview of concepts related to addictions. Both Stevens-Smith, in her chapter on contextual issues, and Conyne, in his review of primary prevention, provide the kind of broad, interdisciplinary perspective that is suggested in the opening chapter.

Part II, **Treating Addictions**, reviews effective strategies for addressing varying addictions and includes chapters on alcohol problems, drug abuse treatment, weight control, eating disorders, smoking cessation, and pathological gambling. The final chapter in this section, "Maintaining Change in Addictive Behaviors," addresses relapse prevention strategies across addictions.

The Pharmacology of Addictions is discussed in Part III, which encompasses chapters on the pharmacology of alcohol, nicotine, and other drugs.

Because family approaches have become widely recognized as treatments of choice for addictions, Part IV, **Families and Addictions**, includes six chapters devoted to this topic. Lawson's overview is followed by descriptions of exciting ideas and strategies that are currently being used in practice.

Additional innovations are described in Part V, **Innovations in Thought and Practice**. Part VI, **Additional Resources**, provides an annotated bibliography of recent work in the addictions field.

Acknowledgments

Many people played important roles in creating and carrying out this project. My special thanks go to the authors who contributed chapters to this book. All of them were chosen because they were known for excellence and all of them lived up to their reputations. Special note should be taken of the chapter by Martin McGurrin, who passed away before he could see this publication come to fruition. His final contribution to the literature on pathological gambling, which appears in this book, exemplifies the high quality that characterized his work throughout his long career.

As this book developed and changed over time, Aspen Publishers, Inc., continually demonstrated a true commitment to the project. The talented staff at Aspen, including Stephen Zollo, Acquisitions Editor; Loretta Stock, Assistant Acquisitions Editor; Jill A. Berry, Associate Editor; and Laura Smith, Book Production Manager; worked long and hard to ensure the quality of the final publication. The quality of the book also owes a great deal to the insightful comments and suggestions offered by reviewers, including Jon Amundson, Dr. Loretta Bradley, and Dr. F. James Hoffmann. At Governors State University, two graduate assistants in the addictions program, Jan Engle and D. J. Andrews, provided valuable help in carrying out the ongoing work involved in coordinating the efforts of so many contributors. As always, thanks go to the students and clients who always make sure that our work is based in reality.

Judith A. Lewis

Part I

Conceptualizing Addictions

Chapter 1

The Addictive Process

Judith A. Lewis

The addictive *process* may be centered on any one of a number of specific *objects* (Donovan, 1988). Whether the focus of an individual's addiction is on food or alcohol, gambling or cocaine, nicotine or heroin, the characteristics of addiction remain similar, with addictive behaviors showing commonalities across a variety of compulsive involvements.

> A defining characteristic of addictive behaviors is that they involve the pursuit of short-term gratification at the expense of long-term harm. Often the person is quite aware of damaging consequences, and has resolved to control or abandon the addictive behavior, yet time and again returns to the old familiar pattern. (Miller & Rollnick, 1991, p. ix)

The mere fact that behaviors remain intractable despite the evidence that they are dangerous to self and others gives an indication of the complexity of the addictive process. Despite this complexity, however, we can make some tentative generalizations about addictions. Each of these generalizations helps to point the way toward appropriate directions for treatment.

Any addiction is likely to have biological, psychological, and social components that must be taken into account in order for prevention or treatment to be successful.

A biopsychosocial perspective (Donovan, 1988; Engel, 1977; Schwartz, 1982) recognizes that biological, psychological, and social factors affect all aspects of an individual's health. These factors intertwine in the development of any addiction, regardless of the object. It is generally recognized that biological factors, including genetic vulnerability, play a definite role in the development of alcohol problems (Department of Health and Human Services, 1987) and a possible role in addictions to other drugs. Yet substance use behaviors are also strongly affected by cultural, environmental, interpersonal, and intrapersonal factors (Leigh, 1985). In contrast, non-drug-related compulsions, such as gambling, tend to considered by most people to be psychological or social in nature, but they too are affected by physiology. As Donovan (1988) points out,

3

> The ability to induce dependence, tolerance, craving, and withdrawal is not inherent only in those drugs defined as addictive . . . . It appears difficult for an individual to discontinue any behavior associated with repeated physiological changes or arousal, whether this change is induced by psychoactive drugs or not. (p. 6)

Multiple systems interact both in the development of addictive behaviors and in their treatment. Chiauzzi (1991) suggests that biological, psychological, and social systems hold the key to the individual's ability to maintain positive long-term changes. Recovery can be jeopardized by biological risk factors, including neurological impairments and cravings resulting from cue reactivity; by psychological risk factors, including beliefs and expectancies as well as skill deficits; and by social factors, such as negative life events, poverty, victimization, unemployment, peer group pressures, and family issues.

If each of these components plays a part in forming and sustaining problems, each should also play a part in treatment. For instance, alcohol and drug dependence can be addressed most effectively if the short-term focus on detoxification and interruption of drinking and drug use patterns is joined by longer-term efforts to deal with psychosocial concerns. The general life areas that might be addressed through multidimensional treatment include the following (Lewis, Dana, & Blevins, 1994):

- resolving or avoiding legal problems
- attaining financial stability
- attaining marital or family stability
- setting and meeting career development goals
- setting and meeting educational goals
- improving assertiveness and other social skills
- enhancing physical health and fitness
- learning more effective methods for coping with stress
- developing problem-solving and decision-making skills
- learning relaxation skills
- learning to recognize and express feelings
- adapting to work or school situations
- developing social support systems
- increasing involvement in recreational and social pursuits
- dealing with psychological issues such as depression or anxiety
- increasing general feelings of self-esteem

The first focus of treatment should be on the addictive behaviors themselves, but lasting changes require an emphasis on the context within which these behaviors occur.

Addiction should be viewed in terms of a continuum, rather than in terms of a dichotomy between addiction and nonaddiction.

We have established that addictions involve short-term gratification at the expense of long-term health and well-being and that addictions are also characterized by the affected individual's return to familiar patterns despite efforts to change. Clearly, these kinds of things happen to everyone in the course of a normal life. Each of us has had the experience of indulging in behaviors that are not in our long-term best interests. Each of us has lived through the ordeal of failing to live up to our self-expectations. The pain of addiction involves taking these experiences to an extreme that falls beyond what most of us anticipate. Addiction may differ from normal life difficulties largely in degree rather than in kind.

How, then, can we make a distinction between addictive and nonaddictive behaviors? The attempt to create such a dichotomy may be an oversimplification that fails to recognize the complexity of the addictive process and that interferes with meeting the needs of affected individuals. If we think in terms of a continuum between addiction and nonaddiction, we come to realize that there is no clear dividing line between normal and addictive behaviors. Behaviors clustered near either pole of the continuum are readily diagnosable, but behaviors at other points along the continuum are not. People should be able to receive help in changing behaviors that are problematic for them, whether or not they perceive that these behaviors fall into an addiction category.

Consider, for example, the diagnosis of "alcoholism." Many people assume that they can readily diagnose the disease of alcoholism and that this diagnosis points the way toward a particular course of treatment. In fact, alcoholism is a multivariate syndrome that affects people in different ways. Use of a dichotomous diagnosis—identifying the individual as either alcoholic or nonalcoholic—may actually interfere with treatment planning by masking individual differences.

An either/or diagnosis leads inexorably to a generalized, diffuse treatment package that at worst may be ineffective and at best may meet the needs only of individuals with serious, chronic, long-standing substance abuse disorders. Insistence on a clear diagnosis of "alcoholism," for instance, drives away from treatment many people who are not necessarily dependent on alcohol but who could benefit from assistance in dealing with life problems associated with incipient alcohol abuse. If we wait until people are ready to accept a diagnosis of "alcoholism" or "addiction," we may be missing an opportunity to help people when they are best able to benefit from counseling. (Lewis et al., 1994)

Rather than insisting that a client accept the "addict" label, we should respond to the client's needs as they are presented. An assessment of the individual's current situation can provide an indication of where the client stands on the continuum between addictive and nonaddictive behaviors. Someone whose behaviors have clearly become destructive and uncontrolled can benefit from help, but so can a person whose problems are less severe. We can be more effective by helping clients identify and alter behaviors that interfere with their life goals than by insisting on labels that they may not be ready to accept.

Ambivalence regarding change is characteristic of the addictive process.
We should not find it surprising that people dealing with addictions are often "trapped by ambivalence" (Miller & Rollnick, 1991, p. ix). Short-term pleasure and satisfaction are inherent in the addictive experience, which "provides a potent and rapid means of changing one's mood and sensations because of both direct physiological effects and learned expectations" (Donovan, 1988, p. 7). These immediate effects are sufficiently strong to override rational thoughts about long-term consequences. Additionally, people who have been involved with addictive behaviors over a long period of time may feel fear, anxiety, and uncertainty about the prospect of a life without the addictive object.

This ambivalence about the possibility of change is often interpreted as "denial" or "resistance." Yet there is no evidence that denial is an inherent characteristic of addicts. Miller and Rollnick (1991) suggest that the aggressive confrontations frequently used to "break down denial" actually increase the client's defensiveness. They suggest, instead, using the *motivational interview*, which attempts to balance the scales in favor of positive change through accurate empathy and respect. The counselor provides advice and assessment data, but clients are encouraged to accept final responsibility for their decisions about treatment.

We can also help clients to work through their ambivalence by dealing in a nonjudgmental fashion with their perceptions of the costs and benefits of change. For example, Saunders, Wilkinson, and Allsop (1991) describe a two-session motivational intervention with heroin addicts in treatment. During these sessions, clients discuss their perceptions of the good things and the less good things about heroin, explore their satisfactions and dissatisfactions with their current lifestyles, and address the benefits and costs of continuing drug-use behavior or attempting to change. The counseling process culminates with a discussion of the client's future intentions. Curry and Marlatt (1987) also discuss the importance of helping clients organize their thoughts concerning the commitment to change. Their alcohol-affected clients use a decision matrix format to identify the positive and negative consequences of drinking, considering both immediate and delayed consequences. It is important that counselors remain objective and nonjudgmental as clients work through these steps. Otherwise, clients might keep their very real ambivalence hidden and unexamined.

The individual's sense of self-efficacy is a key factor in recovery from addiction.
The sense of *self-efficacy* (Bandura, 1982) can be defined as an individual's belief that he or she can solve a problem, accomplish a task, or function successfully in a particular area. A client with a positive sense of self-efficacy is one whose judgment about the possibility of success is affirmative. A person who lacks this confidence may tend to avoid challenges or to give up quickly when obstacles are encountered. In contrast, a person with a strong belief in the possibility of success is likely to perform in accordance with this belief. Thus, self-efficacy perceptions translate into actions.

> The higher the level of perceived self-efficacy, the greater the performance accomplishments. Strength of efficacy also predicts behavior change. The stronger the perceived efficacy, the more likely are people to persist in their efforts until they succeed. (Bandura, 1982, pp. 127–128)

Regardless of their level of knowledge or skill, people dealing with any kind of problem are most likely to be successful in finding and acting on solutions when their sense of self-efficacy is high.

Self-efficacy is an especially important variable when the problem being addressed is an addiction. The addictive process itself tends to lessen both self-esteem and self-efficacy. Many addicts describe repeated efforts to change their behaviors without success. This kind of history engenders a sense of the impossibility of change. Unfortunately, the expectation of failure frequently acts as a self-fulfilling prophecy. Clients who believe that they cannot control their addictive behaviors tend to live out this belief in practice.

Purposeful strategies can be used to focus treatment on the enhancement of self-efficacy. Annis (1986), in a discussion of treatment for alcohol problems, says that "a client's judgment of perceived self-efficacy will be the best predictor of future drinking behavior in high-risk situations" (p. 410). Once the client's self-efficacy judgments regarding specific situations have been assessed (Annis, 1982), action can be taken to bring about improvements. Methods that can enhance self-efficacy include the following (Annis, 1986; Curry & Marlatt, 1987; Marlatt & Gordon, 1985):

• Give the client performance assignments for addressing high-risk situations.
• Order the performance tasks from less difficult to more challenging.

- Prepare the client for success in carrying out assignments by using skill training, including modeling and behavior rehearsal.
- Deal directly with the client's cognitions, in addition to his or her behaviors.

Self-efficacy enhancement methods are especially important for increasing the likelihood that desired behaviors will be maintained and relapses prevented.

In dealing with addictive behaviors, the potential for relapse is always a pressing concern.

As Prochaska, DiClemente, and Norcross (1992, p. 1104) point out, "relapse is the rule rather than the exception with addictions." The model developed by Prochaska and his colleagues recognizes that people attempting to change addictive behaviors tend to move through several stages of change: precontemplation, when they do not yet intend to change their behaviors; contemplation, when they become aware that their behaviors are problematic and begin to consider the possibility of change; preparation, when they begin to make minor modifications in their behaviors; action, when successful behavior changes occur; and maintenance, when gains are preserved and relapse is prevented. Because relapse is the norm in addictive behaviors, people do not proceed through these stages in a linear pattern. Most people recycle through earlier stages several times before they achieve long-term maintenance.

Gorski (1990) also views relapse as a stage phenomenon. Once clients have been treated, they move toward stabilization and acute withdrawal; early recovery, when they begin to learn how to live without the drug; middle recovery, when they attempt balanced lifestyles; late recovery, when they can address long-term psychological and family issues; and maintenance, during which they need to remain permanently attentive to the possibility of relapse.

Gorski's model suggests that relapse prevention requires that clients build appropriate skills at each stage. The extensive research on relapse prevention conducted by Marlatt and Gordon (1985) also emphasizes the importance of skill development. Marlatt and Gordon recognize that clients attempting to change addictive behaviors are placed at risk by such situations as negative emotional states, interpersonal conflicts, and social pressures. When individuals have sufficient skills for coping with high-risk situations, their sense of self-efficacy is enhanced and the likelihood of a relapse is lessened. When people find themselves unable to cope with high-risk situations, their self-efficacy decreases and their expectancies for positive outcomes of drug use are heightened. Guilt, dissonance, conflict, and perceived loss of control increase the probability of relapse.

As these models make clear, successful treatment of addictive behaviors requires that attention be paid to long-term maintenance of change from the outset of therapy. Clients are most likely to achieve successful maintenance when they carefully monitor their behaviors, assess which situations are risky for them, and take pains to learn the coping skills they need. Relapse prevention training should be an integral part of treatment.

Despite the commonalities among addictive processes, we need to remember that individualization is the key to treatment effectiveness. Each client brings to the recovery process his or her own strengths and deficits, goals and needs. Addictions treatment can now offer enough alternatives among empirically validated approaches to make true choice possible.

REFERENCES

Annis, H. M. (1982). *Situational Confidence Questionnaire.* Toronto: Addiction Research Foundation.

Annis, H. M. (1986). A relapse prevention model for treatment of alcoholics. In W. R. Miller & N. Heather (Eds.), *Treating addictive behaviors: Processes of change* (pp. 407–434). New York: Plenum.

Bandura, A. (1982). Self-efficacy mechanism in human agency. *American Psychologist, 37,* 122–147.

Chiauzzi, E. J. (1991). *Preventing relapse in the addictions: A biopsychosocial approach.* New York: Pergamon.

Curry, S. G., & Marlatt, G. A. (1987). Building self-confidence, self-efficacy and self-control. In W. M. Cox (Ed.), *Treatment and prevention of alcohol problems: A resource manual* (pp. 117–136). New York: Academic Press.

Department of Health and Human Services. (1987). *Sixth special report to the U.S. Congress on alcohol and health* (DHHS Publication No. ADM 87–1519). Washington, DC: U.S. Government Printing Office.

Donovan, D. M. (1988). Assessment of addictive behaviors: Implications of an emerging biopsychosocial model. In D. M. Donovan & G. A. Marlatt (Eds.), *Assessment of addictive behaviors* (pp. 3–48). New York:Guilford.

Engel, G. L. (1977). The need for a new medical model: A challenge for biomedicine. *Science, 196,* 129–136.

Gorski, T. (1990). The CENAPS model of relapse prevention: Basic principles and procedures. *Journal of Psychoactive Drugs, 22,* 125–133.

Leigh, G. (1985). Psychosocial factors in the development of substance abuse and alcoholism. In T. E. Bratter & G. G. Forrest (Eds.), *Alcoholism and substance abuse: Strategies for clinical intervention* (pp. 3–48). New York: Free Press.

Lewis, J. A., Dana, R. Q., & Blevins, G. A. (1994). *Substance abuse counseling: An individualized approach* (2nd ed.). Pacific Grove, CA: Brooks/Cole.

Marlatt, G. A., & Gordon, J. R. (1985). *Relapse prevention.* New York: Guilford.

Miller, W. R., & Rollnick, S. (1991). *Motivational interviewing: Preparing people to change addictive behavior.* New York: Guilford.

Prochaska, J. O., DiClemente, C. C., & Norcross, J. C. (1992). In search of how people change: Applications to addictive behaviors. *American Psychologist, 47,* 1102–1114.

Saunders, B., Wilkinson, C., & Allsop, S. (1991). Motivational intervention with heroin users attending a methadone clinic. In W. R. Miller & S. Rollnick (Eds.), *Motivational interviewing: Preparing people to change addictive behavior* (pp. 279–292). New York: Guilford.

Schwartz, G.E. (1982). Testing the biopsychosocial model: The ultimate challenge facing behavioral medicine? *Journal of Consulting and Clinical Psychology, 50,* 1040–1053.

Chapter 2
Contextual Issues in Addiction

Patricia Stevens-Smith

This chapter examines addictive behavior within the context of today's society. To understand the extent to which drug use and other behaviors have become addictions, it is necessary to examine the context or cultural atmosphere in which they exist. For the purposes of this chapter addictions include not only drugs but a wide range of risky or addictive behaviors, or process addictions, such as eating disorders, gambling, relational disorders, workaholism, and sexual addiction.

Although process addictions are a relatively new phenomenon, the idea of ingesting substances to alter consciousness is not new. Drug use (both medicinal and experimental) and abuse has been in evidence from the beginnings of recorded time. Therefore, this chapter examines a brief history of drugs in society. The following drugs are discussed: alcohol, amphetamines, cocaine, marijuana, opium, and hallucinogens.

A BRIEF HISTORY OF DRUG USE

It has been documented that early cave dwellers drank the juices of mashed berries that had been exposed to airborne yeast. When they found that these produced pleasant feelings and reduced discomfort, they began to intentionally produce this crude wine (Ray & Ksir, 1990). Egyptian records dating back to 300 B.C. give testimony to beer production. Homer's *Iliad* and *Odyssey* both discuss drinking wine, and both Egypt and Rome had a god or goddess of wine. The Bible gives record of Noah as perhaps the first recorded inebriate. In the 15th century the process of distillation was discovered in Europe, so that beverages contained a higher percentage of alcohol. European settlers brought alcoholic beverages in the form of wine, rum, and beer to the United States. Additionally, alcohol has been used consistently throughout history to induce sleep and by physicians to reduce pain. In a 1988 NIDA survey 85% of the households surveyed said they had used alcohol in their lifetime, and 53% said they had used alcohol within the past month. Twelve percent of the U.S. population are estimated to be heavy drinkers (cited in Payne, Hahn, & Pinger, 1991).

Although coca, like alcohol, has been around for thousands of years, the active agent, cocaine, was not isolated until 1857. Freud experimented with cocaine as a cure for depression and used it himself for a period of time. However, when he became aware of the addictive effects, he discontinued use for himself and his patients. In the 20th century, cocaine grew in popularity as it decreased in cost and then became available in the intensified form of "crack." Estimates of regular users today vary from 4 million to 24 million. A recent government report estimates that 2.2 million people in the U.S. are cocaine addicts (U.S. Senate, Committee on the Judiciary, 1990).

Marijuana has been used recreationally and medicinally for many centuries. As late as the 19th century, it was used as an analgesic, a hypnotic, and an anticonvulsant. With the beginning of Prohibition, individuals began to grow or import "pot" as a substitute for alcohol. After Prohibition, its use declined until the 1960s. Marijuana is now the fourth most commonly used drug after nicotine, caffeine, and alcohol. In 1988 *Playboy* reported that the Asthma and Allergy Foundation had examined air samples in Los Angeles. A reported 40% of the pollen came from marijuana plants being grown in the area (cited in Gitlin, 1990).

The Sumerians over 5,000 years ago referred to opium as "the joy plant" and the Egyptians claimed it cured all illnesses but also recognized it as a poison. As early as 1500 B.C. opium was used to quiet crying children. In 129-199 A.D. there are reports of opium cakes being sold in the streets of Rome. In 1729 China found it necessary to outlaw opium smoking. Morphine, a derivative of opium, was freely used in the Civil War and in other wars both for pain and for dysentery. In the last half of the 19th century the United States had a wave of opiate abuse. Opium was brought to America by Chinese laborers who came to work on the railroads. At this time morphine could still be obtained without a prescription and was thought to be nonaddictive. By 1900 it was estimated that 1% of the population was addicted to opiates (Inanba & Cohen, 1991; Payne, Hahn, & Pinger, 1991).

Amphetamines were discovered in 1887 and used in World War II by American, British, German, and Japanese soldiers. After the war, amphetamines were prescribed for depression, weight loss, and heightening of one's capacity for work. Soon it was realized that these capsules could be broken and their contents injected with a needle. Amphetamines also were used to replace cocaine due to the high cost of purchasing cocaine. By 1970, 8% of all prescriptions were for some form of amphetamines (Payne, Hahn, & Pinger, 1991).

A 1985 National Institute of Drug Abuse random survey reported that 10.4% of individuals surveyed between the ages of 10–25 had used an amphetamine or amphetamine-like substance in the past year.

Hallucinogens have been around for about 3,500 years. Central American Indian cultures used mushrooms in their religious ceremonies. In fact, when the New World was discovered, Spanish priests tried to eliminate the use of the "sacred mushrooms." In 1938 the active ingredient that caused hallucinations was isolated for the first time by a Swiss chemist. He was studying a particular fungus in bread that appeared to create hallucinations. The substance he synthesized during this research was LSD (d-lysergic acid diethylamide). Between 1950 and the mid-1970s LSD was well researched by the government. It was believed that LSD could be used to view the psychotic mind and the subconscious mind. It was used in the treatment of alcoholics, cancer patients, and schizophrenics. It was also one of the drugs of choice during the drug epidemic that began in the 1960s (Ciraulo & Shader, 1991; Payne, Hahn, & Pinger, 1991).

This brief overview of the use of drugs indicates that the desire or need to alter one's consciousness has consistently been an element of human experience. Use of substances for this reason has been commonplace throughout history. However, with the beginning of the 1960s the use of substances became much more widespread and insidious. Use and abuse of drugs developed into addiction on a national scale. And in the 1980s process addictions such as eating disorders, gambling, shopping, and relationship addictions became better assessed and understood. These process addictions are often seen in combination with substance abuse.

It is important to determine factors that have contributed to the deleterious growth and acceptance of these addictive behaviors in society. Different theories of addiction are first presented and followed by a review of the familial and societal context of the past 30 years.

THEORIES OF ADDICTION

The term *addiction* has been used mainly in describing alcohol and drug dependency. Until quite recently drug addiction was treated in isolation from the context of societal influences that promote, support, and maintain addictive behaviors. Process addictions such as eating disorders, relationship addictions, and sexual addictions, although seen as a product of 20th-century social forces, have also been treated without attention to this societal context (Peele, 1989).

During the 1930s and 1940s scientists began to study alcohol and alcoholism. In 1952 E. M. Jellinek published an article that proposed a pattern of behavioral and physiological symptoms defining alcoholism as a disease. The disease concept opened the door for the treatment of alcohol abuse. The development of Alcoholics Anonymous in the 1930s by Bill W. also provided a structure for fellowship and support to alcoholics "recovering" from this disease. The disease of alcoholism was considered to be *within* the individual and not the "responsibility" of the individual. This is both the major strength and the major weakness of this model (Marlatt & Gordon, 1985).

A second perspective investigated to explain addictive behavior is that of genetic transmission. According to this theoretical paradigm, individuals are predisposed to addiction due to genetic makeup (Stabenau & Hesselbrock, 1983). Studies of identical twins reared apart have supported the theory of genetic predisposition (Schuckit, 1981).

Addictive behaviors have also been explained psychologically. This model views the individual's use of drugs or participation in addictive behaviors as a means to relieve stress and achieve emotional satisfaction or interpersonal goals (Kellam, Simon, & Ensminger, 1983). Individuals follow a cycle in which the drugs or the addictive behavior is used to deal initially with the psychological discomfort. As the negative effects of the behavior increase, the addictive behavior is used as a means of coping. In many cases, this downward cycle continues. Rosen and Leitenberg (1984) have applied this model to eating disorders. According to this model, the original goal of thinness is considered a positive goal, but the addictive behavior leads to emotional and physical instability. The behavior is increased to deal with the instability, which in turn increases the instability. This leads to an addictive cycle of behavior.

The biopsychosocial model, the most recent paradigm, is used to explain both drug addiction and process addictions, particularly eating disorders (Reiff & Reiff, 1992; Woodside & Shekter-Wolfson, 1991; Zucker & Gomberg, 1986). This model incorporates the genetic, medical, psychological, and sociocultural aspects of addiction.

Although the earlier models partially explained substance use/abuse and the addictive process, they failed to give weight to the most pervasive aspects of our lives: the family and the culture in which the family exists (Cooper, 1989). To understand the reasons why addictive behaviors have developed and flourished in our society, it is imperative to examine both the familial and cultural context supporting these behaviors.

THE CONTEXT OF FAMILY

Over the past 10 years the importance of family in the treatment of addictions has been increasingly emphasized. In fact, today family therapy is considered the treatment of choice for most addictive behaviors (Lewis, 1989). Addictions are viewed as a "family illness," and the belief that dysfunctional family relationships breed addictive behavior is widely accepted (Ackerman, 1987; Woititz, 1983).

The cycle of addictive behavior passed down through generations related to family dysfunction is well documented. Parents who use substances to cope with feelings of anger, intimacy, shame, sadness, stress, or disappointment teach their children dysfunctional mechanisms for coping with life. The children then often use these dysfunctional, nonproductive patterns of behavior to handle problems they face (Schaef, 1986; Woititz, 1983).

The inability to be intimate, to communicate, and to feel safe or loved within these families also creates issues that must be addressed beyond the actual substance use (Cruse, 1989; Potter-Efron & Potter-Efron, 1991). Much of the process addiction behaviors that are now seen result from these "side-effects" of substance abuse in families.

As the treatment of addictions and addictive families has developed over the past years, it has become increasing apparent that family issues cannot be addressed without examining the larger system in which the family exists. Just as the family supports the individual's behavior within that system, society must support the family's behavior in society. It is therefore necessary to consider addictive behaviors and family patterns in the context of the larger system that has supported and maintained these behaviors.

THE CONTEXT OF SOCIETY

In the early 1960s American society was in the process of change. Several significant events were taking place: the civil rights movement, women's liberation, and the Vietnam war. The economy was flourishing. The country was divided, and the prevailing philosophy was one of protest.

During the 1960s and 1970s individual freedom and personal pleasure were given the utmost importance. The women's movement significantly affected the family structure as women moved out of the home into the workplace. The divorce rate soared, creating single parent, female-headed households in alarming numbers (Goldenberg & Goldenberg, 1990).

There was a large population of "baby boomers" who came of age in the '60s. Although previous youth cultures have certainly existed in history, this culture differed from previous ones in four very important ways:

1. In numbers — The youth culture consisted of the "baby boomer" generation. More children were born in the 6 years after 1946 than in the previous 30 years — almost one-third of the population — and these children reached late adolescent and early adulthood in the sixties (Jones, 1981).
2. In money — Because of the prosperity in the economy and the reaction of Depression-age parents to their own poverty, these young people had an unrivaled amount of money available to them. Because of their significant numbers and affluence, they became the center of marketing and advertising attention.
3. In education — College populations grew by over 5 million between 1950 and 1970 (U.S. Bureau of the Census, 1984).

4. In the sexual revolution — The birth control pill was developed in the early sixties. For the first time in history, women could effectively control their reproduction (Gitlin, 1990).

Within this youth culture, drug use flourished, first on the college campuses and then throughout the general society. Drugs were used within the context of cultural norms that included sexual promiscuity (a combination of the effect of the women's movement and the birth control pill), political opposition (the Vietnam war), and the cultural separatism felt by this population. This separatism was demonstrated through hairstyles, dress, music, and language. Marijuana and LSD were the drugs of choice. These drugs were considered spiritually enhancing but also were used to support the philosophy of individual pleasure. Drugs and sex became the foremost symbols of the rebellion against society and society's values.

As the counterculture lost its momentum in the 1970s and the "baby boomers" matured, they moved into mainstream society and carried with them the hedonistic philosophy of the 1960s. Instant gratification began to take different forms. The youth culture that ridiculed possessions and materialism found themselves becoming the most materialistic and externally controlled population in history.

As America continued to prosper, a comfort-and-convenience, consumer-oriented attitude began to develop as a part of our culture. The "buy now, pay later" credit card option was overwhelmingly embraced. Department stores, shopping malls, and supermarkets emerged as means to present the mass quantity of consumer goods being produced. Self-value too often was externalized to what one owned and how one looked. Drug use became a chemical form of instant gratification that complemented the consumer-oriented philosophy. This illicit use paralleled mainstream society's use of licit drugs such as tranquilizers and alcohol.

Because the "baby boomers" continued to be the largest portion of the American population, their philosophy became the predominant one. The trend toward a separate but unequal society, however, was accelerated during this same timeframe. Just as the "baby boomers" continued to prosper, the inner-city neighborhoods continued to decline (Johnson & Muffler, 1992). The family structure also began a significant shift during this period. Families were considered less stable than in previous history. This fact can be attributed to several factors, including the rising divorce rate, an increase in unwed mothers, and the mobility of the family.

During the late 1970s and 1980s the American economy began to decline. The prosperity of the previous years ended. However, the media continued to portray a lifestyle of abundance.

The Role of the Media

Mass media have proven to be pivotal in defining cultural and behavioral norms. The media reflect the values of the society in which they exist. Messages that are presented consistently and pervasively through the mass media about drugs, values, gratification, and body image influence not only the individual's belief system but cultural norms in a significant way.

The media have provided mass-produced images to match society's values. As the media changed to reflect these changing values, they began to advertise "a way of life" rather than a particular product (Gitlin, 1990).

Advertising

Although advertising reaches most of the population, it seems to have a powerful influence on young people. In 1987 a Weekly Reader survey of 500,000 students from grades 2 through 12 indicated that television and movies were the major source of their information that drug use appears to be fun (Burton & Johnson, 1987). Images of rich and attractive people — macho males and thin, beautiful women — have presented a lifestyle that is unattainable by the majority of society. Alcohol, cigarettes, and licit drugs have become a part of this media image. Advertising promises more than the quality of the product. Freedom, security, pleasure, sexuality, comfort, and respectability all can be obtained according to today's advertisements by the simple act of purchasing a particular product. One needs only to examine the $33-billion-a-year diet market, the $20-billion-a-year cosmetic market, and the $300-million cosmetic surgery market to realize the influence of these images on our society (Wolf, 1991).

Magazine and newspaper ads have associated beer drinking with manliness and sexual attractiveness. These same ads have presented an image of women as sexual objects who must maintain a svelte, thin figure to attract a man. One example is an alcoholic beverage advertisement that shows a suggestively clad female standing over the caption "Two fingers is all that it takes" (Jacobson, Atkins, & Hacker, 1983, p. 119).

Football, baseball, and basketball players in our country are idolized. How they live and what they say greatly influence the young in our society. These sports figures are regularly seen in advertisements for alcoholic beverages. Today beer producers are the major sponsors of athletic events. They sponsor tennis, football, auto racing, and speedboat racing. In fact, in a recent year, Anheuser-Busch alone sponsored over 98 professional and 380 college events (Cahalan, 1987). Miller Brewing Company paid $25 million to sponsor the 1988 summer and winter Olympics. In a 1985 report *The Chronicle of Higher Education* stated that advertisements for beer and liquor comprised a large portion of the advertising in campus newspapers — in some newspapers as much as two-thirds (cited in Gerbner, 1990, p. 86).

Over-the-counter drug advertising on television and in print reminds the individual that there is no need to suffer physical or emotional pain. Fast relief, better sleep, a thinner body are all available through a variety of nonprescription drugs. In fact, 10 of the biggest drug companies control the $7-billion-plus nonprescription drug market today, and $1.5 million of this is spent on advertising (Gerbner, 1990).

A cursory examination of clothing, automobile, soft drink, or any number of other product advertisements, both in print and on television, gives an explanation of the intensity of the expectation that women must be thin, beautiful, and sexual to be attractive. When the implicit content of the advertisements is further explored, the thin and sexually attractive body is connected to many other attributes such as success, intelligence, self-worth, independence. For example, a woman may be shown as working, but she is still "beautiful, young, rich, and thin" (Anderson, 1988, p. 28). (Are any of the Virginia Slim models not slim?) These images impact on the growing number of young females who are diagnosed with eating disorders.

Television, Movies, and Popular Music

Drug use, violence, disrespect for authority, and stereotypical images of gender are portrayed through the media of television, movies, and popular music with surprising frequency. Violence, drug use, and the treatment of women as submissive sexual objects are glamorized. Implicit as well as explicit messages establish the cultural norm of drug use, violence, and gender stereotyping.

Television has become a powerful medium. Ninety-six percent of the American homes are equipped with at least one television, and these sets are on for an average of 6 hours per day. By the time an American child finishes high school, he or she will have spent approximately 24,000 hours in front of a television set (Fox & Forbing, 1992).

Movies present a thrill-packed, sensational view of life that is far from reality. The intense sensory gratification presented through the movies is not possible to obtain in real life. Within this context, the representation of drug use as glamorous has a profound impact. Although many movies portray drug users involved in murder and crime, these same movies associate the drug use with a lifestyle whose components are wealth and glamor. These messages support the idea that happiness is found through self-indulgence.

The messages given to men and women concerning gender stereotyping are as pervasive as the messages about drug use (Anderson, 1988). Men and women are consistently portrayed in traditional roles. Men are usually shown in high-status roles and women are portrayed as submissive or as helpers. In popular music, the portrayal of women as sex objects and possessions of men continues to be the norm (Cooper, 1989).

The lives of the stars, both screen stars and rock stars, add to the perception of grandiosity and glamor. The stars live life on a grander scale than anyone else (Ewan, 1988). The perfect bodies of these men and women, their wealth, and their irresponsible use of substances again present a lifestyle far removed from reality.

CONCLUSION

Drug use and addictive behavior must be placed within the context of today's culture as reflected in mass media and advertisements. Given the overwhelming intrusiveness of the media into our lives, we find ourselves unable to escape the messages being given. We are surrounded with images of a lifestyle that is unrealistic, both monetarily and physically. The frustration and confusion created by this continuous barrage of messages lead some to cope through the use of addictive behaviors. Relief from the confusion is temporary, and the addictive cycle guarantees the continuation of the behavior. Living in our society guarantees support of the confusion.

There is apparent evidence that the contextual influences of society help to maintain addictive behaviors. It is imperative that counselors working with an addictive client today address these issues in a forthright and honest manner. Just as we have come to accept the individual's responsibility in addiction and the familial influence on the addict, we must now accept the societal influence.

REFERENCES

Ackerman, R. J. (1987). *Same house, different homes: Why adult children of alcoholics are not all the same.* Pompano Beach, CA: Health Communications, Inc.

Anderson, M. L. (1988). *Thinking about women: Sociological perspectives on sex and gender.* New York: Macmillan.

Burton, T., & Johnson, L. (1987). *The Weekly Reader national survey on drugs and drinking.* Middletown, CT: Field.

Cahalan, D. (1987). *Understanding America's drinking problem.* San Francisco: Jossey-Bass.

Ciraulo, D.A., & Shader, R.I. (1991). *Clinical manual of chemical dependence.* Washington, DC: American Psychiatric Press, Inc.

Cooper, S. E. (1989). Chemical dependency and eating disorders: Are they really so different? *Journal of Counseling and Development, 68,* 102–105.

Cruse, S.W. (1989). *Another chance: Hope and health for the alcoholic family.* Palo Alto: Science and Behavior Books, Inc.

DeFoe, J., & Breed, W. (1979). The problem of alcohol advertisements in college newspapers. *Journal of American College Health Association, 27,* 195–199.

Ewan, S. L. (1988). *All consuming passions: The politics of style in contemporary culture.* New York: Basic Books.

Fox, C.L., & Forbing, S.E. (1992). *Creating drug-free schools and communities.* New York: Harper Collins.

Gerbner, G. (1990). Stories that hurt: Tobacco, alcohol, and other drugs in the mass media. In H. Resnick (Ed.), *Youth and drugs: Society's mixed messages* (pp. 53–128). (OSAP Monograph No. 6) Rockville, MD: Office for Substance Abuse Prevention.

Gitlin, T. (1990). On drugs and mass media in America's consumer society. In H. Resnick (Ed.), *Youth and drugs: Society's mixed messages* (pp. 31–52). (OSAP Monograph No. 6) Rockville, MD: Office for Substance Abuse Prevention.

Goldenberg, H., & Goldenberg, I. (1990). *Counseling today's families.* Pacific Grove, CA: Brooks/Cole.

Inanba, D.S., & Cohen, W.E. (1991). *Uppers, downers, and all arounders.* Ashland, OR: CNS Publications.

Jacobson, M., Atkins, R., & Hacker, G. (1983). *The booze merchants: The inebriating of America.* Washington, DC: Center for Science in the Public Interest.

Jellinek, E. M. (1952). Phases of alcohol addiction. *Quarterly Journal of Studies on Alcohol, 13,* 673-684.

Johnson, B. D., & Muffler, J. (1992). Sociocultural aspects of drug use and abuse in the 1990s. In J. H. Lowinson, P. Ruiz, R. B. Millman, & J. G. Langrod (Eds.), *Substance abuse: A comprehensive textbook* (pp. 118-137). Baltimore: Williams & Wilkins.

Jones, L. Y. (1981). *Great expectations and the baby boom generation.* New York: Ballantine.

Kellam, M. L., Simon, M. B., & Ensminger, M. E. (1983). Antecedents of teenage drug use and psychological well-being: A ten-year community wide prospective study. In D. Ricks & B. S. Dohrenwend (Eds.), *Origins of psychopathology: Research and public policy* (pp. 17–42). Cambridge, MA: Harvard University Press.

Lewis, R. A. (1989). The family and addictions: An introduction. *Family Relations, 38,* 254–257.

Marlatt, G. A., & Gordon, J. R. (1985). *Relapse prevention: Maintenance strategies in the treatment of addictive behaviors.* New York: Guilford.

National Institute of Drug Abuse (1985). *National household survey on drug abuse: Main Findings.* Rockville, MD: Author.

Payne, W. A., Hahn, D. B., & Pinger, R. R. (1991). *Drugs: Issues for today.* St. Louis: C.V. Mosby.

Peele, S. (1989). *The diseasing of America.* Boston: Houghton Mifflin.

Potter-Efron, R.T., & Potter-Efron, P.S. (1991). *Anger, alcoholism, and addiction.* New York: W.W. Norton & Company.

Ray, O., & Ksir, C. (1990). *Drugs, society, and human behavior.* St. Louis: Times Mirror/Mosby.

Reiff, D.W., & Reiff, K.K.L. (1992). *Eating disorders: Nutrition therapy in the recovery process.* Gaithersburg, MD: Aspen Publishers.

Rosen, J., & Leitenberg, H. (1984). Exposure plus response prevention treatment of bulimia. In D. M. Garner & P. E. Garfinkel (Eds.), *A handbook of psychotherapy for anorexia and bulimia.* New York: Guilford.

Schaef, A. W. (1986). *Co-dependence: Misunderstood, mistreated.* Minneapolis: Winston.

Schuckit, M. S. (1981). Psychopharmacological elements of drug dependence. *Journal of the American Medical Association, 206,* 1263–1266.

Stabenau, J., & Hesselbrock, V. M. (1983). Family pedigree of alcoholic and control patients. *International Journal of Addictions, 18,* 351-363.

U. S. Bureau of the Census. (1984). *Statistical abstract of the United States: Colonial times to 1970.* Washington, DC: U.S. Government Printing Office.

U. S. Senate, Committee on the Judiciary. (1990). *Hardcore cocaine addicts: Measuring — and fighting — the epidemic.* 101st Congress. Washington, DC: U.S. Government Printing Office.

Woititz, J. G. (1983). *Adult children of alcoholics.* Pompano Beach, CA: Health Communications, Inc.

Wolf, N. (1991). *The beauty myth.* New York: Doubleday.

Woodside, D. B., & Shekter-Wolfson, L. (Eds.). (1991). *Family approaches in treatment of eating disorders.* Washington, DC: American Psychiatric Press.

Zucker, R.A., & Gomberg, E.S.L. (1986). Etiology of alcoholism reconsidered: The case for a biopsychosocial approach. *American Psychologist, 41*, 783–793.

Reviewing the Primary Prevention of Substance Abuse: Elements in Successful Approaches

Robert K. Conyne

The good news in substance abuse prevention is that progress was made during the 1980s in lowering the use of tobacco, alcohol, and many illicit drugs, at least in certain populations. Several health goals set in 1979, with a 1990 target (Department of Health, Education and Welfare, 1979), have been at least partially accomplished. For instance, lowered use of substances for teenagers and young adults and overall mortality reductions due to unintentional injuries (such as traffic accidents) have been documented.

The bad news is that we have a very long way to go. The most recent national data just released (Johnston, O'Malley, & Bachman, 1994), collected in their annual survey from 51,000 eighth, tenth, and twelfth graders, suggest that drug use may be rising after more than a decade of steady decline. Additionally of concern is that underlying beliefs and attitudes of those students sampled about drug use seem to be shifting in a more positive direction. The effects of substance abuse are devastating at personal and societal levels. Further, the trend through the 1980s of lower drug abuse for American youth has not been realized among groups from lower social economic status, those with the least amount of education, and minority populations (Johnston, O'Malley, & Bachman, 1988).

Primary prevention strategies have contributed directly to the reductions realized in substance abuse risk factors. Since 1980, public awareness of the health and economic problems associated with tobacco, drug, and alcohol abuse became more acute, leading to a social climate that became increasingly intolerant of substance abuse. An intolerant social climate spurred the development of community-based approaches to prevention (Office for Substance Abuse Prevention [OSAP], 1989) and to legislative and policy actions, particularly concerning drinking and driving. Companion activity occurred in the development of competency enhancement primary prevention programs (e.g., Price, Cowen, Lorion, & Ramos-McKay, 1988; Rhodes & Jason, 1988), where life skills training in problem solving and other important competencies were made available to designated populations.

Through these and other efforts it has become clear that effective substance abuse prevention programs are those that not only focus on the targeted population itself, such as adolescents, but also consider the ecological context in which the population functions. Thus norms, social policies and institutions, peer influences, opportunity structures, and other community factors all strongly affect pro-drug or anti-drug behavior.

As the title of this chapter indicates, I identify and describe important elements of successful contemporary substance abuse prevention programs. Awareness of these elements may be helpful in facilitating future efforts. First, however, a brief review is presented of the present status of alcohol- and other drug-related problems, including tobacco usage. This kind of information is important because it provides a baseline against which substance abuse prevention programs can be framed and implemented.

ALCOHOL AND OTHER DRUG-RELATED PROBLEMS

Though advances have been made in reducing levels of substance abuse and their effects, much remains to be done. The abuse of alcohol and other drugs contributes in a major way to such problems as AIDS, violent crime, child abuse and neglect, and unemployment. Problems associated with alcohol and drug abuse weaken the social fabric of society, costing in lost productivity, destruction of families, and lives (Blum, 1987). To illustrate, the Research Triangle Institute (1984) calculated the economic cost to society of alcohol and other drug problems at $177 billion per year.

Alcohol

Regarding alcohol, 18.5 million Americans abuse alcohol and 105,000 alcohol-related deaths occur each year. Thousands of these alcohol-related deaths are preventable, including motor vehicle fatalities; some cancers, such as liver and esophageal cancer; homicides and suicides; and cirrhosis of the liver. Alcohol also is the major preventable cause of birth defects. Heavy alcohol consumption during pregnancy is associated with increased risk for fetal alcohol syndrome, inclusive of growth retardation, mental retardation, facial malformations, and dysfunctions of the central nervous system (Department of Health and Human Services [DHHS], 1991).

The average age of first use of alcohol (and marijuana) is 13, although pressure to drink begins at even earlier ages. Elementary school students report pressure from other students to drink beer, wine, and liquor. Twenty-six percent of fourth graders and 40% of sixth graders reported that many of their fellow students had tried wine coolers, beer, and liquor (National Institute on Drug Abuse [NIDA], 1989). For high school students, in 1989 about 60% reported drinking alcohol during the preceding month; 33% reported incidents of heavy drinking, having five or more drinks on one occasion during the last 2 weeks (NIDA, 1989). Among college students, in 1991 approximately 88% had used alcohol during the last 12 months; 43% reported heavy drinking (Johnston, Bachman, & O'Malley, cited in Bacchus, 1992). Moreover, concerning selected campus and behavioral problems involving college students, in a survey of student affairs professionals (Anderson & Gadaleto, 1992), alcohol abuse was said to account for 70% of the violent behavior on campus, 41% of academic failure, 44% of emotional difficulties, 68% of residence hall damage, 62% of campus policy violations, and 28% of student attrition.

Other Drugs

Regarding some drugs other than alcohol, there are an estimated 1 to 3 million regular users of cocaine, 900,000 users of IV drugs, and 500,000 users of heroin, and there are 375,000 drug-exposed babies (DHHS, 1991). Among high school seniors (Beschner, 1986), drugs other than alcohol reported to have been used at "some time in their life" included stimulants (27%), cocaine (16%), hallucinogens (15%), sedatives or barbiturates (14%), inhalants (14%), tranquilizers (13%), opiates (other than heroin) (10%), LSD (9%), and amyl and butyl nitrates (8%). Most recent data for eighth grade and high school students (Johnston, O'Malley, & Bachman, 1994) report increases in 1993 from two to four percentage points over 1992 data for use of marijuana, LSD, and inhalants, the latter especially a problem for middle school students. In terms of the total population, although alcohol and other drug abuse appears to be declining, use of crack cocaine is increasing, particularly in certain urban areas. In terms of human cost, drug abuse is associated with violent crime, transmission of the HIV virus, developmental problems in infants, and a host of other behavioral and academic problems.

Tobacco

Drug abuse in adolescence or adulthood is associated with early use of tobacco, alcohol, and marijuana. Smokers are beginning the behavior at increasingly younger ages. Of high school seniors who have ever smoked, about one-fourth smoked their first cigarette by grade 6, over one-half by grades 7 or 8, and three-fourths by grade 9. The earlier a cigarette smoker begins, the more diffi-cult it is to quit. Though the prevalence of smoking decreased among high school students from about 29% in 1976 to 19% in 1981, the use of snuff and chewing tobacco has increased some 15-fold from 1970 to1986. This is a rising concern. As was pointed out above, the trend of steady decrease in drug use seems to be beginning to reverse for this sample. This change also appears to apply to cigarette smoking (Johnston, O'Malley, & Bachman, 1994). According to that national study, 8% of eighth graders, 14% of tenth graders, and 19% of seniors reported smoking cigarettes daily in 1993. These figures are up by one to two percentage points over 1992 data.

Cigarette smoking is a significant risk factor for heart disease, stroke, and some forms of cancer, such as lung cancer. It is responsible for one of every six deaths in the United States, some 390,000 each year. Though the overall rate of smoking has declined in this society from 40% in 1965 to under 30% in 1990 (saving nearly 800,000 lives between 1964 and 1985), more than 50 million Americans still smoke, with highest rates among blacks, Hispanics, blue-collar workers, and the less educated. All smokers, and these groups in particular, are at increased risk of disease, and smoking remains the single most important pre-ventable cause of death in our society (DHHS, 1991).

This brief review of alcohol, other drug, and tobacco usage yields six major points: (a) the personal and societal cost of problems with alcohol and other drugs, including smoking cigarettes and chewing tobacco, is enormous; (b) in the last decade, some reductions in substance abuse have been realized; (c) reductions in substance abuse are associated with decreases in mortality rates for certain diseases; (d) specific attention needs to be given to high-risk groups, including certain minorities and the less educated; (e) primary prevention and health promotion strategies have facilitated these reductions; and (f) levels of substance abuse remain excessive.

PRIMARY PREVENTION OF SUBSTANCE ABUSE

Evolution of General Approaches Used, 1960s-1980s

Substance abuse (and use) prevention programs have evolved over the last 30 years. In the 1960s, these programs tended to emphasize the presentation of information about the harmful consequences and bodily effects of drug use. These informational programs typically were one-way presentations, frequently including distorted statistics and scare tactics. These approaches were ineffec-tive; some data suggest that they may have promoted, rather than reduced, the use of substances among program recipients (Swisher, 1979).

During the 1970s, prevention programs relied upon affective educational approaches that focused on self-awareness, self-esteem, and learning the basic causes of substance abuse. However, affective approaches of this kind were shown to be generally ineffective in inhibiting substance use and abuse (Schaps, DiBartolo, Moskowitz, Palley, & Churgin, 1981).

Approaches to alcohol and other drug prevention in the 1980s tended to emphasize social influence and social skills training. These programs were either narrow in scope (e.g., "Just Say No") or multifaceted, including environmental, social, and personal components. Useful programs of this kind have been documented, including elements of the life skills training of Botvin and associates (e.g., Botvin & Tortu, 1988). This program combined many facets, including knowledge and information about the realities and myths of substance use, decision making and independent thinking, media influences and advertising techniques, self-image, self-improvement, self-directed behavior change, coping with anxiety, and training in specific social skills.

Some Important Conceptual Frameworks

No absence of conceptual foundations exists for substance abuse prevention (for more detailed discussions, see Gonzalez, 1989; OSAP, 1989; Rhodes & Jason, 1988). Space allows for only a brief discussion of some frameworks that have demonstrated utility in guiding substance abuse prevention projects.

Learning frameworks emphasize the role of cognitions, attitudes, beliefs, values, and social influences on behavior. Social learning theory (Bandura, 1969, 1977), for instance, attends to the role of opportunities, social influences, and rewards on performance. Substance abuse is understood as a socially learned, goal-directed behavior that results from an interaction of personal and social-environmental factors.

Behavioral Development frameworks include several varieties. Developmental approaches rely upon models such as Erickson's (1960) to examine movement from one developmental stage to the next and its relationship to substance use or abuse. Social development models (e.g., Hawkins & Weis, 1985) are concerned with addressing critical risk factors for alcohol and other drug use at specific developmental points. In the health belief model (Rosenstock, 1974), personal perceptions of a problem, such as substance abuse, and of one's susceptibility to experiencing the problem, are thought to strongly determine a person's actions. The problem behavior theory (Jessor & Jessor, 1977) suggests that the propensity for alcohol and drug abuse is associated with an overall tendency for problem behavior, and that behavior, personality, and the perceived social environment are determining factors. In multiple risk factor theory (e.g., Newcomb, Maddahian, & Bentler, 1986), alcohol and other drug problems are thought to result from a number of identifiable risk factors found in domains of personality, behavior, the perceived environment, the social environment, and biology. This model has been extended to examine protective factors found in similar domains as well.

Systems frameworks applied to alcohol and other drug use prevention (OSAP, 1989) include interpersonal and social influences, the community, and the general environment. These factors are conceptualized as interdependent parts, serving to influence individual behavior regarding alcohol and drugs.

Social stress as a framework for substance abuse prevention (Rhodes & Jason, 1988) emerges from the work of Albee (1982) on reducing the incidence of psychopathology. The social stress model was developed in relation to adolescent drug usage. In this model, the risk for substance abuse is considered to be a function of an individual's capacity to withstand stress through strong attachments with family and others, adequate coping skills, and good resources in the community.

The Integrated Theoretical Model for Alcohol and Other Drug Abuse Prevention (ITMADP) (Gonzalez, 1989) organizes the behavioral principles contained in the health belief model, social learning theory, and problem behavior theory and applies them to substance abuse prevention on the college campus. From the perspective of the ITMADP, reduced substance abuse problems result from the dynamic interaction among a person's individual characteristics and competencies, motivations, perceptions, and environment.

Elements in Successful Contemporary Approaches

Contemporary approaches to substance abuse prevention have evolved from and incorporate various aspects of the foregoing frameworks. Although presentation of a comprehensive, empirically based conceptual model is presently premature, practice and research do allow for the identification of elements that tend to comprise state of the art programs. I have organized these elements by (a) perspectives and premises that guide the approaches; (b) method used; and (c) target population considerations. The elements are presented in Exhibit 3–1 and are discussed below.

Perspectives and Premises

Incidence Reduction

Remediation of substance abuse problems, that is, correcting problems already existing, is not primary prevention. Rather, primary prevention concerns

Exhibit 3–1 Elements of Successful Programs

Elements of Successful Programs

Perspectives and Premises

Incidence reduction
Group and population centered
Collaborative ethic
Empowerment goal
Social ecology framework

Method

Multifactorial

Target and Setting Considerations

Systemic focus: family, community, and neighborhood
Risk and protective factors
Minority group representation
Target group validity

---

itself with the reduction of problems prior to onset. It is a before-the-fact approach (Albee & Joffe, 1977; Conyne, 1987; Cowen, 1985). This reduction in the number of new cases of substance abuse is what is meant by incidence reduction, and it is a central feature of primary prevention.

Group and Population Centered

The primary prevention of substance abuse does not take the single individual as the level of intervention. Instead, consistent with the public health model, primary prevention is provided to a group or a population of people who are presently free of substance abuse (Bloom, 1979; Caplan, 1964).

Collaborative Ethic

Primary prevention programs in substance abuse should be done not *to* a targeted group of people, but *with* them (Rappaport, 1981). To assist in realizing this maxim, the design and implementation processes can be accomplished in ways that involve members of the identified population throughout the evolving phases of the project (Conyne et al., in press). Prevention specialists are competent in a number of important areas. But members of the targeted population are also competent, often in other areas. For example, the specialists understand theory, research, and best practices in the area of substance abuse prevention, but they may not appreciate the ecology of the setting. Conversely, members of the population may not understand much about theoretical formulations surrounding substance abuse, but they could be viewed as experts about substance abuse in their neighborhood. The collaborative ethic calls for legitimizing both realms of expertise and finding workable ways to incorporate both.

Empowerment as a Superordinate Goal

The ethic of collaboration promotes participant empowerment. Collaboration inhibits passive receipt of services that are provided by experts from elsewhere because it facilitates active involvement and participation. Empowerment should be a superordinate goal of primary prevention programs, including those in substance abuse. Empowerment means that substance abuse prevention programs, in addition to reducing the new cases of abuse, seek to strengthen the self-efficacy of population members. Through empowerment, members develop a greater sense of agency, an improved locus of control. By taking part in the creation and application of the program and seeing it work, they feel more powerful, more robust, and more resilient.

Social Ecology Framework

Most substance abuse prevention work has emanated from models rooted in individual change (Rhodes & Jason, 1988). Intrapersonal characteristics, affect, cognitions, perceptions, and individual behavior have been the focus of research, theory, and application. Deemphasized, if not ignored, has been attention to the social ecology of substance use and abuse.

As Lewin (1936) observed, behavior is a function of persons transacting with their environment. In recent years, those involved with the substance abuse prevention field have begun producing conceptual and applied work that seems finally to be catching up with the "Lewinian dictum," that is, of including persons' transactions with the environment as a necessity for understanding behavior. The social ecology of substance abuse is being accorded importance. As Biglan observed, "We need to get at the context for these problems, not just focus on the people who exhibit them" (cited in Hayes, 1992, p. 13).

Social ecology (Insel & Moos, 1974; Moos & Insel, 1974) is a term that refers to "human milieus." It is the "personality" of a setting, its psychosocial climate. Though varying perspectives exist about what comprises the social ecology of a setting, such as a neighborhood, family, or organization, a variety of interacting elements contribute. These elements include social interactions; attachments; resources; opportunities for growth; regulations, laws, policies procedures, and rules; physical properties, such as crowdedness or the availability and comfort of furniture; characteristics of the persons within the setting, such as ethnicity; community dynamics, such as involvement; political issues; and economic conditions. These and other factors interact to yield a fairly stable yet changeable social ecology (Conyne & Clack, 1981).

Method

Multifactorial Approaches

The single, unimodal approach to substance abuse prevention has given way to multifactorial approaches. In the latter, an interrelated set of approaches that act on differing aspects of the problem to be reduced are bundled. For example, a successful multiple component program in substance abuse prevention (Pentz et al., 1989) was comprehensive and community focused. It included a set of intervention modes, such as social influence resistance skills training for sixth- and seventh-grade students, homework for their parents, a review of school policies, news coverage, training community leaders in how to organize drug abuse prevention task forces, and more. Which kinds of approaches seem most generally effective? Based on a meta-analysis of over 143 different program approaches for adolescents, Tobler (cited in Benard, 1989) found the following: (a) peer programs were more effective than any other for the average adolescent, and (b) alternative programs were most effective for high-risk adolescents. Though it is not clear that these components are equally potent for other populations, including peers and alternative programming as part of the multidimensional mix seems generally sensible.

Target and Setting

Systemic Focus: Family, Neighborhood, and Community

The primary focus for substance abuse prevention programs has shifted from groups of individuals to the family and the community. Cooperative networks are now frequently established in substance abuse prevention programs, allowing for the creation of multidimensional efforts. In a comparison of pre-1978 to present programs funded by NIDA, for instance, the percentage of those focused on the family grew from 1% to 44% and of those focused on the community from 9% to 18%. Consistent with the social ecology perspective, increased attention is being devoted, also, to environmental contributions to drug abuse, such as neighborhood and peer influences. Imbedding programs within family and community is respectful of cultural and contextual considerations, while allowing for existing social support to be harnessed naturally. By contrast, removing individuals from their local settings to participate in a structured program offered elsewhere ignores the protective and empowering features of family, neighborhood, and community.

Risk and Protective Factors

Considerable work is being devoted to identifying risk factors and protective factors for substance abuse (e.g., Hawkins, Catalano, & Miller, 1992). These factors can be traced to biology/genetics, social environment, perceived environment, personality, and behavior. Risk factors, such as poverty and racial inequality, can lead to risky behavior or lifestyles involving substance abuse, which, in turn, can result in a range of health- or life-compromising outcomes. Protective factors, such as a cohesive family or valuing achievement, can moderate the risk factors, serving to inhibit or prevent undesirable lifestyle or outcomes.

Targeting risk groups or populations has been proposed commonly in the primary prevention literature. Targeting groups or populations that are vulnerable to multiple risk factors is further recommended because evidence suggests that the greater the number of risk factors present, the greater the risk of drug abuse (Bry, McKeon, & Pandina, 1982). Examples of such risk factors include poor child rearing, social influences encouraging drug abuse, few expectations for academic achievement, poverty, and diminished social skills, among others. Likewise, programs seeking to enhance multiple protective factors are to be encouraged. Such protective factors include involvement in school, religious, or community activities, providing positive peer and role models, valuing achievement, training in competency development, and social support, among others.

Minority Group Representation

Members of minority groups, such as Hispanics and African-Americans, are disproportionately represented among abusers of "hard" drugs, such as heroin and intraveneous drugs. Interactions of a variety of economic, social, biological, and psychological factors contribute to this situation. Unfortunately, little past research of substance abuse prevention has been directed at low SES and minority populations (Rhodes & Jason, 1988). However, and positively, increased attention is beginning to be devoted to substance abuse prevention in minority communities. For instance, before 1978 2% of NIDA-funded programs included minority groups, whereas at present 18% of such programs include minority group members.

Target Population Validity

The development and introduction of substance abuse prevention programs needs to be informed by certain sensitivities that are germane to the target population (Rhodes & Jason, 1988). These sensitivities include developmental, cultural, and ethnic validity.

Multifactorial approaches that are aimed at multiple risk and protective factors in a designated group of people need to be developmentally adjusted. That is, recognition of the developmental issues generally being faced by a particular target group, such as elementary school children or senior citizens, needs to inform and guide the goals and methods for any substance abuse prevention program.

Multicultural concerns (e.g., Pederson, 1991) need to be consciously considered and responded to in substance abuse prevention. As Sue and Sue (1977) observed, for instance, factors related to language, class-bound values, and culture-bound values often are particular to different cultures. Gearing a prevention program to mesh sensitively within the culture of the targeted population is necessary.

As an example, the Three-Community study to reduce heart disease used mass media as its main method (Maccoby & Alexander, 1979). Census data revealed that 30% of the population segment were Hispanic. In addition to use of Spanish, examination showed that this population tended to exhibit certain risk factors that were different from the Anglo population, involving less smoking and heavier relative weight. These facts led the program team to create and deliver two different campaigns, one in English and the other in Spanish, with each emphasizing components unique to the two cultures. The Three-Community study example shows how cultural and ethnic validity improves the possibility that the targeted population will accept the program (Barnett, 1983; Lateer & Curtis, 1991).

CONCLUSION

Gains in substance abuse prevention programs are being realized. Much more needs to be accomplished, particularly in reaching lower income and minority populations with programs that are sensitive to their needs and conditions.

Developing a formal conceptual model that is comprehensive, based on consistent research evidence, and generically applicable remains premature. Nonetheless, the elements of successful programs that have been identified in this chapter provide a basic blueprint for designing and conducting substance abuse prevention programs. The organization of these elements into (a) perspectives and premises, (b) method, and (c) target/setting provides the program designer or evaluator with general guidance.

The basic blueprint includes these features:

- Think systemically and ecologically.
- Intervene before the fact.
- Aim the programs at populations, not individuals.
- Work collaboratively.
- Empower.
- Use an interconnected set of methods, not one approach.
- Imbed programs within naturally occurring settings.
- Include risk and protective factors relevant to target.

• Expand to include minority and low income targets.

• Make programs culturally sensitive and valid.

Implementation of these elements will prove to be challenging to the practitioner. It is unreasonable to expect that any single professional possesses the experience, training, competency, or resources to execute them all. What is required is the realization that these elements are necessary, followed by forming collaboratively based interdisciplinary teams whose members can combine different skills interdependently. Once such teams are formed, it becomes critical that they are able to work together, across boundaries, jointly merging diverse skills effectively and efficiently. Skills in working together may prove to be the most important element of all in producing effective substance abuse prevention programs.

REFERENCES

Albee, G. (1982). Preventing psychopathology and promoting human potential. *American Psychologist, 32*, 150-161.

Albee, G., & Joffe, J. (Eds.). (1977). *Primary prevention of psychopathology, Vol. 1: The issues.* Hanover, NH: University Press of New England.

Anderson, D., & Gadaleto, A. (1992). *Research highlights: 1991 Campus Alcohol Survey.* Fairfax, VA: George Mason University.

Bacchus. (1992, March). Recent studies chronicle alcohol use, attitudes, and policy. *The Bacchus Beat, 2*–5.

Bandura, A. (1969). *Principles of behavior modification.* New York: Holt, Rinehart & Winston.

Bandura, A. (1977). Self-efficacy: Toward a unifying theory of behavior change. *Psychological Review, 84*, 191-215.

Barnett, D. (1983). *Nondiscriminatory multifactored assessment.* New York: Human Sciences.

Benard, B. (1989). A few words about prevention program evaluation research. In Office for Substance Abuse Prevention (Ed.), *Prevention Plus II: Tools for creating and sustaining drug-free communities* (pp. 497–513). Rockville, MD: Office for Substance Abuse Prevention.

Beschner, G. (1986). Understanding teen drug use. In G. Beschner & S. Friedman (Eds.), *Teen drug use* (pp. 1–18). Lexington, MA: D.C. Heath.

Bloom, B. (1979). Prevention of mental disorders: Recent advances in theory and practice. *Community Mental Health Journal, 15*, 179-191.

Blum, R. (1987). Contemporary threats to adolescent health in the United States. *Journal of the American Medical Association, 257*, 3390-3395.

Botvin, G., & Tortu, S. (1988). Preventing adolescent substance abuse through life skills training. In R. Price, E. Cowen, R. Lorion, E.J. Ramos-Kay (Eds.), *Fourteen ounces of prevention: A casebook for practitioners* (pp. 98–110). Washington, DC: American Psychological Association.

Bry, B., McKeon, P., & Pandina, R. (1982). Extent of drug use as a function of number of risk factors. *Journal of Abnormal Psychology, 91*, 273–279.

Caplan, G. (1964). *Principles of preventive psychiatry.* New York: Basic Books.

Conyne, R. (1987). *Primary preventive counseling: Empowering people and systems.* Muncie, IN: Accelerated Development.

Conyne, R., & Clack, J. (1981). *Environmental assessment and design: A new tool for the applied behavioral scientist.* New York: Praeger.

Conyne, R., Wagner, D., Hadley, T., Piles, M., Schorr-Owen, V., & Enderly, M. (in press). Applying primary prevention to campus substance abuse programs. *Journal of Counseling & Development.*

Cowen, E. (1985). Person-centered approaches to primary prevention in mental health: Situation-focused and competence-enhancement. *American Journal of Community Psychology, 13,* 31–49.

Department of Health, Education, and Welfare (DHEW). (1979). *Healthy people: The Surgeon General's report on health promotion and disease prevention* (DHEW Publication No. 79-55071). Washington, DC: Author.

Department of Health and Human Services (DHHS). (1991). *Healthy people 2000: National health promotion and disease prevention objectives* (DHHS Publication No. 91-50212). Washington, DC: Author.

Erickson, E. (1960). *The course of healthy personality development.* Midcentury White House Conference on Children and Youth. New York: Holt, Rinehart & Winston.

Gonzalez, G. (1989). An integrated theoretical model for alcohol and other drug abuse prevention on the college campus. *Journal of College Student Development, 30,* 492–503.

Hayes, S. (1992). Changing the culture: An interview with Tony Biglan. *The Scientist-Practitioner, 2,* 10–16.

Hawkins, J., & Weis, J. (1985). The social development model: An integrated approach to delinquency prevention. *Journal of Primary Prevention, 6,* 73–97.

Hawkins, J., Catalano, R., & Miller, J. (1992). Risk and protective factors for alcohol and other drug problems in adolescence and early adulthood: Implications for substance abuse prevention. *Psychological Bulletin, 112,* 64–105.

Insel, P., & Moos, R. (Eds.) (1974). *Health and the social environment.* Lexington, MA: D.C. Heath.

Jessor, R., & Jessor, S. (1977). *Problem behavior and psychosocial development: A longitudinal study of youth.* New York: Academic Press.

Johnston, L., O'Malley, P., & Bachman, J. (1988). *National trends in drug use and related factors among American high school students and young adults.* Rockville, MD: National Institute on Drug Abuse.

Johnston, L., O'Malley, P., & Bachman, J. (1994, January). *Monitoring the future study: 1993.* Institute for Social Research: The University of Michigan, Ann Arbor, Michigan.

Lateer, A., & Curtis, M. (1991, March). *Cross-cultural consultation: Responding to diversity.* Paper presented at the Annual Meeting of the National Association of School Psychologists, Dallas, TX.

Lewin, K. (1936). *Principles of topological psychology.* New York: McGraw-Hill.

Maccoby, N. & Alexander, J. (1979). Reducing heart disease risk using the mass media: Comparing the effects on three communities. In R. Munoz, L. Snowden, & J. Kelly (Eds.), *Social and psychological research in community settings* (pp. 69–88). San Francisco: Jossey-Bass.

Moos, R., & Insel, P. (Eds.) (1974). *Issues in social ecology: Human milieus.* Palo Alto, CA: National Press.

National Institute on Drug Abuse. (1989). *National survey results from high school, college, and young adult populations, 1975-1988.* Washington, DC: Author. DHHS Publication No.(ADM)89-1638.

Newcomb, M., Maddahian, E., & Bentler, P. (1986). Risk factors for drug use among adolescents: Concurrent and longitudinal analyses. *American Journal of Public Health, 76,* 525–530.

Office for Substance Abuse Prevention. (OSAP). (1989). *Prevention Plus II: Tools for creating and sustaining drug-free communities* (DHHS Publication No. (ADM)89-1649). Washington, DC: Author.

Pederson, P. (Ed.). (1991). Special Issue: Multiculturalism as a fourth force in counseling. *Journal of Counseling & Development, 70.*

Pentz, M., Dwyer, J., MacKinnon, D., Faly, B., Hansen, W., Wang, E., & Johnson, C. (1989). A multi-community trial for primary prevention of adolescent drug abuse: Effects on drug use prevalence. *Journal of the American Medical Association, 262,* 3259–3266.

Price, R., Cowen, E., Lorion, R., & Ramos-McKay, J. (1988). *Fourteen ounces of prevention: A casebook for practitioners.* Washington, DC: American Psychological Association.

Rappaport, J. (1981). In praise of paradox: A social policy of empowerment over prevention. *American Journal of Community Psychology, 9,* 1–25.

Rhodes, J., & Jason, L. (1988). *Preventing substance abuse among children and adolescents.* New York: Pergamon.

Research Triangle Institute. (1984). *Economic costs to society of alcohol and drug abuse and mental illness.* Chapel Hill, NC: Author.

Rosenstock, I. (1974). The Health Belief Model and preventive health behavior. *Health Education Monograph, 2,* 328–335.

Schaps, E., DiBartolo, R., Moskowitz, J., Palley, C., & Churgin, S. (1981). A review of 127 drug abuse prevention program evaluations. *Journal of Drug Issues, 22,* 17–43.

Sue, D. W., & Sue, D. (1977). Barriers to effective cross-cultural counseling. *Journal of Counseling Psychology, 24,* 420–429.

Swisher, J. (1979). Prevention issues. In R. Dupont, A. Goldstein, & J. O'Donnell (Eds.), *Handbook on Drug Abuse* (pp. 49-62). Washington, DC: National Institute on Drug Abuse.

BIBLIOGRAPHY

Funkhouser, J., & Amatetti, S. (1987, January). *Part two: Alcohol and drug abuse prevention: From knowledge to action.* Lexington, KY: Task Force on Alcohol and Drug Abuse Hearing.

Chapter 4

Issues of Gender and Culture in Substance Abuse Treatment

Judith A. Lewis

The separate lives of individual clients are best understood when viewed from the vantage point of a broad cultural perspective. In fact, the attitudes and behaviors of individual clients may often seem incomprehensible to a counselor who has failed to consider the powerful influence of social factors that are beyond the client's own control. It is only recently, however, that addictions professionals have become truly cognizant of the impact of culture on addictive behaviors.

> Until recently the bulk of information about substance abuse treatment was based on research carried out with white male subjects. Many of the generalizations accepted by substance abuse counselors were therefore severely limited. Most counselors have now come to accept the fact that their clients may be members of highly diverse groups with varying goals, needs, and social pressures. (Lewis, Dana, & Blevins, 1994, p. 19)

It is widely recognized that, in order to meet the needs of this diverse client population, treatment providers need to take into account the effects of gender and culture on the development and maintenance of substance abuse problems. Less widely recognized—but just as important—is the fact that gender and culture affect the kinds of treatment approaches to which clients are likely to respond. Learning about other cultures is an important first step, but counselors also need to examine the cultural biases that may be inherent in their own helping strategies. Treatment providers need to be especially sensitive to the impact of such factors as racism, gender socialization, inequality, discrimination, and victimization on their clients' ability to benefit from services. Successful services require treatment providers who are *culturally competent*.

37

CROSS-CULTURAL COUNSELING COMPETENCIES

Sue, Arredondo, and McDavis (1992) suggest that cross-cultural counseling competencies fall into three general areas: the counselor's awareness of his or her own assumptions, values, and biases; the counselor's understanding of the worldview of the culturally different client; and the counselor's ability to develop appropriate intervention strategies and techniques.

Awareness of Assumptions, Values, and Biases

Sue et al. contend that culturally skilled counselors possess the following beliefs and attitudes (p. 482):

1. Culturally skilled counselors have moved from being culturally unaware to being aware of and sensitive to their own cultural heritage and to valuing and respecting differences.
2. Culturally skilled counselors are aware of how their own cultural background and experiences, attitudes, values, and biases influence psychological processes.
3. Culturally skilled counselors are able to recognize the limits of their competencies and expertise.
4. Culturally skilled counselors are comfortable with differences that exist between themselves and clients in terms of race, ethnicity, culture, and beliefs.

Although beliefs and attitudes form the basis for cross-cultural skills, they must be complemented by *knowledge* of differing cultural heritages, by *awareness* of the impact of racism and oppression, and by *skills* in applying understanding to practice.

Culture and Worldview

Cultural diversity creates differences in values that are so basic as to constitute alternate worldviews. For instance, Carter and Helms (1987) state that cultures vary in terms of their orientations toward the following factors: *human nature, person/nature, time sense, activity,* and *social relations.* In terms of *human nature,* cultures vary widely, with some teaching that people are born with evil inclinations that must be controlled and others inculcating in their members a belief that people are basically good. The differences among cultures are even more apparent when we consider the *relationship between person and nature.* Some cultures believe in the subjugation of humans to nature and suggest that people cannot expect to control natural forces. Other cultures, in contrast, are built on the assumption that humankind can gain mastery over nature. An alternate worldview suggests that people can achieve partnership and harmony with nature. *Time sense* is also central to cultural worldviews, with some cultures valuing the traditions of the past and others focusing on planning for the future. Closely associated with time sense is the orientation toward *activity.* Cultures that focus on *being* emphasize spontaneous self-expression, while those that focus on *doing* emphasize achievements that are measurable by external criteria. Finally, orientations toward *social relations* run the gamut from an acceptance of clearly established lines of authority, to an emphasis on collective decision making, to an assumption that individuality and autonomy are more important than group goals.

On the basis of a review of numerous studies, Carter (1991) points out that "in general, these researchers have found significant differences between the dominant White middle-class value orientation and those of the cultural and ethnic groups with which they were compared" (p. 167). The value system of white middle-class Americans is characterized "by a belief in mastery over nature, future time, doing-oriented activity, and individual relationships" (p. 165). Studies of Latin cultures, Native American cultures, Asian cultures, African cultures, and Mediterranean cultures have pointed toward major value differences in all of these categories. It should be noted that within cultures, value differences exist between females and males. Studies by Carter and Helms showed that "in comparison to Black men, Black women showed a stronger preference for Subjugation to Nature and Present Time" and "White women in comparison to White men had higher preferences for Good in the Innate Character of Human Nature orientation, Subjugation to Nature, Being Human Activity, and Present Time," suggesting that "men and women may have different worldviews irrespective of race and culture" (Carter, 1991, p. 169). What Carter terms the "White Middle-Class American" worldview may in actuality be the "White, Middle-class, American *Male* World View."

Interventions and Techniques

Differences in worldview can lead to mismatches between helping approaches and client expectations. As Sue et al. (1992) point out, "helping styles and approaches may be culture bound" (p. 483). In addition to studying cultural teachings, treatment providers must also recognize the limitations of their own helping skills and adapt their techniques to their clients' cultural values.

As Ivey (1991) explains, counselors can develop culture-specific strategies for working with their clients. He suggests that the following general steps be taken (pp. 216-217):

1. Study the culture in general. . . . Seek to learn how the culture views the world. . . .
2. Select key aspects of the culture and summarize them. . . .
3. Using this information as a base, identify how the culture has traditionally solved problems and provided help for those in need.
4. Identify concrete skills and strategies that the culture has traditionally used in the helping relationship. . . .
5. Test the theory in practice; change and adapt it as new information becomes available.

As this approach makes apparent, culturally competent counseling is based both on general knowledge about the client's culture and on knowledge about the specific helping strategies that characterize the culture's traditions.

IMPLICATIONS FOR ADDICTIONS TREATMENT

Some of the methods that are used routinely in addictions treatment are based on a worldview that is perceived as "mainstream" but that actually reflects the values of the dominant white, male, American culture. Treatment providers who are interested in reaching a diverse client population may need to make alterations in practices that have remained unquestioned in the past.

For example, standard alcoholism treatments in the United States tend to be based on the assumption that alcoholism is a primary disease and that clients must focus on this issue alone until recovery is well underway. Bell (1993), however, points out that black culture "resists seeing addiction as primary, at least in terms of causality." His viewpoint is that African-Americans, as well as people in other nondominant cultures, tend to see addiction issues as secondary to such problems as racism and poverty. Although Bell does not see racism as the *cause* of alcohol or drug abuse, he does suggest that "treatment based on the disease theory needs to develop a mechanism to allow chemically dependent individuals to talk about racial identity issues and cultural differences" rather than dismissing clients' attempts to raise these issues as diversionary tactics (Bell, 1990, p. 3).

Women clients also need the chance to focus on the cultural context of their addictions. In fact, they should be actively encouraged to explore issues related to gender and oppression because their substance abuse tends to be rooted in the gender socialization process.

Women's use of substances occurs within the context of their relationships with men. . . . The illegal as well as the legal drug distribution system is largely controlled and accessed by men. Men who use substances are likely to be introduced to drugs by male peers, to buy their own drugs, to acquire their drugs from people they do not know well, to use IV drugs alone, and to inject the drugs themselves. Women who use substances are likely to be introduced and initiated into substance use through a male friend or partner, or in the case of psychotherapeutic drugs, a male physician. It is through their relationships with men who purchase the substance, prepare the substance for use, and dispense or, with intravenous use, inject the substance that most women continue their use of substances. Within the drug-using subculture, gender role norms pervade (Mejta, 1993, p. 4)

Treatment providers who work with women also need to be aware of the high correlation between addiction and experiences of sexual victimization, including childhood sexual abuse (Root, 1989). In fact, Root suggests that "the prevailing treatment goal of immediate abstinence from the problem substance before addressing the sexual assault and its aftermath is unrealistic and, indeed, destined for failure" (p. 543).

This is not to suggest that women should cope with past trauma by turning to alcohol, drugs, or food. Rather, it is to question prevailing approaches to addiction, rooted in a narrow specialization, that almost invariably make abstinence from substance abuse the priority in treatment. These methods of coping have adaptive qualities for some women who do not have a repertoire of positive skills for coping with the negative affect, images, and cognitions accompanying unresolved sexual trauma. Thus, attempts to remove the substance are likely to result in relapse, and subsequent labeling of the client as a treatment failure. (Root, 1989, p. 546)

People who view addiction as an internal state that can be clearly identified and categorized frequently use direct confrontation to press clients into acceptance of their diagnoses. Covington (1993), however, says that although confrontation may be useful in addressing grandiosity and deflating male clients' egos, this process should be reversed for women. Confrontation, she suggests, is contraindicated for women, who are likely to come into treatment with a sense of powerlessness and low self-esteem. Among the approaches that are more helpful for women are the following (Mejta, Lewis, & Engle, 1993):

• Collaborative relationships that are respectful and safe
• Personal empowerment strategies
• Positive approaches to behavior management

- Self-esteem training
- Supportive women's groups
- Gender-sensitive family and couples counseling

Direct confrontation as a motivational technique may be contraindicated not only for women but also for clients from ethnic or cultural groups that eschew this form of interaction. Native American cultures, for instance, tend to emphasize cooperation over competition and permissiveness over coercion. Hill and Hill (1992) state that "most American Indian groups and families consider interference in another's behavior to be disrespectful" and that "Indians usually prefer not to confront an antagonist and will often avoid interpersonal contact instead" (p. 497). In this cultural milieu, harsh confrontational interventions are unlikely to succeed.

Hill and Hill (1992) also point out that in the extended Indian family, "kinship extends beyond the nuclear family system to include grandparents, parents, aunts, uncles, siblings, and cousins. . . . as well as other members of the clan or tribal unit" (p. 498). Traditional Hispanic families may also be characterized by emphasis on the extended family, as well as by multigenerational concerns related to acculturation. In recent years, most substance abuse treatment facilities have begun to emphasize work with family systems. Often, however, these services focus narrowly on the traditional nuclear family. As they increase their attention to gender and culture, treatment providers will need to reexamine their definitions of *family*. Only then will they be able to attend to their clients' worldviews, deal with the intrafamilial power inequities brought about by gender socialization, and recognize the possibility that true families may be united by psychosocial, rather than biological, factors.

Culture and gender are also salient factors in service accessibility. Routes to treatment are clearly affected by gender and ethnicity. Bell (1990, 1993) points out that whereas white substance abuse clients are frequently referred by family, friends, or employee assistance programs, African-American clients are likely to enter treatment through the courts. African-American clients could be reached earlier and more effectively through multiple points of entry. Bell recommends an emphasis on such possibilities as client assistance programs in community agencies and recreational facilities, employee assistance programs in minimum-wage industries, and church-based programs such as "Chemical Awareness Sundays."

Access to treatment is also affected by gender. Women substance abusers are less likely than men to reach treatment because of employer referral or arrest for driving under the influence of alcohol. They are more likely to be identified when seeking medical help or because of pressures related to the welfare of their children. Yet traditional treatment facilities have tended to overlook women's special health problems, to ignore the pressing need for child care, and to disregard the fact that female substance abusers are poor and underinsured. Most substance abuse treatment providers are committed to meeting the needs of an increasingly diverse population of clients. In order to accomplish this goal, however, we may need to question some of our most cherished assumptions about the nature of the addictive process, about the quality of treatment, and about ourselves.

REFERENCES

Bell, P. (1990). *Chemical dependency and the African-American: Counseling strategies and community issues.* Center City, MN: Hazelden.

Bell, P. (1993 July). *Chemical dependency and the African-American.* Presentation to the annual conference of the National Association of Drug and Alcohol Counselors, Chicago.

Carter, R. T. (1991). Cultural values: A review of empirical research and implications for counseling. *Journal of Counseling & Development, 70,* 164–173.

Carter, R. T., & Helms, J. E. (1987). The relationship of Black value orientations to racial identity attitudes. *Measurement and Evaluation in Counseling and Development, 19,* 185–195.

Covington, S. (1993 July). *Women and addictions.* Presentation to the annual conference of the National Association of Drug and Alcohol Counselors, Chicago.

Hill, A., & Hill, V. (1992). Substance abuse prevention programs for American Indian youth. In G. W. Lawson & A. W. Lawson (Eds.). *Adolescent substance abuse: Etiology, treatment, and prevention* (pp. 381–390). Gaithersburg, MD: Aspen.

Ivey, A. E. (1991). *Developmental strategies for helpers: Individual, family, and network interventions.* Monterey, CA: Brooks/Cole.

Lewis, J. A., Dana, R. Q., & Blevins, G. A. (1994). S*ubstance abuse counseling: An individualized approach* (2nd ed.). Monterey, CA: Brooks/Cole.

Mejta, C. L. (1993). Substance abuse among women: A review of the literature. In C. L. Mejta, J. A. Lewis, & J. A. Engle, *Training the gender-competent substance abuse counselor.* Training manual completed under funding from the Office of the Lieutenant Governor, Illinois.

Mejta, C. L., Lewis, J. A., & Engle, J. A. (1993). *Training the gender-competent substance abuse counselor.* Training manual completed under funding from the Office of the Lieutenant Governor, Illinois.

Root, M. P. P. (1989). Treatment failures: The role of sexual victimization in women's addictive behavior. *American Journal of Orthopsychiatry, 59,* 542–548.

Sue, D. W., Arredondo, P., & McDavis, R. J. (1992). Multicultural counseling competencies and standards: A call to the profession. *Journal of Counseling & Development, 70,* 477–486.

Part II
Treating Addictions

Chapter 5

Treating People with Alcohol Problems

Judith A. Lewis

Miller (1992) points out that in the treatment of alcohol problems, "standardization appears to be on the way out" and we are "headed toward a society in which treatment is designed to fit the individual" (p. 118). The need for tailoring treatments to individual clients has become apparent to all who recognize the complexity of alcohol-related problems. At the same time, an expanding body of research is pointing us toward a number of potentially effective treatments, allowing for the possibility that each client can choose from among a variety of options. Thus "we are moving toward treatments that are both more effective and more individualized" (Miller, 1992, p. 118).

THE CASE FOR INDIVIDUALIZATION

The Institute of Medicine (1990) defines alcohol problems as "those problems that may arise in individuals around their use of beverage alcohol and that may require an appropriate treatment response for their optimum management" (p. 25). As this broad definition indicates, alcohol problems are very diverse, differing in terms of their duration, their severity, and their effects.

> The manifestations of these problems will sometimes be primarily physical, sometimes social, sometimes psychological; most often they will be variable combinations of all of these. Alcohol problems also vary greatly in terms of the kinds of treatment responses that may be appropriate, responses ranging from simple advice to elaborate combinations and/or sequences of biological, social, and psychological interventions. (Institute of Medicine, 1990, p. 25)

There is no possibility that a single type of treatment could be appropriate for the wide range of individuals affected by alcohol problems. Even when we focus specifically on people whose problems are sufficiently serious that they have received diagnoses of *alcohol abuse* or *alcohol dependence,* we can see that the differences among them are as apparent as their commonalities.

The most commonly used approach to diagnosis is based on the American Psychiatric Association's Diagnostic and Statistical Manual (3rd ed., rev. [DSM III-R]; American Psychiatric Association, 1987). The *DSM-III-R* makes a distinction between alcohol abuse and alcohol dependence. For alcohol, as for other psychoactive substances, a client is diagnosed as being *dependent* on the substance only if at least three of the following nine criteria are met (American Psychiatric Association, 1987, pp. 167-168):

1. Substance often taken in larger amounts or over a longer period than the person intended.
2. Persistent desire or one or more unsuccessful efforts to cut down or control substance use.
3. A great deal of time spent in activities necessary to get the substance, . . . take the substance . . . , or recover from its effects.
4. Frequent intoxication or withdrawal symptoms when expected to fulfill major role obligations at work, school, or home (e.g., does not go to work because hung over, goes to school or work "high," intoxicated while taking care of his or her children), or when substance use is physically hazardous (e.g., drives when intoxicated).
5. Important social, occupational, or recreational activities given up or reduced because of substance use.
6. Continued use despite knowledge of having a persistent or recurrent social, psychological, or physical problem that is caused or exacerbated by the use of the substance.
7. Marked tolerance: need for markedly increased amounts of the substance (i.e., at least a 50% increase) in order to achieve intoxication or desired effect, or markedly diminished effect with continued use of the same amount. . . .
8. Characteristic withdrawal symptoms. . . .
9. Substance often taken to relieve or avoid withdrawal symptoms.

The criteria regarding the severity of dependence on alcohol or other substances include the following (p. 168):

Mild: Few, if any, symptoms in excess of those required to make the diagnosis, and the symptoms result in no more than mild impairment in occupational functioning or in usual social activities or relationships with others.
Moderate: Symptoms or functional impairment between "mild" and "severe."

Severe: Many symptoms in excess of those required to make the diagnosis, and the symptoms markedly interfere with occupational functioning or with usual social activities or relationships with others.
In Partial Remission: During the past 6 months, some use of the substance and some symptoms of dependence.
In Full Remission: During the past 6 months, either no use of the substance, or use of the substance and no symptoms of dependence.

In the *DSM-III-R*, the diagnostic category of *psychoactive substance abuse,* including *alcohol abuse,* is used for an individual whose patterns of use are maladaptive but whose use has never met the criteria for *dependence.* A "maladaptive pattern" is indicated by at least one of the following (p. 169):

1. continued use despite knowledge of having a persistent or recurrent social, occupational, psychological, or physical problem that is caused or exacerbated by use of the psychoactive substance
2. recurrent use in situations in which use is physically hazardous (e.g., driving while intoxicated)

As is readily apparent, there is no simple, dichotomous definition of "alcoholism." Even among people with the diagnosis of alcohol dependence, alcohol problems are multivariate, and "drinkers vary in terms of consumption, physical effects of alcohol, patterns of drinking behavior, life consequences of drinking, personality, social environment, gender, culture, and a variety of other variables" (Lewis, Dana, & Blevins, 1994).

Clearly, people with alcohol problems form a heterogeneous group. For this reason, the treatment community has been forced to move away from the standardized treatment packages that characterized earlier approaches. Individualized treatment will soon become the norm.

EFFECTIVE ALTERNATIVES FOR TREATMENT

In a recent landmark effort, Holder, Longabough, Miller, and Rubonis (1991) reviewed numerous published reports of controlled studies, each of which assessed the effects of specific modalities on alcohol-related outcomes. The authors reviewed these studies of clinical effectiveness in order to create a picture of the cumulative evidence available for the effectiveness of particular approaches. They identified six modalities that showed good evidence of positive effect on alcohol consumption or drinking-related outcomes: (a) social skills training, (b) self-control training, (c) brief motivational counseling, (d) behavioral marital therapy, (e) the community reinforcement approach, and

(f) stress management training. Each of these modalities yielded positive results in a number of controlled trials. These modalities also have in common the fact that they can be offered at relatively low cost.

Certainly, these approaches do not provide the new panacea. Rather, they represent treatments that should be considered as options for clients before more expensive or less rigorously tested modalities are implemented.

Social Skills Training

The development of social skills is important to alcohol-affected individuals for several reasons. First, these skills can be used for coping with specific situations that might normally be associated with drinking. The client's ability to respond effectively when others pressure him or her to drink can mean the difference between relapse and maintenance of recovery. Social skills can also be used as clients seek to develop or enhance social support networks, which are central to healthy functioning. As Monti, Abrams, Kadden, and Cooney (1989) note, many clients either have failed to learn social skills or have lost the use of what skills they had during years of heavy drinking.

These abilities can be rekindled through training programs, especially when offered to clients in group settings. For instance, the program implemented by Monti and his colleagues focuses on helping alcohol-dependent clients gain the following interpersonal skills: (1) starting conversations, (2) giving and receiving compliments, (3) nonverbal communication, (4) "feeling talk" and listening skills, (5) assertiveness, (6) giving criticism, (7) receiving criticism about drinking, (8) drink refusal skills, (9) refusing requests, (10) close and intimate relationships, and (11) enhancing social support networks. The skills are taught through the use of skill guidelines, role-played modeling, behavior rehearsals, and practice exercises.

Similar strategies can be used in training programs that focus on a specific skill, such as assertiveness. Assertiveness training normally begins with guidelines that help clients distinguish among assertiveness, aggressiveness, and passivity. Group discussion can focus on the usefulness of assertive responses for drink refusal, as well as on the possible relationships between nonassertiveness and drinking problems. Sometimes people drink when their lack of assertiveness has prevented them from achieving their goals. Many clients also use alcohol in the mistaken belief that assertiveness is impossible to achieve in a sober state. Once clients have conceptualized the importance of assertiveness, they are ready to move ahead to skill-building and behavior rehearsal.

In a group exercise designed for clients with alcohol-related problems (Lewis et. al., 1994), group members first practice assertive drink refusal. First, one of the group members role plays offering a drink while the group leader models assertive refusal. Participants then role play similar situations, alternating between the roles of drink offerer and assertive refuser. Repetition, coaching, and feedback are used to enhance group members' skills. Once drink refusal behaviors have been rehearsed, group members move on to practice assertive behaviors they may need for dealing with other issues in their real-life situations.

The importance of this general approach lies in the fact that effective social skills can give clients important tools to be used in their recovery, whereas deficits in this area can place recovering clients in jeopardy.

> Social skills deficits may restrict alternatives of actions in a social situation, minimize an individual's control over the situation, and decrease the individual's access to desired resources. . . . Such deficits may prevent the individual from obtaining social and emotional support from others that may be necessary to maintain abstinence. Social skills deficits may also increase intrapersonal risk factors—for example, by producing increased anxiety or tension in social encounters. . . . If social skills deficits are chronic over the course of psychosocial development, the individual's potential for abusive drinking may increase. (Monti et al., 1989, p. 11)

Self-Control Training

Through behavioral self-control training, clients learn how to make behavioral changes that can help them meet their own goals. Individuals learn to interrupt their drinking behaviors by analyzing and monitoring their drinking and by using self-reinforcement and stimulus-control methods on their own.

One important aspect of self-control training involves clients' identification of the situations that they normally associate with drinking. Usually, clients identify these situations by monitoring their day-to-day behaviors or by recollecting their past behaviors. Clients may also use the Inventory of Drinking Situations (Annis, 1982), a self-administered inventory that categorizes the kinds of experiences that place individuals at high risk for drinking. Once clients have identified the situations that put them at highest risk, they can select and practice strategies for coping with them more effectively in the future. One alternative, of course, is avoiding situations that are overly difficult. Ideally, however, individuals can move purposefully from moderately difficult to more challenging situations, gaining confidence with each success.

Sanchez-Craig, Wilkins, and Walker (1987) suggest that the coping strategies used by clients can be categorized as cognitive or behavioral. Cognitive strategies include self-statements such as reappraisals or reminders about their commitment to change. Behavioral methods include alternative behaviors or use of skills such as relaxation or assertiveness. A key component of self-control training is planning. Clients learn to plan carefully for anticipated situations and to engage in repeated rehearsals of the coping strategies they have selected. All clients need to have a large enough repertoire of alternative coping skills available so that they have choices when dealing with difficult challenges.

Clients can use self-control training methods whether their goals are abstinence or moderation. Working toward moderation is difficult and complex, but treatment providers need to discuss goals openly and objectively with their clients. "The shortcoming of an automatic insistence on abstinence as the only acceptable goal is that many clients who feel unable to share their real feelings with counselors may hold onto an unrealistic belief that they can control their drinking on their own or may refuse to enter into treatment at all" (Lewis et al., 1994). Treatment providers can help clients set realistic goals if they themselves are familiar with the characteristics associated with success in maintaining either moderation or abstinence. The client who is a good prospect for success in obtaining a moderation outcome is likely to be one who is young and healthy, who does not appear to be physically addicted to alcohol, who has not developed many life problems related to alcohol, and whose problem is of relatively short duration. People whose problems are longstanding and severe, who have health problems, and who have shown signs of physical dependence on alcohol tend to be more successful in achieving a goal of abstinence. In behavioral self-control training, as in all other treatment strategies, individualization is critical.

Brief Motivational Counseling

People are often surprised to learn that "relatively brief interventions of one to three sessions are comparable in impact to more extensive treatments for alcohol problems" and that brief interventions are "substantially more effective than no treatment in altering problem drinking" (Miller & Rollnick, 1991, p. 31). The efficacy of the brief intervention seems to be based on the success of the interview in motivating clients to make further changes on their own. This modality depends on the use of an effective and realistic approach to client motivation.

As the Institute of Medicine has found, "research has generally failed to support a trait view of alcoholics as poorly motivated, prone to particular defense mechanisms (e.g., denial), inherently resistive, or possessing a characteristic personality" (1990, p. 533). The myth that people with alcohol problems must always be harshly confronted in order to "break down their denial" is being replaced by the notion that motivation can be engendered through a positive and supportive counselor-client relationship.

The concept of *motivational interviewing,* which was developed by Miller and his associates (Miller, 1983, 1985; Miller & Rollnick, 1991), provides an alternative to the traditional confrontation. Miller suggests that treatment providers who actively press clients to accept the view that alcoholism underlies all of their problems tend to encounter resistance that becomes more entrenched as the debate continues. In contrast, motivational interviewing provides encouragement to the client by avoiding labels and accepting the notion that the client holds the final responsibility for making treatment decisions. Although the treatment provider shares the results of any assessment that is completed, the client ultimately decides how to use the data.

> What motivational interviewing does is to overcome the myth that substance abuse clients are so different from others that the usual principles of human behavior fail to apply to them. As long as we assume that people with alcohol or drug problems are unable to make responsible choices and must therefore be told what to do, we will be forced to deal with defensiveness and denial. If we recognize the unassailable truth that behaviors are based on individuals' choices—not therapists' wishes—we are more likely to see motivated clients. (Lewis, 1992, p. 31).

Behavioral Marital Therapy

Family cohesion has a major impact on long-term treatment outcomes for clients with alcohol problems (Moos, Finney, & Cronkite, 1990). This fact is not surprising, given the reciprocal effects of family systems and alcohol use. An individual's alcohol use affects the functioning of his or her family system, even to the point of becoming a central organizing factor. At the same time, family patterns that have arisen as adaptations to the alcohol problem may enable an alcohol-dependent member to continue his or her drinking.

Alcohol-related behaviors sometimes appear to serve a purpose in helping families maintain their stability through problem avoidance.

> These behaviors have come to play a crucial role in helping the family deal, in the short run, with the myriad problems that arise in day-to-day living. Many of these problems are internal to the family—sexual difficulties between spouses, the need to control explosive feelings, role conflicts, and so on. Others have to do with the relationship between the family and its community—conflicts with neighbors, demands at work, needs for more assertive behavior, and so on. . . . The family believes that the behaviors it uses to deal with these prob-

lems are *only* possible when alcohol is present. (Steinglass, Bennett, Wolin, & Reiss, 1987, p. 155)

If we believe that drinking behaviors are embedded in family systems, we need to consider the family, or at least the couple, as an appropriate unit of treatment. In fact, several studies have shown promising results in using behaviorally based couples counseling with alcohol-affected clients in early recovery (O'Farrell, 1992). For example, McCrady, Noel, Abrams, Stout, and Nelson (1986) compared three treatments as part of their Program for Alcoholic Couples Treatment (PACT) study. Couples were assigned at random to one of three treatments: (1) minimal spouse involvement; (2) alcohol-focused spouse involvement, which trained spouses in skills for dealing with alcohol-related situations; and (3) alcohol behavioral marital therapy, which added the use of behavioral therapy to increase positive activities and to teach communication and negotiation skills. All of the treatments were associated with decreases in alcohol use, but the behavioral family therapy also led to more stability and satisfaction in the couples' marriages. Another project, Counseling for Alcoholics' Marriages (CALM), was carried out by O'Farrell, Cutter, and Floyd (1985). Again, the combination of behavioral skill building with a focus on the couple relationship brought about positive results, both in terms of marital adjustment and in terms of drinking behaviors. The results of these and other studies of couples therapy led O'Farrell (1991) to suggest that couples-based interventions can be used effectively to:

- motivate an initial commitment to change in the alcoholic
- help stabilize the marital relationship and support improvements in the alcoholic's drinking during the year after treatment entry
- reduce deterioration and support maintenance of marital and drinking gains during long-term recovery (pp. 43-44)

Community Reinforcement Approach

The Community Reinforcement Approach has long been considered one of the best-documented attempts to provide multifaceted treatment for alcohol-affected clients. The program, which was designed for an inpatient, state hospital program for male alcoholics, is unusual in its comprehensiveness. Treatment has traditionally included the following components (Azrin, 1976):

- *Job Counseling* (efforts to help clients find permanent, full-time jobs that would help prevent a return to drinking after release from the hospital)

- *Marital Counseling* (providing couples counseling for married clients as well as "synthetic families" to aid in the recovery of unmarried clients)
- *Resocialization and Recreation* (providing postrelease alcohol-free social and recreational activities to complement Alcoholics Anonymous referrals)
- *Problem-Prevention Rehearsal* (training clients in ways to cope with situations that might otherwise lead to relapse)
- *Early Warning System* (using a mail-in "Happiness Scale" to be completed by clients on a daily basis)
- *Disulfiram* (developing supportive mechanisms enabling clients to use Antabuse for the purpose of impulse control)
- *Group Counseling* (implementing supportive group sessions during treatment and encouraging the development of social/recreational groups after release)
- *Buddy Procedure* (developing a mechanism to allow recovering people to act as peer advisors for clients)
- *Contracting* (formalizing agreements between treatment providers and clients through written contracts that spell out both program procedures and client responsibilities)

This general approach was designed to address the difficult challenges inherent in the transition from treatment to community environments. When clients return to their social, family, and work environments, they confront constant pressures to return to familiar drinking patterns. The Community Reinforcement Approach recognizes this factor.

Newly acquired social skills are subject to multiple environmental influences. For example, the physical environment (mass media, advertising, sensory cues for drinking) is structured to increase the likelihood of drinking, and drinking is associated with such social activities as conversation, recreation and dating. Under these environmental influences recovering alcoholics may not only lose existing support, but receive negative sanctions from former drinking associates. Finally, many recovering alcoholics do not have the personal resources (e.g., transportation, family, friends, employment) necessary to engage in new social situations. . . . An alternative approach is to create a new social system in the alcoholics' natural environment that provides wide varieties of social and recreational activities and reinforces the acquisition of appropriate social behaviors. (Mallams, Godley, Hall, & Meyers, 1982, p. 1116)

Stress Management Training

Stress management plays an important role in recovery from alcohol problems not because stress *causes* alccohol abuse but because so many clients have routinely used drinking or drug use as their only means of coping with stress. These individuals may never have learned alternate methods for dealing with the stressors of everyday life, let alone for handling major upheavals. When a stressful situation arises, even the most highly motivated client may be put at risk. As Washton (1989) points out, the buildup or onset of stress often serves as the first link in the "relapse chain" (p. 118).

In the context of treatment for alcohol problems, stress management training focuses on helping clients learn how to deal more effectively with environmental demands. Alcohol-affected clients, like all people, can cope with stress by directly altering the environment through problem solving; by changing their cognitions concerning stressors; or by interfering with nervous system activation through such methods as relaxation training. Clients with a greater number of stress management skills in their repertoires are more likely to be successful because they can choose from among several alternatives.

Training in problem-solving techniques can help clients prevent minor difficulties that might otherwise explode into disasters. When clients participate in training sessions, they learn that problem-solving skills can be used both to deal with alcohol-related dilemmas and to address more general concerns. Discussions and practice sessions can be used to help clients work through hypothetical situations related to alcohol use (e.g., how to avoid becoming intoxicated at a holiday celebration or how to cope with coworkers' invitations to join them for drinks after work). Clients can also learn to apply their skills to problems that do not appear on the surface to be alcohol-related (e.g., how to make ends meet financially). Practice allows individuals to become skillful at solving real-life problems when they present themselves, thus interrupting stress patterns at their onset.

Clients may also choose to work on their cognitive reactions to stressors. Sometimes situations engender stress responses because individuals interpret them as demanding, not because they are universally stress inducing. Cognitive restructuring helps clients recognize that their own assumptions and thought patterns may mediate arousal. For instance, individuals may assume that they will lose their jobs if they do not participate in alcohol-related social events. Thus an invitation to a social event may arouse feelings of intense but unnecessary anxiety. Affected individuals can make conscious decisions to think more rationally about the problems, to challenge unrealistic fears, and to identify and rehearse alternate self-messages.

Stressors remain a part of everyone's life, regardless of our attempts to prevent or reinterpret them. Clients need to be able to intervene at the point of the physiological stress response through such methods as muscle-relaxation procedures. For clients who are especially tense or anxious, relaxation training may become a central focus of treatment. Ideally, this method should be used to deal with the anxiety while other techniques are used concurrently to help clients prevent the problem from arising.

Treatment Choices

All of the options discussed above lend themselves to individual choice. Clients can be offered an array of possibilities so that the method used relates to identified skill deficits and personal goals. Clearly, the future research on treatment of alcohol problems will focus on individual differences.

> There is no single superior treatment approach for all persons with alcohol problems. . . . Reason for optimism about alcohol treatment lies in the range of promising alternatives that are available, each of which may be optimal for different types of individuals. Rather than seeking to establish the superiority of a single approach by testing specific interventions in heterogeneous populations, treatment outcome studies should delineate the characteristics of the subpopulation for whom particular modalities are maximally effective. (Institute of Medicine, 1989, p. 197)

Given the current state of the art, treatment providers should emphasize the methods that meet individual clients' goals with the least expense and disruption possible. The most successful treatment plans are likely to be those designed through an active partnership between treatment provider and client.

REFERENCES

American Psychiatric Association (1987). *Diagnostic and statistical manual of mental disorders* (3rd ed. rev.). (DSM III-R). Washington, DC: Author.

Annis, H. M. (1982). *Inventory of Drinking Situations*. Toronto: Addiction Research Foundation.

Azrin, N. (1976). Improvements in the community-reinforcement approach to alcoholism. *Behavior Research and Therapy, 14*, 339-348.

Holder, H., Longabough, R., Miller, W. R., & Rubonis, A. V. (1991). The cost effectiveness of treatment for alcoholism: A first approximation. *Journal of Studies on Alcohol, 52*, 517-540.

Institute of Medicine (1989). *Prevention and treatment of alcohol problems: Research opportunities*. Washington, DC: National Academy Press.

Institute of Medicine (1990). *Broadening the base of treatment for alcohol problems*. Washington, DC: National Academy Press.

Lewis, J. A. (1992, Winter). Applying the motivational interviewing process. *The Family Psychologist, 8* (1), 31-32.

Lewis, J. A., Dana, R. Q., & Blevins, G. A. (1994). *Substance abuse counseling: An individualized approach* (2nd ed.). Pacific Grove, CA: Brooks/Cole.

Mallams, J. H., Godley, M. D., Hall, G. M., & Meyers, R. J. (1982). A social-systems approach to resocializing alcoholics in the community. *Journal of Studies on Alcohol, 43*, 1115-1123.

McCrady, B. S., Noel, N. E., Abrams, D. B., Stout, R. L., & Nelson, H. F. (1986). Comparative effectiveness of three types of spouse involvement in outpatient behavioral alcoholism treatment. *Journal of Studies on Alcohol, 47*, 459-467.

Miller, W. R. (1983). Motivational interviewing with problem drinkers. *Behavioral Psychotherapy, 11*, 147-172.

Miller, W. R. (1985). Motivation for treatment: A review with special emphasis on alcoholism. *Psychological Bulletin, 98*, 84–107.

Miller, W. R. (1992). The evolution of treatment for alcohol problems since 1945. In P. G. Erickson & H. Kalant (Eds.), *Windows on science* (pp. 107-124). Toronto: Addiction Research Foundation.

Miller, W. R., & Rollnick, S. (1991). *Motivational interviewing: Preparing people to change addictive behavior.* New York: Guilford.

Monti, P. M., Abrams, D. B., Kadden, R. M., & Cooney, N. L. (1989). *Treating alcohol dependence: A coping skills training guide.* New York:Guilford.

Moos, R. H., Finney, J. W., & Cronkite, R. C. (1990). *Alcoholism treatment: Context, process, and outcome.* New York: Oxford University Press.

O'Farrell, T. J. (1991). Using couples therapy in the treatment of alcoholism. *Family Dynamics of Addiction Quarterly, 1*(4), 39–45.

O'Farrell, T.J. (1992). Families and alcohol problems: An overview of treatment research. *Journal of Family Psychology, 5*, 339–359.

O'Farrell, T. J., Cutter, H. S. G., & Floyd, F. J. (1985). Evaluating behavioral marital therapy for male alcoholics: Effects on marital adjustment and communication from before to after therapy. *Behavior Therapy, 16*, 147–167.

Sanchez-Craig, M., Wilkins, D. A., & Walker, K. (1987). Theory and methods for secondary prevention of alcohol problems: A cognitively based approach. In C. W. Cox (Ed.), *Treatment and prevention of alcohol problems* (pp. 287–331). New York: Academic Press.

Steinglass, P., Bennett, L. A., Wolin, S. J., & Reiss, D. (1987). *The alcoholic family.* New York: Basic Books.

Washton, A. M. (1989). *Cocaine addiction: Treatment, recovery, and relapse prevention.* New York: Norton.

Chapter **6**

Drug Abuse Treatment: Approaches and Effectiveness

Cheryl L. Mejta, Carol L. Naylor,
E. Michael Maslar

According to a recent study of the nation's drug use patterns and associated problems, an estimated 5.5 million people are in need of drug abuse treatment (Institute of Medicine, 1990a). The detrimental effects of drug abuse on society, the drug abuser, and his or her family are widely recognized. Drug abuse is a significant factor in accidents, crimes and violence, illness and disease, disability, suicide and homicide, and lost productivity (Frances & Miller, 1991). Societal costs of drug abuse are estimated to be around $72 billion (Institute of Medicine, 1990a). Recognizing the serious health consequences of drug abuse, *Healthy People Year 2000* cited reduction of drug abuse and its associated problems as among the primary national health objectives (Institute of Medicine, 1990b).

Concurrent with the recognized need and demand for drug abuse treatment are concerns about the costs associated with providing this treatment. To control costs and prevent abuses of the third-party payment system, managed health care groups and peer review/quality assurance committees are increasing (Frances & Miller, 1991). Within the context of escalating costs, reduced appropriations, increased health consequences, and increased demand, developing and providing effective drug abuse treatment is critical.

This chapter provides an overview of currently used drug abuse treatment programs and approaches. It also addresses the following questions: (a) Is drug abuse treatment effective? (b) Are some treatment modalities and approaches more effective than others? (c) Who seems to do best in treatment? (d) What kinds of counselors seem to be most effective? and (e) What are some innovations in drug abuse treatment?

DRUG ABUSE TREATMENT EFFECTIVENESS: OVERVIEW OF DRUG ABUSE TREATMENT OUTCOME STUDIES

As noted by the Institute of Medicine (1990a), the objectives of drug abuse treatment differ according to the perspective of the invested party (e.g., drug abuse treatment programs; regulatory, licensing, or monitoring agencies; agencies providing coverage for treatment expenses; law enforcement/criminal justice organizations; drug abusers and their families). There are, however, some commonly recognized and, at least within the treatment community, commonly agreed upon goals of drug abuse treatment. The primary goal of drug abuse treatment is to eliminate or reduce client's illicit and licit drug use. Secondary goals of drug abuse treatment often include (a) decreasing criminal activity; (b) increasing educational level and improving vocational skills; (c) attaining steady employment; (d) achieving stable social and familial relationships; (e) developing coping, social, and communication skills; (f) improving physical and psychological health; and (g) eliminating or reducing the client's health risk behaviors, especially those associated with HIV transmission and infection.

How effective are our current drug abuse treatment programs in accomplishing these goals? In a review of treatment outcome studies, Tims, Fletcher, and Hubbard (1991) stated, "The available evidence from treatment outcome studies shows that drug abuse treatment works for significant numbers of clients who enter treatment" (p. 93). Two major national, longitudinal treatment outcome studies conducted within the past two decades support this contention. The first study, the Drug Abuse Reporting Program (DARP), was conducted by the Institute for Behavioral Research at Texas Christian University. Over 44,000 clients admitted into 52 federally funded treatment programs between the years 1969 and 1974 were interviewed at intake and bimonthly during treatment. Follow-up interviews were conducted with samples of these clients 6 and 12 years after treatment admission. The results of this study indicated that drug abuse treatment was effective in reducing or eliminating drug use and criminal activity. Across the major treatment modalities studied (methadone maintenance, therapeutic community, and outpatient drug-free), 26% of the clients showed no drug use and no criminal activity, and 38% of the clients showed no daily drug use and no major criminal activity at 1 year post-treatment (Simpson & Sells, 1982a).

The second study, the Treatment Outcome Prospective Study (TOPS), was conducted by Research Triangle Institute. Over 11,000 clients admitted into 41 federally funded drug abuse treatment programs between 1979 and 1981 were studied at intake, 1 month after treatment admission, and every 3 months during treatment. Follow-up interviews were conducted with a sample of clients at 3 months, 1 year, 2 years, and 3 to 5 years after treatment discharge. The results of this study also indicated that drug abuse treatment was effective in eliminating or reducing clients' drug use. Across the major treatment modalities (methadone maintenance, therapeutic community, outpatient drug-free), about 89% of the regular heroin users, about 87% of the regular cocaine users, about 84% of the regular users of nonmedical psychotherapeutics, and about 55% of the regular users of marijuana were no longer using their primary drug 1 year after treatment discharge (Hubbard et al., 1989, pp. 99-119).

The results of the TOPS and DARP studies clearly demonstrate that positive behavioral changes are associated with drug abuse treatment. Drug abuse treatment resulted in reduced use of licit and illicit drugs during and after treatment, reductions in criminal activity, and increases in employment (Craddock, Bray, & Hubbard, 1985; Hubbard et al., 1989; Simpson & Sells, 1982b). These results were consistent across the three primary treatment modalities.

An additional national treatment outcome study, Drug Abuse Treatment Outcome Study (DATOS), funded by the National Institute on Drug Abuse (NIDA) and conducted by Tims, Fletcher, and Hubbard, currently is underway. This study will examine the major drugs of abuse in the 1990s (cocaine, opioids, polydrug abuse), will examine treatment processes, and will explore client-treatment matching variables (Tims et al., 1991).

Hubbard et al. (1989) stated, "There is no question that treatment works, but much more needs to be known about how and why treatment works" (p. 43). The following sections examine the literature on treatment modalities, techniques, and approaches.

DRUG ABUSE TREATMENT MODALITIES

Until recently, four primary drug abuse treatment modalities existed: detoxification programs, methadone maintenance programs, residential drug-free programs or therapeutic communities, and outpatient drug-free programs. More recently, two additional treatment modalities emerged: chemical dependency (CD) programs (short-term, 21 to 28 day, inpatient, hospital-based programs) and intensive outpatient programs. This section provides a brief description of these major treatment modalities and their effectiveness.

Detoxification

Detoxification programs usually supplement the other primary drug treatment modalities. Clients who are physiologically dependent on a drug often enter a detoxification program prior to entering drug-free outpatient treatment or residential treatment. The goal of detoxification is to eliminate the acute physiological dependence on a drug. This is accomplished through supervised withdrawal in which symptomatic relief from the withdrawal syndrome is provided to the client. The length of time in detoxification depends upon the physiological withdrawal syndrome associated with the specific drug. Newman (1979) provides a more detailed description of detoxification programs. Compared to the other treatment modalities, detoxification alone was not found to be effective in reducing or eliminating subsequent drug use (Hubbard et al.,

1989). It should be noted, however, that detoxification programs, designed to focus primarily on the physiological aspects of addiction, are better conceived as adjuncts to treatment regimens designed to address the psychological, sociological, and familial aspects of addiction.

Methadone Maintenance

Methadone maintenance programs originated in the 1960s as a treatment for opiate-dependent clients. (See Dole and Nyswander, 1965, and Dole, Nyswander, and Warner, 1968, for an initial description of the use and effectiveness of methadone for the treatment of heroin addiction.) Methadone is a long-acting synthetic opiate substitute. Administered orally in doses averaging between 20 and 100 milligrams, methadone eliminates the withdrawal symptoms associated with abstinence from opiates without producing euphoria or toxicological side effects (Hargreaves, 1986; Kreek, 1983).

The Food and Drug Administration (FDA) established regulations specifying the conditions for the use of methadone maintenance and detoxification treatment (Federal Drug Register [FDR], 1989, 21 CFR Part 291). To meet the eligibility criteria for methadone a client must be at least 18 years old, must have at least a 1-year history of opiate use, and must currently be physiologically dependent on opiates. The regulations also specify acceptable methadone dose ranges (no daily dose greater than 100 mg without physician justification), minimum staffing patterns (counselor:patient ratio no greater than 1:50), minimum program services available to patients (inclusion of medical and rehabilitative services), and minimum standards for treatment plan reviews (every 90 days during the first year and twice yearly subsequently).

As stated by Kreek (1991), the goals of methadone maintenance are: (a) reduction or cessation of illicit narcotic use; (b) voluntary retention in treatment for several years; (c) reduction or cessation of other drugs, including alcohol; (d) reduction in diseases transmitted by the use of unsterile injection equipment; (e) reduction in criminality and antisocial behaviors; and (f) improvement in socialization and productivity.

McLellan (1986) noted that there have been over 275 published reports evaluating the effectiveness of methadone maintenance. He concluded, "the weight of evidence indicates that the majority of opiate dependent patients show significant improvements in opiate and nonopiate drug use, employment, and illegal activity during methadone maintenance" (p. 500). In a review of studies examining the health consequences of methadone, Kreek (1983) concluded, "there are minimal side effects that are clinically detectable in patients during chronic methadone maintenance treatment. Toxicity related to methadone during chronic treatment is extraordinarily rare" (p. 474). Follow-up studies at 1 year posttreatment discharge show abstinence rates between 68% (Tims et al., 1991, p. 101) and 83% (Hubbard et al., 1989, pp. 99-119).

Not all clients, however, do well in methadone maintenance treatment. A review of studies by McLellan, Luborsky, Woody, O'Brien, and Druley (1983) indicated that between 15% and 35% of methadone maintenance patients drop out within 12 months of entering treatment. McLellan et al. (1983) also reviewed client predictors of treatment retention, adjustment, and outcome of methadone maintenance clients. Clients most likely to be retained in methadone treatment were black, married, and over the age of 25. Earlier dropout from treatment was associated with a history of criminality, greater severity of psychological problems, and poorer employment. Client predictors of successful outcome were employment, stable family relations, the ability to stabilize on low dosages of methadone immediately before detoxification, and longer length of time on methadone.

There is some controversy about the use of methadone even though studies have proven its effectiveness. Because methadone produces its own physiological dependence, there is some concern about its long-term use with clients (Allison, Hubbard, & Rachal, 1985, p. 11).

Outpatient Drug-Free Treatment Programs

The Institute of Medicine (1990a) noted the heterogeneity among outpatient drug-free programs with respect to their treatment processes, philosophies, staffing patterns, and clients. Generally, outpatient drug-free programs serve clients who have less severe drug-related problems (drug abuse rather than drug dependence), clients who are reentering the community after residential treatment, or clients who relapsed after previous treatment (Kleber & Slobetz, 1979). Outpatient programs usually are between 6 to 9 months in duration with the primary therapeutic interventions consisting of individual and group counseling (Allison et al., 1985).

In a survey of outpatient drug abuse programs, Price et al. (1991) identified the following treatment goals: (a) abstinence from alcohol and other drugs; (b) steady employment; (c) stable social relationships; (d) positive physical and emotional health; (e) improved spiritual strength; and (f) adhering to legal mandates/requirements as applicable. Clearly, these goals are similar to those of other treatment modalities.

Both the TOPS (Hubbard et al., 1989) and DARP (Simpson & Sells, 1982b) results indicate that outpatient drug-free treatment programs are effective in reducing drug use and improving employment. Retention in outpatient treatment, however, is low. Only about 18% of the clients who enter treatment complete the program (Hubbard et al., 1989).

Intensive Outpatient Programs

Intensive outpatient (IO) programs are structured programs that consist of individual counseling, group counseling, and attendance at self-help groups. Clients attend the program 4 to 5 days a week, but they return home in the evening. The effectiveness of these programs has not been established yet (Institute of Medicine, 1990a).

Therapeutic Communities

Therapeutic communities (TCs) are longer term (6- to 24-month) residential treatment communities for drug abusers with longstanding negative and deficient behavioral patterns. Within the TC framework, drug abuse is viewed as "a deviant behavior, reflecting impeded personality development and/or chronic deficits in social, educational and economic skills" (DeLeon, 1986, p. 7). Consistent with this view of drug abuse, the goals of TCs involve more global and comprehensive lifestyle changes including altering negative patterns of behaving, thinking, and feeling and developing a responsible, drug-free lifestyle (DeLeon, 1986; DeLeon & Rosenthal, 1979).

To accomplish the goals of resocializing and habilitating drug abusers, TCs simulate a model family with a hierarchical structure, a system of clear and explicit behavioral norms and rules, and clearly specified rewards for adhering to the rules and consequences for violating the rules (Institute of Medicine, 1990a). Clients usually progress through a series of treatment phases that include increasing responsibilities, privileges, and status within the TC. Movement through the phases is based upon demonstrated changes in behavior. The TC treatment regimen typically includes highly confrontive encounter groups, individual counseling, group counseling, remedial and formal education, and residential job functions (DeLeon & Rosenthal, 1979). The staff, mostly recovering paraprofessional counselors, rely heavily on the peer group to participate in the treatment process.

Follow-up studies support the effectiveness of TCs in reducing drug use, reducing criminality, and increasing employment among clients who graduate from the program (DeLeon, 1985; Institute of Medicine, 1990a). It should be noted, however, that only about 10% of the clients entering a TC complete treatment (Bale et al., 1980). Simpson et al. (1979) found that length of stay was a strong predictor of post-treatment outcomes; a minimum of 3 months was needed to produce positive outcomes with further improvements occurring with increasing lengths of time in treatment up to 18 months.

Chemical Dependency Programs

Chemical dependency (CD) programs are short-term (21 to 28 days), privately financed, hospital-based programs initially developed for alcohol-dependent clients. More recently, clients with other drug dependencies have been treated in CD programs. CD programs view alcohol and other drug dependencies as diseases that are progressive and fatal if untreated. Because the drug dependent person is perceived as having no control over his or her addiction, the treatment goal is total abstinence from alcohol and other drugs. Disease-oriented, 12-step, self-help philosophies underlie CD programs' therapeutic model. While in treatment, clients attend educational groups on chemical dependency, attend self-help group meetings, receive individual counseling sessions, participate in other topic-focused groups, and work the 12 steps. They also meet with other professionals (e.g., physicians, psychiatrists, psychologists, social workers) as needed. Cook (1988a, 1988b) provides a more detailed description of chemical dependency programs.

Currently, there is little available information about the effectiveness of CD programs. Some research results suggest that clients with primary drug problems have poorer outcomes than clients with primary alcohol problems at post-treatment follow-up (Institute of Medicine, 1990a).

COMPARATIVE EVALUATION OF TREATMENT MODALITIES

Are there differences in treatment effectiveness across treatment modalities? In general, the treatment outcome research has not demonstrated one treatment modality to be more effective than another treatment modality. No significant differences in outcome were found among three of the four major treatment modalities in the DARP study; similar positive changes in drug use and criminal activity were found across treatment modalities. Clients in detoxification, however, did not show positive treatment outcomes (Hubbard et al., 1989, p. 7). Results of the TOPS study also demonstrated that drug abuse treatment is effective in producing substantial reductions in drug use, declines in criminal activity, improvements in many negative behaviors associated with drug use, and improvements in employment across treatment modalities. The goal of abstinence from all drugs, however, seems more difficult to attain (Hubbard et al., 1989, p. 124). Comparisons with chemical dependency programs and intensive outpatient programs are not yet available.

In part, treatment outcome may not differ by treatment modality because client characteristics are not considered when assigning clients to treatment modalities. Hansen and Emrick (1983) found that clients were assigned to treatment modalities on the basis of what modalities were available at the treatment program, rather than on the basis of clients' presenting problems and needs.

Although there currently are no conclusive research findings indicating which clients will do best in which treatment modality, guidelines for referring clients to the appropriate level of care have been proposed by the American Society of Addiction Medicine (1992) and Gray (1989). Outpatient treatment is indicated for clients who are not at risk for withdrawal, who are free of any significant medical and emotional problems, who show motivation for treatment, who are able to maintain abstinence with minimal support, who have a supportive recovery environment, and who have a reasonably stable work and family life. Intensive outpatient treatment is recommended for clients who are at minimal risk for withdrawal, who have no or manageable medical problems, who have mild emotional or behavioral problems, who show some resistance to treatment, who need close monitoring and support to sustain abstinence, and who need some environmental support and structure to pursue recovery goals. Chemical dependency programs (28-day hospital programs) are recommended for clients who are at risk for withdrawal, who have medical conditions requiring monitoring, who have emotional and/or behavioral conditions necessitating a 24-hour structured setting, who show little motivation for treatment, who have a history of relapse in outpatient treatment, and whose current environment is unsupportive of recovery. Therapeutic communities or residential drug-free programs are indicated for clients who lack permanent living situations, who have experienced many negative drug-related consequences, who need to learn socialization skills and basic living skills, and who have little, if any, family, social, or job support.

LENGTH OF TIME IN TREATMENT

Though treatment effectiveness did not differ across the major modalities, length of time in treatment was a predictor of treatment outcome. The DARP study results indicated that a minimum of 3 months in treatment was needed to produce positive treatment outcomes; treatment outcomes improved further in direct proportion to additional time spent in treatment (Simpson, 1988; Simpson & Sells, 1982b). Simpson (1988) concluded that good client outcomes are more a function of the amount of time spent in treatment rather than the specific treatment modality provided to the client. The TOPS study results also found that time in treatment predicted treatment outcome; however, the minimum time in treatment necessary to produce positive treatment outcomes was found to be 6 to 12 months (Hubbard et al., 1989). It should be noted that although time in treatment is a predictor of outcome for drug abuse it is not a predictor for alcohol abuse (Miller & Hester, 1986).

DRUG ABUSE TREATMENT APPROACHES

Although there is evidence that drug abuse treatment is effective, empirical evidence establishing a relationship between specific techniques and overall effectiveness is still under investigation. According to Hubbard et al. (1989), "little is known about how and why treatment works" (p. 43). In order to determine the relationship between techniques and effectiveness, a number of factors need to be considered: (a) the actual techniques utilized in counseling need to be described; (b) the empirical evidence regarding the effectiveness of these techniques needs to be explored; (c) factors contributing to or counterproductive to overall treatment effectiveness need to be determined; and (d) the assumptions underlying the theoretical model upon which the counseling is based need to be validated. It also is important to examine the characteristics of clients who do well in existing treatment programs and the characteristics of counselors who effectively promote clients' behavior change.

Current Drug Abuse Treatment Techniques

Slight variations in drug abuse treatment techniques and approaches are found across the primary treatment modalities. Allison et al. (1985) and Hubbard et al. (1989) examined treatment processes across the primary treatment modalities. In methadone maintenance programs, counselors, who maintain caseloads of 35 to 50 clients, provide weekly, 30-minute, individual counseling sessions focused on problem solving and lifestyle change. In outpatient drug-free programs, counselors, who maintain a caseload of 10 to 35 clients, provide weekly, 45-minute, individual counseling sessions and weekly, 90-minute group counseling sessions focused on coping skills, problem solving and interpersonal skills. In therapeutic communities, counselors facilitate daily community meetings, group discussions, and confrontational encounter groups with the entire TC community (30 to 60 residents) while also providing weekly individual and small group counseling sessions to the 8 to 12 residents on their caseloads. Counseling sessions focus on resocialization, changing dysfunctional behavior patterns, problem solving, and skill development. Across these three modalities, little emphasis was placed on psychotherapy (Hubbard et al., 1989). The traditional intervention strategies used in chemical dependency programs include a combination of individual and group therapy, educational lectures on drug abuse, 12-step assignments, and self-help groups (Miller & Hester, 1986).

Effectiveness of Current Techniques

Although there has been extensive research examining the effectiveness of treatment modalities in treating drug abuse, research examining the effectiveness of specific interventions and techniques used within the treatment modalities is minimal. Little is known about why treatment works when it does. This section reviews available research on the major treatment interventions utilized in drug abuse treatment programs.

Individual Psychotherapy and Counseling

There has been only limited research investigating the effectiveness of individual psychotherapy and counseling in the treatment of drug abuse. "Only a few well-designed investigations on the relative efficacy of different types of psychotherapy with drug abusers have been carried out at this point" (Onken, 1991, p. 268).

Woody et al. (1983) verified the effectiveness of individual psychotherapy, in combination with drug counseling, in the treatment of drug abuse. In a controlled study, opiate-addicted clients were assigned to (a) drug counseling alone; (b) drug counseling and cognitive behavioral therapy; or (c) drug counseling and supportive expressive therapy. The overall results indicated that all three groups had improved outcomes. Those clients receiving psychotherapy in addition to drug counseling showed "greater levels of patient improvement with significantly lower methadone levels and with less use of ancillary medications" at a 7-month follow-up (Woody et al., 1983, p. 644). These results were again verified at the 12-month follow-up (Woody, McLellan, Luborsky, & O'Brien 1987). Woody et al. (1983) noted that those clients in the supportive-expressive form of psychotherapy improved more than the clients in cognitive-behavioral psychotherapy in overall psychological functioning and employment.

The differences among groups may be attributed to the amount of time spent with a therapist. Clients in the supportive-expressive therapy group spent more time with their therapist than the clients in the cognitive-behavioral group. Furthermore, the clients in the psychotherapy groups "spent about 35% more time with a helping person than did the DC [drug counseling] patients" (Woody et al., 1983, p.645).

The effectiveness of individual psychotherapy in the treatment of drug abuse also has been verified by Schiffer (1988). While in a 4-week, inpatient, drug treatment program, nine cocaine abusers began intensive psychotherapy. Successful treatment outcome was associated with (a) the establishment of a nonjudgmental, empathetic therapeutic relationship; (b) the use of supportive therapy emphasizing abstinence and identification of other therapeutic issues; and (c) a focus on understanding the dynamics of personal compulsive behaviors.

Group Therapy and Counseling

Group counseling and therapy frequently are used in the treatment of drug abuse. Currently, however, there are no systematic descriptions of group counseling/therapy approaches with drug abusers, nor are there any controlled outcome studies examining the effectiveness of group counseling/therapy with drug abusers (Galanter, Castaneda, & Franco, 1991).

Family Therapy and Counseling

Family treatment also has been found to be a significant factor in successful recovery outcomes (Todd, 1984). "Recently evidence has been obtained from a controlled treatment outcome study that a family treatment therapy program can have a significant impact on heroin abuse" (Todd, 1984, p. 112). However, it is important to note that only a behavioral family approach has been verified as effective and "that there is no implication that similar results can be obtained with 'garden-variety' family therapy" (Todd, 1984, p. 112).

Self-Help Groups

Although self-help groups such as Narcotics Anonymous (NA) and Cocaine Anonymous (CA) frequently are used as adjuncts to treatment, empirical investigations examining their effectiveness in the treatment of drug abuse are lacking. The few studies that have been conducted focus on the effectiveness of Alcoholics Anonymous (AA) in treating alcoholism. Emrick (1987) found that attendance at AA meetings was associated with better outcomes for some alcoholics.

Predictors of Treatment Outcome

In examining the effectiveness of drug abuse treatment, it is important to consider the characteristics of clients for whom current treatment approaches do and do not work. It also is important to explore the characteristics and qualities of counselors who work effectively with clients to produce behavior change.

Client Predictors of Treatment Outcome

Longbaugh and Lewis (1988) summarized a growing list of client descriptors that are of potential use in efforts at treatment matching and predicting treatment outcome. These factors include age, gender, prior alcohol consumption, and nature and extent of polydrug use. Pertinent psychological variables include psychiatric diagnoses, psychological health, marital status, employment status, socioeconomic status, environmental stressors and supports, insurance coverage and other resources for payment, pattern of participation in self-help groups, treatment history, family history of alcoholism and alcohol and substance abuse, and presence or absence of possible biological markers of alcoholism. This section summarizes some findings of recent research in several of these areas.

Westermeyer (1989) summarized client and other nontreatment factors related to outcome for drug abusers. Random assignment to self-help group affiliations was not associated with outcome; only 20% of drug abusers affiliate with self-help groups over a long period. Those who do affiliate, however, evidence higher success rates. Clients' reports of arguments with significant others and loss of socially supportive relationships predict drug use. Employment consistently is associated with abstinence or decreased substance abuse. Married individuals consistently do better than other groups. Affiliation with heavy drinking or drug-using subcultures undermines success.

An exploration of coercion into treatment revealed that employer pressure is not as potent as other types of force. Legal coercion may enhance success in groups having more to lose as the result of not complying than in groups such as "skid row" alcoholics and drug users. It is also not clear that treatment is more effective than punishment for groups such as DUI offenders.

Platt (1986) also reviewed client factors associated with treatment outcome. Better treatment outcomes were associated with less involvement in a drug subculture, including fewer drugs used prior to treatment, steady employment, greater work experience, more developed employment-related skills, higher educational level, fewer pretreatment arrests, fewer psychiatric symptoms, being older, and being married.

Hser, Anglin, and Liu (1991) identified a number of predictors related to gender. Young male addicts who indulged in daily drug use during treatment were unemployed and unmarried and exhibited a higher risk of dropping out of treatment. Males in general were more likely to leave treatment. The length of time between treatment admission and termination of drug use and dealing was shorter for women than for men. Client patterns of decline in functioning leading to negative outcome were different for the sexes. Women tended to progress from unemployment to relapse, to a broken significant relationship, and finally to illegal activity. Male patterns showed progression from drug dealing to relapse, to unemployment, and then to illegal activity.

Counselor Predictors of Treatment Outcome

Though some attention has been paid to client predictors of treatment outcome, very little research has been conducted on counselor predictors of client outcome. Early research on counselor predictors focused on the professional status (professional versus paraprofessional counselors) and recovery (recovering versus nonrecovering) status of counselors. The results of these studies suggested that counselors' performances did not differ on the basis of formal education or past history of addiction (e.g., Aiken, Loscuito, Ausetts, & Brown, 1984; Durlak, 1979). Aiken et al. (1984) examined treatment progress for 302 clients in methadone maintenance or outpatient drug-free programs who were working with professional counselors (bachelor's degree and no addiction history), ex-addict paraprofessional counselors, and nonaddict paraprofessional counselors. The results indicated that all three counselor groups were equally effective in producing client change in drug use, criminality, educational activities, and life quality.

A recent study conducted by McLellan, Woody, Luborsky, & Goehl (1988) examined the role of the individual counselor in the treatment of drug abusers. Sixty-one opiate-dependent clients in methadone treatment were randomly assigned to four counselors after the two counselors who previously had been assigned to these cases resigned. Clients' treatment progress, as measured by urinalysis results, methadone dosage, prescriptions for psychotropic medications, employment, and arrest records, was compared for the six-month period before the transfer and the six-month period after the transfer. Statistically significant pretransfer to post-transfer differences were found in urinalysis results (decrease in positive urines after transfer), methadone dose (reductions in methadone dose after transfer), and employment (higher employment rate after the transfer). Marked and consistent differences in client outcome were found among the four counselors to whom clients were transferred. Similar to the results of Aiken et al. (1984), counselors' qualifications and experience did not account for the counselor caseload differences. After an examination of counselors' charts, it was suggested that counseling process variables differentiated effective from less effective counselors. Specifically, it was found that consistent and professional patient management practices (more frequent sessions, attending to changes in methadone dose and prescription of ancillary medications, enforcement of clinic rules, use of program resources such as employment counselor and nurse) coupled with the use of basic psychotherapy techniques (anticipating problems and discussing strategies to deal with anticipated situations) were associated with better client outcomes.

Catalano, Hawkins, Wells, & Miller (1991) conducted a review of controlled studies on adolescent drug abuse treatment. They found that treatment completion rates were positively correlated with the number of years staff had worked in the program, the number of volunteer staff in client contact, and the use of a practical problem-solving approach with clients.

Rohrer, Thomas, and Yasenchak (1992) examined profiles of counselor traits compiled from surveys of clients in residential treatment. Clients described the ideal counselor as understanding, concerned, caring, experienced, honest, certified, a good listener, street-wise, easy to talk to, direct, and open-minded. Clients described ineffective counselors as unable to relate to clients, dishonest, treating clients like children, uneducated, insincere, rude, foul-mouthed, showing favoritism, and unfair. Males preferred counselors with experience, and females disliked counselors with a foul mouth. White clients preferred counselors who cared and disliked counselors who were fake. Black clients most disliked counselors perceived as weak, unfair, and lazy. Clients 43 years old and above preferred counselors who were easy to talk with but not insincere.

Younger clients rated most negatively the counselors who lacked knowledge about drug use.

Although the results above were not correlated with measures of treatment outcome, they may be instructive when coupled with the results of studies cited by Miller (1989). These suggest that success is correlated with client choice regarding counselors. Further research exploring the relationship between client choice of counselor based on desirable counselor traits would be fruitful.

Theoretical Model and Assumptions Underlying Techniques

Counseling approaches and techniques follow from the theoretical assumptions regarding the etiology and treatment of drug abuse. Within the past decade, the disease model of alcoholism has been accepted as the prevailing theoretical model for drug abuse as well (Brower, Blow, & Beresford, 1989; Drew, 1986). The disease model of drug abuse postulates that (a) the disease is within the person; the person is different from others who are not "sick" with the disease of chemical dependency; (b) the disease, by its very nature, is characterized by a loss of control over the drug-taking behavior; (c) the disease is irreversible; (d) the disease may be arrested by abstinence but never cured; and (e) any return to drug-taking behavior will begin the process of loss of control leading inevitably to relapse (Pattison, Sobell, & Sobell, 1977). The disease of chemical dependency as a problematic entity in itself is the focus of treatment rather than any problem of will power or underlying mental disorder (Brower et al., 1989). Within this model the addict's personal acceptance of the disease and the reality of his or her powerlessness over the disease is essential for recovery (Lewis, Dana, & Blevins, 1988).

Brower, Blow, and Beresford (1989) in discussing the advantages of the disease model, note that the model alleviates guilt and places an emphasis on responsibility for care of oneself. In addition, focusing on the chemical dependency as a problem in and of itself avoids the complication of focusing on other problematic life areas while the chemical dependency continues.

In considering the disadvantages of the disease model of chemical dependency, Miller (1991) focuses on the issue of motivation. The underlying belief system of the disease model maintains that recovery will occur only when clients (a) accept the disease as a personal reality, and (b) acknowledge their powerlessness over the disease. Inherent in this belief is the assumption that the drug abuser is in denial and is characteristically resistant to change (Lewis et al., 1988; Miller, 1991). The traditional strategies for intervention based on the disease model involve a combination of Alcoholics or Narcotics Anonymous, educational lectures, and individual and group therapy (Miller & Hester, 1986). The counseling techniques utilized are focused primarily on confronting the denial system of the substance abuser (Lewis et al., 1988; Miller, 1991; Miller & Hester, 1986). However, according to Miller and Hester (1986) there is no current empirical evidence supporting the effectiveness of these intervention strategies. In fact, studies evaluating the effectiveness of aggressive confrontational style in group leadership determined that aggressive confrontation was associated with more negative than positive outcomes (Miller & Hester, 1986). In contrast, research has indicated that the degree to which a counselor communicates empathic listening will have direct bearing on the degree of positive treatment outcomes for as long as 2 years after treatment (Miller, 1991).

Furthermore, research is indicating that motivation for enduring change must ultimately come from within the individual rather than from external sources (Miller, 1983; Prochaska & DiClemente, 1986). In research examining how people change, the internal process of self-liberation was identified as a critical process for change (Prochaska, DiClemente, & Norcross, 1992). Inherent in the process of self-liberation is a sense of self-efficacy, which involves an inner awareness that (a) one is able to succeed at one's efforts, (b) one is able to choose alternatives to addictive behavior, and (c) one is capable of acquiring the skills to obtain his or her chosen goals (Prochaska & DiClemente, 1986). Consequently, traditional models that emphasize the individual's helplessness can be seen as actually counterproductive in motivating the individual from contemplation to action (Lewis et al., 1988; Miller, 1983). Research has indicated that an internal belief in powerlessness may actually contribute to the process of relapse (Marlatt, 1985; Ogborne & Bornet, 1982).

Another noted disadvantage of the disease model is the assumption that the same treatment is applicable to every client with the same disease (Lewis et al., 1988). Hubbard, Marsden, Rachal, Harwood, Cavanaugh, and Ginzburg (1989), in surveying current drug treatment programs, noted that clients were not actively participating in the development of individualized treatment plans. Consistent with the concept of self-liberation, Hubbard et al. (1989) suggested that actively involving clients in the treatment planning process would increase compliance and overall motivation, thereby increasing the overall effectiveness of substance abuse treatment.

EMERGING TRENDS IN DRUG ABUSE TREATMENT

In examining current drug abuse treatment, it is clear that no single treatment modality, approach, or technique has been found to be most efficacious in treating drug abuse. More recent attempts to improve current drug abuse treatment have focused on determining (a) what techniques are most effective at which point in the client's change process (Transtheoretical Model of Change), and (b) what approaches and techniques are most effective for which type of clients (matching).

Transtheoretical Model of Change

The Transtheoretical Model of Change, proposed by Prochaska and DiClemente (1986), provides a framework within which to make clinical decisions about which therapeutic interventions are likely to be effective at different stages of client change. The model was based upon their research that analyzed 18 leading therapeutic systems and investigations of people who changed with and without the aid of therapy. Stages of client change and processes of change were identified. The five stages of change are Pre-Contemplation, Contemplation, Preparation, Action, and Maintenance. In the Pre-Contemplation stage, the person is unaware or underaware of his or her problems and therefore has no intention to change in the foreseeable future. If such an individual enters treatment, it is as a result of pressure from others.

In the Contemplation stage, the person is aware that there is a problem, and he or she is seriously thinking about addressing it. A commitment to change, however, has not yet been made. This stage may last for extended periods of time during which the client may weigh the pros and cons of the problem and its solution.

Clients in the Determination stage have made the decision to change and they are in the process of taking action to make the changes. They have a limited time to initiate action before motivation to change dissipates and they re-enter the Contemplation stage.

During the Action stage, the individual modifies his or her behavior, experience, or the environment in order to overcome the problem. Action is often erroneously equated with change and, as a consequence, the requisite work of preparation and maintenance are overlooked. In the Maintenance Stage, the client works to prevent relapse and consolidate the gains that have been achieved. Traditionally viewed as a static stage, maintenance is a continuation of change. For the addictions, this stage extends from 6 months to an indeterminate length of time past the point of taking action. Because relapse is so prevalent, it is evident that this model, rather than being linear, is spiral in nature. At any point in the process of change, the individual may cycle back to a previous stage.

Prochaska and DiClemente (1986) further proposed that different therapeutic interventions are more effective at different stages of change. Interventions that attempt to increase a person's awareness of his or her problem(s), increase his or her desire to address the problem(s), and increase his or her belief that change is possible are most effective in the earlier stages of change (e.g., Pre-Contemplation, Contemplation, and Determination). Some of the therapeutic processes effective during the earlier stages of change include (a) consciousness raising—increasing client's awareness of self and the problem through feedback, confrontation, and bibliotherapy; (b) dramatic relief—encouraging clients to experience and express feelings about their problems using psychodrama, role playing, etc.; (c) environmental reevaluation—increasing clients' awareness of how their problem affects others through feedback and the development of empathy; (d) self-liberation—increasing clients' belief in their ability to change and strengthening clients' commitment to change using decision-making techniques; and (e) self-reevaluation—encouraging clients to clarify their feelings and thoughts about themselves in relationship to the problem, using value clarification techniques, imagery, and corrective emotional experiences.

Interventions that focus on modifying behaviors are most effective in the later stages of change (e.g., Action and Maintenance). Some of the therapeutic processes effective during the later stages of change include (a) reinforcement management—rewarding changes; (b) helping relationships—discussing problems with someone who cares; (c) counterconditioning—substituting problem behaviors with alternative behaviors; and (d) stimulus control—avoiding cues that elicit problem behaviors. Generally, experiential, cognitive, and psychoanalytic approaches might be best used during the Pre-Contemplation and Contemplation stages, whereas existential and behavioral approaches might best be used during the Action and Maintenance stages.

Matching

In an attempt to improve the effectiveness of treatment, client-treatment matching has received increased attention. The underlying assumptions of matching include the following: (a) substance abusers constitute a heterogeneous population with a mix of psychological, social, and physical problems; and (b) no single treatment will be equally effective for all clients. Gray (1989) describes client-treatment matching as the process of "distinguishing among clients to determine the level of treatment needed, the type of treatment needed, the treatment approach, and the selection of treatment programs or practitioner" (pp. 6-7).

Client-treatment matching can occur across several dimensions and levels. McLellan, O'Brien, Kron, Alterman, and Druley (1980) identified some of the major dimensions. At the program-client level, treatment program choices are made by clients on the basis of location, cost, and referral network. At the client-setting or client-intensity level, there are at least four different options: advice/self-help, brief intervention, outpatient or partial hospitalization, and inpatient or residential. At the client-treatment level, there are fairly discrete treatment components, including group therapy, individual therapy, drug abuse education, and social service assistance. Miller (1991) suggests matching at two other levels: goals of change (abstinence, moderation, or increased functioning) and style of therapist (directive or nondirective).

Currently, empirical investigations on specific matching dimensions and variables are limited. Several reviews of the matching literature, however, are available. McLellan et al.'s (1980) review of outcome research in this area reveals several matching criteria. Success with antidipsotropic medication was associated with high social stability, treatment and compliance, married status, and absence of depression. Clients with high conceptual level, high therapist empathy, and high self-image tended to do well in group treatment. A more complex relation between client and therapist in individual therapy indicated that clients without diagnoses of antisocial personality and depression did particularly well with counselors exhibiting high levels of empathy and technique purity. Relapse prevention seemed to work best with clients having differential environment risk for drug or alcohol use. Clients who were more authoritarian, religious, conforming, and absent depression showed positive outcome in self-help groups.

Hester and Miller (1988) also reviewed the existing literature on client/treatment interactions in the areas of psychopathology, cognitive style, neuropsychological functioning, self-esteem, social stability, and clients' involvement in treatment selection and focus. In the area of psychopathology, the authors found that clients with low levels of psychiatric symptoms had better treatment outcomes than clients with high levels of psychiatric symptoms. Improvements in treatment outcomes occurred for clients with higher levels of psychiatric symptoms and clients with clinical depression if additional therapy was provided. In the area of cognitive style, the authors found that clients who had low conceptual levels (e.g., who preferred simpler rules and were more dependent on authority) had better treatment outcomes in programs that used a structured and directive approach. Clients who had high conceptual levels (e.g., were more independent and complex in their thought processes) had better treatment outcomes in programs that used a less structured and nondirective approach. It also was found that clients with neuropsychological impairments had poorer treatment outcomes. Confrontational group therapy was effective for clients with high self-esteem, but it had detrimental effects on clients with low self-esteem. A broad-based treatment program was more effective in working with clients who were less socially stable. Finally, the authors found that treatment satisfaction, compliance, and outcome were greater with clients who were able to choose the goals and type of treatment.

Brower et al. (1989) described therapist-client match. In a mismatch, client and therapist do not believe in the same model and, unless the mismatch is addressed and resolved, the relationship will be countertherapeutic. Two typologies of match were described: collusion and alliance. In collusion, therapist and client agree on the operative model but mutually deny problems that do not fit their beliefs. This relationship is countertherapeutic. In alliance, therapist and client agree on the model and address all pertinent problems over time. It is suggested that the integrative and multivariant models of drug abuse, because of their greater inclusiveness, allow for more flexibility in achieving alliance.

Integration that occurs only at the level of technique will not be effective and must also occur at the theoretical level.

In reviewing treatment matching variables, it appears that client factors are more predictive of outcome and differential treatment effect than treatment process. This may be true because client evaluation is more sophisticated than treatment evaluation at this time. Social, economic, and psychiatric characteristics seem to be most important. Also, few studies matching clients to different program components within a given level of treatment intensity have been conducted.

There are many obstacles to implementing matching ideas (Miller, 1991). First, providers must take plurality seriously; different people may need significantly different approaches beyond minor adjustments to a standard program. A second obstacle involves the availability of real alternatives. Actual ranges of treatment options vary significantly by geographic areas. Matching cannot be carried out when only one or even two approaches are available in a given area. A third barrier, related to economics, is the tendency for organizations to refer clients at the point of initial assessment to their own treatment programs even if other, more effective treatment matches are available in the community. A promising solution to this problem is the establishment of an evaluation service independent of ties to any treatment approach.

SUMMARY AND CONCLUSIONS

Treatment outcome studies have demonstrated that drug abuse treatment is effective in reducing drug use, negative behaviors associated with drug use, and criminality. Treatment outcome has not been found to be associated with treatment modality, technique, or approach. The length of time in treatment, however, is positively correlated with treatment outcome.

Although drug abuse treatment works for some clients, Tims et al. (1991) note that it " does not 'work' as well as we would like; for a significant number of clients it does not work at all, and there is little information to explain why" (p. 93). Across treatment modalities, program completion rates are low; only between 10% and 20% of drug abusers complete treatment (Allison et al., 1985). Furthermore, relapse rates are high; about 70% of drug abusers relapse within 1 year after completing treatment.

Recommendations to improve current drug abuse treatment have emphasized: (a) the development of new, multivariant theoretical models such as the biopsychosocial model to better explain and understand the etiology and treatment of drug abuse (e.g., Brower et al., 1989); (b) the incorporation of empirically supported treatment approaches and techniques into program development and clinical practice (Leukefeld, Pickens, & Schuster, 1991); (c) the expansion of our understanding of what works for whom in order to provide more effective and individualized treatment (e.g., Hester & Miller, 1988; McLellan, Luborsky, Woody, O'Brien, & Druley, 1983); and (d) the utilization of different approaches and techniques based upon where the person is in the treatment and recovery process. Increasingly, clinicians are seeking more effective treatment approaches for drug abuse to confront complex client needs, greater demand for their services, and reduced financial resources to provide these services.

REFERENCES

Aiken, L. S., Loscuito, J. A., Ausetts, M. A., & Brown, B. A. (1984). Paraprofessional versus professional drug counselors. The progress of clients in treatment. *International Journal of the Addictions, 19,* 383–401.

Allison, M., Hubbard, R., & Rachal, J. V. (1985). *Treatment process in methadone, residential and outpatient drug free programs.* Rockville, MD: National Institute on Drug Abuse. [(ADM) 85-1388].

American Society of Addiction Medicine, Inc. (1992). *Patient placement criteria.* Washington, DC: Author.

Bale, R., Stone W., Kuldan, J., Englesing, T., Elashoff, R., & Zarsove, V. (1980). Therapeutic communities versus methadone maintenance. *Archives of General Psychiatry, 37,* 179–193.

Brower, K., Blow, F., & Beresford, T. (1989). Treatment implications of chemical dependency models: An integrative approach. *Journal of Substance Abuse Treatment, 6,* 147–157.

Catalano, R. F., Hawkins, J. D., Wells, E. A., & Miller, J. L. (1991). Evaluation of the effectiveness of adolescent drug abuse treatment: Assessment of risks for relapse and promising approaches for relapse prevention. *International Journal of the Addictions, 25,* 1085–1140.

Cook, C. C. (1988a). The Minnesota Model in the management of drug and alcohol dependency: Miracle, method or myth? Part I. The philosophy and the programme. *British Journal of Addiction, 83,* 625–634.

Cook, C. C. (1988b). The Minnesota Model in the management of drug and alcohol dependency: Miracle, method, or myth? Part II. Evidence and conclusions. *British Journal of Addiction, 83,* 735–748.

Craddock, B. G., Bray, R. M., & Hubbard, R.L. (1985). *Drug use before and during drug abuse treatment: 1979-1981 TOPS admission cohorts.* Rockville, MD: National Institute on Drug Abuse. [(ADM) 85-1387]

De Leon, G. (1985). *The therapeutic community: Study of effectiveness.* Rockville, MD: National Institute on Drug Abuse. [(ADM) 85-1286]

De Leon, G. (1986). The therapeutic community for substance abuse: Perspectives and approach. In G. De Leon, & J. T. Ziegenfuss (Eds.), *Therapeutic communities for addictions* (pp. 5–18). Springfield, IL: Charles C. Thomas.

De Leon, G. & Rosenthal, M. S. (1979). Therapeutic communities. In R. L. DuPont, A. Goldstein, & J. O'Donnell (Eds.), *Handbook on drug abuse* (pp. 39–48). Rockville, MD: National Institute on Drug Abuse.

Dole, V. P. & Nyswander, M. (1965). A medical treatment for diocetylmorphine (heroin) addiction: A clinical trial with methadone hydrochloride. *Journal of American Medical Association, 193,* 80–84.

Dole, V. P., Nyswander, M. E., & Warner, A. (1968). A successful treatment of 750 criminal addicts. *Journal of American Medical Association, 206,* 2708–2711.

Drew, L. (1986). Beyond the disease concept of addiction: Drug use as a way of life leading to predicaments. *Journal of Drug Issues, 16,* 263–274.

Durlak, J. (1979). Comparative effectiveness of paraprofessional and professional helpers. *Psychological Bulletin, 86,* 80–92.

Emrick, C. D. (1987). Alcoholics Anonymous: Affiliation processes and effectiveness as treatment. *Alcoholism: Clinical and Experimental Research, 11,* 416–442.

FDR (1989, March 2). Methadone: Rule, proposed rules, and notice. 21 CFR Part 291. *Federal Register,* pp. 8954–8979.

Frances, R. J., & Miller, S. I. (1991). Addiction treatment: The widening scope. In R. J. Frances & S. I. Miller (Eds.), *Clinical textbook of addictive disorders.* (pp. 3-22) New York: Guilford.

Galanter, M., Castaneda, R., & Franco, H. (1991). Group therapy and self-help groups. In R. J. Frances and S. I. Miller (Eds.), *Clinical textbook of addictive disorders* (pp. 431–451). New York: Guilford.

Gray, M. (1989). Case management. In National Institute on Drug Abuse (Ed.), *Drug abuse curriculum for employee assistance program professionals* (pp. 1–98). Rockville, MD: National Institute on Drug Abuse [(ADM) 89-1587]

Hansen, J., & Emrick, C. D. (1983). Whom are we calling "alcoholic?" In W. R. Miller (Ed.), *Alcoholism: Theory, research and treatment* (pp. 389–398). Lexington, MA: Ginn.

Hargreaves, W. A. (1986). Methadone dosage and duration for maintenance treatment. In J. R. Cooper, F. Altman, B. Brown, & D. Czechowicz (Eds.), *Research on the treatment of narcotic addiction: State of the art* (pp. 19–79). Rockville, MD: National Institute on Drug Abuse. [(ADM) 87-1281]

Hester, R. K., & Miller, W. R. (1988). Empirical guidelines for optimal client-treatment matching. In E. R. Rahdert & J. Grabowski (Eds.), *Adolescent drug abuse: Analyses of treatment research.* (pp. 27-38). Rockville, MD: National Institute on Drug Abuse. [(ADM) 88-1523]

Hser, Y., Anglin, M. D., & Liu, Y. (1991). A survival analysis of gender and ethnic differences in responsiveness to methadone maintenance. *International Journal of the Addictions, 25,* 1295–1315.

Hubbard, R. L. Marsden, M. E., Rachal, J. V., Harwood, H. J., Cavanaugh, E. R. & Ginzburg, H. M. (1989). *Drug abuse treatment: A national study of effectiveness.* Chapel Hill: University of North Carolina Press.

Institute of Medicine. (1990a). *Treating drug problems* (Vol. 1). Washington, DC: National Academy Press.

Institute of Medicine. (1990b). *Healthy people year 2000:Citizens chart the course.* Washington, DC: National Academy Press.

Kleber, H.D., & Slobetz, F. (1979). Outpatient drug-free treatment. In R. Dupont, A. Goldstein, J. O'Donnell, & B. Brown (Eds.), *Handbook on drug abuse* (pp. 31-47). Rockville, MD: National Institute on Drug Abuse.

Kreek, M. J. (1983). Health consequences associated with the use of methadone. In J. Cooper, F. Altman, B. Brown, & D. Czechowicz (Eds.), *Research on the treatment of narcotic addiction: State of the art* (pp. 456-482). Rockville, MD: National Institute on Drug Abuse. [(ADM) 87-1281]

Kreek, M. J. (1991). Using methadone effectively: Achieving goals by application of laboratory, clinical, and evaluation research. In R. Pickens, C. Leukefeld, & C. Schuster (Eds.), *Improving drug abuse treatment* (pp. 245-266). Rockville, MD: National Institute on Drug Abuse.

Leukefeld, C. G., Pickens, R. W., & Schuster, C. R. (1991). Improving drug abuse treatment: Recommendations for research and practice. In R. W. Pickens, C. G. Leukefeld, & C. R. Schuster (Eds.), *Improving drug abuse treatment* (pp. 394–406). Rockville, MD: National Institute on Drug Abuse. [ADM) 91-1754]

Lewis, J., Dana, R., & Blevins, G. (1988). *Substance abuse counseling.* Pacific Grove, CA: Brooks/Cole.

Longbaugh, R., & Lewis, D. C. (1988). Key issues in treatment outcome studies. *Alcohol Health and Research World, 12*, 168–173.

Marlatt, A. (1985). Relapse prevention: Theoretical rationale and overview of the model. In A. Marlatt & J. Gordin (Eds.), *Relapse prevention: Maintenance strategies in the treatment of addictive behaviors* (pp. 3–70). New York: Guilford.

McLellan, A. T., O'Brien, C. P., Kron, R., Alterman, A. I., & Druley, K. A. (1980). Matching substance abuse patients to appropriate treatment: A conceptual and methodological approach. *Drug and Alcohol Dependence, 5*, 189–195.

McLellan, A., Woody, G., Luborsky, L., & Goehl, L. (1988). Is the counselor an "active ingredient" in substance abuse rehabilitation? An examination of treatment success among four counselors. *Journal of Nervous and Mental Disease,176*, 423–430.

McLellan, T. (1986). Patient characteristics associated with outcome. In J. Cooper, F. Altman, B. Brown, & D. Czechowicz (Eds.), *Research on the treatment of narcotic addiction: State of the art* (pp. 500–523). Rockville, MD: National Institute on Drug Abuse. [ADM] 87-1281]

McLellan, A. Luborsky, L. Woody, G., O'Brien, C., and Druley, K. (1983). Increased effectiveness of substance abuse treatment: A prospective study of patient-treatment "matching." *Journal of Nervous and Mental Disease, 171*, 597–605.

Miller, W. (1983). Motivational interviewing with problem drinkers. *Behavioral Psychotherapy, 11*, 147–172.

Miller, W.R. (1989). Increasing motivation for change. In R. K. Hester & W. R. Miller (Eds.), *Handbook of alcoholism treatment approaches* (pp. 67–89). New York: Pergamon.

Miller, W. R. (1991). Emergent treatment concepts and techniques. *Annual Review of Addictions Research and Treatment, 1*, 1–14.

Miller, W. R., & Hester, R. K. (1986). The effectiveness of alcoholism treatment: What research reveals. In W. R. Miller & N. Heather (Eds.), *Treating addictive behaviors: Processes of change* (pp. 121–174). New York: Plenum.

Newman, R. G. (1979). Detoxification treatment of narcotic addiction. In R. Dupont, A. Goldstein, & J. O'Donnell (Eds.), *Handbook on drug abuse* (pp. 21–29). Rockville, MD: National Institute on Drug Abuse.

Ogborne, A., & Bornet, A. (1982). Brief report: Abstinence and abusive drinking among affiliates of Alcoholics Anonymous: Are these the only alternatives? *Addictive Behaviors, 7*, 192–202.

Onken, L. (1991). Using psychotherapy effectively in drug abuse treatment. In R. Pickens, C. Leukefeld, & C. Schuster (Eds.), *Improving drug abuse treatment* (pp. 267–278). Rockville, MD: National Institute on Drug Abuse. [(ADM) 91-1754]

Pattison, E. M., Sobell, M., & Sobell, L. (1977). *Emerging concepts of alcohol dependence.* New York: Springer.

Platt, J. J. (1986). *Heroin addiction: Theory, research, and treatment* (Vol. I.) (pp. 187–218). New York: John Wiley.

Price, R. H., Burke, A. C., D'Aunno, T. A., Klingel, D. M., McCaughain, W. C., Rafferty, J. A., & Vaughn, T. E. (1991). Outpatient drug abuse treatment services, 1988. Results of a national survey. In R. Pickens, C.G. Leukefeld, & C. Schuster (Eds.), *Improving drug abuse treatment* (pp. 63–91). Rockville, MD: National Institute on Drug Abuse. [(ADM) 91-1754]

Prochaska, J. O., & DiClemente, C. O. (1986). Toward a comprehensive model of change. In W. Miller & N. Heather (Eds.), *Treating addictive behaviors: Processes of change* (pp. 3–27). New York: Plenum.

Prochaska, J. O., DiClemente, C. O., & Norcross, J. C. (1992). In search of how people change: Applications to addictive behaviors. *American Psychologist, 47*, 1102–1114.

Rohrer, G. E., Thomas, M., & Yasenchak, A. B. (1992). Client perceptions of the ideal addictions counselor. *International Journal of the Addictions, 27*, 727–733.

Schiffer, F. (1988). Psychotherapy of nine successfully treated cocaine abusers: Techniques and dynamics. *Journal of Substance Abuse Treatment, 5*, 131–137.

Simpson, D. D., Savage, L. J., & Lloyd, M. R. (1979). Follow-up evaluation of treatment of drug abuse during 1969–1972. *Archives of General Psychiatry, 36*, 772–780.

Simpson, D.D., & Sells, S.B. (1982a). Effectiveness of treatment for drug abuse: An overview of the DARP research program. *Advances in Alcohol and Substance Abuse, 2*, 7–29.

Simpson, D. D., & Sells, S. B. (1982b). *Evaluation of drug abuse treatment effectiveness: Summary of the DARP follow-up research.* Rockville, MD: National Institute on Drug Abuse. [(ADM) 82–1207]

Simpson, D. D. (1988). National Treatment System Evaluation based upon the Drug Abuse Reporting Program (DARP) followup research. In F.M. Tims & J.L. Ludford (Eds.), *Drug abuse treatment evaluation: Strategies, progress, and prospects* (pp.29–41). Rockville, MD: National Institute on Drug Abuse. [(ADM) 88-1329]

Tims, F. M., Fletcher, B. W., & Hubbard, R. L. (1991). Treatment outcomes for drug abuse clients. In R. Pickens, C. Leukefeld, and C. Schuster (Eds.), *Improving drug abuse treatment* (pp. 93–113). Rockville, MD: National Institute on Drug Abuse. [(ADM) 91-1754]

Todd, T. (1984). A contingency analysis of family treatment and drug abuse. In J. Grabowski, M. Stitzer & J. Henningfield (Eds.), *Behavioral intervention techniques in drug abuse treatment* (pp. 104–114). Rockville, MD: National Institute on Drug Abuse. [(ADM) 84-1282]

Westermeyer, J. (1989). Nontreatment factors affecting treatment outcome in substance abuse. *American Journal of Drug and Alcohol Abuse, 15*, 13–29.

Woody, G., Luborsky, L., McLellan, A., O'Brien, C., Beck, S., Blaine, J., Herman, I., & Hole, A. (1983). Psychotherapy for opiate addicts: Does it help? *Archives of General Psychiatry, 40*, 639–645.

Woody, G., McLellan, A., Luborsky, L., & O'Brien, C. (1987). Twelve-month follow-up of psychotherapy for opiate dependence. *American Journal of Psychiatry, 144*, 590–596.

Chapter 7

Helping People Control Their Weight: Research and Practice

Len Sperry

Of all the areas of lifestyle change, losing weight, and maintaining weight loss is undoubtedly the most difficult and perplexing area. Weight loss is a lifestyle change because it requires more than simply losing weight or changing eating behaviors. Often, the changes require altering a person's life well beyond diet modification. For example, just one relatively simple dietary change, such as reducing the daily consumption of soft drinks, might involve a series of unexpected changes: changes in shopping habits to modify the routine purchase of soft drinks; the development of assertiveness skills to handle well-meaning friends who expect and continue preference for soft drinks; time management skills if other beverages are not readily available at the conveniently located soda machine; knowledge acquisition concerning the nutritional content of soft drinks versus other beverages; and some experimentation and emotional considerations in finding a suitable replacement for the soft drink (Laquatera & Danish, 1988). It is no exaggeration, then, to suggest that weight loss is a complex, difficult lifestyle change.

This chapter provides an overview of both theoretical and clinically useful information on weight control. It briefly reviews pertinent research on how obesity develops and can be classified. Practical clinical suggestions for counseling the obese client are offered.

OBESITY: DEFINITIONS, CLASSIFICATIONS, AND THEORIES

Overweight and obesity are not synonymous. Obesity specifically refers to excess body fat stores, whereas overweight refers to excess body weight (Stunkard, 1984). Obesity seems to be related to both the number and size of fat cells (Bjorntorp, 1986). Hypertrophic obesity refers to an increase in body weight associated with an increase in fat cell size, but not cell number. On the other hand, hyperplastic obesity involves both an increase in fat cell size and an increase in cell number.

Whereas hypertrophic obesity appears to be completely reversible, hyperplastic obesity is not. Once the body has produced new fat cells, it appears to retain them for life. Thus individuals with severe hyperplastic obesity tend to remain overweight despite the most rigorous of dieting and exercise. In order for such individuals to return to their ideal weight, they would have to reduce the size of their individual fat cells so far below normal limits that they would literally be in a state of semistarvation. Obesity that begins in childhood usually involves both hypertrophic and hyperplastic fat cells, whereas obesity that begins after the age of 20 is usually characterized by hypertrophic obesity. Once formed, fat cells are permanent and are not decreased in number by weight reduction, probably explaining why childhood obesity often persists into adulthood and why it is so difficult for patients with this syndrome to lose weight.

Genetic and psychosocial determinants also play a role in the development of obesity. There is a high correlation between obesity in parents and subsequent obesity in their children. Overeating may be an inappropriate response to a variety of different stimuli, such as the sight of appetizing foods; the time of day, such as bedtime snacking; or particular settings, such as TV watching. For some individuals, overeating is used as a method of coping with stress or boredom. Finally, less than 2% of obesity is attributed to endocrine or "gland" problems. Of these, hypothyroidism and hyperadrenocorticism are the most common (Bjorntorp, 1986).

CLASSIFICATION OF OBESITY

Stunkard (1984) has proposed a schema of three types of obesity that have practical clinical significance. The three types are:

1. *Mild Obesity:* In this type, patients are 20 to 40% over their ideal weight. This type represents hypertrophic obesity and a diet program with a behavioral or cognitive-behavioral approach to weight control appears to be the treatment of choice.
2. *Moderate Obesity:* In this type, patients are 41 to 100% over their ideal weight. This type can represent elements of both hypertrophic and hyperplastic obesity. Diet therapy, particularly a very low calorie diet (VLCD), needs to be combined with a behavioral or cognitive-behavioral approach for weight loss and maintenance to be successful.
3. *Severe Obesity:* In this type, patients are more than 100 percent or 100 pounds above their ideal weight. They represent both hypertrophic and hyperplastic obesity, and many are hyperplastically obese. As a rule, these individuals have tried and failed at several programs. It is an unusual patient in this category who has not lost many pounds, sometimes as much as 50 to 100, and then regained that weight. Gastric bypass surgery or stomach stapling may be considered when the severely obese client has failed less invasive forms of treatment.

THEORIES OF OBESITY

Various theories have been proposed to explain the phenomenon of obesity. Although none provides a complete explanation, each provides important concepts a counselor should know and understand.

Set Point Theory

Kessey (1986) proposed that individuals have a "set point" at which weight is held within a particular range. The amount of fat one carries is automatically regulated, and some individuals have more fat than others for genetic reasons. The set point mechanism, which may receive information from fat cells, hormones, and enzymes, strives to maintain a given amount of weight, fat, lean body mass, and related factors. Obesity is thought to result from a homeostatic process that acts to maintain body weight and fat at a high level. An attempt to lose weight is then opposed by strong biological processes. An obese individual starting a diet to overcome the set point or a thin person trying to overeat to gain weight fights a difficult battle. Various studies (Kessey & Corbett, 1984) attest to the remarkable tenacity of the body to maintain a fairly constant weight range and a preordained amount of fat.

The theory of set points has yet to be proven. Because there are many factors that can change the set point, the utility of this theory has been questioned. However, the notion that the body may regulate weight is helpful in approaching patients who consistently remain in specific weight ranges.

Fat Cell Theory

In the previous discussion of hypertrophic and hyperplastic obesity, it was noted that in weight loss, fat cells can reduce in size, but no fat cells are lost (Bjorntorp, 1986). It has been speculated that individuals strive to achieve a specific fat cell size and that efforts to decrease size below average result in lipid depletion. The cell can then initiate a physiological mechanism to replenish the energy stores. This fat cell theory maintains that weight loss beyond the point in which cells reach normal size will be met with great resistance.

In keeping with the fat cell theory, early intervention would seem preferable to waiting for hyperplasticity to occur. Because the set point changes and resets over a long period with exposure to foods high in fat or sweetness and is also sensitive to exercise, it may be helpful to modify the individual's diet to decrease high-fat and sweet foods, while increasing physical activity.

Weight Cycling Theory

The "yo-yo" phenomenon, in which weight has been lost and regained many times, is the basis of the weight cycling theory. Research points to an increased food efficiency in the individual, creating a dieting-induced obesity. The weight cycling theory postulates that food efficiency increases as weight is lost, regained, and lost. As increased efficiency is maintained in each successive diet, along with slower losses, more rapid regain of each loss, and decreased resting metabolic rate. In short, as the individual diets, the body compensates by losing weight more slowly with each diet, and less time is required to regain the weight once dieting ceases. Therefore, with decreased metabolic rate, the same body weight is maintained on fewer calories than before dieting began. At present, it is unknown whether prolonged weight maintenance and exercise produce an upward adjustment of the resting metabolic rate and a decrease in efficiency in formerly obese patients (Brownell, Greenwood, Stellar, & Shrager, 1986). Clinically speaking, if the weight cycling theory is correct, it is of utmost importance to ensure that the patient's motivation is high before embarking on any weight control treatment. Otherwise, exposing the patient to repeated dieting may only make weight loss more difficult in the future.

BIOLOGICAL FACTORS IN OBESITY

Buckmaster and Brownell (1989) indicate that there are five factors involved in weight control. They are (a) exercising; (b) nutrition training; (c) changing the act of eating; (d) cognitive retraining; and (e) developing support systems. From a biopsychosocial perspective all five are integral in understanding the change process. Nutrition training and exercise are clearly biological factors and will be discussed in detail in this section.

Exercise

Patients who exercise while engaging in a behavioral treatment program maintain weight loss better than patients who do not (Pi-Sunyer, 1989). It appears that even moderate amounts of exercise are useful. For instance, it has been shown that obese children will increase their energy expenditure by 200 to 400 calories by walking more or using stairs rather than elevators, and are more likely to maintain their weight loss than those participating in programmed aerobic activity (Epstein et al., 1982). In modifying activity level, treatment must begin with a level of exercise that is reasonable given the individual's attitude about exercise and physical condition. As with eating, self-monitoring and reinforcement are important components of changing exercise behavior. In addition to physiological benefits, there are considerable psychological benefits to regular exercise.

Nutrition

Because improper nutrition can lead to loss of lean body tissue as well as other physical problems, nutrition is important for optimal weight reduction and maintenance. Generally speaking, most weight management groups do not forbid particular food groups because mandated abstinence only seems to enhance the desire and cravings for certain foods. Also, most programs tailor diets to incorporate patients' food preferences. Not to do so only encourages the patient to return to old eating patterns and thus to regain any weight loss on the prescribed diet.

Simply prescribing a more nutritious diet is usually not enough to guarantee weight maintenance. Individuals need to increase their nutritional literacy as well. For this reason, many weight control programs educate participants in the fundamentals of nutritional science in the form of lectures, individual consultation education, or reading materials. Helpful diets provide sufficient amounts of all essential nutrients for the body's metabolic needs. In addition to water, food contains five types of chemical components that provide specific nutrients for bodily functioning. The five types of components in the metabolism are: carbohydrates, lipids, proteins, vitamins, and minerals.

Food also contains fiber, which is not considered a nutrient but is still needed in the process of digestion. Individuals can get all the nutrients and fiber they need by eating diets that contain a variety from the basic food groups (Nelson, 1984; Suitor & Hunter, 1980).

PSYCHOLOGICAL FACTORS IN OBESITY

According to the Buckmaster and Brownell schema (1989), modification of eating behavior and cognitive training would be considered psychological factors. To these we would add lifestyle convictions and other psychodynamic aspects of weight control.

Modification of Eating Behavior

The first application of behavior modification to weight control was reported by Ferster, Nurnberger, and Levitt (1962) nearly 30 years ago. Traditional behavioral techniques were utilized in early behavioral weight control programs to minimize excessive eating. Such techniques were self-monitoring, stimulus control, preplanning, slowing eating, and so on. For example, in self-monitoring the patient would be asked to keep a daily record of calories and amount eaten. These records would then be checked by the health counselor to assess accuracy and detect problem areas. Stimulus control techniques often included sitting in only one place when eating; not engaging in other activities while eating, such as reading or watching television; eating from a smaller plate; or storing food out of sight. Preplanning was another commonly used technique. With this technique patients were helped to anticipate the what, when, and where of meals. For instance, if the patient decided to eat at 5:30 P.M. at home and have the proper ingredients available, the likelihood of eating other foods would be decreased. Preplanning also reduced the chance of impulsive eating. Slowing the act of eating would allow the patient to experience satiety, or a sense of fullness before overeating. The purpose of these techniques was to help patients develop an awareness of their eating habits as well as the structure of their environment and to minimize eating cues that might lead to excessive eating. Unfortunately, these early applications of behavioral techniques are not particularly effective and have been mockingly characterized by the oversimplified adage of "put your fork down and chew each mouthful 20 times."

Today, behavioral or, more correctly, cognitive-behavioral approaches deal with all behaviors that affect weight loss, gain, and maintenance. The same principles that could be applied to eating (shaping, goal setting, self-monitoring for feedback, reinforcement, stimulus control, etc.) can also be used for changing exercise patterns, food selection, and self-defeating thoughts, and for engendering social support from others in the patient's environment.

Cognitive Training

The cognitive component includes goal setting, restructuring dysfunctional beliefs about eating, self-image, coping with mistakes, and motivation. Emphasis is placed on the patient's attitudes towards treatment, especially in the later stages when relapse prevention is of particular concern. The cognitive component in weight control programs primarily seeks to emphasize positive attitudes and enhance adherence to the exercise, lifestyle, and nutritional parts of the program (Brownell & Foreyt, 1985).

Psychodynamic Aspects

Although there has been only limited interest in obesity by psychoanalytic and psychodynamic therapists, there are a few contributions from this orientation that a health counselor may well heed. An early concept that emerged from psychoanalytic theory was the oral character structure. Conflicts over the satisfaction of libidinal and aggressive urges through sucking or biting were felt to be related to obesity. Hilde Bruch's (1973) ongoing experience with obese individuals offers an important perspective on motivation for weight loss. Two forms are noted: reactive and developmental.

The reactive form of obesity is characteristic of relatively psychologically mature individuals who eat more when they are worried, tense, or anxious. It develops usually after the death of a family member, separation from home, loss of a love object, or other situations involving the fear of abandonment. Individuals with reactive obesity have difficulties with aggressive feelings and tend to become depressed and overeat in response to aggression and other undesirable emotions.

Bruch found that individuals who were developmentally obese suffered from disturbances in psychological function often noted by late childhood or early adolescence. Rather than developing a positive concept of their bodily identity, obese adolescents tended to have serious adjustment problems whereby inactivity and overeating became integral parts of their personal development. For developmentally obese individuals, commitment to a sustained, systematic, but gradual weight loss program is very difficult because of their family's magical expectations for quick, painless cures.

Closely related to the psychoanalytic approach to obesity is the view of Adlerian psychology, which emphasizes mistaken convictions or cognitions about self, other people, and life. Obesity is understood as the purposeful maintenance of body weight through overeating. It is viewed as a lifestyle that protects, excuses, and silently communicates dependency—and fear of dependency—or independence—and fear of independence. Nearly always, overweight serves a family function: the unconscious goal of the obese person is to focus attention away from a parental or family problem and onto themselves. The obese individual focuses on food rather than issues, weight rather than judgment, and unreality rather than decision. Obesity then comes to symbolize the control issues, denial, avoidance, excesses, and emptiness of the family (Casper & Zachery, 1984).

SOCIAL FACTORS IN OBESITY

Social factors play an important role in both the etiology and the treatment of obesity. Among the most influential social factors are social support systems, particularly marriage and family relations. Research shows that social support can decrease attrition or early termination from treatment programs, improve weight loss, and improve weight loss maintenance (Morton, 1988).

Marital Factors

Marital factors not only are a causal factor of obesity but also influence treatment outcomes. Based on extensive research, Stuart and Jacobson (1987) offer some intriguing reasons why married women overeat. They found that many women believed that once married, they could relax and stop worrying about keeping their weight down, and enjoy the trust and security of their marriage. When things were going smoothly and weight didn't interfere with their self-esteem, they had little motivation to lose the inevitable weight they gained. For many women who had not been overweight before marriage, the responsibilities and stresses of being a wife and a mother translated into weight gain. Women who didn't hold outside jobs consistently had a more difficult time losing weight than those who worked outside the home. When marital and sexual problems were present, weight problems were compounded. Women in unhappy marriages gained 2.5 times more weight than women who reported being in happy marriages—18.4 pounds gained over 13 years of a happy marriage compared to 42.6 pounds over the same period in an unhappy marriage.

Being overweight served four purposes in a marriage. First, overweight served to allay women's fears of becoming too sexually attractive or even promiscuous. Second, weight gain served to diminish a husband's sexual interest and inhibited the woman's own sexual desire. The end result was that consciously or not, weight gain served as a means of avoiding intimacy. Next, weight gain served to control anger and neutralize the husband's efforts to overcontrol his wife. These women internalized anger by "swallowing it." Some gained weight to rebel at their husbands' insistence that they become thin. Thus the woman's body may become the battleground in a power struggle that neither she nor her husband wins. Finally, weight gain is used to hide a women's fear that she will become a failure—or even success—in life. Weight becomes a convenient scapegoat for insecurity and other problems in the woman's life.

Stuart and Jacobson also studied the husband's view of overweight women. Insecure husbands often blocked and sabotaged their wives' efforts to lose weight. On the basis of survey data and their clinical observations, these researchers found five reasons why a husband wanted his wife to remain overweight. These husbands were unwilling to change comfortable routines, to tackle their own weight problems, or to deal with their own addictive behavior such as drinking or gambling. Sometimes, a man might use his wife's weight to divert attention from marital or sexual problems in the relationship. Furthermore, some men feared that their wives would become unfaithful or leave them after weight loss.

Finally, Stuart and Jacobson found that approximately half of the women wanted their husbands' positive collaboration and support in losing weight, and the other half did not. Clinical experience shows that when a woman wants and expects her husband to be a collaborator in a weight loss program, the woman is more likely to maintain weight loss.

Family Influences

Mahoney and Mahoney (1976) have described four negative patterns that characterize eating atmosphere in a family where the patient is attempting to lose weight. In Pattern I, family members tease the individual about being overweight and criticize attempts at weight loss. In Pattern II, the family openly discourages weight loss efforts and openly sabotages these efforts. Strategies in the next two patterns are more indirect and insidious. In Pattern III, family members ignore the individual's change efforts and somehow communicate their pessimism. Finally, in Pattern IV, family members verbally encourage the individual's efforts, but nonverbally discourage and even sabotage them. Knowledge of patterns like these can be very helpful to counselors and their clients.

ASSESSMENT IN WEIGHT CONTROL

The initial interview involves information gathering and the assessment of the client's psychological status and motivation for treatment. It is assumed that the client has had a thorough medical evaluation and is medically cleared to begin a weight control program before your evaluation.

Weight History

Weight history can provide important information, including clues to the degree of fat cell hyperplasia and hypertrophia. Usually the counselor begins by asking when the patient first became significantly overweight. Childhood onset of obesity is generally associated with greater body weight as an adult and with excess fat cell number. On the other hand, weight gain in adulthood in a previously normal weight person is generally not associated with an increase in fat cell number. Therefore the prognosis for returning to ideal body weight is more favorable in persons with adult-onset than childhood-onset obesity. This is not to say that severely overweight individuals with childhood onset may not lose significant amounts of weight, but they are likely to fall far short of reaching ideal weight and have greater difficulty maintaining the weight loss. Next the counselor asks if there is a family history of obesity. Studies of twins and adoptees suggest that obesity is highly related to heredity. If neither parent is obese, the likelihood of one of their children becoming obese is only 8%; if one parent is obese, the likelihood jumps to 40%; and if both parents are overweight the probability rises to 80%. Severely overweight patients with positive family histories of obesity, as well as childhood onset, almost invariably have hyperplastic obesity.

Next, the counselor inquires about the patient's dieting history. Patients who are moderately or severely overweight and have repeatedly lost weight and regained it are likely to have excess fat cell numbers. In addition, behavioral and emotional factors may also contribute to this rebound in body weight.

Eating Diary

Comprehensive eating diaries go beyond listing the foods eaten and the calories consumed. Among the kinds of factors that might be included are the setting in which eating takes place; the degree of hunger; the mood state preceding eating; and the cognitive self-talk involved before, during, and after the meal.

Eating in response to emotional disturbances—called emotional eating—or eating more when food cues are happening—external eating—are common features of eating styles in individuals of all weight levels and are not specific to obesity. However, emotional eating and external eating need to be assessed and modified as part of the treatment program. This is especially necessary after prolonged dietary restrictions, when emotional or external cues can result in relapse. If the food binging is excessive, the impact of days of dietary restriction can be lost in only a few hours. The patient is asked to complete a daily food intake diary for at least 1 week that provides the counselor with sufficient information to determine general patterns of eating. The counselor reviews the diary considering the factors time of eating, place of eating, activity, degree of hunger, mood, and self-talk while eating. All will be important behaviors that can become a target for habit change.

Assessing Psychological Factors

Following the weight history, the counselor next turns to how the patient's weight affects and is affected by intimate relations, social functioning, and occupational and leisure pursuits. Although psychological inventories generally do not predict weight loss, the MMPI or a similar instrument may be helpful if administered at the onset of treatment. Results of such testing can alert the counselor to personality or emotional factors that may emerge during the course of treatment. In addition to assessing the patient's current psychosocial functioning, the counselor should address several issues specifically related to weight and weight loss.

The counselor may begin by eliciting the patient's feelings about his or her size, focusing on the way it affects social life or work. Next, the client should be queried about why he or she is seeking to lose weight now, and for whom. In many instances, clients indicate that they are losing weight for themselves so as to feel better physically and psychologically. Other clients may be losing weight solely because of their doctor's orders or a spouse's insistence. Treatment tends to be less successful among these clients. When motivation is based on the spouse's insistence, the counselor would do well to meet conjointly with the client and the spouse to determine what marital issues are underlying the pressure toward weight loss.

The counselor then elicits the client's expectations for treatment. Some are interested in weight loss as a means to an end. If the end, such as improving one's social life or finding a new job, can be clearly articulated at the onset of treatment, the counselor can take steps to increase the likelihood that it will be attained. Some clients, like persons of normal weight, are shy and unassertive. Therefore no matter how well they look after substantial weight loss their social lives are unlikely to improve, particularly if their expectations are unrealistic. Some expect to return to their ideal weight in a matter of weeks or months. The counselor needs to spend as much time as necessary educating the patient about the health risks of rapid weight loss, the need for slow, gradual weight loss with subsequent change in eating patterns and self body image, and the ways in which magical thinking and unrealistic expectations foster relapse.

The counselor inquires as to the client's previous experience with dieting, weight loss, and maintenance of weight loss. Typically, clients seeking help with weight control have experimented with six or more diets or even formal weight loss programs before their current consultation. It is important to review these efforts to determine what worked, what went wrong, and what needs to happen differently to improve the patient's chances for being successful in this treatment endeavor. Often clients bring negative expectations with them that they anticipate the counselor will confirm. All expectations, negative and positive, need to be examined at the outset so that the counselor can realistically determine if he or she has something different to offer this patient than previous professionals or programs.

Finally, the counselor does well to address the "why?" Why does the person eat to excess? Why does he or she maintain the image of an obese person? An assessment of the patient's health beliefs and health behaviors as well as past and current gains or payoffs for their obesity can provide important information.

Assessing Social Factors

Because social factors appear to play a significant role in the etiology and treatment of obesity, it is important to assess their impact (Brownell & Foreyt,

1985). Earlier we've suggested that family, social, and cultural factors affect not only the process of weight gain and loss but, more importantly, weight maintenance. Therefore it is essential that the counselor assess the spouse's expectations and feelings about the client's desire to lose weight. In addition, the counselor should inquire as to the spouse's degree of encouragement and cooperation as well as any overt or covert indications of sabotage of the client's weight control program.

It is also useful to characterize the eating atmosphere in the family of the patient who wishes to begin a therapeutic weight control program. Mahoney and Mahoney's criteria (1976) for family patterns I to IV is quite useful in this regard. Combining this information with previous elicited family weight history and spousal support can be useful in anticipating problems in the course of treatment, particularly relapse.

WEIGHT CONTROL TREATMENT PROTOCOL

The behavioral or cognitive-behavioral component of most weight control programs involves essentially the same techniques with slightly different protocols. Usually programs differ in the sequence in which topics and techniques are covered and in the relative emphasis on specific components. The treatment protocol developed by Brownell (1979, 1985) is probably the model program upon which most others have been based. Brownell provides an extensive treatment manual that gives a step-by-step description of a 16-week training program (1979). Brownell's program can be utilized in either a small group or an individual format. His LEARN program (acronym for Lifestyle, Exercise, Attitudes, Relationships, Nutrition) is a refined version of the original program and contains a useful instrument, the *Diet Readiness Test* (Brownell, 1985).

A second treatment protocol has been described by Fremoux and Heyneman (1984). This program is designed to last a total of 10 sessions, in which the first session is an orientation followed by six weekly sessions of active treatment and three monthly follow-up sessions. Each session lasts about 90 minutes. Group size is usually about three to six persons, although the program has also been administered individually or to larger groups. Fremoux and Heyneman have found this protocol particularly useful in the community mental health setting. The components of this program include the following:

• *Session 1:* The first session involves an introduction of patients to each other and an introduction to the logistics of the program. Then the process of self-monitoring is described and clients begin work on their eating diaries.

• *Session 2:* This session provides the rationale for the cognitive-behavioral approach and the group learns to identify negative self-statements and problem situations. Group members examine their eating diaries from the previous week. Considerable group reaction is usually generated when negative self-statements are discussed. Other aspects of eating diaries are also examined and discussed.

• *Session 3:* Patients are weighed in and diaries are checked for compliance, as are the self-monitoring instructions and other homework. This session focuses on the concept of coping statements as well as alternate activities that can be used in conjunction with cognitive coping statements. A list of five activities is generated to serve as homework tasks.

• *Session 4*: Previous assignments are reviewed. A planned binge is prescribed in which the patients intentionally overeat when they are not under stress.

• *Session 5:* This session focuses on the Abstinence Violation Effect and is discussed in terms of examples from each patient. The group contracts for a second planned binge, choosing a situation that is slightly more difficult than in the previous week.

• *Session 6:* This session focuses on the effects of mood on eating. Negative self-statements relating to negative moods are discussed, targeting depression, boredom, and anger. The group also contracts for a final planned binge.

• *Session 7:* The focus of this session is on the general review of the program materials. This section focuses on making new commitments to work on each of the areas that have been presented.

• *Follow-Up Sessions:* Three follow-up sessions are scheduled for 4 weeks, 8 weeks, and 12 weeks following completion of treatment. These sessions focus on group discussion around shared problems, strategies, and "troubleshooting" of individual concerns.

Relapse Prevention

One of the greatest challenges in treating obese patients is keeping them involved in treatment. The attrition in behavioral and cognitive behaviorally based weight control programs is far lower, with dropout rates averaging 13.5 percent (Wilson & Brownell, 1980). Because relapse and noncompliance with treatment is such a major issue with weight control treatment, the health counselor is encouraged to become an expert in relapse prevention. Whether in the formal course of the weight control program or in its maintenance phase, inevitably a patient will lapse or slip. Patients will eat foods they feel they should have avoided, they will want to give up dieting at some point, or they will gain weight. Most initial relapses by dieters are the result of two high-risk factors: 50% of patients slip when experiencing negative emotions such as anxiety, boredom, or depression. The other 50% slip in interpersonal situations, often positive events like parties, when their guard is down and social pressure to eat is high. In many cases, the relapse of the slip itself is much less important than the thought and feeling that it engenders. Invariably the patient believes that the relapse is a signal that more relapses will occur. This weakens restraint and increases the likelihood of further eating, which weakens restraints even more, and so on.

Relapse prevention must be a component of any weight control program. The patient is helped to prevent relapses by identifying high-risk situations, developing coping skills for these high-risk situations, practicing coping with potential relapses, developing cognitive coping strategies for use immediately following a relapse, and developing a more balanced lifestyle (Marlatt & Gordon, 1985). The health counselor works with the patient to restructure the environment with stimulus control restructuring techniques. The patient needs to anticipate troublesome negative thoughts or statements and to counter them with more positive thoughts or statements. There are dozens of countering statements, and they must be matched to the patient's needs. The key is to have patients prepared for relapses by rehearsing the negative statements and their positive counterstatements (Brownell & Foreyt, 1985).

Morton (1988) notes that there are a number of other strategies to ensure maintenance. The first of these is exercise. Exercise may prevent relapse because it can serve as a positive replacement for a problem behavior, it positively influences the patient's self-concept, and it can remove the patient to a safe setting. In addition, it becomes a constructive means for managing stress and other negative emotions while enabling the patient to metabolize a greater number of calories than otherwise would be possible. A second is continued self-monitoring. Stuart (1980) found that those who maintain their weight more successfully continue many of the techniques to reach their weight goal, particularly self-monitoring. The third strategy was post-treatment support. Finally, positive social support from significant others in the patient's life has been shown to foster long-term management better than lack of support.

REFERENCES

Bjorntorp, P. (1986). Fat cells and obesity. In K. D. Brownell & J. P. Foreyt (Eds.), *Handbook of eating disorders* (pp. 116–131). New York: Basic Books.

Brownell, K. D. (1979). *Behavior therapy for weight control: A treatment manual*. Philadelphia: University of Pennsylvania Press.

Brownell, K. D. (1985). *The LEARN Program for Weight Control*. Philadelphia: University of Pennsylvania Press.

Brownell, K. D., & Foreyt, J. P. (1985). *Obesity*. In D. Barlow (Ed.), *Clinical handbook of psychological disorders* (pp. 217–239). New York: Guilford.

Brownell, K. D., Greenwood, M., Stellar, E., & Shrager, E. E. (1986). The effects of repeated cycles of weight loss and regain in rats. *Physiological Behaviors, 38*, 459–464.

Bruch, H. (1973). *Eating disorders*. New York: Basic Books.

Buckmaster, L., & Brownell, K. D. (1989). Behavior modification: The state of the art. In R. Frankle & M. Yang (Eds.), *Obesity and weight control* (pp. 68–79). Rockville, MD: Aspen.

Casper, D., & Zachery, D. (1984). The eating disorders as a maladaptive conflict resolution. *Individual Psychology, 40,* 445–452.

Epstein, L., Wing, R., Roseke, R., & Simon, L. (1982). A comparison of lifestyle change and programmed aerobic exercise on weight and fitness changes in obese children. *Behavior Therapy, 13*, 651–665.

Ferster, G.B., Nurnberger, J., & Levitt, E. (1962). The control of eating. *Journal of Mathematics, 1*, 87–109.

Fremoux, W., & Heyneman, N. (1984). Obesity. In M. Hersen (Ed.), *Outpatient behavior therapy: A clinical guide* (pp. 137–151). New York: Grune & Stratton.

Kessey, R. E. (1986). A set-point theory of obesity. In K. Brownell & J.P. Foreyt (Eds.), *Handbook of eating disorders* (pp. 128–143). New York: Basic Books.

Kessey, R. E., & Corbett, S. (1984). Metabolic defense of the body weight set-point. In A. J. Stunkard & E. Stellar (Eds.) *Eating and its disorders* (pp. 143–167). New York: Raven.

Laquatera, J., & Danish, S. J. (1988). A primer for nutritional counseling. In R. T. Frankle & M. Yang (Eds.), *Obesity and weight control* (pp. 72–93). Rockville, MD: Aspen.

Mahoney, M., & Mahoney, K. (1976). *Permanent weight control: A total solution to the dieter's dilemma*. New York: Norton.

Marlatt, G., & Gordon, J. (1985). *Relapse prevention: Maintenance strategies in the treatment of addictive behaviors*. New York: Guilford

Morton, C. J. (1988). Weight loss maintenance and relapse prevention. In R. Frankle & M. Yang (Eds.), *Obesity and weight control* (pp. 182–209). Rockville, MD: Aspen.

Nelson, G. E. (1984). *Biological principles with human perspectives* (2nd ed.). New York: Wiley.

Pi-Sunyer, F. X. (1989). Exercise in the treatment of obesity. In R. Frankle & M. Yang (Eds.), *Obesity and weight control* (pp. 46–73). Rockville, MD: Aspen.

Stuart, R. (1980). Weight loss and beyond: Are they taking it off and keeping it off? In P. Davidson & S. Davidson (Eds.), *Behavioral medicine: Changing health lifestyles* (pp. 136–152). New York: Brunner/Mazel.

Stuart, R. ,& Jacobson, B. (1987). *Sex, weight and marriage*. New York: Norton.

Stunkard, A.J. (1984). The current states of treatment for obesity in adults. In A. J. Stunkard & E. Stellar (Eds.), *Eating and its disorders*. New York: Raven Press.

Suitor, C., & Hunter, M. (1980). *Nutrition: Principles and applications in health promotion*. Philadelphia: J.B. Lippincott.

Wilson, G., & Brownell, K. D. (1980). Behavior therapy for adults: An evaluation of treatment outcomes. *Advances in Behavior Research and Therapy, 3*, 49–86.

Helping People with Eating Disorders: Research and Practice

Linda Paulk Buchanan

The prevalence of bulimia and anorexia appears to be increasing by epidemic proportions. The incidence of eating disorders during the early 1980s was reportedly 5 to 6% of females; however, more recent studies have found 9 to 12% of this population had some form of an eating disorder (Berg, 1988; Carter & Duncan, 1984). Because 95% of all individuals with eating disorders are female and very little research has been done regarding males with eating disorders, the pronouns *she* and *her* will be used in this chapter when referring to these clients.

Currently, two types of disorders receive the eating disorder diagnosis in the *Diagnostic and Statistical Manual of Mental Disorders* (3rd ed., rev.) (*DSM-III-R*; American Psychiatric Association [APA], 1987): anorexia nervosa and bulimia nervosa. To describe bulimia and anorexia as two separate eating disorders, however, is somewhat arbitrary. Many of the dynamics, food-related behaviors, and thought processes are similar for bulimics and anorexics. Most studies that have compared the subgroups have found more similarities than differences (Buchanan, 1993). However, there are differences between these disorders; thus each is described separately.

DESCRIPTION OF EATING DISORDERS

The term *bulimia* literally means "ox-hunger" or voracious appetite, but in recent years has come to mean binge eating. Typically, bulimics binge on food and then purge by forced vomiting, fasting, or laxative abuse. They have a preoccupation with food and dieting and a fear of gaining weight. It is becoming more and more accepted that the binging and purging are the consequences of excessive dieting (Laessle, Tuschl, Waadt, & Pirke, 1989) and that factors that influence dieting behaviors directly increase the incidence of eating disorders (Hsu, 1989).

99

Several research efforts have been directed to understanding the specifics of the binge-purge cycle itself. Though consumption of large amounts of high-calorie food is common, it is also common for clients to label consumption of very small amounts of a forbidden food (e.g., one cookie) as a binge (Mizes, 1983). In addition to binge eating, bulimics often alternate between binging and restricting and may use other forms of purging such as laxatives and excessive exercise.

Binge eating may effectively divert one's attention from upsetting thoughts, as well as induce relaxation (Mizes, 1983). The purge also seems to be a way of reducing guilt after the binge. In essence, a highly reinforcing sequence is enacted that is characterized by pre-binge anxiety, anxiety reduction during the binge, post-binge anxiety for having binged, and anxiety reduction via vomiting (Mizes, 1983).

Anorexia nervosa occurs predominantly in adolescent girls, with 95% of all cases being females. Although hospitalization is often utilized to prevent death by starvation, there is still a 5 to 18% mortality rate (DSM-III-R, 1987). Actually, the term *anorexia* is a misnomer because people suffering from this disorder generally do not report loss of appetite, as the name implies. In fact, they resemble people dying of starvation in that they are obsessed with eating and food. However, they also have a relentless craving to be thin.

Bruch (1985) suggested that their addiction to thinness is more than the culturally prescribed goal of thinness and a diet that gets out of control. Anorexics, according to Bruch, use their refusal to eat as a solution to personality difficulties and problems in living. Long before these girls begin to refuse to eat, they feel helpless and ineffective in conducting their lives. They focus on the demands of others, which leads to a lack of ability to identify their own needs and feelings. A concrete number, their weight, becomes their only measure of success and self-esteem.

Bruch sees their defiance toward eating as a defense against the feeling of not having a core personality of their own. The paradox of this is that their excessive need for control ultimately causes them to lose all control. Conversely, to gain control of their lives, they must give up the one thing that ever gave them a sense of control: that is, their exaggerated form of discipline with regard to restricting food.

TREATMENT OF EATING DISORDERS

Eating disorders have several components in common with other addictive disorders (Zweben, 1987). The obvious component is the compulsive behavior, either the compulsive restricting of food or the compulsive overeating of food. Additionally, there is a sense of powerlessness and fear that if the eater takes one bite of forbidden food, she will be unable to stop or control herself. The eating-disordered person is also obsessed with thoughts of food, such as when, where, and what to eat. Another aspect of eating disorders common to addictive behaviors is the learned ability to avoid aversive feelings through the abuse of food and the simultaneous relief. There are several useful aspects of 12-step programs such as Overeaters Anonymous for people suffering from an eating disorder: the philosophy of "one day at a time"; a focus on having the destructive behaviors cease before other problems are addressed; an emphasis on spirituality, which gives many eating disordered individuals relief from their internal emptiness; a focus on physical recovery and stabilization; and a reframing of the problem as a disease as opposed to lack of character.

One dissimilarity between an eating disorder and an addiction must not be overlooked. Unlike other substances that can be abused, food is a substance that cannot be given up. Therefore treatment must involve management of, not abstinence from, the feared and loved object: food. Vandereyken (1990) warns that rather than abstinence from food, the abstention target should primarily concern all abnormal attempts at weight reduction and should focus on the individual's deficits rather than the "excesses" of overconsumption. Unfortunately, there is no research to date to demonstrate which aspects of a 12-step approach are effective interventions for eating disordered individuals. It is suggested here that the addiction model is inadequate in and of itself to successfully treat eating disorders.

Regardless of whether a woman has bulimia or anorexia, several issues are important for effective therapy. A thorough physical examination must be conducted by a physician knowledgeable in the treatment of eating disorders. The therapist may suggest that a session early in treatment with all members of the treatment team be held in the physician's office and that clear goals be established in terms of medical stabilization.

There must also be a thorough psychological assessment made with each eating-disordered client. At the minimum, there should be a complete psychosocial history that includes a sexual history and a history of abnormal eating behavior. The latter should include a history of dieting as well as the psychosocial context in which overconcern for weight and eating developed. There has been some support for the idea that a subgroup of women with eating disorders may also have a personality disorder (Sansone, Seuferer, Fine, & Bovenzi, 1989). Additionally, there is some support for the idea that women with eating disorders have a higher incidence of having been sexually abused (Tice, Hall, Beresford, Quinones, & Hall, 1989), have high levels of dissociation (Buchanan, 1993), and may be in need of antidepressant medication (Mitchell, 1988). It is very important that thorough assessments be made in these areas when working with these individuals.

Finally, what little research has been conducted to date on the outcome of various therapies for eating disorders has suggested that family therapy is indicated for younger (below age 18) individuals with eating disorders, whereas individual and group therapy is indicated for older individuals (Andersen, 1987; Dare, Eisler, Russell, & Szmukler, 1990; Minuchin, Rosman, & Baker, 1978). However, a multidimensional approach incorporating aspects from various disciplines, orientations, and treatment modalities is suggested (Andersen, 1987; Garner & Bemis, 1982; Stager, 1989) to allow for comprehensive treatment without sacrificing the unique needs of each individual.

Unfortunately, most of what has been written to date has focused either on cognitive-behavioral treatment, with little attention paid to personality dynamics, or on psychodynamic treatment, in which the family or past experience takes precedence, with little attention paid to symptom management. For people with eating disorders, the cognitive-behavioral phase of treatment must not be overlooked. This disorder involves behaviors that are hazardous to the client's health and may be fatal, and these behaviors must be brought under control. Behavioral treatments have been successful in initially helping the anorexic gain weight, but follow-up studies of behavioral treatments still indicate a high failure rate. For many clients, there is much work still to be done after the eating behaviors have been improved if relapse is to be prevented.

Family therapy has traditionally been indicated for anorexics because they often presented for treatment during adolescence. It should be noted, however, that Minuchin and his associates (Minuchin et al., 1978) often treated anorexics individually after the family therapy stabilized the anorexic symptoms. Individual psychotherapy focused on age-appropriate developmental issues. Additionally, a rising number of anorexics are presenting for therapy at older ages and are no longer living with their families. Therefore the decision regarding whether to use individual or family therapy is based on several factors, including age and family environment.

INDIVIDUAL TREATMENT OF EATING DISORDERS

Suggested in this chapter is a comprehensive, three-phase model conceptualized and developed by this author. This eclectic model has been expanded since its original publication (Buchanan & Buchanan, 1992) to portray a process that is cyclical rather than linear. It will be described first as linear, however, to allow the reader to conceptualize each phase as distinct with specific techniques, tasks, and goals. When family therapy is indicated, it may be conceptualized as coinciding with the first two phases of this model.

Phase 1: Psychoeducation and Therapeutic Relationship Development

People with eating disorders often present themselves as having most other areas of their life under control and desiring only to work on their behavior with food. A useful response is to ask them to talk about what they know about eating disorders. The first phase of treatment consists of educating the client, providing accurate information. The goal of this phase is that the client will begin to believe that her attempts at self-restraint and perfectionism will eventually backfire as described below.

Eating disorders often start with a female who is interested in losing a few pounds to feel better about herself. Because she is determined, her diet is often too strict and results in a series of physiological and emotional reactions. Her body reacts to the state of hunger by increasing its metabolic efficiency, which inhibits weight loss (i.e., by needing less food to maintain the same weight) until she begins eating normally again. Brownell and his colleagues (Brownell, Greenwood, Stellar, & Shrager, 1986; Steen, Oppliger, & Brownell, 1988) demonstrated that the body's basal metabolic rate (BMR) drops measurably within 24 hours and continues to decline 20% within 2 weeks. Moreover, the enzyme lipoprotein lipase (LPL), which controls how fat is stored in fat cells, becomes more active with reduced caloric intake. More active LPL makes the body become more efficient at fat storage. Weight cycling also increases the risk of heart disease, increases the proportion of fat to lean tissue in the body, redistributes body fat (shifting fat from the thighs and hips to the abdomen), and increases the desire for fatty foods (Brownell, 1988).

While dieting, the individual begins to notice that even though she is eating less and less, she is thinking about food constantly. Being a perfectionist, she feels guilty about this obsession with thoughts of food. She needs to hear that this is the second way the body attempts to adapt to a scarcity of food by motivating her to find food. One could say that the body cannot differentiate between a willful restriction of food and a famine. Because she probably experiences her obsession and yielding to eating as a moral issue rather than a biological one, the dieter's self-esteem plummets even further.

For reasons not yet clearly understood, the course of the disorder diverges at this point between anorexics and bulimics. Although the anorexic continues to restrict, the bulimic cannot help binging at times and will learn a way of making up for her "sin" of breaking the diet. Her repentance usually takes the form of forcing herself to vomit. Initially, she feels better in that she has gotten rid of the "sin," but later feels worse as she realizes her helplessness.

Often after years of binging and purging, or excessive restricting, the female's metabolism will have slowed to the point that she really will gain weight even when she eats very little. She will also be constantly obsessed with food, and will have low self-esteem and a myriad of physical problems depending on which type of purging she has used (Pomeroy & Mitchell, 1989). The client must learn that her incessant attempts at controlling her weight through restrained eating are the problem and that binging is a natural consequence of this, not a lack of will power.

Although building a therapeutic relationship continues and deepens through-out all phases of therapy, the therapist builds a foundation during this phase by nonjudgmentally delivering the facts about eating and dieting. Straightforward and respectful discussions about eating behavior and their consequences begin the process of developing trust, which is typically very difficult for eating-disordered individuals.

As this information is being accepted, there is also concurrent assessment that is being conducted. A baseline for the behavior is taken by asking the client in the first session to change nothing for 1 week except for keeping a record of her eating. Also included in the record are where she ate, when, with whom, how she felt before and after eating, and if she purged. The client continues to self-monitor her eating and binging throughout treatment until her symptoms stabilize.

Phase 2: Cognitive-Behavioral Therapy for Symptom Stabilization

The goal of the cognitive-behavioral phase is for the client to begin eating "normally." This goal is achieved by helping the client recognize the false beliefs she holds about herself and eating, by developing a repertoire of alterna-tive behaviors to binging and purging and/or restricting, and by increasing a sense of self-esteem. If improvement is not apparent within 3 months from beginning treatment, hospitalization should be considered. In working individu-ally with anorexics, a contract between the therapist and client should be estab-lished that stipulates the minimum weight necessary for outpatient work. The consequence of dropping below this weight, such as hospitalization, must be clearly labeled.

One of the models most associated with effective treatment of eating disor-ders is the cognitive/behavioral approach, which suggests that cognitive vari-ables play a vital role in maladaptive eating behaviors. Behavioral management without concurrent change in beliefs and attitudes is less effective and/or may lead to rapid relapse (Andersen, 1987; Bruch, 1974; Garner & Bemis, 1982). In reviewing the literature related to the presence of other cognitive difficulties, it was concluded that individuals with eating disorders do not differ from normal populations in their I.Q. levels, ability for abstract reasoning, or incidence of thinking disorders. However, there was some evidence that anorexics, when compared to bulimics, made more logical errors and had lower levels of concep-tual organization. Taken together, these results suggest that these individuals should respond to cognitive therapy, which is based on correcting errors in logic (Buchanan & Buchanan, 1992).

In helping the client recognize and change the misbeliefs she holds, it is use-ful to monitor and challenge automatic, irrational beliefs. For example, the belief that "I've been a *good* girl all day so I deserve one bite of X" (i.e., the forbidden food) may be written down with counterarguments. It is important to note that these clients use words such as "good" and "bad" as perfectionistic labels and that the therapist must be careful not to fall into using such labels in similar ways. The emphasis for cognitive therapy in this phase is more on establishing new beliefs about the consequences of dieting, binging, and/or purging, and less on actual personality change (Phase 3).

For most clients, there seems to be a constant dialogue between a critical parent self (often even more critical than her own parents actually were) and a discouraged or rebellious child self. With a combination of Transactional Analysis and Gestalt techniques, clients become aware of the destructive ways they talk to themselves. As the client begins to limit her destructive self-talk, she also needs to be developing positive self-talk in its place. Keeping a journal can be very helpful in these endeavors. The client can be instructed to write, at least once daily, something that she did or that someone did for her that made her feel good about herself. She can also be instructed to record once a day something that she has done just for fun or pleasure, because people with eating disorders have been known to omit pleasurable activities from their daily activities.

Behavioral interventions are also initiated in this phase of treatment. With the self-monitoring of all food intake that began in the first phase of treatment, patterns and areas of weakness can be identified and targeted for intervention. For example, the client and the therapist can plan a menu together for one day. The client is told to choose one day to follow the menu and told that if she can do it just once in the week, the week will be labeled a success. For clients who restrict, contingency management or contracting for healthier eating is recommended. For example, a client who enjoys going to or renting movies may do so after completing a meal. It must be kept in mind that the changes must be very gradual, with successes labeled as often as possible, to create a lasting change.

For clients who binge, one behavioral technique this author has found to be very helpful includes the use of a kitchen timer. Clients are instructed to set a timer for fifteen minutes when they first have the thought that they have overeaten and are going to throw up. They are asked to sit and explore their feelings during the fifteen minutes and to write them down, after which they may do whatever they like. This task focuses them on the present and they live, at least for 15 minutes, with the consequences of their actions.

Another helpful strategy for some clients is to act "as if" they do not have a problem with eating. Instructing the client to play the part of a created image is often challenging and may result in the client talking and thinking less about food. The more comfortable she begins to feel, the more she incorporates the created image into her self-concept.

A strategic technique for teaching the client to have more control is to have her plan a binge (also known as prescribing the symptom or prescribing a relapse). The planning is very detailed as to when the binge will take place, what will be eaten, and so forth. With this strategy, the client is instructed to plan to eat some "forbidden food" at distinct times during the week. When the client is able to eat formerly forbidden foods without later purging, her fear of forbidden foods decreases and, more importantly, her belief in her own power to control her eating is increased.

Phase 3: Dynamic-Interpersonal Psychotherapy for Treatment Maintenance

The third and final phase of individual therapy is the psychodynamic-interpersonal phase. For some clients the binge-purge syndrome began as a tragic reaction to a prolonged and rigid diet, and with these clients, therapy may be terminated after the second phase of treatment. This is where traditional cognitive-behavioral therapy usually ends and, unfortunately, where most research for treatment ends as well. For many clients, however, the problem is more complex, involving family of origin issues, personality dynamics, perfectionism, guilt, and anger. In determining which clients need to continue to the third phase of treatment, the therapist should consider several factors. These factors include the age of onset, the number of relapses the client has suffered following previous treatment, the ability to maintain significant relationships, presence of a history of sexual abuse, and presence of a personality disorder.

Although the goals of the third phase of treatment must be determined individually for each client, generally an environment should be provided in which the client feels safe to explore the various experiences that have helped to shape her personality. Because of the intimate nature of this phase of treatment, it is less conducive to research and may be more conducive to learning through long-term supervision and personal therapy.

In this phase of therapy, the therapist helps the client understand and modify several aspects of her personality that foster the problem and may contribute to a recurrence of the problem behaviors. In a general sense, these individuals often have had difficulty individuating from their families of origin and need help in their own continuing development. A cluster of personality variables that are interlocked in a powerful, self-destructive belief system seem to be very common among individuals with eating disorders. These broadly include perfectionism, low self-esteem, and high dependency, which tend to lead to unhealthy relationships. The client will often reject the notion that she is a perfectionist because she believes that she rarely lives up to her own standards. Yet this could almost be a definition of perfectionism and it is helpful for her to learn that it is not her ability but where she sets her standards that is leading her to feel guilty and unworthy.

Therapy for the perfectionist consists partly of helping her begin to understand how she developed these beliefs about herself. Often when exploring the family of origin, one finds a parent who was critical while the other parent was often passive (sometimes alcoholic) and did little or nothing to interrupt the negative messages received by the child. One anorexic client realized that she was still believing "the message that my mother gave me, that I wasn't good enough." Additionally, she wondered why her father never protected or took up for her. She had been listening to a critical voice tell her that she was only acceptable if she was thin (like mother) and never questioned or stood up to these messages (like father). Thus she was carrying out in her own mind both of the negative roles that her parents had played and had abolished any of the positive roles they may have played. Her task was to begin nurturing and standing up for the inner child in ways that her parents had not been able to do. This part of therapy is not aimed at blaming the parents because it is often observed that the critical parent, in the client's mind, is "worse" than the actual parent ever was in reality.

The above example illustrates the need for the client to deal with the messages that she received in the past and to take an honest look at how she is still obeying these messages. Visualization techniques may be helpful in changing the power of the old messages. The client is instructed to visualize herself as a child in several settings and then to visualize herself as an adult comforting the child and giving her positive messages in place of the negative ones she originally perceived. The client must begin to realize that this child is still alive inside her and that she is responsible now to nurture her. As she begins to develop compassion for the inner child, she is often less able to be as critical or perfectionistic toward herself.

The second major cluster of personality variables that are attended to in the third phase of therapy involve dependency needs. The bulimic is very unlikely to express anger to others, for she is overly concerned with others' evaluation of her and is likely to hold her own feelings in. She is more comfortable giving than receiving in a relationship and lacks assertiveness. All these variables often lead to a succession of unsuccessful or unsatisfied relationships with others.

A visualization exercise developed by this author (Buchanan & Buchanan, 1992) can be used to assess the client's unique needs. She is asked to imagine herself at a moment when she is feeling a strong urge to binge. Next she is asked to imagine that she has previously activated a "force field" that will last for several hours and will allow her to do anything except eat. The feelings that the client often report are indications of what she needs or is reacting against. For instance, one client reported feeling angry and remembered feeling this when her parents were restrictive, and another felt relief that may have indicated a wish for someone to take more control.

During this phase of treatment, the therapist needs to be consistently monitoring the reactions and feelings she or he feels toward the client. The relationship between the client and the therapist will be the key in understanding how the client behaves in interpersonal relationships outside the therapeutic milieu. The therapist will need to be looking for opportunities to ask how the conversation at hand is meaningful to the client/therapist relationship. For example, one client was talking in boring detail about how her previous therapist had made her angry. The client was encouraged to deal directly with her feelings when the therapist asked what the therapist might do that would make her angry. This was followed by an agreement that the client would speak up if the therapist did anything that made her angry or reminded her of her past experience. The client is encouraged to deal very directly and honestly in a relationship in which the therapist is also willing to deal with the actual feelings. Whereas bulimics often have many unhealthy relationships, anorexics tend to turn inward to cope and have difficulty turning to others, so the therapist-client relationship is even more vital and should be openly evaluated and discussed as often as possible.

In this phase of treatment, the therapist helps the client develop the skills and understanding of what healthy relationships involve. The client is often deeply touched (though anxious) by the therapist's directness. Directness builds trust in a way that the client has never experienced in a relationship. Using the therapeutic relationship to work through past hurtful relationships enables the client to begin to believe in her own power as an individual, care for herself in a healthy way, and develop lasting, satisfying relationships with others.

In conclusion, therapists will find that many clients will need to recycle through these three phases during the treatment process. For example, a client whose symptoms initially stabilized during the cognitive behavioral phase, may become aware of previously denied effect during a psychodynamic phase. The accompanying anxiety may trigger a relapse to eating disordered behaviors and the need for additional cognitive or behavioral intervention. Note that the focus of the first round of cognitive behavioral therapy was on the specific thoughts and behaviors related to eating or restricting, while the second round would focus on the new insight produced as a result of the psychodynamic interventions. A useful metaphor to use with clients is the upward spiral. Each time they cycle up, they may feel as though they've been around this rung before; however, they are actually cycling at a higher level and therefore experiencing it in a new way. This model is intended as a road map which enables the participants to pinpoint where they have been, where they are, and where they still need to go.

FAMILY THERAPY FOR EATING DISORDERS

Minuchin et al. (1978) describe five characteristics of psychosomatic families that can also be seen in the families of anorexics. Although no single family characteristic seems sufficient, the cluster of these transactional patterns is believed to be characteristic of a family process that encourages somatization.

Enmeshment refers to a smothering closeness in which the interpersonal boundaries between people become blurred. In this framework, loyalty and protection take precedence over autonomy and self-realization. Overprotectiveness, a second characteristic, refers to a family's exaggerated concern over the physical and psychological welfare of its members, warranted only for very young children. Third, extreme denial and avoidance of conflict are observed in psychosomatic families. The family presents itself as a unified group devoid of any problems except for the child's "illness," and family members are observed to rarely disagree. The fourth characteristic is rigidity. Extrafamilial stress, such as a loss or change in occupation, may require adaptations that the family cannot make because these might precipitate illness; thus the problems are left unresolved. The final characteristic is the child's involvement in a parental conflict so that the parents avoid or suppress the conflict.

When comparing anorexic families with bulimic families, anorexic families were found to have more interpersonal boundary problems and a stable and conflict-avoidant way of interacting that was experienced as nonconflictual and cohesive by the client and her family (Kog & Vandereycken, 1989). Humphrey (1989) found that parents of anorexics communicated a double message of nurturant affection combined with neglect of their daughters' needs to express themselves and their feelings, whereas bulimic families expressed more negative emotions and were hostilely enmeshed. These findings suggest that honest communication is more restricted in anorexic families but that both groups of families have patterns that reduce the daughter's ability to develop healthy, separate identities.

The structural family therapy approach begins with a thorough evaluation of the system constituted by the client, family, and referring physician or agency to determine both individual and family dysfunction and the need for hospitalization. The indications for psychiatric hospitalization are the presence of suicidal or severe psychotic symptoms in the client, prior or current outpatient failures, and/or relapses after previous inpatient treatment.

The top priority is to eliminate the symptom of refusing to eat and to stimulate progressive weight gain. To do this, the therapist attempts to realign the structure and boundaries between the subsystems of the family. For example, the client may be told that she must gain a minimum of 2 pounds a week to have the privilege of normal weekend activities. The parents are told that it is their responsibility to enforce the rules. Setting the above limits produces a great deal of stress in the family system, causing members of the family to join together to ensure that the client eats.

The family therapy lunch session is a primary tool used to accelerate weight gain. The therapist instructs one parent, then the other, to make the child eat, replaying the failed attempts of the past. With children and younger adolescents, the therapist joins with both parents to help them unite and take a firm stand until the child begins to eat. With older adolescents, the therapist stops the unsuccessful attempts, disengages the parents from further contact with the client about food, and makes eating into a private issue between client and therapist, dealt with in individual sessions.

As the client's weight begins to stabilize, there is a shift in focus from eating and the behavior paradigm to concern about interpersonal issues. Within the family, there is a gradual shift of emphasis to the problems in the marriage. At this point, the parents are seen separately for marital therapy with periodic family sessions as needed. The client is also seen individually to discuss age-appropriate developmental issues, such as the complexities of interpersonal relationships, learning to tolerate frustration, and developing problem-solving skills for home, school, and community. It is at this point that Minuchin's approach more clearly resembles the third phase of treatment advocated by this author with individuals.

Structural family therapy can be adapted for use with families with bulimia as well. The goals of realigning the family structure is to enable the bulimic to achieve a greater sense of self-control, become less protective of her family, become genuinely close to people both inside and outside her family, and let go of the dependent, sickly identity that bulimia symbolizes and maintains.

In summary, therapists who work with individuals with eating disorders must not only adopt an integrated approach to treatment, but also individualize their approach for each client. Although therapy must be individually tailored to meet each client's unique needs, it must involve, for all clients, a combination of treatment goals consisting of trust, education, symptom management, and resolution of psychodynamic and family of origin issues.

REFERENCES

American Psychiatric Association. (1987). *Diagnostic and statistical manual of mental disorders* (3rd ed., rev.; *DSM III-R*). Washington, DC: Author.

Andersen, A. (1987). Contrast and comparison of behavioral, cognitive-behavioral, and comprehensive treatment methods for anorexia nervosa and bulimia nervosa. *Behavior Modification, 11*, 522–543.

Berg, K. (1988). The prevalence of eating disorders in co-ed versus single-sex residence halls. *Journal of College Student Development, 29*, 125–131.

Brownell, K. D. (1988, March). The yo-yo trap. *American Health*, 78–84.

Brownell, K. D., Greenwood, M. R. C., Stellar, E., & Shrager, E. E. (1986). The effects of repeated cycles of weight loss and regain in rats. *Physiology and Behavior, 38*, 459–464.

Bruch, H. (1985). Four decades of eating disorders. In D. M. Garner & P. E. Garfinkel (Eds.), *Handbook of psychotherapy for anorexia and bulimia* (pp. 7–18). NY: Guilford.

Bruch, H. (1974). Perils of behavior modification in the treatment of anorexia nervosa. *Journal of the American Medical Association, 230*, 1419–1422.

Buchanan, L. P., & Buchanan, W. L. (1992). Eating disorders: Bulimia and anorexia. In L. L'Abate, J. Farrar, & D. Serritella (Eds.), *Handbook of differential treatments for addictions* (pp. 165–188). Boston: Allyn & Bacon.

Buchanan, L. P. (1993). *Coping resources, personality, and research design in eating disorder subgroups*. Unpublished doctoral dissertation, Georgia State University.

Carter, J., & Duncan, P. (1984). Binge-eating and vomiting: A survey of a high school population. *Psychology in the Schools, 21*, 198–203.

Dare, C., Eisler, I., Russell, G. F. M., & Szmukler, G. I. (1990). The clinical and theoretical impact of a controlled trial of family therapy in anorexia nervosa. *Journal of Marital and Family Therapy, 16*, 39–57.

Garner, D. M., & Bemis, K. M. (1982). A cognitive behavioral approach to anorexia nervosa. *Cognitive Therapy and Research, 6*, 1–27.

Hsu, L. K. (1989). The gender gap in eating disorders: Why are the eating disorders more common among women? *Clinical Psychology Review, 9*, 393–407.

Humphrey, L. (1989). Observed family interactions among subtypes of eating disorders using structural analysis of social behavior. *Journal of Consulting and Clinical Psychology, 57*, 206–214.

Kog, G., & Vandereycken, W. (1989). Family interaction in eating disorder clients and normal controls. *International Journal of Eating Disorders, 8*, 11–23.

Laessle, R., Tuschl, R., Waadt, S., & Pirke, K. (1989). The specific psychopathology of bulimia nervosa: A comparison with restrained and unrestrained (normal) eaters. *Journal of Consulting and Clinical Psychology, 57*, 772–775.

Minuchin, S., Rosman, B. L., & Baker, L. (1978). *Psychosomatic families: Anorexia nervosa in context*. Cambridge, MA: Harvard University Press.

Mitchell, P. B. (1988). The pharmacological management of bulimia nervosa: A critical review. *International Journal of Eating Disorders, 7*, 29–41.

Mizes, J. S. (1983, March). *Bulimarexia: Clinical description and suggested treatments*. Paper presented at the Annual Meeting of the Southeastern Psychological Association, Atlanta.

Pomeroy, C., & Mitchell, J. (1989). Medical complications and management of eating disorders. *Psychiatric Annals, 19*, 488–493.

Sansone, R., Seuferer, S., Fine, M., & Bovenzi, J. (1989). The prevalence of borderline personality symptomatology among women with eating disorders. *Journal of Clinical Psychology, 45*, 603–610.

Stager, H. (1989). An integrated psychotherapy for eating-disorder patients. *American Journal of Psychotherapy, 18*, 229–237.

Steen, S. N., Oppliger, R. A., & Brownell, K. D. (1988). Metabolic effects of repeated weight loss and regain in adolescent wrestlers. *Journal of the American Medical Association, 260*, 47–50.

Tice, L., Hall, R. C. W., Beresford, T. P., Quinones, J., & Hall, A. K. (1989). Sexual abuse in patients with eating disorders. *Psychiatric Medicine, 7*, 257–267.

Vandereycken, W. (1990). The addiction model in eating disorders: Some critical remarks. *International Journal of Eating Disorders, 9*, 95–101.

Zweben, J. E. (1987). Eating disorders and substance abuse. *Journal of Psychoactive Drugs, 19*, 181–192.

Chapter 9

Multimodal Treatment for Smoking Cessation

Jon Carlson

Although cigarette smoking has continued to decrease over the past two decades, it still remains a major public health problem. Current estimates vary; however, approximately 30% of the U.S. population continues to smoke, with a disproportionately large number of children and adolescents beginning smoking each year. Statements by the U.S. Surgeon General have underlined four general points: (a) smoking has adverse effects on several aspects of health; (b) secondary smoke affects the health of the nonsmoker; (c) nicotine meets the criteria for addiction in a way similar to that of other addictive behaviors; and (d) major and immediate health benefits are achieved by quitting smoking (Iverson, 1987). However, quitting smoking is not very easy to accomplish. Most smokers report wanting to stop and having tried unsuccessfully, with only 25% experiencing any lasting success (Lewis, Sperry, & Carlson, 1993).

Researchers have traditionally focused on the physiological components of addiction rather than on its psychological or social aspects. When smoking is viewed as a total process, researchers begin to examine the client's participation in the process as well as the impact on society. Through this altered way of viewing the smoking problem, a range of psychological, biological, and social interventions have developed. Effective clinical practice requires the utilization of a multimodal approach rather than traditional unimodal ones. In the approach that is presented here, generic hypnotherapeutic suggestions are coupled with behavior modification strategies, as well as adjunctive treatment such as exercise, relaxation, and diet modification. The chapter first provides an overview of intervention approaches and then presents the author's three-step multimodal procedure: (a) assessment, (b) intervention, and (c) treatment adherence/follow-up.

OVERVIEW OF INTERVENTION APPROACHES

Five different smoking intervention strategies have been designed to encourage people to quit smoking and have been identified in the literature: (a) aversion, (b) self-control, (c) a combination of aversion and self-control, (d) pharmacological approaches, and (e) health education (Bloom, 1988).

Aversion strategies can be grouped into four categories: electric shock, rapid smoking, satiation, and cognitive sensitization. None of these methods has been found to be remarkably effective.

Self-control methods include (a) environmental planning, (b) behavioral programming, and (c) cognitive control. Environmental planning involves helping the client change smoking behaviors, either by altering the circumstances in which smoking occurs or by working with others to reinforce each other's smoking-cessation efforts. In the case of behavioral programming, the smoker institutes a self-directed system of rewards and punishments to facilitate smoking cessation. In the case of cognitive control, the smoker attempts to limit smoking behavior by changing his or her way of thinking about smoking.

Pharmacological approaches to smoking cessation are based on the premise that the smoker has become addicted to nicotine. One approach is to provide nicotine to the smoker, mainly in the form of special chewing gum. There is considerable evidence that chewing gum is an effective adjunct in the smoking-cessation program. An aspect of this program that defies logic is that although cigarettes that contain considerable nicotine are freely available to the public, a physician's prescription is currently needed to purchase nicotine gum. Nicotine supplements have been used to lessen the physical symptoms of withdrawal. Gottlieb, Killen, Marlatt, and Taylor (1987) identified the client's expectations as the determinant factor in the effectiveness of nicotine supplements. Their study questions the effectiveness of nicotine supplements and looks at how the client's expectations actually alter the supplements' perceived effects. Other researchers have been experimenting with transdermal clonidine and transdermal nicotine patches. Although these patches have limited applicability, they have been shown to be effective in reducing physical discomforts associated with nicotine withdrawal.

The Food and Drug Administration in 1992 approved several different brands of skin or transdermal nicotine patches. These adhesive pads, about 2 inches square and available by prescription, release a trickle of nicotine through the skin into the bloodstream, thus satisfying the smoker's craving for nicotine. Studies submitted to the FDA indicate that smokers who used nicotine patches for 8 to 12 weeks were about twice as likely to have quit at the end of that period (that is, not to have smoked since the second week of the study) as were those who used dummy patches without nicotine. Quitting rates in different studies ranged from 8% to 92% for the nicotine-patch users, as compared with 3% to 46% for those who got dummy patches (Weiss, 1992).

Unfortunately, quitting smoking is often the easy part. The more difficult problem is not starting again. Many smokers wonder whether the nicotine patch will conquer smoking permanently. So far, research suggests that those who quit with the help of patches relapse at about the same rate as anyone else. The quitting rates for those who use patches seem to be roughly similar to the rates of those who use nicotine gum. The severity of the side effects in both products is comparable: hiccups, sore throat, and jaw aches for gum; minor skin irritation, insomnia, and occasional nightmares for patches. It is important to note that the patches are relatively ineffective unless they are used in conjunction with a smoking-cessation program that includes counseling, relaxation training, hypnosis, or some other form of behavioral therapy. All manufacturers offer forms of psychological support, such as a toll-free hotline, day-by-day motivational suggestions, audiotapes, and a pamphlet to be given to a friend or spouse that contains hints about how to provide support to the quitter.

Edwards, Murphy, Downs, Ackerman, and Rosenthal (1989) studied the use of antidepressants. In their research, Doxepin was identified as an effective agent both in the precessation process and in the active quitting. Researchers have noticed that, because the symptoms of depression and withdrawal are very similar, treatments for depression are likely to be very helpful during the withdrawal process. More comprehensive research should indicate how antidepressants and other medications can be utilized effectively.

Health education is in this context equivalent to psychoeducation. Psychoeducation is provided throughout each session in order to help clients learn the impact of smoking on their lives as well as the skills and strategies necessary to bring about this change.

THE MULTIMODAL APPROACH

Assessment

Information gathered during assessment can give the counselor a perspective of the client's health, strengths, risks, and psychological orientation. The counselor can develop strategies for how the clients' strengths can best be utilized and can prescribe remediation for the clients' weaknesses and skill deficits. Thus a thorough systematic assessment *prior* to direct contact sets the stage for more effective use of the direct counseling contact time. In the assessment phase this involves collecting background information and a smoking history, as well as a wellness and health assessment and lifestyle data. Counselors need to specifically look at some of the psychological, social, and behavioral supports for smoking behavior. This involves assessing the length of time the client has smoked, others in his or her environment who smoke, and presence of any medical problems that could be related to smoking. The counselor is also interested in knowing whether the client has made other successful habit changes. This would help to determine the level of self-efficacy (Bandura, 1987). Bandura has discovered that self-efficacy is the key to helping a person unlearn bad habits and to form good ones. He defines this term as an individual's perception of his or her own ability to do a specific task, such as losing a pound a week, following an exercise program daily, or limiting their alcohol intake. In contrast, self-competence is one's perception of one's general worth and general ability. Studies show that if you believe in your ability to reach a particular goal, you are much more likely to reach it. As Bandura observed, when beset with difficulties, people who entertain serious doubts about their capabilities slacken their efforts or give up altogether, whereas those who have a strong sense of what he terms "efficacy" exert greater effort to master the challenges. It is important in health promotion counseling that individuals are aware of the high level of self-efficacy and success in other areas of their lives. For example, maybe they have not been able to give up cigarettes, but they have been able to do many other things like control drinking and accomplish other successful habit changes. It is important to note that although collecting this information has interesting prognostic value for the counselor, it is also very important to use this information therapeutically by sharing it with the client and explaining how change works in order to create a self-fulfilling prophecy. In multimodal therapy, assessment information is collected not just for the purpose of predicting the effectiveness of treatment, but rather for the purpose of providing action that will improve the outcome of counseling. Assessment should have immediate implications for the conduct of treatment, and it is most valuable when it is linked to a set of clinical procedures that when differentially applied can produce different treatment results.

Assessment can increase clients' motivational level by changing their perception or way of thinking about the smoking problem. For example, asking clients to list the benefits that they plan to receive from quitting can be a very helpful tool. Asking clients to carry the list with them at all times and agree to look at the list before putting another cigarette in their mouth is a way of breaking up the habit process, as well as allowing clients to be clearly aware of their goal.

During the assessment process, it is also helpful to determine the clients' current level of physical and psychological stress and to identify what coping skills they have or need to develop to cope effectively with the stress and meet their goal (Sperry & Carlson, 1993). The level of stress in the client's life influences the treatment process. Lower levels of stress can be a motivational factor that stimulates clients to seek change, but clients who experience high levels of stress are likely to see themselves as not capable of effecting change until some tension is reduced. Clinical instruments are available to assess the client's current level of stress; however, using the simple question "On a scale of 1 to 100, with 1 being low and 100 being high, what would you estimate your current level of stress?" works very effectively. This simple question can help the client assess the present stress, predict the likelihood that their stress is going to change in the future, and better understand whether this is the best time to be considering a smoking cessation program.

Intervention

Once an appropriate assessment has occurred and the counselor determines that the client has committed and is motivated to change, the next task is to match the client with the appropriate treatments and adequate supports. The multimodal approach to smoking cessation attempts to encourage clients to view the smoking problem differently, as well as to offer behavioral alternatives that will support smoking cessation (Carlson, 1989). The handout with smoking cessation prescriptions can be utilized. The suggestions are divided into the physical, behavioral, and psychological, with each having specific activities that need to be accomplished in the next 2 weeks to a month during the difficult stages of the smoking cessation process.

Physical Directives

In the physical dimension, dietary changes are suggested. Clients are suggested to purchase sunflower seeds as something to chew on when they wish to have a cigarette. Sunflower seeds are botanically similar to the tobacco plant and reputedly cause a glandular reaction very similar to that created by tobacco. Specific suggestions based upon the work of Schachter and his colleagues (Fix & Daughton, 1979; Schachter et al., 1977) are given. They observe that there is an acid-alkaline balance in the body and nicotine is a very strong alkaline substance, so that with this pH balance, if one's acidity levels rise, alkaline levels need to change to keep it in balance. When the acidity levels go up or the alkaline levels drop, individuals crave cigarettes. By making dietary changes, it is possible to minimize changes in the pH balance. Suggestions are made to eat more fruits and vegetables; stay away from meat, eggs, and alcohol; reduce sugar intake; and decrease the use of stimulants. The client is also advised to drink lots of fluids such as water and juices to flush their system clean. Vitamin supplements, C and B complex, might also be suggested.

Information is also provided that suggests that the client do deep breathing each hour. Diaphragmatic breathing procedures are taught. They are exactly the opposite of the way we normally breathe. Clients are suggested to put a hand on their chest and one on their belly and breathe in a way that the hand on the belly moves without the hand on the chest changing. It is suggested that this is done each hour, the substitute experience for smoking. This is going to relax the client and help him or her to gain more self-control. When people are stressed, acid is produced. As their acidity levels rise, the acid-alkaline balances change and a craving for alkaline, or nicotine, occurs. Most people report a relapse with smoking occurs when they are in a very stressful situation. It is therefore important to help the client remain as calm as possible. Muscle relaxation is also a very helpful process. This involves stretching a muscle and holding it for 3 to 60 seconds. These procedures are shown to the client, and a handout giving specific suggestions is provided.

Behavioral Directives

One set of changes in the behavioral dimension involves encouraging clients to brush their teeth a lot, use mouthwash, make an appointment to get their teeth cleaned in order to get rid of any residual tobacco stain or taste, and have a fresh, clean mouth. It's important to feel good, and one way is to have a different feeling in one's mouth.

Additionally it is important to break up some of the routines such as where the individual smokes. It's suggested that clients avoid sitting in chairs or areas where they ordinarily smoked. If they have to sit in the same area, it is suggested that if possible the surroundings be rearranged. It is further recommended to get rid of all ashtrays and cigarettes, and to avoid as much as possible people who smoke.

Clients should also increase their daily activity patterns as much as possible, and really become active. They should do things like take walks, showers, go to church, bicycle, pray, swim, make love, play tennis, and engage in activities to keep their hands busy if necessary. Regular aerobic exercise, if medically warranted, can be very effective because it is incompatible with smoking and also helps to restore health and vitality. This is an important aspect in total health promotion. We are not just trying to remove negatives, but also assisting the client to develop positives.

Clients should think of times when it will be difficult to stop smoking and then schedule things that they can do instead. If it is difficult after meals, they can take a walk, take a shower, or listen to the hypnosis audiotape, all things that are simple to think of and accomplish. All suggestions are made to break up the routines and patterns that support smoking and encourage the development of positive addictions.

Psychological Directives

Hypnosis is an important component to lifestyle change in that it helps create a positive psychological mindset. Crasilneck (1990) reports a 1 year follow-up cessation rate of 81% through the use of hynotic techniques, combined with psychoeducation and reinforcers meted out by the counselor and mutual-aid groups. This author's hypnosis program uses standard breathing, relaxation, and guided imagery, along with directives about smoking cessation. The exercise is recorded, and the client is given a copy of the 10- to 12- minute tape for personal use outside the session. The client is requested to listen to this tape at least once a day for the first 2 weeks following treatment. This will reinforce what has occurred in the counseling session. Clients are also able to relax during the hypnosis session because they don't think they have to remember everything. They don't have to pay total attention. They know it is going to be on tape, so this will increase the likelihood of compliance.

In addition to the standard hypnotic suggestions on the audiotape, a sheet with positive affirmations is also given to the client. Clients are asked to verbally repeat the affirmations several times a day or to write out the affirmations. Sample affirmations are: All of my senses are clear and alive. I am more productive and creative than when I was a smoker. I give myself permission to relax, feel good, breathe deeply and fully, and enjoy being a healthy nonsmoker at all times and in all circumstances. I have no habits that control or influence me in any harmful way. I am in control of myself and everything I do. I always do what is best for me, myself, and my future.

Clients need to learn cognitive vigilance as an asset in the cessation process. By learning to recognize the thought processes at work, the client can successfully intervene when faulty thinking occurs. Through psychoeducation, the client can effectively program new cognitive responses.

Other Treatment Considerations

Group versus individual treatment. Most smoking-cessation treatment is provided in small groups of five to 10 people. There appears to be no evidence that groups are superior to individual treatment. However, many clients who have participated in groups report that the group support was central in achieving and maintaining abstinence. Groups are also more cost-effective than individual sessions. However, there are certain pitfalls in group treatment. First, relapse can sometimes be contagious, especially if those who relapse are vocal or have achieved high informal status in the group. Second, group members sometimes give each other permission to fail. Last, if group members are poorly matched or antagonistic to one another, attendance rates can be poorer than in individual sessions.

Abrupt versus gradual quitting. We recommend abrupt cessation because it is most congenial with the methods that we have found helpful. We ask smokers to set a quit date and to stop smoking completely on that day. Many smokers will cut down gradually before that day, and some will continue to smoke right up until the last moment. We have not noticed any difference in outcome as a function of which strategy was used.

Treatment Adherence

It is easy for some people to stop smoking; however, these are not the people who usually seek the help of formal treatment programs. The clients who wish smoking cessation usually represent the more physically and psychologically dependent smokers. For these clients, quitting smoking is often a difficult process that involves readjustment in the physical, intrapsychic, and social domains. If smokers fail to acknowledge these potential problems when quitting smoking, they are poorly prepared for the difficulties involved and are at a higher risk for relapse. Relapse may occur because (a) ex-smokers are not aware that the acute discomfort they are experiencing is time limited and fear they must endure it indefinitely; (b) they believe the problems they are experiencing are uncommon and so relapse because they feel alone and helpless to deal with the problems; and (c) they do not develop appropriate cognitive and behavioral strategies (Hall & Hall, 1987).

It is important for counselors to realize that it is not enough to help the client quit; rather, it is imperative to help the client maintain long-term abstinence. The counselor's real work seems to begin after smoking stops. Research indicates that the majority of relapse occurs within the first 3 months following cessation.

Marlatt and Gordon (1980) developed the following list of situations that can result in relapse. It is important for the counselor to prepare the client for alternative responses in each of these situations.

1. Eating is a frequent stimulus for smoking and a prominent antecedent of relapse (Shiffman, 1982). Smoking after meals or with coffee is so common that these occasions must be considered high risks for all smokers.
2. Times of stress or upset are also frequently associated with smoking and relapse. In these situations, the smoker seems to use cigarettes to blunt unpleasant emotions.
3. Alcohol consumption is strongly associated with smoking. Smokers are almost always drinkers, and laboratory experiments have demonstrated that smoking facilitates drinking.
4. Social situations are also common triggers for smoking. In addition to being cued by other smokers, many smokers seem to use smoking to manage feelings of awkwardness in social situations.
5. Boredom is also associated with smoking. Smokers who are bored may see it "as something to do" or may seek the stimulating pharmacological action of nicotine. In our experience, boredom is often used to describe a condition of mild depression.
6. Positive affect situations are also conducive to smoking. Although smoking is more common when one is in the grip of negative emotions, some smokers are especially likely to smoke when they feel good, claiming that smoking accentuates their positive feeling.

7. Food substitution is another function that cigarettes often serve. Smokers sometimes have a cigarette instead of food. Fear, sometimes justified, of weight gain after quitting often undermines clients' motivations to stay abstinent.

Research seems to support the idea that it is important to help the client plan what he or she is going to do. The proactive rather than reactive stance will decrease the likelihood of relapse. Very clear first-line strategies need to be developed to cope with temptations to smoke. These should include avoidance, escape, distraction, and delay. It is important that clients develop cognitive and behavioral coping responses to counter very specific high-risk situations. Some cognitive procedures are imagery, cognitive restructuring, and self-talk, and some behavioral procedures are physical activity, relaxation, and other substitute behaviors.

CONCLUSION

A multimodal treatment approach was presented in this chapter. In this, counseling was paired with other interventions to produce an effective treatment option. Sound assessment, psychoeducation, hypnosis, and relapse prevention strategies are the important aspects of this health change process.

It is important to note that although virtually anyone can and at some point does quit, the maintenance of cessation is the heart of success in a multimodal smoking cessation program. Relapse prevention is an essential component to achieving this end. Relapse prevention requires a thorough initial assessment, a solid understanding of the psychoeducational process, and a tailored treatment plan based on the initial assessment. The counselor's careful work in the relapse prevention stage can ensure that the maintenance of cessation has a solid chance.

REFERENCES

Bandura, A. (1987, May). Self-efficacy. *University of California-Berkeley Wellness Letter,* pp. 1–2.

Bloom, B. L. (1988). *Health psychology: A psychosocial perspective.* Englewood Cliffs, NJ: Prentice Hall.

Carlson, J. (1989). Brief therapy for health promotion. *Individual Psychology, 45* (1 & 2), 220–229.

Crasilneck, H. B. (1990). Hypnotic techniques for smoking control and psychogenic impotence. *American Journal of Clinical Hypnosis, 32,* 147–153.

Edwards, N. B., Murphy, J. K., Downs, A. D., Ackerman, B. J., & Rosenthal, T. L. (1989). Doxepin as an adjunct to smoking cessation: A double blind pilot study. *American Journal of Psychiatry, 146* (3), 373–376.

Fix, A. J., & Daughton, D. M. (1979, April). *Smoking cessation and acid-base balance.* Paper presented at Rocky Mountain Psychological Association, Las Vegas.

Gottlieb, A. M., Killen, J. D., Marlatt, G. A., & Taylor, C. B. (1987). Psychological and pharmacological influences in cigarette smoking. *Journal of Consulting and Clinical Psychology, 55,* 606–608.

Hall, S. M., & Hall, R. G. (1987). Treatment of cigarette smoking. In J. A. Blumenthal & D. C. McKee (Eds.), *Applications in behavioral medicine and health psychology: A clinician's sourcebook* (pp. 301–323). Sarasota, FL: Professional Resource Exchange.

Iverson, D. C. (1987). Smoking control programs: Premise and promises. *American Journal of Health Promotion, 1* (3), 16–30.

Lewis, J. A., Sperry, L., & Carlson, J. (1993). *Health counseling.* Pacific Grove, CA: Brooks/Cole.

Marlatt, G. A., & Gordon, J. R. (1980). Determinants of relapse: Implications for the maintenance of behavior change. In P. O. Davidson & S. M. Davidson (Eds.), *Behavioral medicine: Changing health lifestyles.* New York: Brunner/Mazel.

Schachter, S., Silverstein, B., Kozlowski, L.T., Perlick, D., Herman, C. P., & Liebling, B. (1977). Studies of the interaction of psychological and pharmacological determinants of smoking. *Journal of Experimental Psychology: General, 106* (1), 3–4.

Shiffman, S. (1982). Relapse following smoking cessation: A situational analysis. *Journal of Consulting and Clinical Psychology, 50,* 71–86.

Sperry, L., & Carlson, J. (1993). *Basics of stress management.* Coral Springs, FL: CMTI Press.

Weiss, R. (1992, April 8). Update on nicotine patches: For some it may help. *New York Times,* p. B9.

Chapter 10

Diagnosis and Treatment of Pathological Gambling

Martin C. McGurrin

Pathological gambling is a behavior disorder characterized by repeated failure to resist the impulse to wager money on the uncertain outcome of games or other chance events. It is a chronic and progressive disorder that often results in unmanageable debt, breakdown of family and friendship relations, loss of employment, embezzlement or forgery, and even attempted suicide. Frequently, pathological gamblers deny their gambling problem and its consequences until their life is almost totally disordered. This extreme condition is called "hitting bottom." When pathological gamblers hit bottom, they are usually willing to admit to their problem and seek treatment. Not all pathological gamblers, however, need to hit bottom before seeking treatment, and most persons who begin gambling never become pathological gamblers. Before reviewing the factual information on the etiology, diagnosis, and treatment of pathological gambling, a brief overview of the history of gambling will be useful.

HISTORICAL OVERVIEW OF GAMBLING

Historical documents have established that human beings have engaged in gambling for at least the past 6,000 years. Organized gambling has origins in both the occult aspects of early religious efforts to predict future events and the strategies of politicians to distract public attention from the discomfort of food shortages or other social calamity. For example, the rulers of Lydia in Asia Minor provided dice to the general populace during periods of famine (Fleming, 1978).

Whatever the origins of gambling, with it arose the phenomenon of uncontrollable gambling. In 1190, for example, during the Third Crusade, King

Richard the Lionhearted became so concerned over the strife among his crusaders who gambled at dice that he issued orders prohibiting ordinary soldiers from any dice play and limited knights and clergymen to losses no greater than 20 shillings. Four centuries later, King Henry VIII became so involved in gambling that he once lost the very valuable Jesus bells that hung from the tower of St. Paul's Cathedral while throwing dice with several of his noblemen (Fleming, 1978).

Gambling has been an integral part of American society from its inception. Colonial Americans bet on horse races, dog- and cockfights, and lotteries even though gambling generally was condemned as a moral vice. This emphasis on the immoral nature of gambling was reinforced legally in that each of the original 13 states adopted English law on gambling, which was interpreted in American courts by judges who for the most part supported basically Puritan attitudes against gambling (Blakey, 1979).

In spite of this official prohibitive stance against gambling, it continued as a popular activity among the general population. In fact, economic problems caused by inadequate banking practices and taxation inspired colonial public officials to manipulate public support for lotteries as a means to finance construction of roads, bridges, fortifications, schools, hospitals, and even churches. This method of financing public works continued after 1776 in the form of state-franchised private lottery companies. This success in generating public funds is convincing proof that gambling enjoyed a broad base of social approval in spite of its essentially illegal status. As the 19th century progressed, horse-race betting in the eastern states and casino gambling at eastern spas and along the western frontier became widely established even though laws that prohibited commercial gambling existed.

In the United States, the most widespread rejection of the legal prohibition of gambling has occurred during the 20th century. In 1931, Nevada legalized casino gambling along with most other forms of gambling. During the next decade parimutuel racing was legalized along the eastern seaboard and in several midwestern states. In 1964, New Hampshire began the first modern legal state lottery. By 1984, 22 states authorized lotteries; New York and Connecticut authorized government-operated offtrack betting (OTB); parimutuel Jai Alai spread from Florida to Connecticut, Rhode Island, and Nevada; and New Jersey legalized casino gambling in Atlantic City. In 1989, the Iowa State Legislature passed a law allowing the return of riverboat gambling on the Mississippi River. In several midwestern states, gambling at bingo is a popular pastime for senior citizens. Legalized gambling is a major source of revenue on many American Indian reservations. Gambling on cruise ships along the Florida coast is common, and legal sports betting is being considered by several state legislatures. The trend to expand the varieties of legalized gambling continues unabated (Abt, Smith, & Christiansen, 1985).

The recent professional interest in both normal and pathological gambling began in about 1975. The astonishingly rapid increase in legal opportunities to gamble called attention to the related issue of pathological gambling (Dunne, 1985). Survey research indicates that approximately 60% of the adult population in the United States gamble for money at least occasionally (Commission on the Review of the National Policy Toward Gambling, 1978), yet only about 3% of the adult population become pathological gamblers (McGurrin, 1992). What causes pathological gambling? The remaining discussion in this chapter will attempt to answer this question and provide practical instructions on how to diagnose and treat pathological gambling.

ETIOLOGY

Pathological gambling is located in the *Diagnostic and Statistical Manual of Mental Disorders* (3rd ed., rev.; [*DSM-III-R*] under "Disorders of Impulse Control Not Elsewhere Classified" (American Psychiatric Association [APA], 1987). Although evidence of cognitive (Corny & Cummings, 1985), affective (McCormick, Russo, Ramirez, & Taber, 1984), and biological (Carlton & Goldstein, 1987; Carlton & Manowitz, 1988) causes of pathological gambling are reported in the literature, there is no scientifically validated cause of this disorder or of the personality structure and psychodynamics of the pathological gambler (Taber, 1988).

However, several features often reported by pathological gamblers regarding their gambling activity distinguish it from normal gambling. The features are (a) an inability to resist the impulse to gamble, (b) an increasing physical and psychological tension prior to gambling activity, and (c) an intense pleasure associated with the relief of tension achieved by active involvement in gambling behavior (McGurrin, 1992). The antecedent tension and repeated failure to resist the impulse to gamble led to the general practice of regarding pathological gambling as an obsessive-compulsive disorder (Bergler, 1957; Kusyszyn, 1978). Increased information about pathological gamblers has revealed, however, that they experience their gambling behavior as egosyntonic. Gambling does not cause them to feel guilt or self-reproach until extreme debt, job loss, acute family disruption, or threat of criminal prosecution occurs as a consequence of their pathological gambling (Rosenthal, 1986). These findings tend to invalidate the notion that pathological gambling is essentially an obsessive-compulsive disorder.

Several other characteristics have been found also to be more common among pathological gamblers than among normal gamblers. Awareness of these characteristics and related research findings is useful in understanding and treating pathological gambling. First, pathological gamblers view the outcome of many life events as externally controlled. Research using Rotter's (1966) I-E Locus of Control Scale has shown that pathological gamblers are more externally oriented regarding the forces that control their lives than are normal gamblers or the nongambling public (Kusyszyn & Rubenstein, 1985; McGurrin, Abt, & Smith, 1984; McGurrin, 1986). Typically, pathological gamblers express a sense of fatalism in statements such as "it wasn't intended to happen" or "easy come, easy go." The development of a more realistic internal orientation toward personal control and responsibility should always be made a major treatment goal for the pathological gambler.

Second, pathological gamblers alternate between periods of extreme confidence in their ability to win large amounts of money as well as to achieve success in other areas of life, and periods of acute self-doubt, anxiety, and depression over experienced or potential failure. Also, they often alternate between hypomania and depressive states. The hypomania involves decreased need for sleep, elevated energy level and restlessness, extreme gregariousness, and inflated self-esteem. During depressive periods, the pathological gambler experiences chronic fatigue, insomnia or hypersomnia, feelings of inadequacy, decreased ability to concentrate, social withdrawal, reduced experience of pleasure, loss of interest in sex, and pessimistic attitudes toward the future or brooding over past events. These periods of mood swings are usually separated by months of normal mood and energy level.

Third, many pathological gamblers may have underlying personality disorders, such as Narcissistic Personality Disorder (APA, 1987, sec. 301.81). For example, pathological gamblers' narcissism is manifest in a grandiose sense of self-importance, hypersensitivity to the evaluations of others, fragile self-esteem, and a common lack of empathy for the feelings and experiences of family and close friends (Rosenthal, 1986). Efforts to maintain self-esteem may result in the demand for constant attention and admiration, which obstructs normal interpersonal relationships. Pathological gamblers' narcissism is revealed also in their frequent use of the primitive defense mechanisms of splitting, projection, omnipotence, idealization and devaluation, and denial as protections against basic experiences of powerlessness and lack of self-worth (Rosenthal, 1986).

There are also impressive points of overlap between Pathological Gambling and Antisocial Personality Disorder (APA, 1987, sec. 301.70). In both disorders there is disregard for social norms against lying or conning (especially to acquire money); significant failure to plan ahead and responsibly manage financial obligations; difficulty maintaining intimacy; impulsivity; and an inability to tolerate anxiety, boredom, or depression (APA, 1987).

Fourth, many pathological gamblers view achievement through sustained effort and delayed gratification as inferior to immediate gratification and success (Taber, Russo, Adkins, & McCormick, 1986). They often view normal employment as a personal failure to be overcome by the immediate wealth and high status that they believe they will acquire through gambling. They rationalize their recurrent impulses to take extreme financial risk in gambling with the explanation that basically everyone wants to be wealthy, but wealth always escapes pathological gamblers because they cannot stop gambling after the "big win."

Fifth, pathological gamblers have difficulty maintaining intimate, emotionally expressive relationships with family and close friends. Family members, particularly spouses, report that the pathological gambler goes through recurrent periods of emotional estrangement from the family. During these periods, the gambler fails to attend school or community events which involve his or her children. There is reduced expression of affection toward spouse or children. Sexual activity is minimal even when the spouse requests more frequent sexual activity. Male and female pathological gamblers themselves acknowledge a greatly reduced interest in sexual activity when they are in their most active phases of gambling. In fact, male pathological gamblers sometimes refer facetiously to gambling as "the other woman in my life."

Some recent research on possible biological causes of pathological gambling has found that some pathological gamblers show deficits in EEG differentiation in response to simple verbal versus nonverbal tasks. These results suggest that there may be some abnormal brain functioning that discriminates pathological gamblers from individuals with normal brain functioning (Goldstein, Manowitz, Nora, Swartzburg, & Carlton, 1985).

Similar EEG deficits have been found among children with Attention Deficit Disorder (ADD) (Carlton & Goldstein, 1987). These findings suggest that if adult pathological gambling were affected by childhood ADD, the EEG deficits in adult gamblers may reflect ADD characteristics carried forward from childhood into adulthood. Carlton and Goldstein (1987) tested this hypothesis using a retrospective questionnaire consisting of ADD relevant statements about the respondents' childhood behavior (e.g., "When I was a child, I was nervous"). The mean scores for pathological gamblers on the ADD items were significantly higher than those of the matched controls, indicating a greater frequency of ADD-related behavior during the pathological gambler's childhood.

Finally, because some alcoholics have been ADD children and have a residual form of the disorder in adulthood (Wender, Reimherr, & Wood, 1981; Wood, Wender, & Reimherr, 1983), Carlton and Goldstein suggest that ADD may be a brain function disorder common to pathological gamblers and alcoholics. The frequent comorbidity of pathological gambling and substance abuse may be related to such an underlying trait. Carlton and Manowitz (1988) suggest that the underlying link among ADD, alcoholism, and pathological gambling is inadequate impulse control. Specifically, they are referring to a tendency to act in a situation without forethought and a relative inability to delay gratification until there is a sufficient basis for assuming a minimum risk of an unfavorable outcome. The implication follows that for both pathological gamblers and alcoholics, *pathology* refers to the inability to self-regulate rather than to the specific behavior (i.e., gambling, abusing alcohol). These findings are supportive of the *DSM-III-R* diagnostic classification of pathological gambling as an impulse control disorder and could lead to the development of pharmacological intervention that could be useful in treatment.

Finally, it is important to comment on the common practice of treating pathological gambling as an addiction. Several aspects of pathological gambling suggest that it may be an addictive disorder: (a) the gradual involvement in gambling, with a progressive need to increase amounts wagered in order to achieve tension release; (b) the pathological gambler's increasing preoccupation with acquiring money and arranging opportunities to gamble; and (c) many pathological gamblers' experience of extreme anxiety, depression, and somatic discomfort during initial abstinence from gambling, which somewhat resembles withdrawal reactions found in alcohol and drug addiction.

There is another association between pathological gambling and addictive disorders. It has been found repeatedly that approximately 30% to 50% of persons receiving inpatient treatment for pathological gambling also satisfy diagnostic criteria for alcohol or drug abuse (Ramirez, McCormick, Russo, & Taber, 1984). These findings have inspired continuing research into the phenomenon of the "cross-addicted gambler" (Ciarrocchi, 1987).

Jacobs (1986, 1988, 1989) has developed a general theory of addictions that relates specific addictions to an underlying propensity to addiction. His general theory of addictions relates alcoholism and pathological gambling through the bridging concept of *altered state of identity*. Continuous use of addictive substances or activities is viewed as a means by which addicts detach themselves psychologically from their ordinary reality and become so engrossed in fantasy that they assume an altered state of identity that is hypothesized to be the end product of a self-induced dissociative condition.

An enhanced sense of wellness that occurs during the dissociative state as well as the accentuated experience of characteristics that the addicted person finds most attractive about his or her personality suggests powerful psychological inducements for continuous use of a substance in addition to biochemical properties of the substance that may be operative. Jacobs' theory also provides an explanation for the apparent addictive properties of gambling. For example, persons with low self-esteem and a poor self-image under ordinary circumstances may be able to dramatically increase self-esteem rapidly by a self-induced dissociative state that results from intense episodes of gambling. Jacobs (1989) has systematically tested his general theory of addictions and has reported impressive confirmatory results.

DIAGNOSIS

The professional standard for diagnosis of pathological gambling is the *DSM-III-R* (APA, 1987). The diagnostic perspective includes common psychological characteristics of the pathological gambler such as frequent preoccupation with gambling, as well as social consequences of uncontrolled gambling such as disruption to personal, family, or vocational areas of the gambler's life. As a more complete psychological profile of the problem gambler is developed, additional modifications in diagnostic criteria will occur.

A positive diagnosis of pathological gambling is justified currently by determining that at least four of the following nine indicators in the *DSM-III-R* apply to the person being evaluated (APA, 1987, p. 325):

1. frequent preoccupation with gambling or with obtaining money to gamble
2. frequent gambling of larger amounts of money or over a longer period of time than intended
3. a need to increase the size or frequency of bets to achieve the desired excitement
4. restlessness or irritability if unable to gamble
5. repeated loss of money by gambling and returning another day to win back losses ("chasing")
6. repeated efforts to reduce or stop gambling
7. frequent gambling when expected to meet social or occupational obligations
8. sacrifice of some important social, occupational, or recreational activity in order to gamble
9. continuation of gambling despite inability to pay mounting debts, or despite other significant social, occupational, or legal problems that the person knows to be exacerbated by gambling

The South Oaks Gambling Screen (SOGS) is another excellent instrument for diagnosing pathological gambling and may be used as a supplement to the *DSM-III-R* diagnostic criteria (Lesieur & Blume, 1988). The SOGS is a 20-item scale derived from the *DSM-III* (APA, 1980) diagnostic criteria for pathological gambling. The instrument has been found valid and reliable in distinguishing pathological gamblers among hospital workers, university students, high school students, prison inmates, and inpatients in alcohol and substance abuse treatment programs (Lesieur & Blume, 1988; Lesieur, Blume, & Zoppa, 1986; Lesieur & Klein, 1985, 1987) and has been used in the most valid recent survey research designed to determine the true incidence and prevalence of pathological gamblers (Volberg & Steadman, 1989).

GA has developed a 20-question screening instrument that is useful for evaluating the nature of a person's problem in controlling his or her gambling (see Exhibit 10–1). These questions were developed originally for distribution as public education and self-assessment materials. The questions refer to situations that problem gamblers will recognize as relevant for themselves and other gamblers. The basic face validity of these questions also assists the clinician in

Exhibit 10–1 Twenty Questions about Gambling Behavior

 1. Did you ever lose time from work due to gambling?
 2. Has gambling ever made your home life unhappy?
 3. Did gambling affect your reputation?
 4. Have you ever felt remorse after gambling?
 5. Did you ever gamble to get money with which to pay debts or otherwise solve financial difficulties?
 6. Did gambling cause a decrease in your ambition or efficiency?
 7. After losing did you feel you must return as soon as possible and win back your losses?
 8. After a win did you have a strong urge to return and win more?
 9. Did you often gamble until your last dollar was gone?
10. Did you ever borrow to finance your gambling?
11. Have you ever sold anything to finance gambling?
12. Were you reluctant to use "gambling money" for normal expenditures?
13. Did gambling make you careless of the welfare of yourself and your family?
14. Did you ever gamble longer than you had planned?
15. Have you ever gambled to escape worry or trouble?
16. Have you ever committed, or considered committing an illegal act to finance gambling?
17. Did gambling cause you to have difficulty in sleeping?
18. Do arguments, disappointments, or frustrations create within you an urge to gamble?
19. Did you ever have an urge to celebrate any good fortune by a few hours of gambling?
20. Have you ever considered self destruction as a result of your gambling?

Source: From *Twenty Questions* by Gamblers Anonymous, 1980, Los Angeles, CA: Gamblers Anonymous. Copyright 1980 by Gamblers Anonymous. Reprinted by permission.

establishing credibility with problem gamblers, who often view the clinician as uninformed and easily misled about the true indicators of problem gambling. Although no statistically defined norms have been established for use in diagnosis, affirmative responses to any combination of four or more of these questions is a reliable indication that the client may be a pathological gambler and is no longer normally in control of his or her gambling behavior (McGurrin, 1992).

A third diagnostic technique that is useful in conjunction with the *DSM-III-R* is to interview immediate family members — especially a spouse — to determine their perception of the client and their experiences since the client has begun gambling. Gam-Anon has developed a set of 20 questions that are very useful in directing this type of diagnostic interview (Exhibit 10–2).

Because pathological gambling may exist in conjunction with other psychological disorders such as personality disorders, affective disorders, or substance abuse, it is extremely important that the diagnostician fully evaluate a person who presents as a possible pathological gambler. It is also important to check for the additional problem of pathological gambling among persons who are referred for evaluation because of substance abuse problems, increased anxiety and depression, cyclothymic mood swings, interpersonal problems, or difficulty maintaining employment and family relations.

Exhibit 10–2 Are You Living with a Compulsive Gambler?

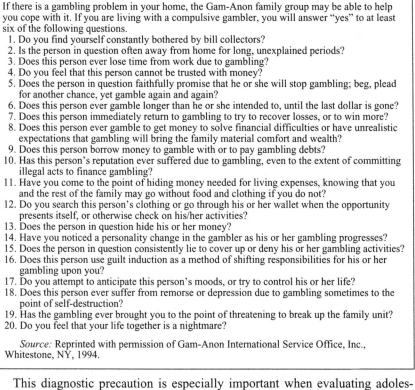

If there is a gambling problem in your home, the Gam-Anon family group may be able to help you cope with it. If you are living with a compulsive gambler, you will answer "yes" to at least six of the following questions.
1. Do you find yourself constantly bothered by bill collectors?
2. Is the person in question often away from home for long, unexplained periods?
3. Does this person ever lose time from work due to gambling?
4. Do you feel that this person cannot be trusted with money?
5. Does the person in question faithfully promise that he or she will stop gambling; beg, plead for another chance, yet gamble again and again?
6. Does this person ever gamble longer than he or she intended to, until the last dollar is gone?
7. Does this person immediately return to gambling to try to recover losses, or to win more?
8. Does this person ever gamble to get money to solve financial difficulties or have unrealistic expectations that gambling will bring the family material comfort and wealth?
9. Does this person borrow money to gamble with or to pay gambling debts?
10. Has this person's reputation ever suffered due to gambling, even to the extent of committing illegal acts to finance gambling?
11. Have you come to the point of hiding money needed for living expenses, knowing that you and the rest of the family may go without food and clothing if you do not?
12. Do you search this person's clothing or go through his or her wallet when the opportunity presents itself, or otherwise check on his/her activities?
13. Does the person in question hide his or her money?
14. Have you noticed a personality change in the gambler as his or her gambling progresses?
15. Does the person in question consistently lie to cover up or deny his or her gambling activities?
16. Does this person use guilt induction as a method of shifting responsibilities for his or her gambling upon you?
17. Do you attempt to anticipate this person's moods, or try to control his or her life?
18. Does this person ever suffer from remorse or depression due to gambling sometimes to the point of self-destruction?
19. Has the gambling ever brought you to the point of threatening to break up the family unit?
20. Do you feel that your life together is a nightmare?

Source: Reprinted with permission of Gam-Anon International Service Office, Inc., Whitestone, NY, 1994.

This diagnostic precaution is especially important when evaluating adolescents. The age group with the greatest increase in incidence and prevalence of pathological gamblers is 11 to 18 years old. Jacobs (1989) reports that in 1988 as many as 7 million youth were gambling in America without adult awareness or sanction, and about 1 million were experiencing problems in controlling their gambling activity. Between 4% and 6% of high school students could be diagnosed as pathological gamblers as compared to 1.4% of adults.

TREATMENT ISSUES

There are currently three basic modes of treating pathological gambling: (a) self-help groups and peer counseling, (b) inpatient or residential rehabilitation, and (c) outpatient psychotherapy and counseling. Most often, the treatment plan for a pathological gambler includes a combination of these three modes over time.

Self-Help Groups and Peer Counseling

The primary self-help group for pathological gamblers is Gamblers Anonymous (GA). GA was formed in 1957 by two pathological gamblers who were members of Alcoholics Anonymous (AA). Because of their success in dealing with their alcohol abuse through AA, they decided to use the AA model of group meetings, sponsors (peer counselors), fellowship (shared commitment to recovery), 12-step recovery, and commitment to total abstinence in an effort to overcome their uncontrolled impulses to gamble. In 1960, family members affected by pathological gamblers' behavior formed Gam-Anon, similar to Al-Anon. There are also groups for the children of pathological gamblers called Gam-A-Teen (Gamblers Anonymous, 1984). Information on local chapters of these self-help groups or chapters in other countries such as Australia, Canada, the Netherlands, and the United Kingdom can be acquired by telephoning the GA International Office, (213) 386-8789, or the National Council on Problem Gambling, Inc., (212) 765-3833 or (800) 522-4700.

The primary treatment effectiveness of GA seems to derive from the fact that during the early stages of recovery (the first 90 days) GA provides the pathological gambler with frequent contact and support from other recovering gamblers. During early recovery, the new member is encouraged to attend daily meetings if possible. The expectation for frequency of attendance is reduced as recovery proceeds, but periodic attendance at GA meetings is a lifetime activity of the recovery process.

According to GA's published statement, their recovery program reaches into all areas of the member's life in order to help the member to achieve an improved sense of self-confidence and self-respect. To begin recovery a new member must be committed to stop gambling because success in the program depends on the individual's motivation to stop gambling and to return to a normal way of life.

The GA Recovery Program is outlined in 12 steps (Gamblers Anonymous, 1984). GA claims that each step is open to individual interpretation and has no official limits of acceptable interpretation for directing action. This claim of unlimited openness of meaning may seem confusing, however, because all systems of theory and practice have boundaries that limit acceptable interpretation. Without boundaries there would be no system. GA's claim regarding the individual interpretation of the 12 steps is an example of the type of issue that may be problematic for professionally trained counselors and psychotherapists, who utilize relatively more specific treatment principles and practices.

The 12 steps are presented below with this author's summary interpretation. This material provides a comprehensive description of the GA recovery program. Somewhat more detailed discussion of specific GA counseling techniques such as personal financial planning, self-evaluation, and sponsorship are available in the literature on pathological gambling (Gamblers Anonymous, 1984; Nora, 1989; Zinberg, 1989).

• *Step 1: We admitted we were powerless over gambling — that our lives had become unmanageable.*

Members admit a powerlessness over gambling and accept that pathological gambling is an incurable illness that can be controlled only through abstinence from gambling.

- *Step 2: Came to believe that a power greater than ourselves could restore us to a normal way of thinking and living.*

Members are asked to believe in a Higher Power that is an external source of strength greater than one's self-will. The Higher Power can be anything a member chooses, such as God or the emotional support from the Fellowship. This step does not ask for belief in any organized religion; it simply asks for a commitment to personal spirituality.

- *Step 3: Made a decision to turn our will and our lives over to the care of this power of our own understanding.*

Members subordinate themselves to the will and care of the Higher Power through faith. Faith coupled with the decision to commit oneself to the care of a Higher Power is believed to lead the members toward recovery.

- *Step 4: Made a searching and fearless moral and financial inventory of ourselves.*

In order to attain a more meaningful life, the pathological gambler must undergo a thorough self-appraisal. Negative characteristics such as selfishness, anger, self-deception, and impatience should be examined. Equally important is the acknowledgment of one's positive characteristics, such as friendliness, optimism, industriousness, and tolerance. Members are urged to make a written inventory of their characteristics.

- *Step 5: Admitted to ourselves and to another human being the exact nature of our wrongs.*

Members acknowledge gambling and related problems to themselves and to someone else. This admission to another person is expected to provide members with a greater objectivity about their problems and a further means to reduce guilt and anxiety.

- *Step 6: Were entirely ready to have these defects of character removed.*

Members are asked to be ready to eliminate their character defects. This is a step of preparation only. It does not ask them to remove their character defects but simply to open themselves to change.

• *Step 7: Humbly asked God (of our understanding) to remove our shortcomings.*

In the same way that members admit their powerlessness to control their gambling, they admit that they are powerless to remove their character defects by themselves. Rather than expecting immediate success, they accept that recovery is an ongoing process and that working toward change is most important.

• *Step 8: Made a list of all persons we have harmed and became willing to make amends to them all.*

Most pathological gamblers acknowledge the financial damage they have caused, but they have difficulty acknowledging the emotional harm they have caused. Step 8 requires members to acknowledge all the emotional pain they have caused for others.

• *Step 9: Made direct amends to such people wherever possible, except when to do so would injure them or others.*

Members are asked to carry out the intention of the preceding step to the best of their ability. By making amends, one transforms the negative behavior of the past into the potential for future positive action.

• *Step 10: Continued to take personal inventory and when we were wrong, promptly admitted it.*

Members are asked to evaluate themselves continuously for wrongdoings that they commit. Members benefit from prompt admission of wrongdoings by creating a catharsis for the anxiety, depression, and sense of loneliness experienced prior to recognizing the wrongdoings.

• *Step 11: Sought through prayer and meditation to improve our conscious contact with God as we understand him, praying only for knowledge of His will for us and the power to carry that out.*

GA claims that their program gives members freedom to choose the means by which they contact the God of their understanding. Through continuous contact with their God, members become more receptive to the potential experience of God's will for them and the strength to live accordingly.

• *Step 12: Having made an effort to practice these principles in all our affairs, we tried to carry this message to other compulsive gamblers.*

The 12th step is regarded as the culmination of the entire recovery program. Members are asked to practice the 12 steps in their lives and in their efforts to convey to other pathological gamblers that they can stop gambling and can achieve self-respect and personal and spiritual growth through the practice of the GA program.

Inpatient Treatment or Residential Rehabilitation

The majority of pathological gamblers begin treatment in specialized inpatient or residential rehabilitation (RR) programs because they will have denied the need for treatment until major life crisis has affected their personal, marital, vocational, and financial functioning. By this point, gamblers may have already experienced several months of increasingly intense and frequent anxiety attacks, insomnia, and recurrent alternation between manic and depressed mood. They recognize the developing crises in their life and their inability to continue escaping the consequences of their gambling activity. Gamblers may also report feelings of derealization that create difficulty in concentrating and completing routine tasks (Kuley & Jacobs, 1988). Thoughts of suicide or threats of suicide are fairly common at this point.

Pathological gambling is rarely the primary diagnosis used to justify an admission of the gambler to an inpatient setting because of the difficulty in acquiring private health insurers' preapproval of payment for inpatient care of pathological gambling. More often the admitting diagnosis is one of the several mood disorders (*DSM-III-R*, sec. 296, 300, 301, or 311) or psychoactive substance use disorders (sec. 303-305), based on the gambler's acute anxiety, depression, suicidal ideation, or need for detoxification because of recent intense abuse of alcohol or drugs. Private hospitals with programs for pathological gamblers often interview the gambler and a family member separately by telephone in advance of admission to determine if the gambler can be admitted under an appropriate diagnosis. If accepted, the gambler is then evaluated and assigned an official diagnosis by a staff psychiatrist as a part of the official admission process.

Most formal inpatient and RR programs are 20 to 30 days in length and have a treatment cost ranging from approximately $10,000 to $28,000. Typically patients receive basic medical and psychological assessments preliminary to their assignment to a treatment team and the development of a treatment plan. Treatment teams usually consist of a staff psychiatrist, a primary therapist or counselor, and a social worker who coordinates and acts as a liaison to family, employers, and other persons who are outside of the hospital. Primary therapists or counselors are often master's-level psychologists, MSWs, psychiatric nurses, or addiction counselors.

During the first week, treatment focuses on stabilizing the patient, selecting medications if indicated, and orienting the patient to treatment program regulations. Patients are required to follow highly structured schedules of daily activity that usually exclude any contact with their family or others outside of the hospital. Telephone use is a scheduled privilege during most of the treatment program. This detention-like atmosphere is intended to block access to alcohol, drugs, or the opportunity to gamble.

By the middle of the first week, the patient is involved in group therapy sessions. Sessions focus on reducing the patients' denial of their inability to gamble in a normal manner. They are confronted with the fact that what they had believed were their own private techniques for beating the odds in gambling are essentially the same unsuccessful techniques employed by the other pathological gamblers in the therapy group. Groups often include a recovering gambler as a means of introducing the patient to the GA concept of peer counseling or sponsorship (Franklin & Ciarrocchi, 1987).

In the second week an educational component is introduced into treatment. Patients attend sessions in which they are counseled on personal finances and money management. Often they develop a time schedule for paying back their gambling debts. It is very important that the recovering gambler accept responsibility for paying back debts without financial assistance from family and friends. This requirement confronts patients with issues they will encounter after they have left the hospital and also discourages resumptions of codependent relationships with family members, which have been interrupted during inpatient treatment.

During the first 2 weeks of treatment, family members are seen collaterally by a member of the treatment team. The sessions are intended to (a) educate them about pathological gambling, (b) inform them about the goals of the patient's treatment plan, (c) allow the treatment team member to develop impressions of family dynamics, and (d) provide initial supportive therapy to family members who may be dealing with mixed feelings of resentment, guilt, and neglect in the face of all the attention that is being directed toward the patient.

By the third week, spouses and other key family members are often included in group sessions with the gamblers. This allows both gamblers and family members to recognize the common features of pathological gambling that have affected other gamblers and their families. As with other pathological behavior, pathological gambling is typically the "great family secret" that the family denies collectively. It is very important to teach these families to acknowledge the problem gambling and discuss it in a constructive manner. Sessions encourage emotional expression, which has often been avoided by the family. The therapist assures the family that such expression can benefit them and that no family member's expression of emotion will be allowed to become destructively out of control during the sessions.

Many programs also schedule GA meetings in the hospital several evenings a week to allow gamblers to begin attending meetings as well as to have further contact with peer counselors.

There is very little theoretical or treatment-based rationale for keeping pathological gamblers in an inpatient or residential program for almost a month (Gambino & Cummings, 1989; Nora, 1989). Considering the cost of these programs and the lack of reliable evidence demonstrating either their treatment or cost effectiveness, they should be carefully evaluated if they continue to be used in treating pathological gambling.

Outpatient Treatment

The most common circumstance that directs pathological gamblers to outpatient psychotherapy is referral to a psychotherapist as part of the gambler's aftercare plan following hospital discharge. Some hospitals refer to their own outpatient program; others refer to private practice professionals. It is increasingly common for these outpatient therapists to be peer counselors or other professionals who have received special training in treating pathological gamblers. The client will usually also have been enrolled in a GA group. The client is typically motivated to attend at least several outpatient sessions because therapy is accepted as a continuation of the inpatient program. The client's family has usually been advised by the inpatient treatment team leader to support follow-up psychotherapy after the pathological gambler has been discharged from the inpatient program.

The client's GA sponsor may also encourage the client to participate in outpatient therapy, depending on the attitude of the sponsor and the particular GA group toward the value of treatment provided by professionally trained counselors and other mental health practitioners. GA's 12-step recovery program often has no practical significance for the independent psychotherapist's treatment techniques. There are times, however, when GA's major emphasis on spiritual subordination to a Higher Power and their rather evangelical themes (public confession before peers, recovery of self-worth through self-criticism and abstinence, dealing with life only one day at a time, and achieving a vaguely defined redemption through surrender to a higher power) may conflict with outpatient treatment goals focused on developing the gambler's sense of internal control and self-reliance.

Pathological gamblers may also enter outpatient psychotherapy without having "hit bottom" and gone through hospital care. These clients are often motivated to seek professional care because of threat of divorce, loss of employment, or other problematic conditions if they do not become involved in therapy. Usually such individuals are not strongly self-motivated to seek help. They may continue to deny that their gambling is out of control. Typically, the client is extremely cordial, expressing a somewhat patronizing and indulgent attitude toward family members who have insisted that the client seek treatment for his or her uncontrolled gambling. The opportunity to exercise a basic control over the therapy situation by skillfully hustling all parties involved becomes a welcome challenge to the client. It is common during the early sessions for the client to volunteer to comply with a self-imposed but limited period of abstinence from gambling to demonstrate a capacity for control and to minimize the seriousness of the problem. The client entering outpatient therapy before hitting bottom is usually far more difficult to work with, at least initially, because of his or her intense denial of the pathological nature of the gambling behavior.

Although there is no agreement yet among professional counselors and psychotherapists regarding the amount of time or number of sessions required for effective treatment of pathological gambling, there is consensus that treatment is a process that can be usually divided into stages (Abt, McGurrin, & Smith, 1985; Miller, 1986; Zinberg, 1989). Each stage is defined in terms of major tasks that must be accomplished before the client is prepared to deal with the next stage. A basic model for this approach to outpatient psychotherapy is presented below. Specific tasks and techniques are suggested for each stage, but individual practitioners are advised that they should view the model as a general structure that can be customized to fit specific treatment situations or client's needs.

Generic Outpatient Model

Stage 1 focuses on inducing gamblers to acknowledge the uncontrolled nature of their gambling behavior and to commit themselves to abstinence. It is crucial at this phase for the therapist to confront the gambler's denial of his or her inability to control gambling. At the same time, it is important that the therapist not become too confrontational because of the risk of the client's premature withdrawal from therapy. The therapist must be authentic, involved, and supportive, but also firm on the issue of abstinence. Anxiety must be managed carefully so that clients remain motivated to change but are not overwhelmed by anxiety related to the thought of discontinuing gambling. The therapist should establish with the client a reasonable balance of expectations for gradual improvement and the likelihood of occasional regressions because pathological gamblers tend to underestimate substantially the amount of time and effort required to resolve their problems. It is also important in this stage to identify concrete goals for therapy, a set of activities that will serve as a replacement for gambling, and an agreement that whenever the client slips back into gambling he or she will notify the therapist.

Stage 2 focuses on enabling the client to identify and confront the problems that have been caused by gambling. Continued abstinence is important, and the therapist should support the client's ability to cope with the increasing distress resulting from abstinence. The focus of sessions will often be on managing impulses and thoughts about gambling. The therapist should avoid discussion with the client about gambling because the client loves to talk about gambling strategy and will attempt to use these discussions to avoid relevant problem solving. Also, the therapist should not waste time trying to convince clients that in the long run the odds cannot be beaten. They know; they just do not care. Engagement is a difficult but crucial issue in this phase. Most pathological gamblers have been so dishonest and manipulative with other people that an honest and open emotional relationship with the therapist may be difficult to develop.

Stage 3 focuses on longer-term problems. Developing greater internal control over behavior, accepting greater intimacy in relationships, and more directly recognizing feelings of anger, sadness, and guilt related to gambling become important issues. Sufficient structure and direction by the therapist must be maintained to prevent regression. The therapist should also anticipate episodes of anxiety, depression, and criticism of the value of therapy around periods of significant sports events (e.g., World Series, championship boxing matches, Super Bowl Sunday, or Triple Crown racing).

In stage 4, therapy may become less structured and similar in process to open-ended, client-centered therapies. Clients should be able to tolerate increasing amounts of anxiety and acknowledge their personal limitations in controlling gambling. This stage is also often a good point to increase the involvement of family members, who presumably have had more limited involvement during the earlier stages.

It is certainly conceivable that additional distinct stages may be developed to define the structure of the therapeutic process. As knowledge about the causes and treatment of pathological gambling continues, redefinition of the structure is highly likely.

Alternative Outpatient Models

A variety of other models of outpatient psychotherapy have been utilized over the past 20 years in treating pathological gambling. Bolen and Boyd (1968) describe successful results with couple's group therapy lasting about 1 year. They claim that there was typically a reduction of chronic anxiety, depression, and destructive criticism within couples. The couples also developed more effective defense techniques, became more spontaneous and authentic in interpersonal relations, and assumed more responsible and appropriate marital roles. Goorney (1968), Barker (1968), and Seagar (1970) report some success with aversion therapy. Tepperman (1985) reports substantive success using short-term (12-week) conjoint group therapy using the Gamblers Anonymous 12-step program materials as topics of group discussion. Each session began with one or more members reading aloud one of the steps and then each group member discussing the meaning the step had for his or her life. Zinberg (1989) provides a more detailed integration of GA's 12 steps into outpatient therapy.

CONCLUSION

Counseling and psychotherapy for pathological gamblers has only about a 30-year history. Much of what is presently regarded as good practice is borrowed from the AA counseling model or other existing counseling and psychotherapy models. The long-range effectiveness of these approaches as applied to pathological gambling has not yet been well evaluated. Estimates of relapse to gambling among persons in abstinence for at least 18 months range from 25 to 80 percent (Gambino & Cummings, 1989). Obviously these evaluators of treatment success are using very different methods and criteria for evaluating remission. Also, it must be stressed that treatment effectiveness criteria for chronic conditions should be conceptualized differently from criteria for acute disorders. There is a great need for more factually based information on pathological gambling, but in the meantime responsible persons must do the best that is possible to aid others who are unable to control their gambling and the destructive consequence it has for them and their families.

REFERENCES

Abt, V., McGurrin, M. C., & Smith, J. F. (1985). Toward a synoptic model of gambling behavior. *Journal of Gambling Behavior, 1*, 79–88.

Abt, V., Smith, J. F., & Christiansen, E.M. (1985). *The business of risk: Commercial gambling in mainstream America*. Lawrence: University of Kansas Press.

American Psychiatric Association (APA). (1980). *Diagnostic and statistical manual of mental disorders* (3rd ed.). Washington, DC: Author.

American Psychiatric Association (APA). (1987). *Diagnostic and statistical manual of mental disorders* (3rd ed. rev.). Washington, DC: Author.

Barker, J. C. (1968). Aversion therapy for compulsive gambling. *Journal of Nervous and Mental Disease, 146,* 285–302.

Bergler, E. (1957). *The psychology of gambling.* New York: Hill & Wang.

Blakey, G. R. (1979). State conducted lotteries: History, problems and promises. *Journal of Social Issues, 35,* 62–86.

Bolen, D. W., & Boyd, W. H. (1968). Gambling and the gamblers. *Archives of General Psychiatry, 18,* 617–630.

Carlton, P. L., & Goldstein, L. (1987). Physiological determinants of pathological gambling. In T. Glaski (Ed.), *A handbook of pathological gambling* (pp. 657–663). Springfield, IL: Charles C. Thomas.

Carlton, P. L., & Manowitz, P. (1988). Physiological factors as determinants of pathological gambling. *Journal of Gambling Behavior, 3,* 274–285.

Ciarrocchi, J. (1987). Severity of impairment in dually addicted gamblers. *Journal of Gambling Behavior, 3,* 16–26.

Commission on the Review of the National Policy Toward Gambling. (1978). *Gambling in America.* Washington, DC: U.S. Government Printing Office.

Corney, W. J., & Cummings, W. T. (1985). Gambling behavior and information processing biases. *Journal of Gambling Behavior, 1,* 64-75.

Dunne, J. A. (1985). Increasing public awareness of pathological gambling behavior: A history of the National Council on Compulsive Gambling. *Journal of Gambling Behavior, 1,* 8-15.

Fleming, A. M. (1978). *Something for nothing: A history of gambling.* New York: Delacorte.

Franklin, J., & Ciarrocchi, J. (1987). The team approach: Developing an experimental knowledge base for the treatment of the pathological gambler. *Journal of Gambling Behavior, 3,* 60-67.

Gambino, B., & Cummings, T. N. (1989). Treatment of compulsive gambling: Where are we now? In H. J. Shaffer, S. A. Stein, B. Gambino, & T. N. Cummings (Eds.), *Compulsive gambling: Theory, research, and practice* (pp. 315–335). Lexington, MA: D. C. Heath.

Gamblers Anonymous. (1980). *Twenty questions.* Los Angeles, CA: Author.

Gamblers Anonymous. (1984). *Sharing recovery through Gamblers Anonymous.* Los Angeles: Author.

Goldstein, L., Manowitz, P., Nora, R., Swartzburg, M., & Carlton, P. I. (1985). Differential EEG activation and pathological gambling. *Biological Psychiatry, 20,* 1232–1234.

Goorney, A. B. (1968). Treatment of a compulsive horse race gambler by aversion therapy. *British Journal of Psychiatry, 114,* 329–333.

Jacobs, D. F. (1986). A general theory of addictions: A new theoretical model. *Journal of Gambling Behavior, 2,* 15–31.

Jacobs, D. F. (1988). Evidence for a common dissociative-like reaction among addicts. *Journal of Gambling Behavior, 4,* 27–37.

Jacobs, D.F. (1989). Teenage gambling. In H. J. Shaffer, S. A. Stein, B. Gambino, & T. N. Cummings (Eds.), *Compulsive gambling* (pp. 249–292). Lexington, MA: D.C. Heath.

Kuley, N. B., & Jacobs, D. (1988). The relationship between dissociative-like experiences and sensation seeking among social and problem gamblers. *Journal of Gambling Behavior, 3,* 190–198.

Kusyszyn, I. (1978). Compulsive gambling: The problem of definition. *International Journal of Addictions, 13,* 1095–1101.

Kusyszyn, I., & Rubenstein, L. (1985). Locus of control and race track betting behaviors: A preliminary investigation. *Journal of Gambling Behavior, 1,* 106–110.

Lesieur, H. R., & Blume, S. (1988). The South Oaks Gambling Screen (SOGS). A new instrument for the identification of pathological gamblers. *American Journal of Psychiatry, 144,* 1184–1188.

Lesieur, H. R., Blume, S., & Zoppa, R. M. (1986). Alcoholism, drug abuse, and gambling. *Alcoholism, 10,* 33–38.

Lesieur, H. R., & Klein, R. (1985, June). *Prisoners, gambling and crime.* Paper presented at the Annual Meeting of the Academy of Criminal Justice Sciences, Las Vegas.

Lesieur, H. R., & Klein, R. (1987). Pathological gambling among high school students. *Addictive Behaviors, 12,* 129–135.

McCormick, R. A., Russo, A. M., Ramirez, L. F., & Taber, J. I. (1984). Affective disorders among pathological gamblers seeking treatment. *American Journal of British Psychiatry, 141,* 215–218.

McGurrin, M. C. (1986, March). *Personality characteristics of pathological gamblers.* Paper presented at the First National Conference on Gambling Behavior, New York.

McGurrin, M. C. (1992). *Pathological gambling: Conceptual, diagnostic, and treatment issues.* Sarasota, FL: Professional Resources Press.

McGurrin, M. C., Abt, V., & Smith, J.F. (1984). Play or pathology: A new look at the gambler and his world. In B. Smoth (Ed.), *The masks of play* (pp. 24–36). West Point: Leisure Press.

Miller, W. (1986). Individual outpatient treatment of pathological gambling. *Journal of Gambling Behavior, 2,* 95–107.

Nora, R. M. (1989). Inpatient treatment programs for pathological gambling. In H.J. Shaffer, S. A. Stein, B. Gambino, & T. N. Cummings (Eds.), *Compulsive gambling: Theory, research, and practice* (pp. 127–134). Lexington, MA: D. C. Heath.

Ramirez, L. F., McCormick, R. A., Russo, A. M., & Taber, J. I. (1984). Patterns of substance abuse in pathological gamblers undergoing treatment. *Addictive Behaviors, 8,* 425–428.

Rosenthal, R. J. (1986). The pathological gambler's system for self-deception. *Journal of Gambling Behavior, 2,* 108–120.

Rotter, J. B. (1966). Generalized expectancies for internal versus external control of reinforcement. *Psychological Monographs, 80,* (1, Serial No. 609).

Seagar, C. (1970). Treatment of compulsive gamblers by electric aversion. *British Journal of Psychiatry, 117,* 545–553.

Taber, J. I. (1988). Compulsive gambling: An examination of relevant models. *Journal of Gambling Behavior, 3,* 219–223.

Taber, J.I ., Russo, A. M., Adkins, B. J., & McCormick, R. A. (1986). Ego strength and achievement motivation in pathological gamblers. *Journal of Gambling Behavior, 2,* 69–80.

Tepperman, J. H. (1985). The effectiveness of short-term group therapy upon the pathological gambler and wife. *Journal of Gambling Behavior, 1,* 119–130.

Volberg, R. A., & Steadman, H. J. (1989). Policy implications of prevalence estimates of pathological gambling. In H.J. Shaffer, S. A. Stein, B. Gambino, & T. N. Cummings (Eds.). *Compulsive Gambling* (pp. 163–174). Lexington, MA: DC Heath.

Wender, P. H., Reimherr, F. W., & Wood, D. R. (1981). Attention deficit disorder (minimal brain dysfunction) in adults. *Archives of General Psychiatry, 38,* 449–456.

Wood, D. R., Wender, P. H., & Reimherr, F. W. (1983). The prevalence of attention deficit disorder, residual type, or minimal brain dysfunction in a population of male alcoholic patients. *American Journal of Psychiatry, 140,* 95–98.

Zinberg, N. E. (1989). The applicability of the twelve-step model to compulsive intoxicant use and other compulsive behaviors. In H. J. Shaffer, S. A. Stein, B. Gambino, & T. N. Cummings (Eds.), *Compulsive gambling: Theory, research, and practice* (pp. 315–335). Lexington, MA: D. C. Heath.

Maintaining Change in Addictive Behaviors

F. James Hoffmann and Charles F. Gressard

One of the few areas of consensus in the addiction treatment field involves the recognition that the maintenance of change in an addictive behavior is often a difficult process and frequently results in high rates of relapse (Annis, 1986). In fact, Prochaska (1984), in discussing his transtheoretical stages of change model, suggests that many addicted individuals require an average of three attempts before attaining a relatively stable addiction-free lifestyle. This chapter will explore three different relapse prevention models that have demonstrated success in assisting clients with the difficult process of maintaining change in such addictive behaviors as alcohol abuse, drug abuse, tobacco abuse, overeating, gambling, and similar compulsive behaviors.

MODELS OF MAINTAINING BEHAVIOR CHANGE

Helping clients maintain behavior change following initial treatment of addictive behavior can be conceptualized and implemented from a number of theoretical perspectives. This section will present three specific conceptual models from which to view the process of maintaining change in the addictive behavior categories in question. Although these three models were developed in response to alcohol and drugs, they have since been applied to the other addictive behaviors already mentioned with success.

Cognitive–Social Learning Model

Based on the principles of social learning theory and cognitive psychology, this biopsychosocial model is primarily attributed to the work of Marlatt and his colleagues (Cummings, Gordon, & Marlatt, 1980; Marlatt, 1978, 1979, 1982;

Marlatt & Gordon, 1980, 1985) and is increasingly supported by a number of other addiction researchers (Annis, 1990; Miller, 1991; Prochaska & DiClemente, 1988). Commonly thought of as a model of relapse prevention, Marlatt's (1985) conceptualization stands in contrast to the disease model. Typically, the disease model views *any* use of drugs or return to the addictive behavior following an abstinence-oriented treatment program as indicative of relapse or "failure." As Marlatt (1985) pointed out, this outlook tends to ignore the influence of situational and psychological factors as potential determinants in the relapse process. From a cognitive–social learning perspective, however, a single relapse event is viewed as a slip or "lapse" in the individual's behavior change-maintenance process. A primary assumption of Marlatt's relapse prevention model (RP) is that "the cognitive and affective *reactions* to the first slip/lapse after a period of abstinence exert a significant influence that may determine whether or not the lapse is followed by a full return to the former behavior or habit (relapse)" (Marlatt, 1985).

The material to follow is an overview of Marlatt's RP model of the relapse process, together with its focus on the precipitating determinants, covert antecedents, lifestyle balance issues, and intervention procedures gleaned from research and clinical practice. Marlatt (1985) cautioned, however, that an important constraint in the model is that it applies only to those individuals who have made a *voluntary* choice or decision to change; the implications of the theory for enforced or involuntary abstinence have not as yet been determined.

The RP model focuses on the therapist's adoption of a collaborative, colleague role in helping clients identify and anticipate situations when they might be at increased risk for problematic levels of exhibiting the addictive behavior. These high-risk situations can be intrapersonal or interpersonal in nature. Cummings, Gordon, & Marlatt (1980) identified three categories of high-risk situations associated with the highest relapse rates: (a) negative emotional states, (b) interpersonal conflict, and (c) social pressures. An important aspect of the RP model involves helping clients assess their own high-risk situations using daily self-monitoring of their addictive behavior.

Once the client's high-risk situations have been identified, the counselor works collaboratively with him or her to help develop coping skills for managing the high-risk situations without the need to engage in the addictive behavior (i.e., alcohol, drugs, tobacco, overeating, gambling). Such skills are carefully chosen in collaboration with the client and designed to fit the client's individual dynamics. These skills might include behavioral strategies such as engaging in alternative behaviors or practicing assertive behaviors in social situations (e.g., drink refusal). Cognitive strategies are also employed, including the use of cognitive restructuring, imagery, and self-talk to overcome urges. Increasing the individual's coping skills repertoire is specifically designed to enhance a sense of self-efficacy for responding effectively to high-risk situations in a variety of settings.

The RP model also works to modify the individual's positive outcome expectancies for engaging in the addictive behavior. For example, such positive expectancies for the effects of consuming alcohol have been linked to alcohol use (Marlatt & Rohsenow, 1980). In addition, Marlatt draws a distinction between the process of lapsing and the outcome of relapse. In this way, a lapse/slip is reframed as a learning experience. The lapse is used as an opportunity to carefully assess the overt and covert antecedents leading to the lapse and to formulate a strategy for coping more effectively in the future.

The final stage in this approach to behavior change maintenance emphasizes the importance of a balanced lifestyle as a means of facilitating lifestyle change. Clients are taught to conduct a careful "shoulds" (i.e., responsibilities, things they have to do) and "wants" (i.e., things they do for themselves to obtain pleasure) assessment, because a preponderance of "shoulds" places the client at high risk for the return to addictive behavior styles. Counselors then help the client develop "positive addictions" (Glasser, 1976) such as aerobic exercise, relaxation exercises, and other such pleasurable leisure activities of particular interest to the client. Such lifestyle intervention strategies are designed to strengthen the client's overall coping capacity and to reduce the frequency and intensity of urges and cravings that are often the product of an unbalanced lifestyle (Marlatt, 1985).

Developmental Model of Maintaining Behavior Change

The predominant developmental model of maintaining behavior change in addictive behavior can be attributed to Terrance Gorski and his colleagues (Gorski, 1986, 1990; Gorski & Miller, 1982, 1986). This model, known as the CENAPS Model of Relapse Prevention, integrates the fundamental principles of AA and the Minnesota Model of Treatment (Downing, 1989) and is employed most frequently with individuals recovering from chemical dependency. Little published work has appeared describing its use with such addictive behaviors as smoking, overeating, or gambling. However, the conceptual framework of the CENAPS Model would, with some modification, appear to hold promise as a relapse prevention strategy for other addictive behaviors.

Within the CENAPS Model framework, chemical dependence is viewed as a biopsychosocial disease, involving the complex interaction of physical, psychological, and social components. Conceptually, chemical dependence is viewed as a chronic disease having a tendency toward relapse. Gorski (1990) stated that because chemical dependencies create dysfunction at each component level, maintenance of behavior change should focus on the diagnosis and treatment of dysfunction at each level. Additionally, total abstinence as well as personality and lifestyle changes are viewed as essential elements for full recovery. As is the case with Marlatt's cognitive–social learning model, Gorski views client motivation and the ability to participate in RP therapy as an important precursor.

Gorski (1989) posited a developmental model of recovery (DMR) involving six stages. During the *transition* stage, the individual experiences progressively severe addictive symptoms, recognizes the need for, and seeks treatment. During the *stabilization* stage, clients resolve immediate crises threatening recovery. During the *early recovery* stage clients learn to interrupt their chemically dependent thinking and manage their emotions without engaging in the addictive behavior. During the *middle recovery* stage clients are helped to develop healthy balanced lifestyles. At the point the client enters *late recovery* they complete intensive psychotherapy dealing with core psychological issues threatening sobriety. The *maintenance* stage is a life-long process of honing coping skills to deal effectively with adult life transitions, and guard against relapse.

Gorski (1990) articulated nine principles specifically designed to guide the relapse prevention (RP) treatment process, each of which has its own RP procedure. The first RP procedure includes helping clients develop a daily structure, including stress management, diet management, exercise, contact with a therapist, and self-help groups. A second RP procedure involves teaching the client to conduct ongoing self-assessments as a means of understanding their relapse history and its causes. The third RP procedure involves structured relapse education concerning the biopsychological model of addictive disease. The fourth RP procedure teaches clients the process of identifying their warning signs of relapse. The fifth procedure involves helping clients learn how to manage or cope with their own unique warning signs as they occur. Here management training focuses on the situational-behavioral, cognitive-affective, and underlying psychological issues. The sixth RP procedure involves development of a schedule of recovery activities to help clients recognize and manage warning signs. The seventh RP procedure teaches relapse-prone clients to monitor compliance of their recovery program and check for the emergence of relapse warning signs. The eighth RP procedure requires the therapist to involve significant others (e.g., family members, 12-step sponsors, Employee Assistance Program [EAP] counselors) in the structured relapse prevention planning process. The ninth RP procedure involves a continuing collaboration between counselor and client during which they update the client's relapse prevention plan monthly during the initial 3 months, quarterly for the remainder of the first year, and semiannually for the next 2 years. Because relapse warning signs typically change as the client progresses from one recovery stage to another, the emergence of new warning signs requires the development of new and frequently more sophisticated coping strategies in order to ensure maintenance of an addiction-free lifestyle.

Maintaining Change in Addictive Behaviors 147

Alcoholics Anonymous Model

Alcoholics Anonymous (AA) began in 1935 when two alcoholics found that they could maintain sobriety by sharing their experiences (their "stories") as alcoholics and by following a set of principles that eventually became the familiar 12 steps of AA. Since that time, AA has provided alcoholics with a program for attaining sobriety and for prevention of relapse. Gorski's model borrows much from the principles of AA, but it is important that counselors be aware that the methods of AA constitute a comprehensive relapse prevention program by themselves. An understanding of these methods can help counselors become more effective in guiding addicted clients through the recovery process.

Many of AA's methods of change are contained in the 12 steps. Probably the most powerful and least understood methods of change are contained in the first three steps. The first three steps read:

1. We admitted that we were powerless over alcohol—that our lives had become unmanageable.
2. Came to believe that a Power greater than ourselves could restore us to sanity.
3. Made a decision to turn our will and our lives over to the care of God as we understood Him. (Alcoholics Anonymous, 1976)

Essential to the understanding of these steps is the paradox of gaining control over one's behavior by giving up control to a higher power. This paradox is the cornerstone of the AA method and is usually the focus of most inpatient and outpatient treatment programs. It is important to note that most AA members and most addiction counselors emphasize that even though God is mentioned in these steps, it is important for addicted individuals to use whatever concept of higher power makes sense to them.

The first three steps appear to be the most essential of all the AA methods, but there are others that contribute to the process of recovering from addiction. Steps 4 through 7 encourage addicted individuals to undertake a comprehensive process of self-examination by making a "searching and fearless moral inventory" and then discussing the inventory with another person. Steps 8 and 9 help addicted individuals to alleviate guilt and tie up loose ends by making amends to those they may have harmed in some way. The eleventh step encourages AA members to stay in touch with their higher power through prayer and meditation, and the twelfth step helps members continue their sobriety by helping others. By practicing the last step, AA members also help perpetuate the helping process by encouraging a personal contact with potential new members.

Although the 12 steps are the cornerstone of the AA process, other important factors contribute as well. Probably the most important of these is group support. Although not specifically stated in the steps, implicit in the actions of AA is the belief that addiction is best confronted by a group. Group meetings are the primary AA medium, and early progress for those who are learning to cope with addiction is often measured by the number of meetings they attend. Progress is also often measured by the extent of involvement with the group and by the involvement with a mentor or "sponsor." This emphasis on social support is consistent with the idea presented in the first three steps that individuals cannot cope with addiction on their own but need the help of something greater than themselves. Relying on the support group is probably as important as the reliance on the higher power.

Another component of the AA model for maintaining sobriety is the daily reminder or meditation. AA uses various slogans, meditations, and prayers to serve as reminders of what was learned in the first three steps: namely, the paradox and the need for humility in the face of the powerful disease of alcoholism. Without these reminders, veteran AA members have found that it is easy to forget this learning and therefore be susceptible to returning to the addictive behavior. From the AA view, recovery from addiction requires a constant awareness of the disease and the recovery principles.

There are therefore five main components of the AA model: learning the paradox of giving up control to gain control, self-examination and discussion of problems, making amends, extensive group support and working with a sponsor, and the daily reminders in the form of slogans, prayers, and meditations. The combination of these factors comprise a comprehensive system for coping with addiction and promoting recovery. Although each by itself can be an effective technique, the factors are probably most effective when combined in a synergistic system in which each component reinforces the others. It is also important to note that the components are presented in a noncoercive atmosphere where an individual can make the choice to participate or not. This method of involvement by attraction undoubtedly increases the effectiveness of the method.

MAINTENANCE STRATEGIES: THE MODELS IN ACTION

Cognitive–Social Learning Maintenance Strategies

The intervention procedures described by Marlatt and Gordon (1985) and elaborated upon by MacKay and Marlatt (1991) are intended to provide a working template that counselors can employ with clients in developing a change maintenance program. In carrying out these interventions it is important to tailor their use to the individual client's cognitive and affective strengths and weaknesses because some areas of client functioning are likely to be more open to change than others.

The following case vignette is used to illustrate how a counselor might apply Marlatt's relapse prevention strategies with individuals who are concerned about their ability to maintain a reasonably addiction-free style of life.

Case Study—John

John is a recently divorced Caucasian male in his early 30s with a 15-year history of alcohol and nicotine abuse. His chronic abuse of alcohol led not only to his divorce but also to loss of employment and three DUIs. Following his most recent DUI conviction, John's attorney urged him to seek treatment for his problem drinking. He successfully completed a comprehensive inpatient alcohol treatment program and had been successful in maintaining sobriety for some 8 months. With the support and assistance of his state's vocational rehabilitation agency he had enrolled in a career training program to prepare him for a career in architectural drafting. During the Christmas holiday, while he was spending time with his 9-year old son, his son angrily told him he thought John would always be a bum, just as his mother had said. John was unable to cope effectively with this, subsequently had an angry exchange with his ex-wife, and immediately experienced a slip and got drunk. It was at this point that John sought a referral for help with his slip.

The first step in helping a client develop a personally effective relapse prevention program involves working to develop a collaborative helping relationship between counselor and client. John's counselor accomplished this through the use of a number of motivational interviewing procedures described by Miller and Rollnick (1991). Specifically, the counselor opened the first session with John by asking a series of open-ended questions and followed up on John's responses with "reflective-listening responses," as shown in the following excerpt from the first session:

> Counselor: I understand you have some concerns about your recent return to drinking. Tell me about them.
> John: Well, I am really scared. I thought I had this drinking thing licked, but then this business with my son happened, and boom, I lost it and got drunk. I feel like a total failure!
> C: You were somewhat surprised by your own reaction to that incident, and it seems to you like you're back to square one.
> J: You bet! That whole business made me realize I still have a way to go before I can be free of this drinking problem.

The counselor's use of such interviewing strategies allowed John to feel that his concerns were being accurately heard and understood. This served as a collaborative springboard from which the counselor was able to suggest that John self-monitor and keep a daily log of situations, moods, and interactions with people that led either to drinking or to an increased urge to drink. Although John and his counselor had collaboratively agreed that the primary focus of a relapse prevention program would be on helping John develop the ability to cope effectively with those high-risk situations that would be likely to spur a return to alcohol use, his smoking behavior was included in the monitoring process because both John and the counselor viewed his smoking as an "early warning signal."

During a subsequent session, John and the counselor reviewed the daily log in order to identify his high-risk situations and any attendant patterns. This process helped John and his counselor learn that his high-risk situations primarily involved interpersonal conflict (e.g., arguments with his ex-wife regarding such issues as visitation, disagreements with his roommate) and negative emotional states (e.g., frustration and anxiety whenever his work was criticized by his instructor or he was assigned a project he perceived as "too difficult"). With this information available, the counselor encouraged John to describe and assess the ways in which he had been coping with these high-risk situations in the past. This aspect of the counseling process proved particularly helpful to John in that it functioned to focus his awareness on the specific limitations of his current coping strategies. In essence, John's primary style of coping with both types of high-risk situations outlined above was to immediately defend himself while simultaneously experiencing high levels of physical tension, anxiety, and/or anger.

Employing a $2 \times 2 \times 2$ decision matrix procedure suggested by Marlatt (Marlatt & Gordon, 1985, p. 58), the counselor also helped John explore and learn more about his own "positive outcome expectancies" for using alcohol as a coping device. This intervention further helped John identify both the positive and negative consequences of his drinking behavior. For example, working through the decision matrix collaboratively with his counselor allowed John access to the awareness that his drinking slips frequently followed a critique of his class work and served to temporarily blunt his feelings of anxiety and sense of failure. He was also able to verbalize an important negative consequence as well, namely, feelings of guilt for having been unable to successfully control the urge for immediate gratification.

Employing a cognitive reframing procedure, the counselor congratulated John on his skill in successfully identifying the immediate determinants and covert antecedents surrounding his high-risk situations. Doing so allowed John to begin viewing his slip as a positive opportunity to learn effective strategies for contending with similar situations in the future. Continuing the collaborative therapeutic focus, John's counselor "tentatively" suggested that a combination of structured coping skills training such as that espoused by Davis, Eshelman, and McKay (1988) and scanning relaxation training (Charlesworth & Nathan, 1984) might prove effective for John. John expressed interest in this approach, and the counselor further suggested that a good first step might involve John's reading some descriptive material about the procedures as a means of arriving at his own decision. This style of intervention reinforced the notion that the counselor perceived John as fully capable of determining if certain change processes were a good "fit."

Subsequently, eight skill training and monitoring sessions were conducted with John during which the counselor employed modeling, videotaped feedback, and behavioral rehearsal to help John acquire appropriate coping and relaxation skills that could be employed prior to, during, and following the type of high-risk situations he frequently encountered. John was encouraged to actively look for ways to use these new skills in his interactions with only his roommate and instructor and to share the results during subsequent sessions. This "restraining" message was given purposefully as a means of suggesting that John not impulsively attempt to achieve success in too many high-risk settings too quickly. John's reported coping successes were so pronounced that the counselor cautioned him against sliding into a "false sense of security." However, after 3 months of reasonably enduring successful coping, John informed the counselor that his sense of self-confidence was "his constant companion" even when he failed to respond to a high-risk situation as well as he might have wanted.

In addition, the counselor introduced the concept and value of John's engaging in a number of "lifestyle balancing" techniques as an additional means of helping "insulate" himself from the daily stressors linked to his personal high-risk situations. Collaborative exploration of John's leisure interests suggested a number of activities of genuine interest to John, such as biking, hiking, and listening to music. Rather than prescribe an exercise/leisure activity program for John, the counselor described the important role such activities play in helping a client reestablish a healthy "shoulds/wants" balance. The counselor suggested John might find it helpful to construct and implement his own stress-reducing exercise/leisure activity regime. During their next session, John reported having returned to regular 5-mile bike rides four afternoons a week as well as joining a weekly exercise class at the local YMCA. He also remarked having "forgotten" his cigarettes each morning since his last counseling session, indicating that he considered this a "signal" to himself that it was time to quit smoking.

Mackay and Marlatt (1991), drawing on the work of Prochaska's (1984) stages of change model point out that some clients will, at times, fail to use effective coping strategies coupled with adequate exercise or leisure activities and experience a slip. At such times, the sooner a counselor can intervene, the greater the probability of preventing a full-blown relapse. Mackay and Marlatt (1991) suggest that such a slip or lapse is not in itself reason for a client to feel like a failure. However, failure to discuss the slip and learn from it is clearly problematic.

Gorski's Developmental Change Maintenance Strategies

Application of the CENAPS Model is predicated on the use of the nine relapse prevention procedures outlined by Gorski (1990). Gorski's relapse prevention model becomes the primary focus for clients who have been unable to maintain abstinence in spite of having successfully completed primary treatment. Gorski indicated that not all clients are good candidates for relapse prevention therapy (Gorski, 1990). Consequently, counselors who practice this developmental model typically screen potential clients using the following four criteria: (a) whether the client has cognitively integrated basic biopsychosocial information about his or her addictive behavior, (b) effectiveness of his or her past recovery efforts, (c) a history of relapse warning signs during past periods of abstinence, and (d) expression of the motivation and ability to participate (Gorski, 1990). Clients meeting these criteria are considered the most appropriate candidates for developmental relapse prevention therapy.

The following case vignette illustrates the application of the CENAPS Model of relapse prevention with an individual having a history of marijuana and cocaine dependence.

Case Study—Mary

Mary is a single 32-year-old young woman with a 12-year history of first marijuana and then cocaine abuse that eventually led to dependence. Since dropping out of high school at age 16, she has worked in a number of low-paying food service jobs ranging from cook to waitress. Following a drug-related conviction at age 30, Mary successfully completed an intensive outpatient treatment program, and until more recently had maintained regular attendance at NA. Although at the time of her referral she was again living at home with her mother, she had lived on her own a number of times. Just prior to returning to live with her mother, she and her fiancé terminated their relationship after living together for 3 years. It was, in fact, the termination of this relationship that precipitated Mary's most recent slip and renewed cocaine use. Because of the most recent slip, the intense feelings of rejection growing from the termination of her relationship with her fiancé, and considerable interpersonal conflict with her mother, Mary's NA sponsor had urged her to seek therapy.

Mary was seen in a community-based outpatient addictions treatment program that employed the CENAPS Model of relapse prevention. Employing the screening criteria recommended by Gorski (1990), her therapist assessed Mary to be an appropriate relapse prevention candidate. During the second treatment session the counselor and Mary worked together to develop an initial treatment plan that would help Mary stabilize physically, psychologically, and socially. Mary agreed to participate in random drug screens and her counselor encouraged her to return to her regular NA attendance. As the treatment progressed, they also explored what she considered to be her most significant sources of stress, specifically her ongoing arguments with her mother and her continuing rumination about the break-up of her relationship. Mary's counselor shared with her the direct relationship that often occurs between such stressors and the increased likelihood of continued drug use, and suggested using a part of each of their early sessions to monitor her diet, implement a regular exercise program, and practice such stress management procedures as relaxation training and the use of 12-step meditations. In addition, the counselor used a portion of these early sessions to challenge some of her irrational thinking and work to develop a more realistic self-appraisal. For example, the counselor actively challenged Mary's irrational thought that the break-up of her relationship was proof that she was incapable of maintaining a reasonably healthy, intimate relationship with a man, asking her instead to reflect on and describe those times during the relationship when their interactions reflected normal healthy intimacy. This process proved helpful to Mary in regaining a more realistic view of her skills as a mate.

During subsequent sessions, Mary's counselor worked with her to reconstruct her historical past, particularly those aspects that appeared to have contributed to her drug use and abuse. For example, employing the Gestalt "empty chair" technique with Mary allowed her to begin resolving the painful feelings she had experienced each time her mother had been critical of her appearance, choice of friends, and school work. The counselor also guided Mary through a detailed assessment of initial recovery and relapse history. This process proved particularly helpful in helping Mary gain a more realistic awareness of the progress she had made following each relapse and in her initial treatment program. The counselor built on Mary's increased awareness by providing a number of educational interventions, including information concerning common complicating factors encountered by recovering people and warning-sign identification (i.e., impulsive behavior, irritation with friends, and dissatisfaction with one's life).

Consistent with Gorski's observation that the risk of relapse will decrease as a client's ability to recognize his or her personal relapse warning signs increases, the counselor helped Mary make use of the 37 common warning signs of relapse as a method for developing her own personal list of warning signs. For each warning sign that Mary identified, the counselor helped her gain an awareness of the accompanying irrational thoughts, related unmanageable feelings, and self-defeating behavior she had engaged in. For example, two of the personal warning signs identified by Mary (i.e., periods of depression following an argument with her fiancé and irregular NA meeting attendance) were connected to her irrational thought that she was totally worthless unless her fiancé was always loving and attentive. Reconstruction of this scenario helped Mary realize that such warning signs were early indicators that typically led to her using marijuana or cocaine as a means of coping with the emotional pain. With this new learning fresh at hand, the therapist employed a number of coping skill training procedures to help Mary develop more effective ways of responding in such high-risk situations. For example, Mary and her counselor role played situationally appropriate cognitive and behavioral strategies she could employ at those times she felt unfairly criticized by her mother or coworker. Some weeks later she happily reported a situation in which her mother was intensely critical of her numerous unsuccessful attempts to maintain a drug-free lifestyle, and indicated how effective she had felt when she thanked her mother for her continued concern and then pointed out the numerous positive behavioral lifestyle changes she had been able to make since entering relapse prevention counseling. Typically, counselors working from this developmental model find it helpful to focus their skill training on the cognitive-affective, situational-behavioral, and core psychological issue levels during this phase of relapse prevention counseling. In Mary's treatment, she and her counselor worked together to link specific recovery activities to each of her personal warning signs.

Once Mary began to experience an increased sense of effectiveness in coping with difficult situations, her counselor introduced the importance of Mary's doing a daily written inventory as a means of monitoring her own progress as well as checking for the emergence of a relapse warning sign. Specifically, Mary was encouraged to identify and record in her inventory each day three goals for that day. In the evening she reviewed her goals and assessed the extent to which she had been able to accomplish each. This process allowed her to concretely assess her level of change and identify problematic patterns that might lead to relapse. Both on her own and with the help of her counselor, Mary successfully used this developmental process to steadily increase her awareness of the positive changes she had been making.

Consistent with Gorski's developmental model, once Mary reported success in coping with her mother's criticisms, the counselor suggested it might be time to more actively involve her mother and her NA sponsor in her relapse prevention treatment plan. Although her mother saw no reason to become more actively involved in Mary's recovery process because this was, "after all, completely Mary's problem," Mary's NA sponsor was quite open and supportive of being more involved. With Mary's concurrence, the therapist invited her sponsor to attend a session bimonthly and become actively involved in Mary's relapse prevention planning process.

The final phase of Gorski's developmental model of relapse prevention involves helping clients update their relapse prevention plan, quarterly during the first year of relapse prevention counseling and then semiannually during the next 2 years. Typically, a client's relapse warning signs change as they move from one stage of recovery to another and from one stage of adult development to another. Relapse prevention update sessions focus on helping the client anticipate and monitor these shifts in early warning signs. As a part of Mary's relapse prevention counseling process her counselor conducted these periodic updating sessions, during which they (a) reviewed her original assessment, warning sign list, coping strategies, and recovery plan, (b) updated that assessment by documenting significant progress or problems since the previous update, (c) revised the warning sign list where necessary, (d) worked together to help her develop coping strategies to deal effectively with these new warning signs, and (e) revised her recovery program to add activities needed to support her continued recovery. For example, during their 18-month update session, a period of brief couples therapy proved particularly helpful to Mary and a man she had been dating for some time by providing communication skills training.

Alcoholics Anonymous Change Maintenance Strategies

In order to maintain the behavior change that has occurred, whether it be weight loss or abstinence from alcohol, cigarettes, or other drugs, the AA or 12-step viewpoint would advocate utilizing the five components of changes that are outlined in the 12 steps: learning the paradox of giving up control to gain control, self-examination and discussion of problems, making amends, extensive group support and working with a sponsor, and the daily reminders in the form of slogans, prayers, and meditations. Although these were not developed with counselors in mind, it is not difficult for counselors to integrate these relapse prevention strategies into their counseling practice. The following case vignette illustrates relapse from an AA program and suggests what counselors can do to prevent it.

Case Study—Sam

Sam was a 28-year-old male. He had completed alcoholism treatment three times, and this last time he had been sober for about 9 months. He was seeing an outpatient counselor once every 2 weeks for follow-up. Sam was married with two children, and he worked as a car salesman. Starting around the eighth month of sobriety the counselor began to notice some changes. Sam began to seem more confident in his sobriety. He stated that he had learned so much more this time around and that he was really understanding the AA program this time. Although he went to four meetings a week after treatment, he was attending two and stated that he didn't need the meetings as much because he was feeling better and was busier at his job. He also stated that he did not need as many meetings because he completely understood the AA program and would not need as many meetings in the future because he was in control of his drinking. The counselor also noted that Sam was disclosing less about his feelings in the counseling sessions, stating that he finished the fourth step and he had resolved "all those problems." He also felt that he would not need as many counseling sessions. When asked when Sam last saw his sponsor, he replied, "About 3 weeks ago. It's hard to get in touch with him and there's not that much to talk about anyway. He keeps bugging me about the ninth step (making amends) and that gets irritating. I've done as much as I need to do. I'm not drinking and that's all that counts." Sam also stated that he had lost his daily meditation book, but that he didn't need to use it any more. He was very optimistic about his future, and he was spending an increasing amount of time playing sports and spending time with his old poker buddies. Two weeks after receiving his 9-month chip, Sam relapsed. What happened?

Sam showed signs of relapse in all five components of change. Although counselors might not see symptoms in all five components in each client, they should be aware of what these symptoms look like.

The AA Paradox

The paradox of giving up control to gain control is often one of the most difficult of these strategies for the client to understand and to maintain. Even after initially obtaining the desired behavior change, there is a strong tendency, after a period of success, for clients to begin to feel that they are in control of the behavior and that there is no longer a need for sticking with a humble attitude toward the behavior change. It is therefore important for the counselor to look for signs of overconfidence in the client and for indications that the client is beginning to take matters into his or her own hands rather than following the relapse prevention program. Some indications of this problem are statements such as "I think I have this licked" or "I haven't had an urge to [engage in undesirable behavior] for some time. I think I can back off the counseling and the group meetings." When counselors begin to hear these type statements in the early stages of the recovery process, it is important for them to remind clients of the difficulty of behavior change and the need to continue cooperating with the program. It is also important for them to remind clients of the importance of the paradox and to state that too much confidence may be a sign the client is developing a mind-set that may lead to relapse. Keeping the paradox fresh in the client's mind is an important component of relapse prevention from the 12-step perspective. Sam's over-confidence should have been a red flag for his counselor.

Self-Examination

Once sobriety is achieved and stabilized, the 12-step model for relapse prevention encourages a thorough "inventory" or self-examination. This fourth step of AA encourages the recovering person to take a "fearless" look at the characteristics that have caused problems in the past. This component is an effective step in relapse prevention because often personal issues arise after the addictive behavior has ceased for a period of time. Whether the behavior is smoking, gambling, overeating, or alcohol and other drug use, the cessation of the behavior often forces the client to examine feelings that he or she may have avoided while engaging in the addictive behavior. Working through these feelings with a counselor or other members of the support system not only helps alleviate the possible anxiety associated with these feelings but lays the groundwork for permanent change in the client.

The counselor can obviously play an important role in this process. By encouraging the client to face rather than repress the feelings as they arise and by helping the clients to face facets of their personalities that have created problems in the past, the counselor is helping to ensure that these feelings, problems, and characteristics do not play a role in a return of the undesired behaviors.

Sam stopped this self-examination process. The cessation of this process after only 8 months of sobriety should have been a clue to the counselor that there was a problem. Individuals who successfully maintain behavior change usually continue the process of self-examination for years.

Making Amends

One of the problems associated with addictive behavior is the guilt that is often created by the negative effect addictive behavior has had on those close to the addicted client. If the guilt is not alleviated, it can seriously affect addicted clients' feelings toward their support system and feelings of those in the support system toward the addicted client. In order to deal with this "unfinished business," 12-step programs encourage their members to make a list of all those they may have harmed and make amends for that harm if possible. Although this process has been advocated by AA for 50 years, it is a part of the 12-step relapse prevention process that has not often been used by counselors. Perhaps it is too directive for many counselors. But because it both alleviates guilt and improves the support system for the client, it is an important step in decreasing the probability for relapse. Sam's reluctance to get involved with this process was a sign that his sobriety lacked a firm foundation.

Group Support and Working with a Sponsor

Probably the most important part of the AA relapse prevention process is the development of social support and the reliance on someone to act as a guide through the recovery process. Both of these components help keep addicted clients in touch with the concept that they cannot succeed in this process by themselves. It also provides a group of other recovering individuals to learn from and the support and comfort needed to get them through rough times.

Sponsors provide another level of support. They provide a more intense level of guidance and feedback about how the client is faring with the recovery process. They also provide a valuable source of feedback when the client is displaying symptoms of relapse. This intensive involvement with a group is often necessary to combat relapse and goes beyond what most counselors can provide.

Fortunately for counselors, the client's involvement in a self-help group makes the relapse prevention process significantly easier. Unfortunately, counselors often feel threatened by the client's involvement in a self-help group. Counselors are often concerned about losing their clients to the self-help group or about the client's getting contradictory information or advice from the sponsor or other group members. In order to take advantage of this type of relapse prevention program, counselors are advised to learn as much as possible about the 12-step process and to deal with their own insecurity about working with another potent therapeutic entity.

Once counselors deal with their own issues, they can begin to take advantage of the assistance that the program can provide with their client. They should encourage clients to be involved with the groups and a sponsor and help the client work through resistance to involvement. This does not mean that counselors should be "salespersons" for the 12-step process but that they should help their clients take advantage of a powerful assistance to their recovery. Also, if a client is attending meetings, the meeting attendance can provide counselors with an accurate predictor of relapse. Any time a client significantly reduces his or her attendance at 12-step meetings, this is an indication of a potential relapse problem. Counselors should therefore stay in touch with meeting attendance patterns.

Work with a sponsor can sometimes be problematic. Counselors need to be aware of the value of the sponsor and to encourage the client to utilize this important relapse prevention tool. There is potential, though, for conflict with the sponsor because both the counselor and the sponsor are providing guidance to the client at the same time. It is important that the counselor be aware of this potential conflict and work to keep this relationship a smooth one. This can be difficult because the sponsor and the counselor will usually never meet each other.

Sam's decrease in time spent with his sponsor and his involvement in non-AA activities was a sign of possible relapse. At 8 months' sobriety, involvement with AA should be a priority, and with Sam it clearly was not. The counselor could have encouraged Sam to get together with his sponsor and increase the number of meetings per week.

Daily Reminders

A final component of the 12-step relapse prevention program is the use of daily reminders or daily meditations. With any addictive behavior there is a strong tendency for relapse. The relapse often occurs because addicted individuals tend, over time, to slowly forget or take for granted the lessons they have learned about avoiding the addictive behavior. The use of slogans, daily reminders, or daily prayers or meditations is one method of combating this potentially destructive tendency. Again, it is important that counselors support this concept or perhaps devise their own form of daily reminders. Clients' avoidance or neglect of these reminders can also serve as an indication of potential relapse. If counselors detect this avoidance, it is important that they inquire about it and encourage the client to get more involved in the relapse prevention program. Sam's loss of the daily reminder book was an indication that he was not taking this component seriously.

The 12-step model provides a comprehensive program for relapse prevention and for the detection of potential relapse. Counselors who work with addictive behavior are encouraged to learn more about this process by reading 12-step materials and by attending the open sessions of the meetings.

CONCLUSION

Over the last two decades, change maintenance intervention programs such as those described above have provided clients with valuable and effective options for maintaining a more balanced, addiction-free lifestyle. Counselors in a variety of clinical settings can now choose to select a relapse prevention model consistent with their client's cognitive, affective, and behavioral capabilities.

REFERENCES

Alcoholics Anonymous. (1976). *Alcoholics Anonymous: How many thousands of men and women have recovered from alcoholism* (3rd ed.). New York: Alcoholics Anonymous World Services.

Annis, H. M. (1986). A relapse prevention model for treatment of alcoholics. In W. R. Miller & N. Heather (Eds.), *Treating addictive behaviors: Processes of change* (pp. 407–421). New York: Plenum .

Annis, H. M. (1990). Relapse to substance abuse: Empirical findings within a cognitive-social learning approach. *Journal of Psychoactive Drugs, 22,* 117–124.

Charlesworth, E. A. & Nathan, R. G. (1984). *Stress management: A comprehensive guide to wellness.* New York: Atheneum.

Cummings, C., Gordon, J. R., & Marlatt, G. A. (1980). Relapse: Strategies of prevention and prediction. In W. R. Miller (Ed.), *The addictive behaviors* (pp. 291–321). Oxford, U.K.: Pergamon.

Davis, M., Eshelman, E. R., & McKay, M. (1988). *The relaxation and stress reduction workbook* (3rd ed.). Oakland, CA: New Harbinger.

Downing, C. D. (1989). *Triad: The evolution of treatment for chemical dependency.* Independence, MO: Independence Press.

Glasser, W. (1976). *Positive addictions.* New York: Harper & Row.

Gorski, T. T. (1986, Fall). Relapse prevention planning — A new recovery tool. *Alcohol Health and Research World, 12,* 186–193.

Gorski, T. T. (1989). *Passages through recovery: An action plan for preventing relapse.* Center City, MN: Hazelden.

Gorski, T. T. (1990). The CENAPS model of relapse prevention: Basic principles and procedures. *Journal of Psychoactive Drugs, 22,* 125–133.

Gorski, T.T., & Miller, M. (1982). *Counseling for relapse prevention.* Independence, MO: Independence Press.

Gorski, T. T., & Miller, M. (1986). *Staying sober: Guide to relapse prevention.* Independence, MO: Independence Press.

Mackay, P. W., & Marlatt, G. A. (1991). Maintaining sobriety: Stopping is starting. *International Journal of Addictions, 25,* 1257–1275.

Marlatt, G. A. (1978). Craving for alcohol, loss of control, and relapse: A cognitive-behavioral analysis. In P. E. Nathan, G. A. Marlatt, & T. Loberg (Eds.), *Alcoholism: New Directions in behavioral research and treatment* (pp. 271–314). New York: Plenum.

Marlatt, G. A. (1979). Alcohol use and problem drinking: A cognitive–behavioral analysis. In P.C. Kendall & S. D. Hollon (Eds.), *Cognitive–behavioral interventions: Theory, research, and procedures* (pp. 320–334). New York: Academic Press.

Marlatt, G. A. (1982). Relapse prevention: A self-control program for the treatment of addictive behaviors. In R. B. Stuart (Ed.), *Adherence, compliance, and generalization in behavioral medicine* (pp. 87–99). New York: Brunner/Mazel.

Marlatt, G. A. (1985). Relapse prevention: Theoretical rationale and overview of the model. In G. A. Marlatt & J. R. Gordon (Eds.), *Relapse prevention: Maintenance Strategies in the Treatment of Addictive Behavior* (pp. 104–105). New York: Guilford.

Marlatt, G. A., & Gordon, J. R. (1980). Determinants of relapse: Implications for the maintenance of behavior change. In P. O. Davidson & S. M. Davidson (Eds.), *Behavioral medicine: Changing health lifestyles* (pp. 410–452). New York: Brunner/Mazel.

Marlatt, G. A., & Gordon, J. R. (Eds.). (1985). *Relapse prevention: Maintenance strategies in the treatment of addictive behaviors.* New York: Guilford.

Marlatt, G. A. & Rohsenow, D. J. (1980). Cognitive processes in alcohol use: Expectancy and the balanced placebo design. In N. K. Mello (Ed.), *Advances in substance abuse* (Vol. 1) (pp. 284–301). Greenwich, CT: JAI.

Miller, W. R. (1991). What motivates people to change? In W.R. Miller and S. Rollnick (Eds.), *Motivational interviewing: Preparing people to change addictive behavior* (pp. 14–30). New York: Guilford.

Miller, W. R. & Rollnick, S. (1991). *Motivational interviewing: Preparing people to change addictive behavior.* New York: Guilford.

Prochaska, J. O. (1984). *Systems of psychotherapy: A transtheoretical analysis* (2nd ed.). Homewood, IL: Dorsey.

Prochaska, J. O., & DiClemente, C. C. (1986). Toward a comprehensive model of change. In W. R. Miller & N. Heather (Eds.), *Treating addictive behaviors: Processes of change* (pp. 3–27). New York: Plenum.

Part III

The Pharmacology of Addictions

Chapter 12

The Pharmacology of Alcohol Use

Jill Littrell

Most people, and certainly people working in the addictions field, are aware of the more dramatic life-threatening physical consequences of consuming large amounts of alcohol over several decades. Alcoholic cirrhosis ending in liver failure in a hospitalized patient with a bloated appearance is pretty well recognized. The Korsakoff's patient who cannot retain information or remember longer than about 3 minutes and thus must be confined to a nursing home comes to mind when the public thinks of the ravages of long-term alcoholism. The impact of heavy alcohol consumption is, however, not limited to these more dramatic effects. Alcohol affects every system in the body. In addition to the prototypically alcoholic pathways to death, heavy alcohol consumption can result in an array of disabilities. It can compromise vigor and well-being. Even short-term bouts of heavy consumption can have drastic consequences. This discussion will spell out the ways in which short-term as well as long-term heavy alcohol consumption can diminish quality of life. Although some addiction counselors will be working with end-stage alcoholics, the more modal alcoholic in treatment, who has not yet totally devastated his or her life, may be experiencing the less dramatic but debilitating effects of alcohol without recognizing that alcohol use is the cause. Commitment to sobriety can be enhanced when clients realize that their aches and pains are attributable to their drinking habits.

As most clinicians know, before sharing the bad news about behavior patterns, it is important for the clinician to understand what the client thinks, or feels, is being gained by his or her lifestyle. Therefore this chapter reviews the general effects of alcohol, both good and bad. Most of the positive consequences are found in the short-term effects, which are reviewed first.

IMMEDIATE EFFECTS OF ALCOHOL ON THE BODY

In low doses, alcohol does exert an arousing effect on functioning. It increases activity level, gregariousness, amount of talking, and sheer quantity (although not quality) of mental associations (Babor, Berglas, Mendelson, Ellingboe, & Miller, 1983; Young & Pihl, 1982). It even improves memory

163

(Esposito, Parker, & Weingartner, 1984). Researchers concerned with why people find drug consumption to be compelling have advanced the theory that alcohol, like other drugs associated with compulsive use, stimulates the ventral tegmental area of the brain. Stimulation of the ventral tegmental area manifests behaviorally as increased activity and exploration of the environment. Stimulation of this brain area does seem to be pleasurable, as evidenced by the fact that rats will work for the effect (Di Chiara & Imperato, 1988; Wise & Bozarth, 1987).

Perhaps associated with this arousal effect, alcohol does seem to make experience of many types more riveting. This probably accounts for the fact that people believe they can use alcohol to alter mood. Alcohol makes it easier for those who are in a dysphonic state to become absorbed in a neutral or pleasurable activity. When someone is in a cranky mood, alcohol alone does not help much. But alcohol in combination with a distracting, pleasant task can alter the mood (Steele, Southwick, & Pagano, 1986). The explanation for alcohol's reputation as an anxiety reducer may reside in its impact on attention focus as well. For those in an anxiety-producing situation, alcohol can reduce the acuity or awareness of the anxiety-eliciting stimulus. This will occur if there is a distraction. However, without a distraction, when the person can devote his or her full attention to the fear inducer, alcohol enhances anxiety level (Steele & Josephs, 1988). Beyond this, alcohol does seem to be associated with enhanced intensity of whatever emotional experience is elicited by the situation. Although it is difficult to predict whether any particular individual will be more sad, happy, angry, or charitable given alcohol consumption, it is a good bet that whatever emotion is provoked by the situational context will be experienced with more intensity after drinking (see review in Littrell, 1991).

Alcohol has a reputation as a depressant drug, and this is also true. At higher doses alcohol does sedate (Ritchie, 1980). For the sleep deprived, it will enhance drowsiness and make it harder to stay alert (Roehrs, Zwyghuizen-Doorenbos, Knox, Moskowitz, & Roth, 1992). It is not a very good sleeping potion, however, because after it clears the system, there is a rebound awakening (Hartmann, 1982). This apparently paradoxical quality of being both a sedating and arousing drug makes alcohol difficult to classify and predict. Further, the effect of alcohol does seem to differ depending on the individual. It is known that for those who have a family history of alcoholism, there is an expectation that alcohol will have arousing effect and cause little sedation (Mann, Chassin, & Sher, 1987). Although a study demonstrating more arousal among children of alcoholics has not yet been conducted, the finding of less impairment (sedation) after drinking in offspring of alcoholics has been documented (Goodwin, 1979; Schuckit, 1985).

Some people will be more susceptible to intoxication because they absorb alcohol more rapidly than others. Women lack the stomach enzymes that partially metabolize alcohol before it is absorbed. Hence they will be more affected by less (Lieber, 1988). Aspirin also retards the stomach enzymes that metabolize alcohol (Roine, Gentry, Hernandez-Munoz, Baraona, & Lieber, 1990). Further, Tagamet (prescribed for ulcers) will enhance the absorption of alcohol (Lieber, 1988).

Intoxication itself can be life threatening. At very high blood alcohol levels, the breathing center in the brain stem (medulla) can be depressed so that death can result (Sellers & Kalant, 1976). With extreme intoxication, the risk of accidental inhalation of food or emesis (vomit) is increased. Intoxicated individuals have difficultly coughing up the inhaled material (Chew & Rissing, 1982). Finally, accidents resulting in bone breakage and hemorrhage are increased among the intoxicated (Skinner, Holt, Schuller, Roy, & Israel, 1984).

The impact of alcohol along with other sedating drugs is synergistic. The consumption of over-the-counter medications such as Benadryl along with alcohol can result in marked enhancement of the medicinal effects. Such is the case for other sedative medications as well (Ritchie, 1980).

CONSEQUENCES OF HAVING HAD TOO MUCH TO DRINK ON ONE OCCASION

High blood alcohol levels can induce spasms of the cerebral vasculature. There have been reports of alcohol-provoked strokes induced by particularly high blood alcohol levels. In fact, in younger populations, for whom strokes are rare events, imbibing is often associated with those strokes that do occur (Altura, Altura, & Gebrewold, 1983; Taylor & Combs-Orme, 1985). Another dramatic consequence of heavy consumption over a several-day period can be rhabdomyolysis. Alcohol can cause the breakdown of muscle tissue. The released myoglobin (a component of muscle tissue) can clog up the kidneys and result in kidney failure (Ferguson & Knochel, 1982).

In some persons high blood alcohol levels can induce a state called idiosyncratic intoxication. It has been suggested that seizure activity probably underlies this syndrome (Maletzky, 1976). The manifestations of idiosyncratic intoxication are extreme. Visual hallucinations, aggression, and paranoia can occur (Knott, Beard, & Fink, 1987). Although the aberrant display of behavior may not be recalled later due to a blackout, the consequences may be profound.

The effects of alcohol on carbohydrate metabolism are just now being detailed and appreciated. Heavy drinking can result in hypoglycemia hours later after the alcohol clears the system. In persons operating vehicles, this faulty regulation of blood glucose levels can be dangerous (Ryan, 1983/1984).

In those who subject themselves to bouts of heavy consumption, imbalances in electrolytes caused by the alcohol can alter the pumping action of the heart muscles. Arrhythmias and rapid heartbeat, a condition labeled "holiday heart," can be experienced during intoxication and after the alcohol has cleared the system (Greenspon & Schaal, 1983; Van Thiel & Gavaler, 1985).

A less dramatic consequence of acute consumption is the banal hangover. Whereas in the past not much importance was ascribed to a hangover, the evidence is mounting that performance is impaired. Spatial motor performance decrements have been documented. Pilots induced to consume 5 drinks between 5 and 7 p.m. displayed compromised ability to establish a proper landing angle on the plane the next morning (Yesavage & Leirer, 1986). During a hangover, pulse rate and blood pressure are elevated. Standing steadiness and hand steadiness are impaired. Nystagmus (the eyes jump when tracking a stimulus) may be present. Furthermore, headache, nausea, drowsiness, dizziness, and thirst are experienced (Rydberg, 1977).

Studies in which otherwise normal individuals have been made to sustain blood alcohol levels over day-long periods have demonstrated that anyone can be induced to display withdrawal symptoms (Leroy, 1979; Tabakoff & Rothstein, 1983). In terms of less dramatic manifestations, there are tremors, high blood pressure, sweating (diaphoresis), weakness, anxiety, nausea, diarrhea, and sleep disturbance. Hallucinations (usually auditory) and seizures can occur (Tabakoff & Rothstein, 1983). Withdrawal can also be life threatening, although extreme consequences are a relatively rare event whose probability is enhanced by debilitation. In fact, Whitfield et al. (1978) found that in a sample of 1,024 alcoholics admitted for detoxification but not medicated, one experienced delirium tremens and 12 experienced seizures.

CONSEQUENCES OF HEAVY DRINKING OVER MONTHS OR YEARS: THE LONG-TERM TOLL

Liver Function

Alcohol is notorious for its long-term impact on the liver. In a fairly short period of time (within months), heavy consumers develop a fatty liver. This is due to the change in the chemical environment of the liver created by the mechanisms of alcohol metabolism. The processing of other chemicals in the liver is shifted toward the accumulation of fat (Watson, Mohns, Eskelson, Sampliner, & Hartmann, 1986). Most authorities state that a fatty liver is a benign, asymptomatic condition, although hepatitis development is frequent (Pimstone & French, 1984). A fatty liver does allow for easy detection of heavy drinking. A bloated, enlarged liver is palpable upon physical examination.

Due to the alteration in the function of the body's major chemical-processing plant (the liver), other functional changes are observed in an alcohol processing liver.

1. Rather than producing glucose when glucose blood levels drop, the chemical equilibrium is shifted toward the production of lactic acid. Lactic acid impairs the kidney filtration process so that higher levels of uric acid are observed in the blood. High levels of uric acid do manifest as a clinical syndrome, called *gout*. Persons with gout experience joint pain and inflammation (Korsten & Lieber, 1982).

2. Although it probably will only be a manifest problem in the underfed, in heavy drinkers the liver's capacity for maintaining blood glucose levels is impaired. Acute heavy alcohol consumption, chronic malnourishment, and short-term starvation can result in ketone acidosis. A similar condition (the same functional state, but attributable to a slightly different metabolic pathway) is observed in diabetics. Ketone acidosis is a life-threatening crisis of respiratory changes, confusion, and coma (Williams, 1984).

3. Alcohol interferes with the liver production of certain proteins, some of which are blood-clotting factors. Further, if bile production is impaired in the liver, the lack of bile secretion to the stomach will result in insufficient vitamin K absorption. Vitamin K is required for the liver production of prothrombin, a substance vital in the process of blood clotting. This poor blood-clotting ability will become a problem if the heavy drinker undergoes surgery or if he or she suffers an accident that results in blood release (Van Thiel, 1983).

4. The process of drinking does increase the efficiency of the enzymes in the liver that metabolize alcohol. (Increased metabolic efficiency accounts for some of the observed tolerance to alcohol in regular heavy consumers.) The enzymes operating on the alcohol have other substrates (targets of activity) as well. Alcoholics process some drugs far more efficiently than other people who do not have activated enzyme systems. Heavy-consuming individuals will require higher dosages of medications such as Warfarin, Dilantin, Tolbutamide, and Isoniazid in order to achieve the same effect (Lieber, 1984).

Some environmental toxins are not harmful to persons with normally functioning enzymes. However, in those with enhanced enzyme activity, the toxic metabolites of particular chemicals become more abundant after exposure to the specific chemical. Carbon tetrachloride exposure becomes a larger threat. Alcoholics are more susceptible to liver damage from acetaminophen (Tylenol). It is believed that the mechanism through which alcohol increases the risk for many types of cancers is attributable to its enzyme induction function. Vitamin A, which can be toxic, is another chemical whose toxicity is enhanced by alcohol consumption, possibly due to its more rapid breakdown by induced liver enzymes. Its low storage and deficiency is also a problem in heavy drinkers. A lack of vitamin A results in poor night vision and sexual dysfunction. Treatment via replacement of vitamin A is tricky in alcoholic populations. The vitamin A given to treat deficiency will be utilized in the process of visual perception but also converted more rapidly to a toxic substance (Lieber, 1984).

5. In a malfunctioning liver, intake and storage of vitamins A, C, D, and B-12 are impaired. There is increased storage of iron, which can be damaging (Van Thiel, 1983).

In addition to the above changes, alcohol predisposes to inflammation of the liver (hepatitis) and to cellular damage with a build up of scar tissue (cirrhosis). Both conditions are life threatening. Death results from hepatic insufficiency and associated kidney failure. Toxins build-up in the system when not processed by the liver. Further, when the liver does not function, albumin is not produced. Without albumin, the fluid content of the blood seeps into the body tissues rather than remaining in the bloodstream. The body is bloated; there is insufficient pressure in the bloodstream to maintain adequate circulation. Prior to the time when cirrhosis results in complete hepatic insufficiency, other problems are observed. A hard cirrhotic liver will impair circulation through the organ. The plumbing problem will create engorged blood vessels in the upper part of the body. This is a particular problem in the neck area, where esophageal varices can hemorrhage. Complaints of fatigue, anorexia, weight loss, nausea, and abdominal discomfort may be observed (Korsten & Lieber, 1982; Lieber, 1976; Pimstone & French, 1984).

Recent attention has been focused on those factors that lessen alcohol's ability to induce scar tissue formation. The nutrient found in bean curd (lecithin) seems to retard the process of cirrhosis (Lieber, De Carli, Mak, Kin, & Leo, 1990). Beef fat, as opposed to vegetable fat, also seems to retard scar tissue formation (Takahashi et al., 1991). The existence of such moderating factors may explain why some alcoholics become cirrhotic while others do not.

Gastrointestinal Tract

Parotid gland enlargement can be created by heavy alcohol consumption. The function of the sphincters in the upper body can be altered so that more frequent episodes of heartburn ensue. Alcohol is a stomach irritant. Alcohol enhances stomach motility so that diarrhea is increased. Alcohol can destroy stomach mucosa and result in bleeding. Transport of particular nutrients is impaired by alcohol. D-xylose, thiamine, folic acid, vitamin B-12, calcium, and vitamin A are poorly absorbed. Heavy drinkers are known to be at risk for many types of nutritional deficiency syndromes. The list includes pellagra (niacin deficiency), Wernicke-Korsakoff syndrome (thiamine deficiency), scurvy (vitamin C deficiency), sideroblastic anemia (vitamin B-6 deficiency), bone disease (vitamin D deficiency), and beriberi (thiamine deficiency) (Feldman, 1982). It has been recognized that the calories from alcohol are not the same as calories from other sources of food. Alcoholics consuming calorically adequate diets plus alcohol do not gain weight (Lieber, 1988). In women who are drinkers, there is an inverse relationship between weight and dietary calories consumed from alcohol. The reason for the peculiar impact of alcohol on weight accumulation is not yet clear (Lands, 1991).

Pancreas

Tissue damage to the pancreas develops in heavy drinkers. The pancreas becomes fatty, bloated, and full of pseudocysts. Insufficient production and secretion of stomach enzymes from the pancreas can create malabsorption problems. With pancreatic inflammation, insulin and glucagon (required for blood glucose regulation and utilization) can be deficient. In addition to these functional problems, pancreatic ducts can become plugged for the glands secreting the caustic enzymes that break down foods in the stomach. When this occurs, the pancreas can dissolve itself. This is called pancreatitis. It has a mortality rate of 30% (Korsten & Lieber, 1982; Van Thiel, 1983).

Cardiovascular Effects

One of the few body systems on which alcohol exerts a beneficial effect is the vasculature system. Because of the alteration in liver chemistry, alcohol predisposes to the production of high-density lipoproteins, substances that cleanse the system of cholesterol. Drinking also decreases the level of low-density lipoprotein, the damaging fats (Kervinen, Savolainen, Tikkanen, & Kesaniermi, 1991). Alcoholics do manifest less arteriosclerosis than control populations (LaPorte, Cauley, Kuller, Flegal, & Van Thiel, 1985). People who consume at the level of several drinks per day also derive this beneficial effect (Gallant & Pena, 1992).

Whereas cholesterol levels are decreased by alcohol, alcohol does predispose to spasms of the cerebral vasculature. As mentioned previously, young binge drinkers face increased risk of strokes. Probably due to compromised blood clotting ability, heavy drinkers are more susceptible to hemorrhagic stroke (Shaw, 1987). Drinking in excess of three drinks per day has been associated with high blood pressure (Khetarpal & Volicer, 1981; Klatsky, Friedman, Siegelaub, & Gerard, 1977). In studies of alcoholics entering treatment, blood pressure decreases dramatically after a period of abstinence (Flegal & Cauley, 1985).

The heart muscle itself is damaged by alcohol. The muscle becomes enlarged (cardiomegaly) and unable to pump effectively. Cardiomyopathy (damaged muscle tissue) is a well-established consequence of chronic alcoholism. Abnormalities of left ventricular function can be detected prior to the emergence of diagnosable disease (Khetarpal & Volicer, 1981; Knott et al., 1987). Later symptoms include dyspnea (shortness of breath) and palpitations. Death occurs with congestive heart failure, when the pumping action is compromised to the point where the blood can no longer circulate adequately.

Blood Cell Production

A variety of anemias are observed in heavy drinkers. Because of nutritional deficiencies and the direct impact of alcohol on blood cell production in the bone marrow, anomalous red blood cells are produced. Some of the red blood cells are larger than normal and are inefficient carriers of oxygen (macrocytic anemia). Red blood cells with characteristic iron rings (sideroblastic anemia) can be observed. Spur cell anemia can also occur (Van Thiel, 1983).

In heavy drinkers, the immune system is also compromised. Fewer white blood cells are produced. The processes required to mobilize against pathogens are less readily induced. Liver disease results in less production of complement, a blood component needed to activate white blood cells to attack foreign invaders (Deaciuc, D'Souza, Bagby, Lang, & Spitzer, 1992; Meadows, Wallendal, Kosugi, Wunderlich, & Singer, 1992; Pitts & Van Thiel, 1986). Platelets are a component of blood involved in blood clotting. In alcoholics, fewer blood platelets are produced and those that are produced are less efficient at aggregating (Van Thiel, 1983). Blood changes revert to normal within about a month of abstention (Chanarin, 1982).

Muscles

Nearly half of alcoholics display problems with muscle tissue. Muscle fibers die or become inflamed, and there are alterations in the energy-supplying organelles (mitrochondria) in the muscle cells. Complaints of swollen and tender tissue, cramping, and weakness are predictable. Usually muscles in the hips and shoulders are affected first. As previously discussed, there is an acute condition of rapid muscle tissue breakdown (called *rhabdomyolysis*) that can occur as well. The urine takes on a brown cast as a result of the myoglobin (a component of muscle tissue) that is excreted (Ferguson & Knochel, 1982; Urbano-Marquez et al., 1989).

Bones

In heavy drinkers, bone tissue density decreases due to loss of particular nutrients. Bones become brittle so that breakage is more likely (Bliven, 1982).

Dermatological Effects

Many dermatological conditions are exacerbated by heavy drinking. In a sample of 355 alcoholics, 44% were observed to suffer some type of skin condition (Rosset & Oki, 1971; Whitfield, 1982). The immediate effect of drinking is to cause skin redness and bloodshot eyes. Among those who drink on a regular basis, the ruddiness can remain after alcohol clears the system. Facial edema (puffiness), probably attributable to vasopressin changes, occurs acutely and can take several weeks of abstention before it resolves (Whitfield, 1982). Other alcohol-induced hormonal changes can cause reddening of the palms (palmar erythema) (Van Thiel, 1983).

The W. C. Fields nose (rhinophyma) and dilated blood vessels, enlargement of sweat glands in the nose, and pustules (acne rosacea) can develop if a person is predisposed genetically (Bernstein & Soltani, 1982).

Liver disease is associated with a number of dermatological manifestations. If dead blood cells are inefficiently cleared from blood circulation, itchiness will be experienced. Due to deficit protein metabolism, fingernail production is altered such that characteristic bands in fingernails are observed. Due to changes in iron storage, the skin develops a dark or grayish cast (Whitfield, 1982; Woeber, 1975).

Kidneys

As a result of alcohol's impact on kidney filtration, a number of minerals (zinc, magnesium) are hyperexcreted (Feldman, 1982). Kidney failure is observed secondary to liver malfunction. Even in absence of cirrhosis, damaging deposits of IgA in the kidney have been observed in heavy drinkers (Smith & Tsukamoto, 1992). Bladder and kidney infections are more common because of the compromised immune system functions (Pitts & Van Thiel, 1986).

Respiratory System

Alcoholics are at risk for an array of respiratory diseases including TB, bronchitis, pneumonia, and lung abscesses. The lung protects itself through two mechanisms from contaminants that are inhaled. First, there is a coughing reflex. Second, white blood cells engulf and degrade pathogens. Both of these processes are retarded in the heavy drinker (Lyons, 1982).

Endocrine Disturbances

Acutely, alcohol will stimulate the hypothalamic-pituitary-adrenocortical axis. Eventually the homeostatic regulation of associated hormones is impaired. The dexamethasone suppression test response, often used to diagnose depression or other conditions that entail dysregulation of adrenal gland hormones, is abnormal in heavy drinking persons. Sometimes heavy drinkers exhibit chronically elevated levels of cortisol (an adrenal gland hormone). They may exhibit a condition similar to Cushing's syndrome, a disease usually observed when there is a tumor in the adrenal gland (Stokes, 1982).

Insulin secretion is disrupted among heavy drinkers. When a person is drinking, carbohydrates induce hypersecretion of insulin. However, when a person is sober, not enough insulin is secreted in response to carbohydrate consumption. Alcoholics will function like diabetics on tests of glucose intolerance. After several weeks of sobriety, alcoholics usually reinstate a normal insulin response to carbohydrate consumption (Sereny & Endrenyl, 1978).

Male Reproductive System

Male heavy drinkers do exhibit low levels of testosterone. The low levels of testosterone result through at least four mechanisms. There is increased breakdown of testosterone in the liver; the cells of the testes that produce testosterone are destroyed by alcohol; the synthesis of testosterone is retarded by alcohol breakdown products in existing cells in the testes; there is down-regulation through the pituitary gland. While male drinkers are decreasing their levels of testosterone, due to changes in the liver, estrogen accumulates. The net result of decreased male hormone and increased female hormone is predictable. Breast development (gynecomastia), feminine fat and hair distribution, and decreased sex drive ensue. Impotence and infertility can occur (Alcohol Health and Research World, 1981; Cicero, 1982; Van Thiel, 1983). Although alcohol consumption may be seen as macho behavior (Neff, Prihoda, & Hoppe, 1991), the effects certainly are not. In addition to the feminization changes, the high estrogen levels contribute to palmar erythema (red palms) and spider angiomata (visible small blood vessels) (Fadel & Hadi, 1982).

Due to changes in the testes, sperm production among heavy drinkers is decreased, and the sperm that are produced often are abnormally shaped

(Stokes, 1982). For some yet unexplained reasons, the infants sired by heavy-drinking fathers display lower birth weight and impaired immune system functioning. The effect does not seem to be genetic. In rats, alcohol-consuming male rats sire rat pups that are less active and less readily acquire avoidance learning (Abel & Lee, 1988; Berk, Montgomery, Hazlett, & Abel, 1989; Little & Sing, 1986).

Female Reproductive System

Heavy-drinking females do display increased rates of menstrual disorders, infertility, and miscarriages. Amenorrhea (absence of menstruation) may be observed (Mello et al., 1988). Among heavy-drinking women, a loss of secondary sex characteristics is observed (loss of breast tissue and pelvic fat) (Van Thiel, 1983). At less heavy drinking levels, among postmenopausal women, alcohol is associated with increased levels of estrogen (Gavaler & Love, 1992).

A number of studies have reported an association between social drinking (3.5 drinks per week) and breast cancer. There is still some controversy as to the level of drinking at which the risk for breast cancer is increase l, however (Lowenfels & Zevola, 1989).

Fetal alcohol syndrome has been publicized widely. Drinking during gestation exerts very damaging effects on fetal development. There are aberrations in facial structure formation, heart formation, and brain structure (Murcherjee & Hodgen, 1982; Russell & Skinner, 1988). Fetal alcohol syndrome infants are born with low weights and have difficulty acquiring weight after birth (Fisher, 1991). They possess inefficient immune systems (Tewari, Diano, Bera, Nguyen, & Parekh, 1992). Understandably, there has been a good deal of empirical effort in ascertaining safe levels of alcohol consumption in pregnant women. The best answer seems to be total abstention. The correlation between cognitive deficits and level of alcohol consumption is such that even low levels appear to result in subtle impairment (Streissguth, Barr, Sampson, Darby, & Martin, 1989). Further, there may be critical periods. For example, it is known that the hard-wiring connections in brain circuitry are formed during the first trimester. It is known that alcohol will interfere with this process, causing the migrating neurons to overshoot their appropriate destination (Kotkoskie & Norton, 1988). Thus drinkers learning of an unplanned pregnancy in the second month can be helpless to avoid all deleterious effects.

In addition to fetal alcohol syndrome and cognitive impairment, intoxication can cause the umbilical cord to spasm. A lack of oxygen to the fetus can result (Murcherjee & Hodgen, 1982).

Nervous System

The acute impact of alcohol on the ventral tegmental area was discussed previously. Possibly because heavy drinking diminishes neurotransmitter (brain chemicals) reserve supplies, alcoholics do experience some predictable mood effects when sober (Dongier, Vachon, & Schwartz, 1991; Rossetti, Melis, Carboni, Diana, & Gessa, 1992). Alcoholics who are unrecovered or who are recently sober report depression, oversensitivity, irritability, paranoia, distrust, jealousy, and paranoid delusions. With several weeks of abstention, the dysphoria remits (Overall, Reilly, Kelley, & Hollister, 1985).

In addition to functional alterations, alcohol will affect neuronal hard wiring as well. Alcohol can cause the destruction of the fatty covering around a neuronaxon so that conduction is impaired. Alcohol can cause the atrophy of the connections (dendrites and axons) between neurons without killing the neuronal body. Alcohol can also kill the neuron itself. Recovery from the first two processes can occur with abstention. Dead neuronal cells cannot be replaced (Mayer & Khurana, 1982).

Damage to neurons can occur in all areas of the nervous system. When the autonomic nervous system (the area that controls involuntary functions) is affected, difficult swallowing, hoarseness, problems with temperature regulation, and dizziness upon standing as well as other problems can occur. Peripheral neuropathy (damage to sensory and motor nerves outside the brain and spinal cord) can occur. Usually sensory nerves are affected before motor nerves. Typical findings include complaints of burning or tingling in the extremities. There is often a loss of ability to feel things, explaining why alcoholics often present with cigarette burns on their fingers. Some alcoholics present with an inability to contract the muscle raising their foot (foot drop) (Mayer & Khurana, 1982).

Alcohol also can cause brain damage. Dementia can be severe. Sometimes deficits are subtle so that deficits will not be apparent upon casual observation. Vocabulary levels do not deteriorate. Difficulties are observed on specific types of tasks: breaking set after a series of problems requiring the same cognitive strategy, spatial motor tasks, poor tactile recognition (Risberg & Berglund, 1987; Tarter & Edwards, 1986). Brain atrophy can be observed on CAT scans. Fortunately, with abstention, recovery that can be observed on a CAT scan does occur (Risberg & Berglund, 1987). Practice (thinking) seems to promote the recovery process (Stringer & Goldman, 1988).

There are a number of highly specific forms of brain damage that occur less frequently as well (Wernicke-Korsakoff, Marchiafava-Bignami, cerebellar deterioration, deficiency amblyopia, seizure disorder, chronic hallucinosis). Some of the specific forms result from alcoholism-associated nutritional deficiencies (Mayer & Khurana, 1982).

THE FINGERPRINT OF HEAVY DRINKING

Some fairly characteristic alterations in body chemistry are observed in heavy drinking populations. It should be noted that women are more susceptible to nervous system damage and liver problems than are men (Gallant, 1987; Van Thiel, 1983). In both sexes, checking laboratory findings for elevated liver enzyme scores (SGOT, SGPT, GGT) along with the various blood cell types produced among the heavy drinking can enable identification when people are loathe to disclose the magnitude of their alcohol consumption. Empirical efforts have been directed toward devising a formula of weighted values for discriminating heavy drinkers from the general population (Skinner et al., 1984; Watson et al., 1986). For some, laboratory tests will not be necessary. Unusual accidents, unexplained bruises, complaints of muscle problems, a red face, red palms, and puffy eyelids will already have created suspicion. Changes in drinking behavior can be brought about by discussing inauspicious laboratory findings (Kristenson, Ohlin, Hulten-Nosslin, Trell, & Hood, 1983). Further, after controlling for severity of liver problems and other problem severity, Walsh et al. (1992) found that those who remembered having been warned by a physician about their drinking did display better outcomes 2 years after entry into a treatment program. Monitoring the signs of heavy drinking and intervening is good public health practice.

WHAT CAN BE EXPECTED DURING RECOVERY

With abstention, many of the conditions discussed above do remit. During early recovery, alcoholics may display sleep disturbance. A strict schedule, along with refraining from napping during the day, has been recommended to assist in recovery from insomnia. Many treatment programs provide B vitamins liberally. Engaging in stimulating discussions and activities can also assist in cognitive recovery. For those who maintain sobriety, mortality rates are improved. Although a study by Bullock, Reed, and Grant (1992) excluded subjects with major illness such as diabetes, chronic obstructive pulmonary disease, or clinically significant liver dysfunction, the mortality rates among alcoholics who achieved stable sobriety were not found to differ from nonalcoholic men (Bullock et al., 1992).

REFERENCES

Abel, E. L., & Lee, J. A. (1988). Paternal alcohol exposure affects offspring behavior but not body or organ weights in mice. *Alcoholism: Clinical and Experimental Research, 12,* 349–355.

Alcohol Health and Research World. (1981). *Focus on the fourth special report to the U.S. Congress on alcohol and health.* Rockville, MD: U.S. Department of Health and Human Services.

Altura, B. M., Altura, B. T., & Gebrewold, A. (1983). Alcohol-induced spasms of cerebral blood vessels: Relation to cerebrovascular accidents and sudden death. *Science, 220*, 331–332.

Babor, T. F., Berglas, S., Mendelson, J. H., Ellingboe, J., & Miller, K. (1983). Alcohol, affect and the disinhibition of verbal behavior. *Psychopharmacology, 80*, 53–60.

Berk, R. S., Montgomery, I. N., Hazlett, L. D., & Abel, E. L. (1989). Paternal alcohol consumption: Effects on ocular response and serum antibody response to pseudomonas aeruginosa infection in offspring. *Alcoholism: Clinical and Experimental Research, 13*, 795–798.

Bernstein, J. E., & Soltani, K. (1982). Alcohol-induced rosacea flushing blocked by naloxone. *British Journal of Dermatology, 107*, 59–62.

Bliven, F. E. (1982). The skeletal system: Alcohol as a factor. In E. M. Pattison & E. Kaufman (Eds.), *Encyclopedic handbook of alcoholism* (pp. 215–224). New York: Gardner.

Bullock, K. D., Reed, R. J., & Grant, I. (1992). Reduced mortality risk in alcoholics who achieve long–term abstinence. *Journal of the American Medical Association, 267*, 668–672.

Chanarin, I. (1982). Effects of alcohol on the hematopoietic system. In E. M. Pattison & E. Kaufman (Eds.), *Encyclopedic handbook of alcoholism* (pp. 281–292). New York: Gardner.

Chew, W. H., & Rissing, J. P. (1982). Infectious diseases and the alcoholic. In E. M. Pattison & E. Kaufman (Eds.), *Encyclopedic handbook of alcoholism* (pp. 263–274). New York: Gardner.

Cicero, T. J. (1982). Pathogenesis of alcohol–induced endocrine abnormalities. *Advances in Alcohol and Alcohol Abuse, 1*, 87–112.

Deaciuc, I. V., D'Souza, N. B., Bagby, G. J., Lang, C. H., & Spitzer, J. J. (1992). Effect of acute alcohol administration on TNF–alpha binding to neutrophils and isolated liver plasma membranes. *Alcoholism: Clinical and Experimental Research, 16*, 533–538.

Di Chiara, G., & Imperato, A. (1988). Drugs abused by humans preferentially increase synaptic dopamine concentrations in the mesolimbic system of freely moving rats. *Proceedings of the National Academy of Sciences, 85*, 5274–5278.

Dongier, M., Vachon, L., & Schwartz, G. (1991). Bromocriptine in the treatment of alcohol dependence. *Alcoholism: Clinical and Experimental Research, 15*, 970–977.

Esposito, R. U., Parker, E. S., & Weingartner, H. (1984). Enkephalinergic "reward" pathways: A critical substrate for the stimulatory, euphoric, and memory–enhancing actions of alcohol–a hypothesis. *Substance and Alcohol Actions/Misuse, 5*, 111–119.

Fadel, H. E., & Hadi, H. A. (1982). Alcohol effects on the reproductive function. In E. M. Pattison & E. Kaufman (Eds.), *Encyclopedic handbook of alcoholism* (pp. 293–300). New York: Gardner.

Feldman, E. B. (1982). Malnutrition in the alcoholic and related nutritional deficiencies. In E. M. Pattison & E. Kaufman (Eds.), *Encyclopedic handbook of alcoholism* (pp. 225–262). New York: Gardner.

Ferguson, E. R., & Knochel, J. P. (1982). Myopathy in the chronic alcoholic. In E. M. Pattison & E. Kaufman (Eds.), *Encyclopedic handbook of alcoholism* (pp. 204–215). New York: Gardner.

Fisher, S. E. (1991). Ethanol and fetal/postnatal growth. *Alcoholism: Clinical and Experimental Research, 15*, 903–904.

Flegal, K. M., & Cauley, J. A. (1985). Alcohol consumption and cardiovascular risk factors. In M. Glanter (Ed.), *Recent developments in alcoholism* (Vol. 3), (pp. 165–180). New York: Plenum.

Gallant, D. M. (1987). The female alcoholic: Early onset of brain damage. *Alcoholism: Clinical and Experimental Research, 11,* 1990.

Gallant, D. M., & Pena, J. M. (1992). One more look at alcohol consumption and risk of coronary disease. *Alcoholism: Clinical and Experimental Research, 16,* 350.

Gavaler, J. S., & Love, K. (1992). Detection of the relationship between moderate alcoholic beverage consumption and serum levels of estradiol in normal postmenopausal women: Effects of alcohol consumption quantitation methods and sample size adequacy. *Journal of Studies on Alcohol, 53,* 389–394.

Goodwin, D. W. (1979). Alcoholism and heredity. A review and a hypothesis. *Archives of General Psychiatry, 36,* 57–61.

Greenspon, A. J., & Schaal, S. F. (1983). The "holiday heart": Electrophysiologic studies of alcohol effects in alcoholics. *Annals of Internal Medicine, 98,* 135–139.

Hartmann, E. L. (1982). Alcohol and sleep disorders. In E. M. Pattison & E. Kaufman (Eds.), *Encyclopedic handbook of alcoholism* (pp. 180–193). New York: Gardner.

Kervinen, K., Savolainen, M. J., Tikkanen, M. J., & Kesaniermi, Y. A. (1991). Low density lipoprotein derivatization by acetaldehyde affects lysine residues and the B/E receptor binding affinity. *Alcoholism: Clinical and Experimental Research, 15,* 1050–1055.

Khetarpal, V. K., & Volicer, L. (1981). Alcohol and cardiovascular disorders. *Drug and Alcohol Dependence, 7,* 1–30.

Klatsky, A. L., Friedman, G. D., Siegelaub, A. B., & Gerard, M. J. (1977). Alcohol consumption and blood pressure: Kaiser–Permanente multiphasic health examination data. *New England Journal of Medicine, 296,* 1194–1200.

Knott, D. H., Beard, J. D., & Fink, R. D. (1987). Medical aspects of alcoholism. In W. M. Cox (Ed.), *Treatment and prevention of alcohol problems: A resource manual* (pp. 57–70). New York: Academic Press.

Korsten, M. A., & Lieber, C. S. (1982). Liver and pancreas. In E. M. Pattison & E. Kaufman (Eds.), *Encyclopedic handbook of alcoholism* (pp. 225–244). New York: Gardner.

Kotkoskie, L. A., & Norton, S. (1988). Prenatal brain malformations following acute ethanol exposure in the rat. *Alcoholism: Clinical and Experimental Research, 12,* 831–836.

Kristenson, H., Ohlin, H., Hulten–Nosslin, M. B., Trell, E., & Hood, B. (1983). Identification and intervention of heavy drinking in middle-aged men: Results and follow-up of 24 to 60 months of long-term study with randomized controls. *Alcoholism: Clinical and Experimental Research, 7,* 203–209.

Lands, W. E. M. (1991). Acetate metabolism: New mysteries from old data. *Alcoholism: Clinical and Experimental Research, 15,* 393–394.

LaPorte, R. E., Cauley, J. A., Kuller, L. H.., Flegal, K., & Van Thiel, D. (1985). Alcohol, coronary heart disease, and total mortality. In M. Glanter (Ed.), *Recent developments in alcoholism* (Vol. 3, pp. 157–163). New York: Plenum.

Leroy, J. B. (1979). Recognition and treatment of the alcohol withdrawal syndrome. *Primary Care, 6,* 529–539.

Lieber, C. S. (1976, March). The metabolism of alcohol. *Scientific American,* pp. 3–11.

Lieber, C. S. (1984). Metabolism and metabolic effects of alcohol. *Medical Clinics of North America, 68,* 3–31.

Lieber, C. S. (1988). Biochemical and molecular basis of alcohol-induced injury to liver and other tissues. *New England Journal of Medicine, 319,* 1639–1651.

Lieber, C. S., De Carli, L. M., Mak, K. M., Kin, C–I., Leo, M. A. (1990). Attenuation of alcohol–induced hepatic fibrosis by polyunsaturated lecithin. *Hepatology, 12,* 1390–1398.

Little, R. E., & Sing, C. F. (1986). Association of father's drinking and infant's birth weight. *New England Journal of Medicine, 314,* 1644–1645.

Littrell, J. (1991). *Understanding and treating alcoholism: Biological, psychological, and social aspects of alcohol consumption and abuse* (Vol. 2). Hillsdale, NJ: Lawrence Erlbaum.

Lowenfels, A. B., & Zevola, S. A. (1989). Alcohol and breast cancer: An overview. *Alcoholism: Clinical and Experimental Research, 13,* 109–111.

Lyons, H. A. (1982). The respiratory system and specifics of alcoholism. In E. M. Pattison & E. Kaufman (Eds.), *Encyclopedic handbook of alcoholism* (pp. 325–331). New York: Gardner.

Maletzky, B. M. (1976). The diagnosis of pathological intoxication. *Journal of Studies on Alcohol, 37,* 1215–1228.

Mann, L. M., Chassin, L., & Sher, K. J. (1987). Alcohol expectancies and the risk for alcoholism. *Journal of Consulting and Clinical Psychology, 55,* 411–417.

Mayer, R. F., & Khurana, R. K. (1982). Peripheral and autonomic nervous system. In E. M. Pattison & E. Kaufman (Eds.), *Encyclopedic handbook of alcoholism* (pp. 194–203). New York: Gardner.

Meadows, G. G., Wallendal, M., Kosugi, A., Wunderlich, J., & Singer, D. S. (1992). Ethanol induces marked changes in lymphocyte populations and natural killer cell activity in mice. *Alcoholism: Clinical and Experimental Research, 16,* 474–479.

Mello, N. K., Mendelson, J. H., King, N. W., Bree, M. P., Skupny, A., & Ellingboe, J. (1988). Alcohol self–administration by female macaque monkeys: A model for study of alcohol dependence, hyperprolactinemia, and amenorrhea. *Journal of Studies in Alcohol, 49,* 551–560.

Murcherjee, A. B., & Hodgen, G. D. (1982). Maternal ethanol exposure induces transient impairment of umbilical circulation and fetal hypoxia in monkeys. *Science, 218,* 700–702.

Neff, J. A., Prihoda, T. J., & Hoppe, S. K. (1991). "Machismo," self-esteem, education, and high maximum drinking among Anglo, Black, and Mexican-American male drinkers. *Journal of Studies on Alcohol, 52,* 458–463.

Overall, J. E., Reilly, E. L., Kelley, J. T., & Hollister, L. E. (1985). Persistence of depression in detoxified alcoholics. *Alcoholism: Clinical and Experimental Research, 9,* 331–333.

Pimstone, N. R., & French, S. W. (1984). Alcoholic liver disease. *Medical Clinics of North America, 68,* 39–56.

Pitts, T. O., & Van Thiel, D. H. (1986). Urinary tract infections and renal papillary necrosis in alcoholism. In M. Galanter (Ed.), *Recent developments in alcoholism* (Vol. 4, pp. 341–377). New York: Plenum.

Risberg, J., & Berglund, M. (1987). Cerebral blood flow and metabolism in alcoholics. In O. A. Parsons, N. Butters, & P. E. Nathan (Eds.), *Neuropsychology of alcoholism; Implications for diagnosis and treatment* (pp. 64–75). New York: Guilford.

Ritchie, J. M. (1980). The aliphatic alcohols. In A. G. Goodman, L. S. Goodman, & A. Gilman (Eds.), *The pharmacological basis of therapeutics* (pp. 376–390). New York: Macmillan.

Roehrs, T., Zwyghuizen–Doorenbos, A., Knox, M., Moskowitz, H., & Roth, T. (1992). Sedating effects of ethanol and time of drinking. *Alcoholism: Clinical and Experimental Research, 16,* 553–587.

Roine, R., Gentry, T., Hernandez–Munoz, R., Baraona, E., & Lieber, C. S. (1990). Aspirin increases blood alcohol concentrations in humans after ingestion of ethanol. *Journal of the American Medical Association, 264,* 2406–2408.

Rosset, M., & Oki, G. (1971). Skin diseases in alcoholism. *Quarterly Journal of Studies on Alcohol, 32,* 1017–1024.

Rossetti, Z. L., Melis, F., Carboni, S., Diana, M., & Gessa, G. L. (1992). Alcohol withdrawal in rats is associated with a marked fall in extraneuronal dopamine. *Alcoholism: Clinical and Experimental Research, 16,* 529–532.

Russell, M., & Skinner, J. B. (1988). Early measures of maternal alcohol misuse as predictors of adverse pregnancy outcomes. *Alcoholism: Clinical and Experimental Research, 12,* 824–830.

Ryan, K. (Winter 1983/1984). Alcohol and blood sugar disorders: An overview. *Alcohol Health and Research World, 8,* 2, 3–7.

Rydberg, U. (1977). Experimentally induced hangover. In C. M. Idestrom (Ed.), *Recent advances in the study of alcoholism: Proceedings of the first international Magnus Hull Symposium* (pp. 32–40). New York: Elsevier-Holland.

Schuckit, M. A. (1985). Ethanol-induced changes in body sway in men at high alcoholism risk. *Archives of General Psychiatry, 42,* 375–379.

Sellers, E. M., & Kalant, H. (1976). Drug therapy: Alcohol intoxication and withdrawal. *New England Journal of Medicine, 294,* 757–762.

Sereny, G., & Endrenyl, L. (1978). Mechanism and significance of carbohydrate intolerance in chronic alcoholism. *Metabolism, 27,* 1041–1046.

Shaw, T. G. (1987). Alcohol and brain function: An appraisal of cerebral blood flow data. In O. A. Parsons, N. Butters, & P. E. Nathan (Eds.), *Neuropsychology of alcoholism: Implications for diagnosis and treatment* (pp. 129–149). New York: Guilford.

Skinner, H. A., Holt, S., Schuller, R., Roy, J., & Israel, Y. (1984). Identification of alcohol abuse using laboratory tests and a history of trauma. *Annals of Internal Medicine, 101,* 847–851.

Smith, S. M., & Tsukamoto, H. (1992). Time dependency of IgA nephropathy induction in alcohol ingestion. *Alcoholism: Clinical and Experimental Research, 16,* 471–473.

Steele, C. M., & Josephs, R. A. (1988). Drinking your troubles away II: An attention-allocation model of alcohol's effect on psychological stress. *Journal of Abnormal Psychology, 97,* 196–205.

Steele, C. M., Southwick, L., & Pagano, R. (1986). Drinking your troubles away: The role of activity in mediating alcohol's reduction of psychological stress. *Journal of Abnormal Psychology, 95,* 173–180.

Stokes, P. E. (1982). Endocrine disturbances associated with alcohol and alcoholism. In E. M. Pattison & E. Kaufman (Eds.), *Encyclopedic handbook on alcoholism* (pp. 311–324). New York: Gardner.

Streissguth, A. P., Barr, H. M., Sampson, P. D., Darby, B. L., & Martin, D. C. (1989). IQ at age 4 in relation to maternal alcohol use and smoking during pregnancy. *Developmental Psychology, 25,* 3–11.

Stringer, A. Y., & Goldman, M. S. (1988). Experience–dependent recovery of block design performance in male alcoholics: Strategy training versus unstructured practice. *Journal of Studies on Alcohol, 49,* 406–411.

Tabakoff, B., & Rothstein, J. D. (1983). Biology of tolerance and dependence. In B. Tabakoff, P. B. Sutker, & C. L. Randall (Eds.), *Medical and social aspects of alcohol abuse* (pp. 187–222). New York: Plenum.

Takahashi, H., Wong, K., Jui, L., Nanji, A. A., Mendenhall, C. S., & French, S. W. (1991). Effect of dietary fat on ito cell activation by chronic ethanol intake: A long-term serial morphometric study on alcohol-fed and control rats. *Alcoholism: Clinical and Experimental Research, 15,* 1060–1066.

Tarter, R. E., & Edwards, K. L. (1986). Multifactorial etiology of neuropsychological impairment in alcoholics. *Alcoholism: Clinical and Experimental Research, 10,* 128–135.

Taylor, J. R., & Combs-Orme, T. (1985). Alcohol and stroke in young adults. *American Journal of Psychiatry, 142,* 116–118.

Tewari, S., Diano, M., Bera, R., Nguyen, Q., & Parekh, H. (1992). Alterations in brain polyribosomal RNA translation and lymphocyte proliferation in prenatal ethanol-exposed rats. *Alcoholism: Clinical and Experimental Research, 16,* 436–442.

Urbano-Marquez, A., Estruch, R., Navarro-Lopez, F., Grau, J. M., Mont, L., & Rubin, E. (1989). The effects of alcoholism on skeletal and cardiac muscle. *New England Journal of Medicine, 320,* 409–415.

Van Thiel, D. H. (1983). Effects of ethanol upon organ systems other than the central nervous system. In B. Tabakoff, P. B. Sutker, & C. L. Randall (Eds.), *Medical and social aspects of alcohol abuse* (pp. 79–132). New York: Plenum.

Van Thiel, D. H., & Gavaler, J. S. (1985). Myocardial effects of alcohol abuse: Clinical and physiologic consequences. In M. Galanter (Ed.), *Recent developments in alcoholism* (Vol. 3, pp. 181–187). New York: Plenum.

Walsh, D. C., Hingson, R. W., Merrigan, D. M., Levenson, S. M., Coffman, G. A., Heeren, T., & Cupples, A. (1992). The impact of a physician's warning on recovery after alcoholism treatment. *Journal of the American Medical Association, 267,* 663–667.

Watson, R. R., Mohns, M. E., Eskelson, C., Sampliner, R. E., & Hartmann, B. (1986). Identification of alcohol abuse and alcoholism with biological parameters. *Alcoholism: Clinical and Experimental Research, 10,* 364–385.

Whitfield, C. L. (1982). Skin diseases associated with alcoholism. In E. M. Pattison & E. Kaufman (Eds.), *Encyclopedic handbook of alcoholism* (pp. 275–280). New York: Gardner.

Whitfield, C. L., Thompson, G., Lamb, A., Spencer, V., Pfeifer, M., & Browning–Ferrando, M. (1978). Detoxification of 1,024 alcoholic patients with alcohol–induced cirrhosis. *Journal of the American Medical Association, 239,* 1409–1410.

Williams, H. E. (1984). Alcoholic hypoglycemia and ketoacidosis. *Medical Clinics of North America, 68,* 33–38.

Wise, R. A., & Bozarth, M. A. (1987). A psychomotor stimulant theory of addiction. *Psychological Review, 94,* 469–492.

Woeber, K. (1975). The skin in diagnosis of alcoholism. *Annals of the New York Academy of Sciences, 252,* 292–295.

Yesavage, J. A., & Leirer, V. O. (1986). Hangover effects on aircraft pilots 14 hours after alcohol ingestion: A preliminary report. *American Journal of Psychiatry, 143,* 1546–1550.

Young, J. A., & Pihl, R. O. (1982). Alcohol consumption and response in men social drinkers: The effects of causal attributions concerning relative response control. *Journal of Studies on Alcohol, 43,* 334–351.

Chapter 13

The Pharmacology of Abused Drugs

Gregory A. Blevins

Pharmacology is the study of drugs, including their composition, uses, and effects. Over the past 20 years, our understanding of pharmacological principles has grown considerably. The prospects for further developments are dramatic as new knowledge of how the brain works and is modified by various chemicals accumulates.

In this context, it is essential that helping professionals acquire a basic understanding of pharmacology because drugs can be a cause, cofactor, or cure for many human problem situations. Through an awareness of pharmacology, counselors should be better prepared to interpret client behavior patterns; ask relevant questions; provide feedback and constructive confrontation; motivate clients to contemplate, implement, and maintain behavioral changes; detect high-risk situations; and prevent secondary or indirect risks related to drug-using behavior. Knowledge of how drugs work and their effects should enhance our professional credibility, confidence, and ability to remain current. Finally, awareness of pharmacological principles can affect the attitudes we hold toward drugs and drug users as well as enhance our understanding of the drugs we use ourselves.

In many respects, our society's concerns over drugs and drug use related behaviors are no different than those found in other historical and cultural contexts. For example, the usual justification for intervening in drug use behavior is either purported health or social consequences. However, it must be noted that both the drugs and the types of behaviors that are of concern have varied and continue to vary across sociohistorical contexts. Most of the currently defined abused drugs were originally introduced and gained acceptance for their sacred or medicinal properties, and even recreational use was not always discouraged. Over the past 30 years, an increasingly broad array of drugs have become negatively sanctioned. The major goal of this monograph is to provide the reader with a basic understanding of pharmacological principles that should help separate drug-related facts from mythology.

HOW DRUGS WORK

The mechanism of action for psychoactive drugs focuses on the electrochemical transmission system of neurons. Though a review of neural transmission processes is beyond the scope of this discussion, it should be noted that there are several ways in which drugs can disrupt neural transmission. These include

1. *Neurotoxicity*—the drug or one of its metabolites can destroy neurons.
2. *Neuromembrane permeability*—the neural cell wall becomes less permeable (more permeable), thereby retarding (enhancing) neurotransmission.
3. *Neurotransmitter (NT) synthesis*—the drug may act as a precursor of catalysts to increase the amount of NT available (enhancing neurotransmission) or inhibit synthesis to reduce NT production (retarding neurotransmission).
4. *Mimicking a neurotransmitter*—the exogenous drug may be similar to an endogenous NT and act as an NT.
5. *Release of NT*—the drug may stimulate the release of synthesized NT that is stored in vesicles.
6. *Occupying NT receptors*—the drug may attach to (have affinity for) the NT receptor and can (a) alter the receptor, (b) block access to the receptor, or (c) displace the endogenous NT.
7. *Metabolism of NT*—one way of terminating the endogenous NT's activity is to metabolize it; by blocking this metabolism, the drug prolongs NT activity.
8. *Reuptake of NT*—the second way of terminating an NT's activity is to reabsorb the NT (reuptake); blocking reuptake prolongs NT activity.

Though the behavioral effects of many drugs are generally known, their exact mechanisms of action are often not well understood. For example, an increase in activity in particular NT pathways may result from (a) increased synthesis of the NT; (b) the exogenous drug mimicking the NT; (c) increased release of the NT from storage; (d) depolarization of receptors, making them more responsive to the NT; (e) decreased metabolism of the NT; (f) decreased reuptake of the NT; or (g) some combination of the above. In addition, the observable behavioral effects of drug use can be the result of combinatory and-compensatory changes in two or more NTs. Finally, we must remember that drug effects depend on a variety of factors other than specific chemical structure—neurophysiological relationships (i.e., structure-activity relationships or SARs). Some drug-neurotransmitter relationships are summarized in table 13–1.

UNDERSTANDING DRUG EFFECTS

To understand the variations in drug effects from one user to another or for the same user across time, we need to be aware of the many variables that affect

Table 13-1 Drug-Neurotransmitter Relationships

Drug	Neurotransmitter	Effect
Amphetamine	Dopamine	increase, neurotoxic
	Norepinephrine	increase
	Serotonin	increase
Barbiturates	Gamma Aminobutyric Acid (GABA)	increase
Benzodiazepines	GABA	increase
Caffeine	Adenosine	blocks receptors
Cocaine	Dopamine	increase
	Norepinephrine	increase
	Serotonin	increase
	GABA	decrease
Inhalants	Neuromembranes	initially hypopolarizing, higher doses hyperpolarize
LSD	Serotonin	enhancement
	Dopamine	enhancement
Marijuana	Acetylcholine	increase
	Dopamine	increase
Nicotine	Acetylcholine	dose-related increase or decrease
	Dopamine	increase
	Norepinephrine	increase
Phencyclidine	Acetylcholine	increase and decrease
	Dopamine	increase
	Norepinephrine	increase
	Serotonin	increase
	GABA	increase
	Endorphins	increase
Opioids	Endorphins	increase

a user's response to a drug. These variables can be usefully separated into four categories: (a) pharmaceutical characteristics, (b) physiological variables, (c) psychological factors, and (d) socio-environmental conditions.

Pharmaceutical Characteristics

The dosage pattern, composition, route of administration, and interactions with other drugs or foods all affect the effects a drug may have on a user. The dosage pattern has both quantitative and temporal dimensions. The quantitative dimension is referred to as a dose-response relationship. A typical dose-response curve is presented in Figure 13-1.

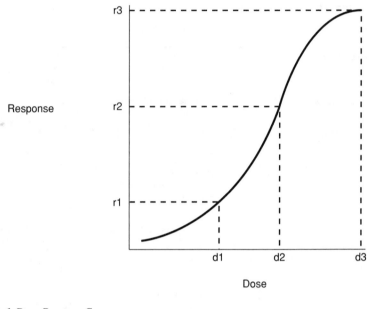

Figure 13–1 Dose–Response Curve

In Figure 13–1, three dosages are of particular importance: d1, the threshold dose, d2, the effective dose, and d3, the dose required to produce maximal efficacy. The threshold dose, d1, is defined as the minimum dose necessary to produce an observable, measurable effect on the user. The effective dose, d2, represents the amount of drug that must be administered to produce a desired effect, where "desired" may be defined by the user (e.g., an altered state of consciousness) or by a clinician, and is generally referred to as the ED for effective dose. The third dose, d3, is defined by the fact that further increases in dosage fail to produce additional changes in the response or behavior. A fourth dose of concern, which is not represented in Figure 13–1, is the lethal dose or LD.

There are three important points to be noted about dose-response relationships. First, d1, d2, and d3 may be very different from one another, as in Figure 13–1, or they may be the same dose, in which case we can speak of an all-or-none response. Second, because most drugs produce more than one response, the dosages may vary with the behavioral response being studied. Finally, for reasons to be considered later, there can be considerable response variation among users or for the same user over time.

To account for individual variations in response to drugs, the effective dose, ED, and lethal dose, LD, are often expressed as percentages. For example, an ED50 would mean that this is the effective dose for 50% of the population, and an LD50 would have a similar meaning. When both the ED and LD are known, it is possible to specify a therapeutic ratio or safety margin for the drug, which is the LD/ED. Unfortunately, for some abused drugs the safety margin is unknown or unclear due to species variation in lethal dosage.

The second dosage pattern dimension is temporal. A typical time-response relationship is diagrammed in Figure 13–2. In Figure 13–2, the dotted line represents the amount of drug in the blood (blood-drug level or BDL), and the solid line represents the strength of the effect over time. From t0 to t1, the BDL is rising and so is the strength of behavioral response (onset). From t1 to t3, the BDL continues to rise (t1 to t2) and then falls (t2 to t3), but the effect of the drug is constant because the maximum efficacy (peak effect) was reached at t1, and the BDL is referred to as overshoot. From t3 to t4, the effect dissipates as the BDL drops. It is during the time period represented by t3 to t4 that withdrawal or rebound effects become increasingly evident. The entire time period from the point when the BDL reaches the threshold until it drops below that point is the duration of the effect. It follows from this discussion that by controlling the frequency of use, the user can affect the quantity of drug in the blood which will, in turn, produce a higher peak effect or longer duration of action than a single dose.

In addition to the quantity and frequency of use, the third aspect of the dosage pattern is duration of use. Though some effects of drugs are identifiable from virtually the first occasion of use (acute effects), other effects derive from repeated use over a period of time (chronic effects). A classic example here is the difference between the nausea and vomiting that can accompany ingestion of alcohol on any particular occasion and cirrhosis that develops over time from repeated use of alcohol.

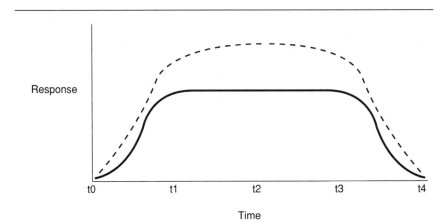

Figure 13–2 Time–Response Curve

The second pharmaceutical characteristic that influences a drug's effects is the composition of the drug. A prescription or over-the-counter compound typically consists of an active chemical and one or more inactive ingredients. The purchaser can generally be assured that the compound contains the listed chemicals in specified amounts and that other chemicals are not present. On the street, the quality, quantity, and purity of drugs is less certain. Street drugs may not contain the alleged drug (e.g., some samples of marijuana are not marijuana). When the alleged drug is present, there can be wide variations in strength (marijuana can contain from 0.5 to 16% THC). Finally, the substitute chemicals, contaminants, and cutting agents can be active chemicals. As a result, the alleged "drug effect" may be from some ingredient other than the drug.

A third pharmaceutical characteristic is the route of administration. Generally, the route of administration affects the onset, peak, and duration of effects. Oral administration has a slow onset (15-30 minutes minimum), relatively low peak effect (some drug is lost to digestive-metabolic processes), and longer duration of effect (due to delayed absorption). Injected drugs have quicker onsets, higher peak effects, and shorter durations of action than oral drugs. Finally, inhaled drugs usually have quicker onsets, greater peak effects, and shorter durations of action than injected drugs.

The final pharmaceutical characteristic concerns the presence of other drugs or foods. The drug effect may result from the interaction of the drug with other drugs or even certain foods. These interactions can take several forms. Additive effects occur when the effects of two or more drugs can be predicted by knowledge of their separate dose-response relationships. Synergistic effects are said to occur when the effects are greater then those predicted on the basis of our knowledge of each drug separately. Potentiation refers to an effect that occurs when one drug enables a second drug to have an effect it would not otherwise have. Finally, antagonistic effects refer to effects from different drugs that oppose one another. Antagonism can occur when the chemicals neutralize each other (chemical antagonism), the drugs energize opposing physiological systems (physiological antagonism), or the drugs compete for the same receptor (pharmacological antagonism). The key point is that some drug effects are the result of drug-drug or drug-food interactions requiring the presence of both substances to occur.

Physiological Variables

The drug user brings to the drug-using occasion a number of physiological variables that influence the effects of the drug. These include the following.

Absorption of a drug refers to its ability to move from the site of administration to the site of action. Generally, to be absorbed, a drug must cross one or more membrane barriers. The ability of the drug to cross these barriers is partly determined by its chemical composition, including lipid solubility, ionization, polarization, pH, molecular size and configuration, and concentration of the drug. However, conditions at the site of administration also influence absorption rates, including the volume of blood flow, impairment of the digestive system for oral drugs, and cardiovascular impairments.

Distribution of a drug is the movement of a drug throughout the body. The distribution of a drug tends to be systemic rather than specific, so the dose is diluted in body tissues. How rapidly a portion of the drug reaches the brain will depend on cardiovascular functioning. Whether enough drug reaches the brain to produce an effect will depend on the dose administered and on the affinity of the drug for various biological components because it may become sequestered in nonreactive areas of the body. Saturation of these nonreactive areas by prior doses of a drug means that successive doses will have greater effects.

Metabolism refers to the chemical alteration of the drug, usually from an active compound to one that is less active or inactive. Though virtually every cell of the body is capable of metabolizing minute amounts of a drug, most metabolism occurs in the liver. Metabolism rates can be affected by disease, damage, nutrition, distribution of the drug to the liver, and sequestration of the drug. Metabolism is also influenced by *inducibility,*or the ability of some drugs to stimulate metabolic processes. Because metabolic processes are the primary way in which a drug's effects are terminated, enhancing metabolism rates shortens the duration of action and may reduce the maximum effect, whereas retarding metabolism has opposite effects.

Excretion is the removal of the drug and its metabolic by-products from the organism. The principal means of excretion are urination and defecation, with small amounts excreted through respiration and perspiration. Impairment of excretory processes allows the drug and its by-products to remain in the body, where they may be reabsorbed into the blood, thereby prolonging the effects of the drug or producing new effects.

Pharmacokinetics is the study of the absorption, distribution, metabolism, and excretion characteristics of drugs. The half-life of a drug is the amount of time required to metabolize and excrete a standard dose of a drug. Thus the half-life gives an indication of pharmacokinetic functioning. Impairment of absorption, distribution, metabolism, or excretion rates will be reflected in an increase in half-life and therefore an increase in the duration of action and possibly the peak effect.

The nature and extent of disease or damage to a user can affect the drug's effects. As mentioned above, disease and damage that affect any of the pharmacokinetic processes can alter a drug's onset, peak, and duration of effects. Similarly, neurological impairments can alter the effect of a drug. Because disease and damage are often direct or indirect results of chronic drug use, regular users may react to a drug very differently from nonusers or occasional users.

Malnutrition can be a contributing factor in drug effects. Because proper nutrition is essential for normal physiological functioning, imbalanced diets can lead to dysfunctions that affect a drug's effects. In particular, the enzymes, catalysts, and other chemicals necessary for metabolizing a drug can be adversely affected by poor nutrition.

Genetic endowment seems to be important in determining some types of individual sensitivity to drugs. Allergic reactions are classic examples of individual susceptibility to drugs. More broadly, pharmacologists have become increasingly interested in the role genetics plays in understanding apparent supersensitivity or relative immunity to the effects of particular drugs.

Biorhythms can also alter individual responsiveness to drugs. Annual, monthly, circadian (daily), and ultracircadian (more than once per day) physiological cycles have been identified. Understanding such cycles and knowing where a person is in a cycle can be important to understanding how the effects of a drug vary.

Age of the user can be an important determinant of drug effects. Age is often used as an index variable to reflect variations in body mass, physiological functioning, neurological development, and psychosocial factors that affect responses to drugs. This is clearly seen in recommended pediatric and geriatric doses for some drugs.

Gender, like age, is often an index variable that reflects several factors. These factors include differences in body mass, body fat, protein, and water proportions; hormones; and psychosocial development that influence individual responses to drugs.

Body mass or weight is one of the most important variables in determining a drug's dosage among medical practitioners. Clearly, the greater the body mass, the greater the dilution factor, and the more drug an individual can or must consume before experiencing a particular effect.

Race, like age and gender, is probably an index variable used to represent some combination of biological and psychosocial variations. Biologically, racial variations in digestion, metabolism, excretion, blood chemistry, and other physiological variables may contribute to differences in drug effects. At the psychosocial level, race may reflect variations in expectations for drug-free and intoxicated states.

Psychological Factors

Specific effects of drugs are those that can be demonstrated through double-blind placebo studies to be the result of biochemical processes. Effects of a drug that are related to other processes are *nonspecific effects*. Generally, psychological factors and socioenvironmental conditions, to be considered in the next section, are assumed to be the major determinants of nonspecific effects. With potent drugs and strong doses, nonspecific effects would be of little importance. However, abused drugs are often either low potency or used in low to moderate dosages, so nonspecific effects can be more important than specific effects. The three major psychological factors of concern are: expectations or set, mood, and task of the user. *Expectations* or *set* refers to what the user believes will or should happen when he or she uses a drug. Expectations for a drug's effects derive from several sources, including prior use of the drug, media accounts, friends' and family members' opinions and experiences, education and training, and professional descriptions. Placebo studies have demonstrated that inactive compounds can alter cognitions, sensations, emotions, and behaviors. Thus, the user's expectations are often a powerful determinant of his or her responses to a drug. In some cases, the drug may actually be used in an attempt to provide a justification for otherwise sanctionable behavior.

Mood refers to a general feeling state that may be either transitory or enduring. Drugs may be used in an effort to either reverse an undesirable mood (e.g., depression) or augment a desirable mood state (e.g., exhilaration). Users often report using drugs in an effort to reverse undesirable mood states. Clearly, expectations play a role in the selection and use of a drug. Unfortunately, the response to a drug may not conform to expectations. For example, a depressant can reduce inhibitions, a stimulant may confer a sense of omnipotence, or a hallucinogen could distort perceptions so that a depressed user considers suicide a reasonable choice and an angry user engages in violence.

Task refers to the behavior a user attempts to engage in following use of the drug. Behaviors can be analyzed along many dimensions, four of which will be considered here. A behavioral task varies from simple to complex, from concrete to abstract, from well learned to recently acquired, and from highly motivated to poorly motivated. Simple, concrete, well-learned, or highly motivated tasks are generally more resistant to drug effects than their more complex, abstract, recently acquired, or poorly motivated counterparts. Thus an assessment of impairment may depend on the methodology used to make the assessment. Moreover, with practice, a user may learn to perform a wide variety of behaviors while under the influence of a drug.

Socioenvironmental conditions or *setting* refers to the physical and social aspects of the drug-using situation. Although these can be treated as separate elements, they interact with one another to define acceptable and unacceptable behaviors.

The *physical environment* consists of all the props and physical elements (e.g., furniture, room size, lighting) present in an environment. Classrooms, for example, have many similarities to one another, but are different from churches, bars, or sporting event locations. Such physical environments enable some types of behavior while simultaneously inhibiting other behaviors. Extending this observation to drug-related behavior, it follows that although the drug and dosage may be the same, the behavior will vary.

The *social environment* is defined by the people and social interaction patterns present in the drug-using environment. This social environment influences drug-related behavior by (a) establishing a general mood or emotional tone, (b) providing models on how and how much drug may be used, (c) serving as a comparison standard for one's behavior, and (d) providing support and sanctions for appropriate and inappropriate behaviors. Thus a person's behavior will be different in the presence of drug-using friends than when he or she is with business associates or others he or she wishes to impress.

Given the variation in pharmaceutical, physiological, psychological, and socioenvironmental influences on drug-related behavior, there can be considerable variability among users or for the same user across drug-using occasions. Among users, unusual drug reactions include *hypersensitivity,* in which small doses result in unusual effects (e.g., allergic reactions); *hyperreactivity,* or exaggerated reactions to average doses as if they were toxic; *hyporeactivity,* or a lack of response to normal dosages; *paradoxical reactions* that are opposite to those expected; and *idiosyncratic reactions,* or unexpected, unpredictable responses unique to the individual.

For the same user on different occasions, two types of drug reactions deserve special mention. First, there is the phenomenon of *kindling.* With kindling, the user becomes increasingly sensitive to the drug (although such sensitivity may go unnoticed) until a reaction occurs. At least some cocaine-related cardiovascular collapses are believed to be the result of kindling.

The second form of repeated use variation is commonly referred to as *tolerance.* When used generically, tolerance refers to a decreased response to the same dose of a drug over time or an increase in dosage to achieve the same effect. Tolerance to different effects of a drug can develop at different rates (e.g., tolerance to narcotic nausea can occur without tolerance to the pinpoint pupils or miosis). There are three different ways in which tolerance to a drug can develop. *Pharmacodynamic* or *neurological* tolerance refers to the adaptation of the nervous system to the presence of a drug. *Dispositional* or *metabolic* tolerance is the ability of the body to more rapidly metabolize a drug. *Behavioral* or *learned* tolerance reflects an individual's ability to perform various activities with the drug in his or her system. Three special types of tolerance deserve mention. *Tachyphylaxis* is acute tolerance that occurs very rapidly, often in as little as one or two doses. *Cross-tolerance* refers to the fact that as tolerance to one drug develops, tolerance also develops to other drugs. Finally, *reverse tolerance* occurs when the user becomes increasingly sensitive to the drug so that lower dosages produce the same effects as higher dosages previously produced.

Withdrawal, when it occurs, generally reflects CNS adjustment to the absence of the drug after pharmacodynamic tolerance has occurred. When a drug is administered, it creates a biochemical imbalance in the CNS. To re-establish homeostasis within the CNS, neurological adaptation occurs. When the drug is no longer available, a biochemical imbalance recurs, and the CNS undergoes readaptation to compensate for the absence of the drug. The intensity and duration of the withdrawal process will depend on the same kinds of variables that influence the effects of the drug (pharmaceutical, physiological, psychological, and socioenvironmental).

CONCLUSION

This discussion has reviewed the pharmacological principles that influence a user's reactions to a drug. Pharmaceutical, physiological, psychological, and socioenvironmental factors were seen to be important in understanding a drug's effects on a user. As a result, readers should be more sensitive to the variations in drug-related behaviors evidenced by users. It follows that there is a continuum of drug-using behaviors whose two poles are nonuse and dependency, with use and abuse falling between. However, the presence of such a continuum does not imply that individuals will inevitably progress along this continuum.

Effective and efficient treatment of drug users should begin with a knowledge of how the behavior was initiated and what maintains it. An understanding of pharmacological principles as they apply to specific drugs is a necessary but not sufficient condition for working with this population.

Chapter 14

How Nicotine Works

Andrea G. Barthwell

PHARMACOLOGY OF NICOTINE

Nicotine, found in the plant *Nicotiana taabacum*, has significant medical importance because of its toxicity, presence in tobacco, and ability to cause dependence. The Surgeon General of the United States recently published an extensive review of scientific studies on abuse liability and physical dependence potential of tobacco and concluded, "The processes that determine tobacco addiction are similar to those that determine addiction to drugs such as heroin and cocaine" (Report of the Surgeon General, 1989). The comparison of nicotine with heroin and cocaine dependence is correct in most regards, particularly because the psychology of addiction is general to all the drugs in question.

The differences involve the relative absence of behavioral toxicity from nicotine and its potent toxicity to biologic tissue when smoked. For example, one can make fully informed decisions on complex matters or operate complex machinery while using nicotine-containing products; this is not the case, in their usual doses, with heroin and cocaine. Some evidence suggests that nicotine increases ability to concentrate, whereas heroin and cocaine impair major mental functions in dose-related fashion.

Nicotine acts on a variety of sites in the body and has both stimulant and depressant phases of action; its ultimate effects are the result of a variety of complex effects, sometimes in opposition. Those effects in the human model are a product of interaction among environmental conditions, the person's history of use (whether the use is acute, with no tolerance, or chronic, with tolerance to some effects), and behavioral factors. Nicotine and cotinine accumulate during the day and persist overnight. Acute and chronic tolerance develops in humans to the effects of nicotine (see the later section in this chapter on tolerance).

Nicotine acts on specific binding sites throughout the nervous system and has actions throughout the neuroendocrine system. Because nicotine alters the bioavailability of several active neuroregulators, evidence suggests that its self-administration allows the modification of affective states or cognitive demands in a reinforcing or rewarding way. The overall effect of nicotine is to give the user, to a remarkable degree, the effect the user seeks.

Nicotine markedly stimulates the central nervous system (CNS). It excites the central respiratory center, but stimulation is followed by depression, and death can result from a failure of respiration; nicotine induces a centrally stimulated vomiting response. Nicotine peripherally stimulates autonomic ganglia and causes the release of catecholamine in a number of isolated organs. It also stimulates a number of sensory receptors.

Nicotine administered intravenously to the dog causes an increase in heart rate and blood pressure. In the human gastrointestinal system it causes nausea, vomiting, and occasionally diarrhea.

Nicotine is readily absorbed from every site on or in the body, including the respiratory tract, buccal and nasal membranes, skin, and gastrointestinal tract (Benowitz, 1986). As a result, people use a variety of nicotine delivery systems, and these have varying pH because absorption is influenced by pH of the absorbing system. The most common way to use nicotine is to burn tobacco in cigarettes and thereby absorb it in the lungs. The alkaline smoke from cigars and pipes is better absorbed in the mouth. Nicotine in spit tobacco is also alkaline and absorbed in the mouth; because it is more slowly absorbed than inhaled nicotine, it has a longer duration of effect. Nicotine pilocrilex (commonly referred to as "nicotine gum") has nicotine embedded in it that is absorbed across the buccal mucosa. It is used for the treatment of withdrawal from nicotine in a nicotine cessation program. Nicotine is available as a 21-mg, 14-mg, or 7-mg patch, where it is absorbed across the skin. A nicotine nasal spray delivers the active ingredient, nicotine, to the nasal mucosa, where it is rapidly absorbed in the membrane.

When compared, the different routes of administration of nicotine vary in their ability to deliver nicotine to the user. As with other drugs, the route of administration or delivery of the nicotine is related to drug reinforcement and dependence potential. Cigarettes produce the most intense, quickest rise in venous nicotine levels. Those levels are slightly delayed with oral snuff or chewing tobacco and more markedly attenuated with nicotine gum (Gritz et al., 1981; Russell, Feyerabend, & Cole, 1976). Transdermal absorption is slowest (Rose, Jarvik, & Rose, 1984). Nicotine nasal spray shows a rapid onset of action mimicking that of smoked tobacco (Russell et al., 1983; West, Jarvik, Russell, & Feyerabend, 1984). A cigarette contains about 10 mg of nicotine; a smoker absorbs about 0 to 3 mg of nicotine from one cigarette, depending only upon how it is smoked. The arterial nicotine levels after a single cigarette are about 2 1/2 times the simultaneous venous nicotine level. The rapid movement of nicotine through the arterial side of the circulation to the site of desired action, the brain and its receptors, allows for a rapid rise and decay of the drug (nicotine) flooding those receptors, thus contributing to the "fingertip titration" of dose and instantaneous satisfaction of demand for the drug. This offers a high level of flexibility to the user in immediately adjusting his or her nicotine level. When faced with different brands and different nicotine levels in the cigarettes, smokers are able to extract a fairly consistent amount of nicotine from different cigarettes to maintain essentially the same nicotine and carbon monoxide blood levels (Benowitz & Jacob, 1984).

A user is cued into a variety of internal and external stimuli, including withdrawal, and will adjust his or her smoking to compensate for preloading with nicotine intravenously (Henningfield, Miyasoto, & Jasinski, 1983; Lucchesi, Schuster, & Emley, 1967), by oral capsule (Jarvik, Gulick, & Nakamura, 1970), or by nicotine gum (Ebert, McNabb, & Snow, 1984; Kozlowski, Jarvik, & Gritz, 1975; Nemeth-Coslett & Henningfield, 1986). Changes in nicotine content in a cigarette will also force changes in nicotine extraction from that cigarette or smoking behavior (Benowitz & Jacob, 1984). Thus addiction to nicotine is a complex compilation of the addiction to the chemical—nicotine, the behavior associated with its use—smoking with fingertip titration of dose versus snorting versus oral administration (dipping snuff), and the tobacco itself—the taste, the touch, the aroma, and so forth. It is easy to understand how everything in the external environment as well as the internal environment can get cued to nicotine use in the chronic user.

DISPOSITION OF NICOTINE

Approximately 80 to 90% of nicotine is biotransformed or metabolized in the liver to about 90% cotinine and 10% nicotine-1'-N-oxide (Benowitz, Porchet, & Jacob, 1989). Nicotine's half life is about 2 hours following inhalation or intravenous administration of the drug. Nicotine and its metabolites are rapidly excreted by the kidney because they are water soluble. Nicotine and its metabolites can also be found in breast milk of lactating women. Nicotine is cleared through the renal route faster when the pH of the urine is acidic (lower pH).

NICOTINE POISONING/OVERDOSE

Acute, severe poisoning with nicotine causes nausea, salivation, abdominal pain, vomiting, diarrhea, cold sweat, headache, dizziness, disturbed hearing and vision, mental confusion, and marked weakness. Death may occur from cardiovascular collapse (loss of blood pressure and regular contractions of the heart), convulsions, and/or respiratory failure.

NICOTINE AS A HEALTH HAZARD

The smoke generated from burning tobacco is a complex mixture of over 3,000 compounds in gaseous and particulate matter phases. Smoking behavior and technique, often called "smoking topography" or "puff behavior," is a major determinant of what is delivered to the smoker. It is possible to quantify the amount of nicotine, "tar," and carbon monoxide delivered by a particular brand of cigarette when it is smoked under constant conditions by a machine, but smokers, as discussed earlier, show great variability in how they smoke. The composition of the tobacco; how it is packed in the cigarette; what kind of filter is present, if any; and how often and how deeply one draws on the cigarette all affect the composition of the smoke from any given cigarette. The components of cigarette smoke most likely to contribute to the health hazards of smoking are carbon monoxide, nicotine, and "tar." Other components of smoke probably contribute to ill health effects as well.

The use of tobacco is the number one cause of preventable death and illness in the United States, responsible for over 400,000 deaths each year. Following a 30-month investigation, the first *Surgeon General's Statement on the Health Consequences of Smoking* was released in 1964 (Public Health Service, 1964). There have been 27 reports of the Surgeon General since. In the original Surgeon General's report, cigarette smoking was considered a form of "habituation," not a pharmacologic dependence or addiction. Today, tobacco cigarette smoking is the most common substance use disorder in the United States (Jarvik & Schneider, 1992).

The Surgeon General's 1964 report found that cigarettes are associated with a 70% increase in the age-specific death rates of men; cigarettes are causally related to lung cancer in men, and data suggest that this is also true for women; cigarettes are the most important cause of chronic bronchitis and probably emphysema; male cigarette smokers have a higher death rate from coronary artery disease than nonsmoking males; pipe smoking is causally related to lip cancer; cigarettes are a causal factor in laryngeal cancer; cigarettes are associated with esophageal and bladder cancer; women who smoke have low birthweight babies; cigarettes are epidemiologically associated with peptic ulcer disease; and the habitual use of tobacco is related to psychological and social drives, reinforced by the pharmacologic actions of nicotine.

More studies over time and reports of the Surgeon General have shown that chronic use of tobacco is causally linked to a variety of serious illnesses (Office on Smoking and Health Education, 1979, 1980, 1981, 1982, 1983, 1984). The likelihood of developing one of the diseases linked with smoking increases with the degree of exposure, which is related to the number of cigarettes smoked per day and the duration of the smoking. Cigar smoking and pipe smoking are associated with these same diseases in general, but the dose-related phenomena are not as robust, probably because less smoke, and therefore fewer constituents of smoke, are inhaled.

DISEASE STATES

The most serious diseases include cardiovascular diseases—coronary artery disease, cerebral vascular disease, and peripheral vascular disease; neoplastic diseases—of the lung, larynx, oral cavity, esophagus, bladder, and pancreas (responsible for regulation of sugar and some digestion); respiratory diseases—emphysema or chronic obstructive pulmonary disease; and reproductive problems—reduction in fertility, increase in premature rupture of the membranes, *abruptio placenta*, spontaneous abortion, reduction in infant birth weight, increases in likelihood of perinatal mortality and sudden death of infants, and, finally, increased risk of acute and chronic respiratory illnesses in children exposed to passive smoke.

If smoking is interrupted, the risk of development of a disease, in general, falls off over time (Department of Health and Human Services, 1990). For most disease, the risk falls off over 5 to 10 years to near the nonsmokers' risk. The lung tissue affected by the smoke cannot regenerate itself, but the continuous decline in function may be arrested if smoking cessation occurs.

TOLERANCE

Tolerance seems to develop to some of the effects of nicotine, though some argue that changes seen following cessation of use are a release of nicotine effect rather than a phenomenon of true tolerance. Chronic treatment with nicotine is accompanied by an increase in the number of nicotinic receptors and results in a chronic desensitization of nicotine receptors (Schwartz & Kellar, 1985); therefore at least metabolic tolerance occurs. Tolerance develops to the effects of most drugs at differential rates, depending upon the site of action of the effect. Thus tolerance to the dizziness, nausea, and vomiting experienced by the nonsmoker occurs with chronic use; however, even the chronic smoker can exhibit increases in blood pressure or heart rate following one or two cigarettes. Smokers tend to metabolize nicotine more rapidly than nonsmokers.

In one study, people with and without histories of drug abuse were given opportunities to self-administer nicotine or saline intravenously. The patterns of lever pressing for the nicotine were similar to those observed for other common reinforcers, such as food or money. At the end of the session, the subjects reported "liking" the nicotine, despite nausea and dysphoria. Two subjects without histories of illicit drug use showed gradual increases in the number of injections self-administered over the course of the seven test sessions (Henningfield et al., 1983). In the nonlaboratory setting, the smoker notes that the first cigarette of the day is able to produce a much greater subjective response than subsequent cigarettes. Most people are not aware of their tolerance, but they are usually aware of their withdrawal.

WITHDRAWAL

Withdrawal can be defined as a set of signs and symptoms that occur together when the drug is abruptly discontinued. The withdrawal or abstinence syndrome can be simply described as adverse physiological (or physical) consequences to drug use cessation, or in some instances, drug use reduction. According to Jarvik and Schneider (1992), "reports of withdrawal from tobacco smoking appeared in the Larson and Silvette studies of the 1960s and 1970s" (p. 335). Nicotine withdrawal, which is rapid in onset, appearing within 24 hours of cessation of drug use, can be characterized by "craving" for the drug, irritability, impatience, agitation, anxiety, restlessness, difficulty in concentration, confusion, lethargy, mood swings, and insomnia. Sometimes drowsiness, headaches and increased appetite are a part of the picture (Cummings, Giovino, Jean & Enrich, 1985; Department of Health and Human Services, 1988; Gilbert & Pope, 1982; Gritz, Carr & Marcus, 1991; Gritz & Jarvik, 1973; Hatsukami, Hughes, Pickens, & Svikis, 1984; Hughes & Hatsukami, 1986; Shiffman & Jarvik, 1976; Schneider, 1986). The withdrawal syndrome varies in intensity from individual to individual. It is not clear what causes the variation, but it is commonly noted across other substances that this variability occurs in both subjective and objective symptomatology. Some of the variability can be explained in terms of the size of dose and duration of exposure and timing since last dose, but not all.

During acute withdrawal from nicotine, the withdrawal symptoms become the dominant cues for smoking, in contrast to the role of environmental and internal cues that sustain use. Nicotine substitution products can offer significant help in the control of the strength and frequency of withdrawal symptoms. This withdrawal control only supervenes when the usual environmental and internal cues are not heeded and behavioral control is in place. Thus integration of treatment components for each level of control (behavioral and physiologic) is needed to avoid resumption of smoking or use of other nicotine-containing tobacco products for a successful smoking cessation program.

TREATMENT RATIONALE

Approximately 90% of those who smoke use more than five (5) cigarettes per day and can be considered dependent upon nicotine (Shiffman, Fischer, Settler-Segal, & Benowitz, 1990). Thirty percent of the population of the United States uses tobacco products, down from 37% in the 1970s. The co-occurrence of cigarettes with alcohol is particularly common: 85% of alcoholics smoke cigarettes, and the overall prevalence rate of alcoholism is 16% in the general population (Miller & Cocores, 1991). The number of smokeless tobacco users is estimated at 12 million. The use of tobacco by females, particularly young females, both in the industrialized West and in the Third World, is of great public health concern. In 1980, among high school seniors in the United States, more females than males smoked cigarettes on a daily basis, a finding that has remained stable through the decade of the eighties. In recent years, general rates of tobacco use are declining, but the decline is much less in females. The gender gap has been replaced by an education gap, in that lower socioeconomic status is associated increasingly with smoking, and a color gap, in that more racial and ethnic minorities commence smoking—both in the United States and world wide.

The primary indication for treating nicotine dependence is the fact that smoking and use of other nicotine delivery systems are associated with more overall morbidity and mortality than any other single drug, including alcohol. There have been 6 million deaths attributable to smoking since 1964 (Report of the Surgeon General, 1989). In the United States on any given day, there are approximately 15 to 25 drug-related deaths associated with use of cocaine, heroin, and PCP; some 350 to 400 deaths associated with alcohol; and over 1,000 deaths associated with nicotine (Centers for Disease Control, 1985; National Center for Health Statistics, 1990; Office on Smoking and Health Education, 1986). An estimated 53,000 people die each year due to passive inhalation of others' smoke (Benowitz, Porchet, Sheiner, & Jacob, 1988b; Henningfield et al., 1983; Perkins, Epstein, Marks, Stiller, & Jacob, 1989). Yet our national strategy against drug abuse is only focused on illegal drug abuse. Treatment can be viewed as having one or more of the following goals: (a) treating withdrawal from nicotine; (b) enabling decreased use of nicotine containing products; (c) preventing relapse to nicotine or prolonging abstinence from nicotine; and (d) reversing chronic toxic effects of nicotine and other constituents of nicotine delivery systems. Safe levels of tobacco use have not been established, nor are there safe levels of nicotine use, as one might get from the use of a nicotine patch or "nicotine gum." Although some of the morbidity and mortality associated with the use of tobacco comes from the nicotine, nicotine substitution therapies have become a promising cornerstone of the pharmacotherapies in use or development for the treatment of nicotine dependence. The decision to use or not use has to be made with a consideration of the risk of continued use and risk from the nicotine alone versus benefits derived from the cessation of the smoking, chewing, "dipping" and other behaviors. Additionally, one needs to consider that the newer nicotine delivery systems have fewer associated potential carcinogens and "problem" chemicals (e.g., "tar," carbon monoxide, etc.) than do nicotine-containing tobacco-based products.

Most treatment centers and professionals do not have experience in treating patients with nicotine dependence, though this is changing. However, for those not actively involved in the treatment of nicotine dependence, a minimal investment in getting the education one needs to provide some treatment can offer a significant payoff. In 1979, it was estimated that 90% of all U.S. smokers wanted to stop but could not (Office on Smoking and Health Education, 1979). For those using organized treatment clinics or specialized techniques, the failure rates can be as high as 70-80% for most therapies at 1 year (Schwartz, 1987).

One set of patients will do well with almost any withdrawal technique used, but unless they make the initial attempt, they will continue to use nicotine-containing tobacco products. A second set of patients appear to be refractory to every technique, although they may, following a treatment episode, reduce the amount of nicotine-containing tobacco products used for a substantial period. Some may eliminate its use for a period of time, then relapse. Finally, a different set of individuals or a subset of the first two will respond to a number of different treatment techniques in series (e.g., hypnosis followed by acupuncture followed by group therapy) or parallel (e.g., nicotine replacement pharmacotherapy with behavior modification therapy with "talk therapy" with group support, all commencing on the "Great American Smoke Out") or both. There may be some cumulative or synergistic effect from the multiple, ongoing efforts at abstinence, such that the penultimate therapy gets credit for working, when in fact, the process was contributory in a significant way. In fact, a review of treatments for nicotine dependence (Kottke et al., 1988) indicates that using multiple intervention is superior to any one intervention alone. This analysis also indicates that there is a dose effect: the more sessions per intervention (e.g., face-to-face counseling, nicotine gum, relapse prevention training) the better. This is the closest we get to really assisting our clients in smoking cessation because currently the appropriate pharmacologic behavior or combination treatment for any given smoker is not known and patients surprise us by being exceptions more often than not.

SMOKING CESSATION

Pharmacologic Treatments

Treatment can consist of the pharmacologic—aimed at the nicotine dependence, withdrawal, and craving—or the behavioral—aimed at the overlearned habit of smoking. With either approach or both combined with equal or greater focus on one technology or the other, the emphasis must also be on long-term maintenance of efforts at abstinence.

Pharmacologic treatments can be replacement/agonists, to replicate or continue the effects of nicotine; antagonists, to block the effects of nicotine, eliminating the return of use; symptomatic, to reduce the objective and subjective complaints of withdrawal without using a cross-tolerant drug; and deterrent, to make the use of nicotine unpalatable or worse (Kottke et al., 1988).

Nicotine Replacement Systems

Nicotine replacement systems are designed to systematically reduce nicotine over time. They vary in their ability to achieve peak level ("fast-acting" nicotine nasal spray or nicotine pilocrilex versus the slow, steady-state nicotine patch system) and to relieve withdrawal and craving. Rapid delivery more closely mimics cigarette smoking; slower delivery produces more gradual reduction in nicotine blood level and better tolerated withdrawal (peak intensity). All systems, with the exception of inhalers, which are "fast acting," unlink smoking behaviors.

Nicotine pilocrilex (nicotine gum) is available in the United States in a 2-mg dose. Fagerstrom's (1988) summary of nicotine gum studies shows consistent findings that although nicotine gum is better than placebo, nicotine treatment with behavior therapy is better than either alone. There have been good results reported in research trials with nicotine gum (Fagerstrom, 1982, 1984, 1988; Fagerstrom & Schneider, 1988; Hughes, Gust, Keenan, Fenwick, & Healey, 1989; Jarvik, Raw, Russell, & Feyerabend, 1982; Russell, Merriman, Stapleton, & Taylor, 1983; Sachs & Leischow, 1991; Schneider et al., 1983; Tonnesen, 1988; Tonnesen et al., 1988a, 1988b); however, there are some problems associated with its use. These include problems at the physician level (failure to prescribe correctly or prescribing to unmotivated patients, underdosing, and/or failure to provide adequate instructions regarding use) and problems in patient compliance (failure to use it properly, failure in absorption or reduced absorption from concomitant coffee or carbonated liquid use and/or access variables [self-purchases versus provided gum]).

The nicotine-containing patch was designed to decrease the withdrawal symptoms resulting from smoking cessation while addressing some of the compliance issues resulting from nicotine pilocrilex use (Transdermal Nicotine Study Group, 1991). Though there are some differences among the patches currently available on the market, they have in common an ability to produce their effect by slow release of nicotine through the skin. The advantages of the patch are (a) its "user-friendly" nature in that it requires no attention after application; (b) the ability to produce a steady-state nicotine level, thus providing relief from withdrawal and craving, versus the variable, "peak-trough," levels achieved with nicotine pilocrilex; (c) the absence of "reinforcing peaks" (Russell & Feyerabend, 1978); (d) the lack of the side effects associated with the pilocrilex; (e) possible use when gum is contraindicated; and (f) physicians' willingness to prescribe. The limitations are in the long time needed to reach peak effective plasma levels and inflexible dosing, except for choice of the strength of the patch. There can be no "fingertip" titration of dose to respond to a crisis, so the patch lacks a perceived immediacy of response.

Though the nicotine patches have only recently been available for broad clinical application, a body of research data exists regarding their efficacy (Tonnesen, Norregaard, Simonsen, & Sawe, 1991). Most clinical trials have shown that nicotine patches are more effective than placebo patches for 6 months or longer, ranging from 22 to 42% versus 2 to 28% at 6 months (Abelin, Buehler, Muller, Vesanen, & Inhof, 1989; Daughton et al., 1991; Hurt, Lauger, Offord, Kotte, & Dale, 1990; Tonnesen et al., 1991; Transdermal Nicotine Study Group, 1991). There is a decline in efficacy after patch cessation that is similar to other treatments (Abelin et al., 1989; Daughton et al., 1991; Hurt et al., 1990; Tonnenen et al., 1991; Transdermal Nicotine Study Group, 1991). In general, success rates are better than for placebo within the early phases of treatment. The lack of long-term efficacy may reflect the lack of relapse prevention strategies.

Nicotine nasal spray (NNS) and nicotine inhalers give a rapid rise response. NNS offers speed and delivery of reinforcement with the ability to self-administer at any point in quitting. The nicotine inhalers, in various stages of development, are promising because they too offer one an intense physical dependency speed of onset, sense of control, and sensory feedback. Both forms, NNS and inhalers, probably have a high potential for dependency. However, these forms and the pilocrilex and patches all deliver nicotine without the tar and other burned particulate matter in inhaled smoke.

Other Pharmacologic Agents

Glassman, Jackson, Walsh, Roose, & Rosenfeld (1984) and Glassman et al. (1988) report an interesting comparison among clonidine, alprazolam, and placebo on the nicotine withdrawal syndrome. Both alprazolam and clonidine reduced many of the symptoms of the withdrawal syndrome, but only clonidine reduced craving. There are inconsistent findings with clonidine.

One common withdrawal complaint is anxiety. Buspirone has shown promise in small open trials (Gawin, Comptom, & Byck, 1989; Robinson, Smith, Cederstrom, & Sutherland, 1991; West, Hajck, & McNeill, in press). Meprobamate and benzodiazepines have received attention in the past (Gritz & Jarvik, 1977).

Depression is an issue in smoking cessation and antidepressants are under study (Edwards, Simmons, Rosenthal, Hoon, & Downs, 1988; Naranjo, Kadlec, Sanhueza, Woodley-Remus, & Sellers, 1990; Wilcox, 1990). The use of pharmacologic agents other than nicotine chewing gum is in an early phase of development, and their use should be confined to controlled studies until we appreciate fully the possible risks and benefits involved.

Behavioral/Nonpharmacological Treatments

Behavior modification techniques such as desensitization, the attempt to release smoking from the control of stressful stimuli; sensitization, the exposure to noxious concentrations of smoke; and contingency contracting, a procedure in which the client agrees to some negative consequences if abstinence is not both achieved and maintained, are being employed increasingly in the treatment of nicotine dependence.

Smoking Cessation at the Doctor's Office

Hurt et al. (1992) propose a comprehensive model for the treatment of nicotine dependence in the medical office. If the physician is in a primary treatment program, a program can be constructed, including a schedule of meetings with the patient. A "quit" date needs to be set, with the patient identifying a time of low life stress. A plan to control weight should be developed, and a program of contacts extending over 1 year or more should be established. The need for nicotine replacement therapy should be assessed. The patient's family may be involved, and breath monitoring for carbon monoxide levels may be employed.

A good patient–service setting match is important to treatment outcomes for all drugs of dependence (Barthwell & Gastfriend, 1992). Because the quit success is dependent upon a complex interaction between physical factors (degree of dependence, withdrawal, etc.) and behavioral factors (response to environmental and internal cues), the program should employ an evaluation of the contribution of both or either element. Fagerstrom's Tolerance Questionnaire (Fagerstrom & Schneider, 1989; Heatherton, Kozlowski, Frecker, & Fagerstrom, 1991; Stolerman, Bunker, & Jarvik, 1974) is a commonly used subjective measure of nicotine withdrawal. Fagerstrom feels that nicotine gum may be more effective in smokers who have a high degree of physical dependence as measured by the questionnaire.

REFERENCES

Abelin, T., Buehler, A., Muller, P., Vasanen, K., & Inhof, P. (1989). Controlled trial of transdermal nicotine patch in tobacco withdrawal. *Lancet, 1,* 7–10.

Barthwell, A., & Gastfriend, D. (1992). Treating multiple substance abuse. In M. Parrino (Ed.), *State methadone maintenance treatment guidelines* (pp. 151–170). Rockville, MD: Center for Substance Abuse Treatment.

Benowitz, N. (1986). Clinical pharmacology of nicotine. *Annual Review of Medicine, 37,* 21–32.

Benowitz, N., & Jacob, P. (1984). Nicotine and carbon monoxide intake from high- and low-yield cigarettes. *Clinical Pharmacology Therapy, 36,* 265–270.

Benowitz, N., Porchet, H., & Jacob, P. (1989). Nicotine dependence and tolerance in man: Pharmacokinetic and pharmacodynamic investigations. *Progress in Brain Research, 79,* 279–287.

Benowitz, N., Porchet, H., Sheiner, L., & Jacob, P. (1988a). Intake from high- and low-yield cigarettes. *Clinical Pharmacology Therapy, 37*, 21–32.

Benowitz, N., Porchet, H., Sheiner, L., & Jacob, P. (1988b). Nicotine absorption and cardiovascular effects with smokeless tobacco use: Comparison with cigarettes and nicotine gum. *Clinical Pharmacology Therapy, 44*, 23–28.

Centers for Disease Control. (1985). State-specific estimates of smoking-attributable mortality and years of potiential life lost—United States. *Morbidity and Mortality Weekly Report (MMWR), 37*, 689–693.

Cummings, K., Giovino, G., Jean, C., & Enrich, L. (1985). Reports of smoking withdrawal symptoms over a 21-day period of abstinence. *Addictive Behaviors, 10*, 373–381.

Daughton, D.M., Heatley, S.A., Prendergast, J., Causey, D., Knowles, M., Rolf, C.N., Cheney, R.A., Hattelid, K., Thompson, A.B., & Renard, S.I. (1991). Effect of transdermal nicotine delivery as an adjunct to low-intervention smoking cessation therapy: A randomized, placebo-controlled, double-blind study. *Archives of Internal Medicine, 151*, 749–752.

Department of Health and Human Services. (1988). *The health consequences of smoking: A report of the Surgeon General.* Washington, DC: U.S. Government Printing Office.

Department of Health and Human Services. (1990). *The health benefits of smoking cessation: A report of the Surgeon General.* Washington, D.C.: U.S. Government Printing Office.

Ebert, R., McNabb, M., & Snow, S. (1984). Effect of nicotine chewing gum on plasma nicotine levels of cigarette smokers. *Clinical Pharmacology Therapy, 35*, 495–498.

Edwards, H., Simmons, R., Rosenthal, T., Hoon, P., & Downs, J. (1988). Doxepin in the treatment of nicotine withdrawal. *Psychosomatics, 29*, 203–206.

Fagerstrom, K. (1982). A comparison of psychological and pharmacological treatment in smoking cessation. *Journal of Behavioral Medicine, 5*, 343–351.

Fagerstrom, K. (1984). Effects of nicotine chewing gum and follow-up appointments in physician-based smoking cessation. *Preventive Medicine, 13*, 517–527.

Fagerstrom, K. (1988). Efficacy of nicotine chewing gum: A review. In O. Pomerleau & C. Pomerleau (Eds.), *Nicotine replacement in the treatment of smoking* (pp. 109–128). New York: Alan R. Liss.

Fagerstrom, K., & Schneider, N. (1989). Measuring nicotine dependence in tobacco smoking: A review of the Fagerstrom tolerance questionnnaire. *Journal of Behavioral Medicine, 12*, 159–182.

Gawin, F., Comptom, M., & Byck, R. (1989). Buspirone reduces smoking. *Archives of General Psychiatry, 46*, 288–289.

Gilbert, R., & Pope, M. (1982). Early effects of quitting smoking. *Psychopharmacology, 78*, 121–127.

Glassman, A., Jackson, N., Walsh, T., Roose, R., & Rosenfeld, B. (1984). Cigarette craving, smoking withdrawal, and clonidine. *Science, 226*, 864–866.

Glassman, A., Stetner, M.S., Walsh, B.T., Covey, L., & Raizman, L. (1988). Heavy smokers, smokers cessation and clonidine. *Journal of the American Medical Association, 260*(11), 1553.

Gritz, E., Baer-Weiss, V., Benowitz, N., et al. (1981). Plasma nicotine and cotinine concentrations in habitual smokeless tobacco users. *Clinical Pharmacology Therapy, 30*, 201–209.

Gritz, E., Carr, C., & Marcus, A. (1991). The tobacco withdrawal syndrome in unaided quitters. *British Journal of Addiction, 86*, 57–69.

Gritz, E..,& Jarvik, M. (1973). Preliminary study: Forty-eight hours of abstinence from smoking. *Proceedings of the 81st Annual Convention of the American Psychological Association*, 1039–1040.

Gritz, E..,& Jarvik, M. (1977). Pharmacological aids for the cessation of smoking. In J. Steinfeld, W. Griffiths, K. Ball, & R. Taylor (Eds.), *Proceedings of the Third World Conference on Smoking and Health* (pp. 575–591). Washington, DC: U.S. Department of Health, Education & Welfare, Public Health Service.

Hatsukami, D., Hughes, J., Pickens, R., & Svikis, D. (1984). Tobacco withdrawal symptoms: An experimental analysis. *Psychopharmacology, 84*, 231–236.

Heatherton, T., Kozlowski, L., Frecker, R., & Fagerstrom, K. (September 1991). The Fagerstrom test for nicotine dependence: A revision of the Fagerstrom tolerance questionnaire. *British Journal of Addiction, 86*, 1119–1127.

Henningfield, J., Miyasoto, K., & Jasinski, D. (1983). Cigarette smokers self-administer intravenous nicotine. *Pharmacology, Biochemistry Behavior, 19*, 887–890.

Hughes, J., Gust, S., Keenan, R., Fenwick, J., & Healey, M. (1989). Nicotine vs. placebo gum in general medical practice. *Journal of the American Medical Association, 261*, 1300–1305.

Hughes, J., & Hatsukami, D. (1986). Signs and symptoms of tobacco withdrawal. *Archives of General Psychiatry, 43*, 289–294.

Hurt, R., Dale, L., McClain, F., et al. (1992). A comprehensive model for the treatment of nicotine dependence in a medical setting. *Medical Clinics of North America, 76*, 495–514.

Hurt, R., Lauger, G., Offord, K., Kotte, T., & Dale, L. (1990). Nicotine-replacement therapy with use of a transdermal nicotine patch: A randomized double-blind placebo-controlled trial. *Mayo Clinic Proceedings, 65*, 1529–1537.

Jarvik, M., Gulick, S., & Nakamura, R. (1970). Inhibition of cigarette smoking by orally administered nicotine. *Clinical Pharmacology Therapy, 11*, 574–576.

Jarvik, M., Raw, M., Russell, M., & Feyerabend, C. (1982). Randomized controlled trial of nicotine chewing-gum. *British Medical Journal, 285*, 537–540.

Jarvik, M., & Schneider, N. (1992). Nicotine. In J. Lowinson & R. Millman (Eds.), *Substance abuse; A comprehensive textbook* (pp. 334–356). Baltimore: Williams & Wilkins.

Kottke, T., Battista, R., DeFriese, G., & Brekke, M.L. (1988). Attributes of successful smoking cessation interventions in medical practice: A meta-analysis of 39 controlled trials. *Journal of the American Medical Association, 259*, 2883–2889.

Kozlowski, L., Jarvik, M., & Gritz, E. (1975). Nicotine regulation and cigarette smoking. *Clinical Pharmacology Therapy, 17*, 93–97.

Lucchesi, B., Schuster, C., & Emley, G. (1967). The role of nicotine as a determinant of cigarette smoking frequency in man with observations of certain cardiovascular effects associated with the tobacco alkaloid. *Clinical Pharmacology Therapy, 8*, 789–796.

Miller, N., & Cocores, J. (1991). Nicotine dependence: Diagnosis, pharmacology and treatment. *Journal of Addictive Diseases, 2*, 51–65.

Naranjo, C., Kadlec, K., Sanhueza, P., Woodley-Remus, D., & Sellers, E. (1990). Fluoxetine differentially alters alcohol intake and other consummatory behaviors in problem drinkers. *Clinical Pharmacology Therapy, 47*, 490–498.

National Center for Health Statistics. (1990). *Annual summary of births, marriages, divorces and deaths, United States, 1989: Monthly Vital Statistics Report.* Washington, DC: U.S. Government Printing Office. (DHHS Publication No. PHS 90-1120).

Nemeth-Coslett, R., & Henningfield, J. (1986). Effects of nicotine chewing gum on cigarette smoking and subjective and physiologic effects. *Clinical Pharmacology Therapy, 39*, 625–630.

Office on Smoking and Health Education. (1979). *Smoking and health: A report of the Surgeon General.* Washington, DC: U.S. Government Printing Office (DHEW Publication No. PHS 79-50066).

Office on Smoking and Health Education. (1980). *The health consequences of smoking for women: A report of the Surgeon General.* Washington, DC: U.S. Department of Health Education and Welfare, Public Health Service.

Office on Smoking and Health Education. (1981). *The health consequences of smoking: The changing cigarette: A report of the Surgeon General,* Washington, DC: U.S. Department of Health Education and Welfare, Public Health Service. (DHEW Publication No. PHS 81-50179).

Office on Smoking and Health Education. (1982). *The health consequences of smoking: Cancer: A report of the Surgeon General.* Washington, DC: U.S. Department of Health Education and Welfare, Public Health Service. (DHEW Publication No. PHS 82-50179).

Office on Smoking and Health Education. (1983). *The health consequences of smoking: Cardiovascular disease: A report of the Surgeon General.* Washington, DC: U.S. Department of Health Education and Welfare, Public Health Service. (DHEW Publication No. PHS 84-50204).

Office on Smoking and Health Education. (1984). *The health consequences of smoking: Chronic obstructive lung disease: A report of the Surgeon General.* Washington, DC: U.S. Department of Health Education and Welfare, Public Health Service. (DHEW Publication No. PHS 84-50205).

Office on Smoking and Health Education. (1986). *Reducing the health consequences of smoking: A report of the Surgeon General.* Washington, DC: U.S. Department of Health Education and Welfare, Public Health Service. (DHEW Publication No. CDC 87-8398).

Perkins, K., Epstein, L., Marks, B., Stiller, R., & Jacob, R. (1989). The effect of nicotine on energy expenditures during light physical activity. *New England Journal of Medicine, 320,* 898–903.

Public Health Service. (1964). *Smoking and health: Report of the Advisory Committee to the Surgeon General of the Public Health Service.* Washington, DC: U.S. Government Printing Office. (DHHS Publication No. PHS 1103).

Report of the Surgeon General. (1989). *Reducing the health consequences of smoking: 25 years of progress.* Washington, DC: U.S. Department of Health and Human Services. (DHHS Publication No. CDC 89-8411).

Robinson, M., Smith, W., Cederstrom, E., & Sutherland, D. (1991). Buspirone's effect on tobacco withdrawal symptoms: A pilot study. *Journal of the American Board of Family Practitioners, 4,* 89–94.

Rose, J., Jarvik, M., & Rose, K. (1984). Transdermal administration of nicotine. *Drug and Alcohol Dependence, 13,* 209–213.

Russell, M., & Feyerabend, C. (1978). Cigarette smoking: A dependence on high nicotine level. *Bol: Drug Metabolism Review, 8,* 29–57.

Russell, M., Feyerabend, C., & Cole, P. (1976). Plasma nicotine levels after cigarette smoking and chewing nicotine gum. *British Journal of Medicine, 1,* 1043–1046.

Russell, M., Jarvik, M., Feyerabend, C., & Ferno, O. (1983). Nasal nicotine solution: A potential aid to giving up smoking? *British Journal of Medicine, 286,* 683–684.

Russell, M., Merriman, R., Stapleton, J., & Taylor, W. (1983). Effect of nicotine chewing gum as an adjunct to general practitioners' advice against smoking. *British Journal of Medicine, 287,* 1782–1785.

Sachs, D., & Leischow, S. (December 1991). Pharmacological approaches to smoking cessation. In *Clinics in chest medicine.* (769–791). Vol. 12, No. 4. Philadelphia: Harcourt-Brace.

Schneider, N. (1986). Use of 2mg and 4mg nicotine gum in an individualized treatment trial. In J. Ockene et al. (Eds.), *The pharmacologic treatment of tobacco dependence: Proceedings of the World Congress, November 4-5, 1985* (pp. 233–248). Cambridge, MA: Institute for the Study of Smoking Behavior and Policy.

Schneider, N., Jarvik, M., Forsythe, A., Read, L., Elliott, M., & Schweiger, A. (1983). Nicotine gum in smoking cessation: A placebo-controlled, double-blind trial. *Addictive Behavior, 8,* 256–261.

Schwartz, J. (1987). *Review and evaluation of smoking cessation methods: The United States and Canada.* U.S. Department of Health and Human Services, Public Health Services, National Institutes of Health, Washington, DC: Government Printing Office.

Schwartz, R., & Kellar, K. (1985). In vivo regulation of [3H] acetylcholine recognition sites in brain by nicotinic cholinergic drug. *Journal of Neurochemistry, 45,* 427–433.

Shiffman, S., Fischer, L., Settler-Segal, M., & Benowitz, N. (1990). Nicotine exposure among non-dependent smokers. *Archives of General Psychiatry, 47,* 333–336.

Shiffman, S., & Jarvik, M. (1976). Smoking withdrawal symptoms in two weeks of abstinence. *Psychopharmacology, 50,* 35–39.

Stolerman, I., Bunker, P., & Jarvik, M. (1974). Nicotine tolerance in rats: Role of dose and dose interval. *Psychopharmacologia, 34,* 317–324.

Tonnesen, P. (1988). Dose and nicotine dependence as determinants of nicotine gum efficacy. In O. Pomerleau & C. Pomerleau (Eds.), *Nicotine replacement: A critical evaluation* (pp. 129–144). New York: Alan R. Liss.

Tonnesen, P., Fryde, V., Hansen, M., Helsted, J., Gunnerson, A.B., Forchammer, H., & Stochne, M. (1988a). Effect of nicotine chewing gum in combination with group counseling on the cessation of smoking. *New England Journal of Medicine, 318,* 15–18.

Tonnesen, P., Fryde, F., Hansen, M., Helsted, J., Gunnerson, A.B., Forchammer, H., & Stochne, M. (1988b). Two and four mg nicotine chewing gum and group counseling in smoking cessation: An open, randomized, controlled trial with a 22-month follow-up. *Addictive Behavior, 13,* 17–27.

Tonnesen, P., Norregaard, J., Simonsen, K., & Sawe, U. (1991). A double-blind trial of a 16-hour transdermal nicotine patch in smoking cessation. *New England Journal of Medicine, 325,* 311–315.

Transdermal Nicotine Study Group. (1991). Transdermal nicotine for smoking cessation. *Journal of the American Medical Association, 266,* 3133–3138.

West, R., Hajck, P., & McNeill, A. (in press). Effect of buspirone on cigarette withdrawal symptoms and short-term abstinence rates in a smokers clinic. *Psychopharmacology.*

West, R., Jarvik, M., Russell, M., & Feyerabend, C. (1984). Plasma nicotine concentration from repeated doses of nasal nicotine solution. *British Journal of Addiction, 79,* 433–445.

Wilcox, J. (1990). Fluoxetine and obsessive-compulsive disorder: A naturalistic study. *Journal of Psychoactive Drugs, 22,* 355–356.

Part IV

Families and Addictions

Chapter 15

Family Therapy and Addictions

Ann W. Lawson

The field of addictions is one with more questions than answers. It is ever evolving with its theories of etiology and treatment. The moral weakness theory was put aside by Jellenick's writing on the disease concept of alcoholism. But the biggest shift in thinking came with the powerful adult children of alcoholics movement of the 1980s. This forced the field to look at addictions from a family model—an intergenerational family model. One certainty exists in the field: addictions run in families. Some are plagued with generations of addictions whereas others are spared altogether. In a review of 39 studies, Cotton (1979) found that regardless of the population studied, an alcoholic was more likely than a nonalcoholic to have a father, mother, or more distant relative who was an alcoholic. Since the discovery of this family phenomenon, researchers have debated the nature versus nurture controversy. Is alcoholism or any addiction biologically inherited or a product of the disrupted family environment? This debate will probably never be settled because for each alcoholic or addict there may be a unique combination of these etiological risk factors. From a family therapy perspective, the important point is that the environmental factors can be modified or changed. Quality of sobriety for families can be enhanced and the risk of intergenerational transmission of alcoholism can be reduced through family intervention.

HISTORY OF THE FAMILY MOVEMENT

The beginning of the paradigm shift to interpersonal ideas about alcoholism began in the 1950s. Whalen (1953) observed four types of wives of alcoholics: the sufferer, who needs to punish herself by living with an alcoholic; the controller, who tries to change her mate; the waverer, who needs to be needed and is fearful and insecure yet competent, and the punisher, who demonstrates her superiority to her mate and drives him to drink. This attempt to understand why women lived with alcoholic men was a beginning of looking at relationships instead of individuals in the treatment of alcoholism. Ironically, the field has returned to studying and treating these "codependent" women—unfortunately, often from an individual model.

Source: Copyright © Ann W. Lawson, 1994.

Family adjustment to the crisis of alcoholism was studied by Jackson (1954), who described seven critical stages in the cumulative family crisis. These early works were concerned with how the family members reacted to the alcoholic as opposed to a systems theory of how alcoholism was developed and maintained by the family system. The field has grown exponentially from these early beginnings. From the idea that alcoholism/addiction is a family illness sprang the idea that children of alcoholics were a high-risk group. The massive adult children of alcoholics movement soon followed, with the creation of self-help groups designed especially for this population. In 1979 one book had been published that was primarily concerned with the alcoholic/addict family system: *Family Therapy of Drug and Alcohol Abuse* (Kaufman & Kaufmann, 1979). Today there are many professional books concerning the alcoholic family system. On the popular scene, entire sections in bookstores are dedicated to family issues of addiction and recovery. The Public Broadcasting System (PBS) has made information about the alcoholic family system available to the public through the John Bradshaw programs.

Because the family plays a part in the etiology, perpetuation, and treatment of addictions, this chapter will address each area. It will further track the family systems model of addiction from its early beginnings of reporting family members' reactions to alcoholics and their rigid role behaviors in response to the alcoholism, through the theory-building work of systems theorists, to the description of the alcoholic family system and the intergenerational transmission of alcoholism, and finally to the clinical application of family systems therapy to the alcoholic family system. The effectiveness and prevalence of family systems treatment with addicted populations will be reviewed, including an analysis of why there is resistance to this treatment and prevention method.

Introduction to Familial Alcoholism

It is common knowledge that alcoholism tends to run in families. Every study of familial alcoholism has reported a higher rate of alcoholism among relatives of alcoholics than among the general population (Goodwin, 1971). When studying alcoholics in treatment, Winokur and Clayton (1968) found that 28% of the women alcoholics had alcoholic fathers and 12% had alcoholic mothers. The men receiving treatment for alcoholism reported that 21% of their fathers and 3% of their mothers were alcoholics.

Cotton (1979) reviewed 39 studies of the incidence of familial alcoholism and summarized the alcoholism rates of parents, grandparents, siblings, and children of 6,251 alcoholics and 4,083 nonalcoholics in these studies. She found that regardless of the population studied, an alcoholic was more likely to have a father, mother, or more distant relative who was an alcoholic than the nonalcoholic comparisons. Two-thirds of the studies found that at least 25% of the alcoholics had fathers who were alcoholics and that the range was 2.5% to 50%. In a later study, Schuckit (1983) discovered that when sources other than the patient were questioned and second-degree relatives were included, only 30% of those hospitalized did not have a family history of alcoholism. In summary, one of the few certainties in the field of substance abuse is that alcoholism has a family connection. It is far more prevalent in some families than in others. The question is: What is the etiological process that maintains alcoholism and other addictions from generation to generation in some families, whereas in others it is absent?

Although these studies support the idea that alcoholism runs in families, they do not answer the important question of whether it is nature or nurture that produces this familial transmission. Because alcoholism does not follow an exact Mendelian mode of inheritance, it is difficult to separate heredity from environment in the etiology of alcoholism. When studying families, environmental and genetic factors are both produced by the parents, making it difficult to separate these influences. The environmental influences, however, are the most important to family therapists because these are areas that can be targeted for prevention and treatment efforts. These environmental influences can be seen in the research with children of alcoholics, alcoholic families versus nonalcoholic families, and intergenerational transmission of addictions.

Psychosocial Influences on Familial Alcoholism

Many of the studies that look at the environmental aspects of the transmission of alcoholism from generation to generation focus on the children who are living with an alcoholic parent or adults who grew up in alcoholic families. An important question of these studies is, how does this environment affect the children, and why are some affected more than others?

There are 28 million Americans with at least one alcoholic parent (National Association for Children of Alcoholics, 1983), and it is becoming widely recognized that some of these children develop a full range of problems as a result of living with an alcoholic parent—problems that continue on into their adult life. These children are at high risk for developing social and emotional problems, and they are twice as likely to develop alcohol-related problems as children of nonalcoholics (Bosma, 1975; Goodwin, Schlosinger, Hermansen, Guze, & Winokur, 1973).

Even if the alcoholic stops drinking, the children do not recover spontaneously. In a study of alcoholic families in Pennsylvania, Booz-Allen and Hamilton (1974) found that "the treatment and recovery of the alcoholic parent does not appear to reduce the problems experienced by the children" (p. 63). These family systems were often out of balance and unable to adjust to the newly sober parent, and the children had not given up their coping roles. In a study of 115 children between the ages of 10 to 16 who lived in alcoholic homes, Cork (1969) found that the children did not consider that family life became significantly better when their parents drinking stopped.

Studies That Focus on Family Relationships

Both longitudinal studies (McCord, McCord, & Gudeman, 1960; Miller & Jang, 1978; Vaillant & Milofsky, 1982) and current or retrospective studies (Booz-Allen & Hamilton, 1974; Chafetz, Blane, & Hill, 1971; Haberman, 1966; McKenna & Pickens, 1981; Wilson & Orford, 1978) have revealed various problems in children who live with alcoholics. Sloboda (1974) found that alcoholic parents often do not live by society's rules; discipline is inconsistent, and the children become confused and unable to predict parental behavior.

Chafetz, Blane, and Hill (1977) compared 100 alcoholic families with 100 nonalcoholic families that were seen at a child guidance center and found that marital instability, poor marital relationships, prolonged separations, and divorce were considerably more prevalent in the alcoholic families (41% vs. 11%). In addition, these researchers discovered more serious illnesses and accidents as well as more school problems in alcoholic families than in nonalcoholic families. Children from alcoholic homes externalized conflict and were more often involved with police or the courts. According to Chafetz et al. (1971), "This suggests that children of alcoholics have a difficult time becoming socially mature and responsible adults" (p. 696).

Hecht (1973) focused on the alcoholic family and concluded that communication in the alcoholic family was often incongruent and unclear, and led to the isolation of family members. Watching as their parents said one thing and did another, the children received two messages and did not know which message to follow. If these messages became "double binds," the children could not win with either choice. Spouses of alcoholics often "protected" children with half-truths about the alcoholic; unfortunately, however, the children came to believe that parents could not be trusted. To survive in this environment, the children learned to ignore verbal messages and watch for actions and deeds. Similarly, the children imitated the parental communication style of fighting and hostile sarcasm, often acting out their impulses. Children living in these family systems felt alone and had difficulty trusting others.

Studies have revealed a wide range of child and family problems that occur in alcoholic families, depending on the nature of the study and the questions asked. There appear to be two foci, an individual focus on the problems of children and a second focus on family relationship problems. Lawson, Peterson, and Lawson (1983), in reviewing these studies, have grouped the problems that children experience when living with an alcoholic parent and the problems of the alcoholic family. Children's problems can be sorted into four groups: (a) physical neglect or abuse, (b) acting-out behaviors, (c) emotional reactions to alcoholism and chaotic family lives, and (d) social and interpersonal difficulties. Likewise, family problems can be divided into (a) marital relationship problems, (b) parental dysfunctions, and (c) cross-boundary or parent-child relationship difficulties. Although these problems are not exclusive to alcoholic families, they are frequently found in families where alcoholism has disrupted the family system.

ROLE BEHAVIOR THEORIES

In all families, members take on role behaviors. In alcoholic families, however, normal role behavior becomes rigid as family members cope with alcoholism (Black, 1979; Booz-Allen & Hamilton, 1974; Nardi, 1981; Wegscheider, 1981a, 1981b). Virginia Satir, a pioneer in family therapy, identified role behaviors that family members play when they are under stress (Bandler, Grender, & Satir, 1976). Wegscheider (1981a, 1981b), a student of Satir's, identified role behaviors specific to an alcoholic family: the dependent or alcoholic; the enabler or spouse; the family hero, usually the oldest or most responsible and a high achiever; the scapegoat or problem child; the lost child, who is a loner and lives in a fantasy world; and the mascot or clowner who pretends to be carefree. Family members work hard at these roles to save the family system at the expense of their own emotional and physical health. The roles hide the true feelings of these people and interfere with clear, congruent communication. When these role behaviors fail and the stress continues, family members change roles in a desperate attempt to cope.

Although these roles have obvious negative aspects, such as self-denial, repression of feelings, and denial of needs, several investigators (e.g., Nardi, 1981; Thornton & Nardi, 1975; Wilson & Orford, 1978) have asserted that they may help children of alcoholics develop important life skills such as responsibility, initiative, independence, and insight into people's problems.

Of all of the theories of family substance abuse, the idea of "role behaviors" has been the most popular. The idea that a child of an alcoholic was a family hero or a scapegoat or any of the other roles gave meaning to the adult children of alcoholics' struggle. If the clinical notion that adult children of alcoholics have an identity problem is correct, then these adult children of alcoholics can claim one from the list of role behaviors. However, identifying each child with a role behavior does not help the clinician or the family to understand the family dynamics that helped to set the stage for alcoholism in a family member nor to understand the dynamics that maintain the symptom or the problems of recovery. The field of chemical dependency has stopped short in the understanding of alcoholism/addiction as a family system problem by identifying each member as diseased and in need of individual treatment. This is counterproductive to healing the system and halting the intergenerational transmission of addiction, and it is harmful to the individuals in the system who are searching for an identity.

Role behaviors are a natural part of living in a family. They become harmful only when they are acted out in a rigid manner with little or no other option for problem solving. Roles are only one of several parts of systems theory. It is equally important to understand family rules, family values, cultural issues, alliances, coalitions, homeostatic mechanisms, and intergenerational transmissions and projections.

THE ALCOHOLIC FAMILY SYSTEM

Wegscheider (1981b) made a leap from the role theory to describe family homeostasis with her description of the family mobile:

If one flicks one of the suspended parts, energy, the whole system moves to gradually bring itself to equilibrium. The same thing is true of a family. In a family where there is stress, the whole organism shifts to bring balance, stability, survival. (p. 37)

The survival roles described by Black (1979) and Wegscheider (1981b) are best understood as parts of a mobile that become rigid in the service of the family stability and survival. This idea of parts of a family that are controlled by a homeostatic balance, rules for operation, and an intergenerational transmission process is one of the connecting pieces between individual diagnoses of family members and the understanding of how a system operates and can perpetuate the addictive process.

The history of the family and addictions field began with the theorists who made the connection between the addiction and the family dynamics. Bowen (1974) and Bateson (1971) were among the first to look at alcoholism from a systemic perspective. Clinicians then began to study the alcoholic family system and to describe what they were finding. These descriptions were often very global and reported commonalities in all alcoholic/addict families. During the 1980s researchers and clinicians began to see the differences in this population. Gender issues were raised. Ethnicity was examined. Family typologies were created. The field began to examine which families were transmitters of alcoholism and which produced resilient children.

TYPES OF ALCOHOLIC FAMILY SYSTEMS

It was important to identify common characteristics of alcoholic families so that assessments and treatment strategies could focus on recovery of the entire system. Many investigators have looked at the alcoholic family environment (Bowen, 1974; Davis, Stern, & Vandeusen, 1978; Killorin & Olson, 1984; McLachlan et al., 1973; Pringle, 1976). McLachlan et al. (1973) found that a sense of secure family cohesiveness clearly differentiated the adolescents in the control group from the adolescents in alcoholic families. Pringle (1976) reported that the alcoholic families of origin in her study were controlling, closed systems that provided little room for self-expression and strongly encouraged competition and achievement, whereas the nonalcoholic families of origin were more cohesive, provided more support, and had less open expression and autonomy.

Kaufman (1980, 1984, 1986) described four types of family reactivity patterns: (a) the functional family system in which family members have the ability to wall off and isolate alcoholic behavior; (b) the neurotic, enmeshed family system, in which drinking behavior interrupts normal family tasks, causes conflict, shifts roles, and demands new adaptation; (c) the disintegrated family system, in which the alcoholic is separated from the family, but family members are still available for family therapy; and (d) the absent family system, which is marked by total loss of family of origin. He further stated, "There is now substantial evidence to conclude that family systems play a significant role in the genesis of alcoholism, as for example in the transmission of marital and family roles of alcoholism from one generation to the next" (Kaufman, 1984, p. 7). Kaufman (1980) also pointed out that families of drug abusers are very similar to families of alcohol abusers; however, the drug abuser may be a child, whereas the alcohol abuser may be the adult. In more than half of the families in which there is an identified patient with a drug problem, there is also a parent who is alcoholic. He also cautioned about overgeneralizing about alcoholic families and added that they vary according to ethnic background, sex of the alcoholic, and stage of life cycle of the family. He concluded that there is a need for more research in the area of the substance-abusing family environments and implications for directions in family therapy.

Kaufman (1991) recently updated his theory of subgroups of alcoholic/addict families. He thought there are far less of the "functional families systems," who are able to wall off and isolate alcoholic behavior, than he first believed. Berenson (1976) also proposed a two-category system for classifying families with alcohol problems. Category 1 was similar to Kaufman's functional family. These families agreed that alcohol was not a problem or a minor problem; that the problem was acute as opposed to chronic; that there was only occasionally a family history of alcoholism; and that the drinker's behavior change when drinking was slight and infrequent. The Category 2 family had high conflict about drinking; saw it as a chronic problem; usually had a family history of alcoholism; and stated that the drinker often had intense behavior change when drinking. It is interesting to note that Berenson describes the amount and pattern of drinking in both of these categories of families as variable. This differentiation of categories was important because different treatment models were proposed for each category.

ADAPTIVE CONSEQUENCES OF ALCOHOLISM

A differentiation was also made between various states of operating within a single family in an attempt to understand the alcoholic family dynamics. Steinglass, Davis, and Berenson (1977) observed that families tend to maintain alcoholic behaviors. They studied the adaptive consequences of alcoholism by observing videotapes of families when the alcoholic was in a "dry" state and when he or she was drinking, the "wet" state. They found the family to be more relaxed and talkative when the alcoholic was intoxicated and more rigid and closed during dry states. Steinglass et al. (1977) further developed a model to demonstrate the way in which drinking behavior is maintained. They based their model on three concepts: "interactional behavior cycling between the sober state and the intoxicated state; patterning of behavior that has reached steady state; and the hypothesis that alcohol use in the alcoholic family has become incorporated into family problem solving behavior" (Steinglass, 1979, p. 167). In addition, Steinglass (1980) pointed out that chronic alcoholism distorts the normative family life cycle. Davis, Berenson, Steinglass, and Davis (1974, p. 210) postulated that the adaptive consequences of alcohol abuse "are reinforcing enough to maintain the drinking behavior, regardless of its causative factors. These adaptive consequences may operate on different levels including intrapsychic, intracouple, or to maintain family homeostasis."

Killorin and Olson (1984) believe that as a result of these adaptive consequences, the function of the symptom of alcoholism and the family style varies. Even though the families may have a common symptom, the way in which the system interacts can take many forms. Using Olson's circumplex model for evaluating family environment, these researchers found that alcoholic families fell into all 16 types of family systems (Olson & Killorin, 1987). They found disengaged as well as enmeshed systems, and chaotic as well as rigid systems. On the scale of cohesion, approximately one-third of the chemically dependent families perceived their families as disengaged, compared to 7% of the nondependent families. In terms of family adaptability, more than 40% of the chemically dependent families saw themselves as chaotic, whereas only 8% of the nondependent families rated themselves as chaotic.

The idea of adaptive consequences of alcoholism and varying behavior patterns in families was an important finding for family therapists. It suggested that there were rigid patterns in alcoholic families that would be resistant to change yet were harmful to all family members and could be part of a multigenerational transmission process.

INTERGENERATIONAL TRANSMISSION OF ALCOHOLISM

A consistent finding in the field of families and addiction is the multigenerational aspects of the addictions. The most important question for the field of addiction prevention is: How do alcoholism and other addictions transmit from generation to generation or even jump generations in families? Families that seem to function in the face of addiction and do not transmit these addictions to the offspring are important to prevention and treatment.

In an attempt to determine how the family environment may be a transmitter of alcoholism, several researchers investigated the importance of family rituals (Bennett, Wolin, Reiss, & Teitelbaum, 1987; Steinglass, Bennett, Wolin, & Reiss, 1987; Wolin & Bennett, 1984; Wolin, Bennett, & Noonan, 1979, 1980). Wolin et al. (1979) studied a group of 25 families of middle- and upper-class background and of European origin. All families included at least one parent who met their criteria for the identification of an alcoholic or problem drinker. Structured individual interviews that covered personal history of the interviewee and the continuity of family heritage from the grandparents' generation into the current nuclear family provided information into seven areas of family rituals: (1) dinnertime, (2) holidays, (3) evenings, (4) weekends, (5) vacations, (6) visitors in the home, and (7) discipline. These investigators defined family rituals as patterns of behavior that have meaning beyond their practical outcome or function. "Patterned behavior is behavior that is repetitive, stable with respect to roles, and continues over time" (Wolin et al., 1979, p. 590). They believed that these rituals were important because they "stabilize ongoing family life by clarifying expectable roles, delineating boundaries within and without the family, and defining rules so that all family members know that 'this is the way our family is'"(Wolin et al., 1979, p. 590). Steinglass et al. (1987) stated, "family rituals are, in effect, condensed, prepackaged training modules intended to convey to all family members the important facts about family identity" (p. 309). They identified three types of families: distinctive families, in which rituals did not change during drinking episodes; intermediate subsumptive families, which rejected intoxicated behavior when it was present; and subsumptive families, in which drinking changed the "fabric of the family" and highly disrupted the family life. They found that families whose rituals were disrupted or changed during the period of heaviest drinking by the alcoholic parent were more likely to transmit alcoholism to the younger generation than were families whose rituals remained intact. The more that alcoholism became a central organizing force and a disruption to the family rituals, the more the children were at risk for developing alcoholism. The nontransmitter families had one outstanding quality in common: "a rejection of the intoxication of the alcoholic parent through such means as confronting the alcoholic parent openly or privately, or talking about his or her behavior disapprovingly" (Wolin et al., 1979, p. 591).

To follow up this study, Bennett et al. (1987) interviewed 68 married children of alcoholic parents and their spouses regarding dinnertime and holiday rituals in their families of origin and in the couples' current generations. They identified 14 predictor variables that contributed significantly ($p < .01$) to the couples' alcoholism outcomes. The children of alcoholics who remained nonalcoholic had limited attachments to their families of origin or selective disengagements, and the families of origin had been able to separate the rituals from the alcoholism.

In summation of these ritual studies, Steinglass et al. (1987) said,

> We believe that the transmission of alcoholism from one generation to the next involves the whole family system over time. The context for transmission is the sum total of interactions, attitudes, and beliefs that define the family. The process is ongoing and dynamic, and has no particular beginning, end, or pivotal event. And it often goes on outside the awareness of the participants involved, the "senders" as well as the "receivers." (p. 304)

Another concept that Bennett, Wolin, and Reiss (1988) have proposed as a risk-reducing factor is deliberateness. They

> argued that families with serious problems, such as parental alcoholism, which can still impose control over those parts of family life that are central to the family's identity, communicate important messages to their children regarding their ability to take control of present and future life events. These messages, in turn, can play an important role in the extent to which the offspring are protected from developing problems in childhood, as well as alcoholism in adolescence and adulthood.(p. 821)

Spouse selection in a deliberate way, establishment by the couple of their own family rituals and heritage, participation in institutions of the community, and selective disengagement from the families of origin are strategies proposed by this group of researchers to reduce the transmission of alcoholism across generations. This is important information for family therapists working with newly constituted families who are concerned about their own risk for addictive disorders and transmission of these disorders to their own children. A common theme in research on intergenerational transmission of familial alcoholism is that a "supportive other" or cohesion in the family is less often reported as present by those children of alcoholics who become alcoholic (Booz-Allen & Hamilton, 1974; Lawson, 1988; O'Sullivan, 1991; Simmons, 1991). Booz-Allen and Hamilton (1974) listed "having a supportive person" in the family as a risk reducer for children of alcoholics. Lawson (1988) found that adult children of alcoholics who were not alcoholic perceived their families of origin as more cohesive and supportive than adult children of alcoholics who were alcoholic. In looking at these supportive others, O'Sullivan (1991) related the presence of a childhood mentoring relationship to resiliency in adult children of alcoholics. Even in families with alcoholic fathers and families with psychiatrically disturbed fathers, the presence of a "healthy" mother produced young adults who appeared as well adjusted as the control group of young adults whose parents had neither alcoholism nor psychiatric problems (Simmons, 1991). Healthy mothers were defined in this study as having no diagnosis of substance abuse or psychiatric disorder. The common message of these studies seems to be that children can emerge from dysfunctional, substance-abusing families with some degree of resilience if they receive some nurturing and guidance from someone in the family or even someone outside of the family system. From a prevention standpoint, this cohesion and support in families seems to provide a buffering effect against the damage done to children in dysfunctional families.

Another group of investigators (Jacob, Seilhamer, & Rushe, 1989) observed intact families under a broad range of conditions, including laboratory observations involving experimental drinking procedures and naturalistic home observations focused on dinnertime interactions. They were interested in the impact of alcoholism on the process and structure of family life, the degree to which varying patterns of family interaction served to potentiate or inhibit the development of alcoholism in children of alcoholics, and the degree that patterns varied in relation to alcoholism versus depression. In observing episodic versus steady and in-home versus out-of-home drinking behaviors, they found that steady, in-home drinkers seemed to have a positive impact on family life. The steady, in-home drinkers and their wives engaged in more productive problem solving during the drink versus nondrink conditions. This is consistent with the "adaptive consequences" theory of alcoholism. They admit that causality cannot be determined, but the study did underscore how the interplay of familial stressors associated with alcohol abuse, parental psychiatric status, and the mother's ability to mediate negative effects impacts on the child.

In viewing adult children of alcoholics' responses to parental drinking styles, Tarter (1991) found that the same drinking style that Jacob et al. (1989) found to be a productive problem-solving style for the alcoholic couple was the most problem-creating style for the adult child of an alcoholic who grew up in this drinking style family. As compared to adult children of alcoholics from "binge drinker at home," "binge drinker away," and "daily away drinker" groups, daily at-home drinkers produced adult children of alcoholics who rated their families of origin as the most unhealthy of the four groups (on the Family of Origin Scale). These adult children of alcoholics who had daily at-home drinking parents reported that they had more alcohol problems (MAST) and depression (Beck Depression Scale) than members of the other three groups.

The family system studies have added another dimension to the nature versus nurture controversy in the etiology of alcoholism. It is quite possible that there is no one etiological prescription for alcoholism. Genetics may play a major role in the father-son transmission of alcoholism, whereas family environment may have more of an impact on women's alcoholism. The importance of finding family environment patterns that predispose children for alcoholism is that it may be possible to prevent alcoholism in these children by changing the patterns through family therapy and parent training.

TREATMENT MODELS

Resulting from the theories and the researchers' work, models for treating the alcoholic family were created (Steinglass et al., 1987; Szapocznik, Rio, Perez-Vidal, Santiseban, & Kurtines, 1989; Treadway, 1989; Usher, 1991). Steinglass et al. (1987) described a family therapy model of treating alcoholism within a developmental perspective that drew from more than 10 years of intensive research, including in-depth interviews and home observations. Treadway (1989) used the work of Berenson (1976) with the chronic alcoholic system and devised a treatment model for cooling off the emotional system that included several stages of work with the couple and family over a long period of time. The steps include disengagement, differentiation, negotiation, conflict management, and intimacy. Family Effectiveness Training, developed by Szapocznik, Rio, Perez-Vidal, Santiseban, & Kurtines (1989), is an example of direct intervention designed to change family interaction styles and to reduce adolescent risk of drug abuse. This training involves 13 lessons offered simultaneously to parents and children. Recently, Usher (1991) proposed a treatment model for couples and families that does not stop at the point of getting the alcoholic "dry." She drew from her previous work (Usher, Jay, & Glass, 1982) to develop a four-phase model that included learning, reorganization, and consolidation.

Family therapy has also shown great promise in working with adolescent substance abusers. Todd and Selekman (1991) have presented several models of therapy for working with this population, including brief problem-solving models.

These are only a few examples of the growing number of therapy models. As these models develop, they bring new questions of treatment effectiveness: Are they more effective than individual approaches? Are they effective for minority and ethnic populations? Do they work as well for single-parent or blended families as for intact families? Do they prevent substance abuse in children and siblings?

TREATMENT OUTCOME STUDIES

The field of family therapy has consistently called for treatment outcome studies. Due to the many variables of family type, problem type, treatment theory, and treatment provider, there are few certainties about the effectiveness of family therapy with substance abuse. Many theoretical orientations are difficult to measure with the current instruments. Thus behavioral and structural theories may be represented in the research literature, whereas intergenerational theories, which are more difficult to measure, are missing.

The earliest research in treatment outcome for alcoholism compared treatment with and without spouse involvement. Researchers have found strong evidence for involving at least a spouse and other family members in the treatment process. Berger (1981) found that the number of family members involved affected the outcome in a positive direction. Spouse involvement might mean a separate-parallel program, conjoint therapy, or education for the spouse. Spouse and family involvement in the Johnson Institute "intervention" process of three or four educational sessions before a confrontation session with the alcoholic about his or her drinking with a strong recommendation for treatment is widely accepted in the field. Inclusion of the spouse in alcoholic/addict's treatment is less common. Evidence is accumulating, however, that marital and family therapy stabilizes relationships and supports improvements in alcoholics' drinking during the 6-month period following treatment entry for alcoholism. A promising approach is behavioral marital therapy that combines both a focus on the drinking and work on more general marital relationship issues. This method instigates positive couple and family activities and teaches communication and conflict resolution skills (e.g., McCrady et al., 1986; O'Farrell & Choquette, 1991; O'Farrell & Cutter, 1982; O'Farrell, Cutter, & Floyd, 1985). McCrady et al. (1986) compared treatment of alcoholics and their spouses in three outpatient treatment conditions: minimal spouse involvement (MSI), alcohol-focused spouse involvement (AFSI), and alcohol-focused spouse involvement plus behavioral marital therapy (ABMT). The ABMT group were more compliant with homework assignments, decreased their drinking more quickly during treatment, relapsed more slowly after treatment, and maintained marital satisfaction better.

In comparing couples group therapy and individual treatment, Bowers and Al-Redha (1990) found that conjointly treated alcoholics had significantly lower rates of alcohol consumption than the standard group at 6-month follow-up and higher relationship ratings at the 6-month and 1-year follow-up.

The other area of interest in family therapy outcome research is in the treatment of adolescent substance abuse. This has been influenced by the National Institute on Drug Abuse (NIDA) funding of several projects to test the effectiveness of family therapy with this problem. The Purdue Brief Therapy Model (Lewis, Piercy, Sprenkle, & Trepper, 1991; Piercy & Frankel, 1989) was one of the projects that integrated family therapy theories that had previously demonstrated their effectiveness and applied this model to adolescent substance abuse. The models included theory from Stanton and Todd (1982), who demonstrated the effectiveness of structural-strategic family therapy with adult heroin addicts; Szapocznik and his colleagues (Szapocznik, Kurtines, Foot, Perez-Vidal, & Hervis, 1983, 1986) at the University of Miami School of Medicine, who found strategic therapy effective in decreasing adolescent drug abuse; Minuchin, Rosman, and Baker (1978), who found that structural family therapy decreased symptoms of psychosomatic illnesses such as asthma and anorexia nervosa; Alexander (1974) and his colleagues, who used functional family therapy to work with juvenile delinquents; and Patterson (1982) and his colleagues, who repeatedly demonstrated the effectiveness of behavioral contracting with delinquent adolescents. This brief 12-session model is geared to help change the entire family into a healthier, more supportive environment. Its goal is to stem the current drug abuse of an adolescent and prevent the development of drug abuse by a younger sibling.

The Purdue Brief Therapy Model was compared to a family drug education program, the Training in Parenting Skills (TIPS) Program and individual-based drug counseling of adolescents. The results indicated that the two brief, family-based drug interventions together appeared to reduce the drug use of nearly one-half (46%) of the adolescents who received them. In commenting on this success, Lewis (1991) stated:

> We suspect that this success was due partly to the fact that both of these outpatient interventions focused on the systemic treatment of *entire* family groups. In contrast, however, the family therapy intervention seems to have been more effective in significantly reducing adolescent drug use for a greater percentage of the adolescents (54.6%) than the family education intervention (37.5%). An even more dramatic result of the study was this: Although more than twice as many adolescents in the family therapy condition (40%) were hard drug users at their pretest, *twice as many of these hard users (44.4%) moved to no use at all* by the posttest time, compared to only the 25% of the hard users in the family education condition who moved to no drug use. (pp. 2–3)

This project is also analyzing data about how this model works for minorities, lower socioeconomic groups with less education, or single parent families.

Additionally, they are doing a long-term follow-up to determine if this model is effective in preventing substance abuse for the younger siblings in the families.

Several other family systems models for working with adolescent substance abusers are showing promise and positive outcomes (Friedman, Tomko, & Utada, 1991; Liddle & Diamond, 1991; Quinn, Kuehl, Thomas, & Joanning, 1988; Szapocznik, Kurtines, and contributors, 1989). One of these studies (Joanning, Quinn, Thomas, & Mullen, 1992), funded by NIDA, compared the effectiveness of three models of adolescent drug abuse treatment. Family Systems Therapy (FST) was compared to Adolescent Group Therapy (AGT) and Family Drug Education (FDE) with Anglo and Hispanic youth living in and around Lubbock, Texas. FST appeared to be more effective in stopping adolescent drug abuse than AGT or FDE, with twice as many (54%) apparent drug-free clients than FDE (28%) and three times as many as AGT (16%). Interestingly, all three treatment conditions improved perceived intergenerational communication; however, the dropout rate for group therapy was much higher ($n = 29$) than for family education ($n = 14$) or family therapy ($n = 9$). The adolescents in the group therapy condition were often able to convince their parents that the treatment was not working and they should stop attending, whereas this was not as possible when the family was involved in the treatment.

PREVALENCE OF FAMILY TREATMENT IN ADDICTIONS

Until about 12 years ago, very few drug treatment programs and fewer alcohol treatment programs involved spouses or other family members in the treatment of the identified patient. According to Stanton (1979a, 1979b), although 93% of drug treatment programs acknowledged some interest in the clients' families, very few directly included them in therapy. In a national survey, Coleman and Davis (1978) studied the involvement of the drug abuse treatment agencies with family therapy. Although they discovered that 98% of the Phase I agencies had some type of family program, with 75% seeing entire families, the level of expertise and training of the therapy providers was low. There is evidence that those facilities that utilize systemic approaches often do so only as a peripheral part of the program and/or use therapists minimally trained (Coleman & Davis, 1978). A comparison of the drug field with the alcohol field showed much keener interest in the drug abuse treatment field than in the alcoholism treatment field. In a recent interview-style survey of five prominent southern California inpatient alcoholism treatment programs that advertised family programs, only two of these programs actually conducted family systems therapy (Wilson, 1991). This was, however, not a standard part of the program and not applied uniformly. The average number of hours of conjoint family therapy provided by the five programs was 2.1 hours of the 32.6 total treatment hours.

None of the counselors providing the family therapy were licensed marriage and family therapists.

There are various dynamics that account for this reluctance to embrace family therapy by the alcohol field. Alcohol counselors avoid family therapy for several reasons: (a) they may not have training in family therapy; (b) they may believe that family therapy is opposed to Alcoholics Anonymous; (c) they may see it as incompatible with the disease concept of alcoholism; (d) they may be unsupported by their employers in their efforts to use family therapy; and (e) due to the large amount of inpatient treatment of alcoholism, the family may be unavailable or unwilling to participate. The family may scapegoat the alcoholic to wash their hands of the problem.

Currently a problem for all treatment providers is the unwillingness of insurance companies to pay for family therapy as a treatment for substance abuse. The American Psychiatric Association's *Diagnostic and Statistical Manual of Mental Disorders* (3rd ed., rev.; *DSM III-R*) codes diagnose individual pathology, not family systems problems, and these are the codes used to bill insurance companies. Although family therapy is more cost effective than treating each member individually, it is not a mainstream treatment approach in the addiction field. Another reason that it is not enthusiastically adopted by alcoholism treatment providers is that alcohol counselor training programs often do not provide sufficient family therapy training. Finally, many counselors working in the alcoholism treatment field are recovering alcoholics, adult children of alcoholics, and spouses of alcoholics. They may resist working with families because of their own unresolved family of origin or nuclear family issues.

FAMILY THERAPY AND AA

One of these resistances is not valid. Family therapy and Alcoholics Anonymous attendance are quite compatible. Although family therapy and Alcoholics Anonymous (or other 12-step programs) may seem to be working at cross-purposes, with AA and Al-Anon focusing on the individual with a disease, in apparent contradiction to the family systems approach, which identifies addiction as a family dysfunction and treats the entire family, these self-help groups and family therapy actually have several common factors. They agree that (a) family members other than the alcoholic suffer; (b) change can occur when significant others are engaged in the process; (c) family members can resist change by the alcoholic; (d) if the alcoholic recovers emotionally and the other family members do not, a crisis may occur; and (e) the individual is responsible for personal change.

Some therapists insist on attendance of self-help groups as a prerequisite for therapy. Others make distinctions in which clients are encouraged to attend AA.

Because attendance at AA meetings may not be appropriate for all problem drinkers, a rigid position on AA attendance may rule out help for some families who might benefit from family therapy alone or who, after an intervention period, are receptive to trying self-help groups. David Treadway (1989) often uses a drinking contract to reduce an alcoholic's denial of the drinking problem while he sends the spouse to Al-Anon to cool off the marital subsystem and reduce the "enabling" behavior. Once the alcoholic breaks his or her drinking contract, he or she is more open to admitting the problem and attending self-help groups. Choices are also a good idea. If a client refuses to attend AA meetings, therapists can give their clients choices of other self-help groups such as Rational Recovery, Women for Sobriety, or specialized AA or NA groups where they will feel more connected.

A pitfall of using both approaches simultaneously may occur when a difficult issue arises in either therapy or the self-help group. The family or individual may escape working on this issue by fleeing from one approach into the other. This can be avoided by coordination efforts between the therapist and the 12-step sponsor.

Therapists also worry that too much 12-step attendance is replacing one addiction with another that is equally harmful to family life. This is an issue that can be addressed in family therapy. Berenson (1976) believes that

> continuation in AA and Al-Anon is up to the client, with the therapist being careful that an early decrease in attendance may be a warning of an impending resumption of drinking, and that continued and frequent attendance for many years may become a stress in the marriage. (p. 292)

Family therapists have the opportunity to increase the effectiveness of self-help groups. Bowen (1974) described alcoholism as a fusion with "other," in this case alcohol. His prescription for treatment is self-differentiation, not only from the alcohol but from the alcoholic's family of origin. In many cases the alcoholic with low levels of differentiation and high levels of fusion may lower his or her level of differentiation with a fused identification with a self-help group. Regina and Simmons (1992) suggest that a Bowen approach in family therapy promotes detriangulation and a development of a solid self, while encouraging continued attendance at self-help groups.

CONCLUSION

Because it is commonly agreed that children of alcoholics are at high risk for developing their own addictions and other relationship problems, family systems therapy with the entire family plays the dual role of treating the immediate addiction and preventing future addictions in the other family members. Given the vast amount of research on the problems of children of alcoholics, the intergenerational transmission of addictions, and the problems of the alcoholic family system, it is impossible to ignore the role of the family environment in the etiology and perpetuation of addictions. These problems of children, dysfunctions of the family system, and intergenerational transmission can be altered through family systems therapy.

REFERENCES

Alexander, J. F. (1974). Behavior modification and delinquent youth. In J. C. Cull & R.E. Hardy (Eds.), *Behavior modification in rehabilitation settings*. Springfield, IL: Charles Thomas.

Bandler, R., Grender, J., & Satir, V. (1976). *Changing with families*. Palo Alto, CA: Science and Behavior Books.

Bateson, G. (1971). The cybernetics of "self": A theory of alcoholism. *Psychiatry, 34,* 1–18.

Bennett, L. A., Wolin, S. J., & Reiss, D. (1988). Deliberate family process: A strategy for protecting children of alcoholics. *British Journal of Addiction, 83,* 821–829.

Bennett, L. A., Wolin, S. J., Reiss, D., & Teitelbaum, M. A. (1987). Couples at risk for transmission of alcoholism: Protective influences. *Family Process, 26,* 111–129.

Berenson, D. (1976). Alcohol and the family system. In P. Guerin (Ed.), *Family therapy: Theory and practice* (pp. 284–297). New York: Gardner .

Berger, A. (1981). Family involvement and alcoholics' completion of a multiphase treatment program. *Journal of Studies on Alcohol, 42*(5), 517–521.

Black, C. (1979, Fall). Children of alcoholics. *Alcohol Health and Research World*, pp. 23–27.

Booz-Allen & Hamilton, Inc. (1974). *An assessment of the needs of and resources for children of alcoholic parents*. Rockville, MD: National Institute on Alcohol Abuse and Alcoholism.

Bosma, W. (1975). Alcoholism and teenagers. *Maryland State Medical Journal, 24,* 62–68.

Bowen, M. (1974). Alcoholism as viewed through family systems theory and family psychotherapy. *Annals of the New York Academy of Science, 233,* 115–122.

Bowers, T. G., & Al-Redha, M. R. (1990). A comparison of outcome with group/marital and standard/individual therapies with alcoholics. *Journal of Studies on Alcohol, 51*(4), 301–309.

Chafetz, M., Blane, H., & Hill, M. (1977) . Children of alcoholics: Observations in a child guidance clinic. *Quarterly Journal of Studies on Alcohol, 32,* 687–698.

Coleman, S. B., & Davis, D. (1978). Family therapy and drug abuse: A national survey. *Family Process, 17,* 21–29.

Cork, M. (1969). *The forgotten children*. Toronto: Alcoholism and Drug Addiction Research Foundation.

Cotton, N. S. (1979). The familial incidence of alcoholism: A review. *Journal of Studies on Alcohol, 46,* 89–115.

Davis, D. J., Berenson, D., Steinglass, P., & Davis, S. (1974). The adaptive consequences of drinking. *Psychiatry, 37,* 209–215.

Davis, P., Stern, D. R., & Vandusen, J.M. (1978). Enmeshment-disengagement in the alcoholic family. In F. Seixas (Ed.), *Currents in alcoholoism. Vol. IV: Psychological, social & epidemiological.* New York: Grune & Stratton.

Friedman, A. S., Tomko, L. A., & Utada, A. (1991). Client and family characteristics that predict better family therapy outcome for adolescent drug abusers. *Family Dynamics of Addiction Quarterly, 1*(1), 77–93.

Goodwin, D. W. (1971). Is alcoholism hereditary? A review and critique. *Archives of General Psychiatry, 25,* 545–549.

Goodwin, D. W., Schlosinger, F., Hermansen, L., Guze, S. D., & Winokur, G. (1973). Alcoholism problems in adoptees reared apart from alcoholic biological parents. *Archives of General Psychiatry,281,* 238–243.

Haberman, P. W. (1966). Childhood symptoms in children of alcoholics and comparison group parents. *Journal of Marriage and the Family, 28*(2), 152–154.

Hecht, M. (1973). Children of alcoholics. *American Journal of Nursing, 10,* 1764–1767.

Jackson, J. K. (1954). The adjustment of the family to the crisis of alcoholism. *Quarterly Journal of the Studies on Alcohol, 15,* 562–586.

Jacob, T., Seilhamer, R. A., & Rushe, R. H. (1989). Alcoholism and family interaction: An experimental paradigm. *American Journal of Drug and Alcohol Abuse, 15*(1), 73–91.

Joanning, H., Quinn, W., Thomas, F., & Mullen, R. (1992). Treating adolescent drug abuse: A comparison of family systems therapy, group therapy, and family drug education. *Journal of Marital and Family Therapy, 18*(2).

Kaufman, E. (1980). Myths and realities in the family patterns and treatment of substance abuse. *American Journal of Drug and Alcohol Abuse, 7* (3 & 4), 257–279.

Kaufman, E. (1984). Family system variables in alcoholism. *Alcoholism: Clinical and Experimental Research, 8*(1), 4–8.

Kaufman, E. (1986). The family of the alcoholic patient. *Psychosomatics, 27*(5), 347–358.

Kaufman, E. (1991). An interview with Edward Kaufman, M.D. *Family Dynamics of Addiction Quarterly, 1*(3), 1–11.

Kaufman, E., & Kaufmann, P. (1979). *Family therapy of drug and alcohol abuse.* New York: Gardner.

Killorin, E., & Olson, D. (1984). The chaotic flippers in treatment. In E. Kaufman (Ed.), *Power to change: Alcoholism.* New York: Gardner.

Lawson, A. (1988). *The relationship of past and present family environments of adult children of alcoholics.* Doctoral dissertation, United States International University.

Lawson, G. W., Peterson, J. S., & Lawson, A. W. (1983). *Alcoholism and the family: A guide to treatment and prevention.* Gaithersburg, MD: Aspen.

Lewis, R. A. (1991). Testimony before the House Select Committee on Children, Families, Drugs and Alcoholism. *Hearing on adolescent substance abuse: Barriers to treatment.* 101st Congress. Washington, DC.

Lewis, R. A., Piercy, F. P., Sprenkle, D. H., & Trepper, T. S. (1991). The Purdue brief family therapy model for adolescent substance abusers. In T. Todd & M. Selekman (Eds.), *Family therapy approaches with adolescent substance abusers* (pp. 29–48). Needham Heights, MA: Allyn & Bacon.

Liddle, H., & Diamond, G. (1991). Adolescent substance abusers in family therapy: The critical initial phase of treatment. *Family Dynamics of Addiction Quarterly, 1* (1), 55–68.

McCord, W., McCord, J., & Gudeman, J. (1960). *Origins of alcoholism.* Palo Alto, CA: Stanford University Press.

McCrady, B. S., Noel, N. E., Abrams, D. B., Stout, R. L., Nelson, H.. F., & Hay, W. M. (1986). Comparative effectiveness of three types of spouse involvement in outpatient behavioral alcoholism treatment. *Journal of Studies on Alcohol, 47*(67), 459–466.

McKenna, T., & Pickens, R. (1981). Alcoholic children of alcoholics. *Journal of Studies on Alcohol, 42,* 1021–1029.

McLachlan, et al. (1973). *A study of teenagers with alcoholic parents* (Donwood Institute Research Monograph N3). Toronto: Donwood Institute.

Miller, D., & Jang, M. (1978). Children of alcoholics: A 20 year longitudinal study. *Social Work Research and Abstracts, 13,* 23–29.

Minuchin, S., Rosman, B., & Baker, L. (1978). *Psychosomatic families: Anorexia nervosa in context.* Cambridge, MA: Harvard University Press.

Nardi, P. (1981). Children of alcoholics: A role-theoretical perspective. *Journal of Social Psychology, 115,* 237–245.

National Association for Children of Alcoholics Charter Statement. (1983, June). *Alcoholism,* 18.

O'Farrell, T. J., & Choquette, K. (1991). Marital violence in the year before and after spouse-involved alcoholism treatment. *Family Dynamics of Addiction Quarterly, 1*(1), 32–40.

O'Farrell, T. J., & Cutter, H. S. G. (February 1982). Effect of adding a behavioral or an interactional couples group to individual outpatient alcoholism counseling. In T. J. O'Farrell (Chair), *Spouse involved treatment for alcohol abuse.* Symposium conducted at the Sixteenth Annual Convention of the Association for the Advancement of Behavior Therapy, Los Angeles.

O'Farrell, T. J., Cutter, H. S. G., & Floyd, F. J. (1985). Evaluating behavioral marital therapy for male alcoholics: Effects on marital adjustment and communication from before to after therapy. *Behavior Therapy, 16,* 147–167.

O'Sullivan, C. (1991). Making a difference: The relationship between childhood mentors and resiliency in adult children of alcoholics. *Family Dynamics of Addiction Quarterly, 1*(4), 46–59.

Olson, D. H., & Killorin, E. A. (1987). *Chemically dependent families and the circumplex model.* Unpublished research report, University of Minnesota, St. Paul.

Patterson, G. R. (1982). *A social learning approach to family intervention: Coercive family process.* Eugene, OR: Castalia.

Piercy, F. F., & Frankel, B. R. (1989). The evolution of an integrative family therapy for substance-abusing adolescents: Toward the mutual enhancement of research and practice. *Journal of Family Psychology, 3*(1), 5–25.

Pringle, W. J. (1976). *The alcoholic family environment: The influence of the alcoholic and nonalcoholic family of origin on present coping styles.* Doctoral dissertation, California School of Professional Psychology, Fresno.

Quinn, W. H., Kuehl, B. P., Thomas, F. N., & Joanning, H. (1988). Families of adolescent drug abusers: Systemic interventions to attain drug-free behavior. *American Journal of Drug and Alcohol Abuse, 14*(1), 65–87.

Regina, W., & Simmons, G. (1992, October). *Beyond recovery: Healing addictions through differentiation,* Paper presented at the meeting of the American Association of Marriage and Family Therapists, Miami.

Schuckit, M. A. (1983). Alcoholic men with no alcoholic first-degree relatives. *American Journal of Psychiatry, 140*(4), 439–443.

Simmons, G. M. (1991). Interpersonal trust and perceived locus of control in the adjustment of adult children of alcoholics. Doctoral dissertation, United States International University.

Sloboda, S. (1974). The children of alcoholics: A neglected problem. *Hospital and Community Psychiatry, 25,* 605–606.

Stanton, M. D. (1979a). Drugs and the family. *Marriage and Family Review, 2,* 1–8.

Stanton, M. D. (1979b). Family treatment approaches to drug abuse problems : A review. *Family Process, 18,* 251–281.

Stanton, M . D., & Todd, T. C. (1982). *The family therapy of drug abuse and addiction.* New York: Guilford.

Steinglass, P. (1979). Family therapy with alcoholics: A review. In E. Kaufman & P. Kaufmann (Eds.), *Family therapy of drug and alcohol abuse*, (pp. 147–186). New York: Gardner.

Steinglass, P. (1980). Life history model of the alcoholic family. *Family Process, 19*(3), 211–226.

Steinglass, P., Bennett, L. A., Wolin, S. J., & Reiss, D. (1987). *The alcoholic family*. New York: Basic Books.

Steinglass, P., Davis, D., & Berenson, D. (1977). Observations of conjointly hospitalized "alcohol couples" during sobriety and intoxication for theory and therapy. *Family Process, 16*, 1–16.

Szapocznik, J., Kurtines, W. M., Foot, F., Perez-Vidal, A., & Hervis, O. (1983). Conjoint versus one person family therapy: Some evidence for the effectiveness of conducting family therapy through one person. *Journal of Consulting and Clinical Psychology, 51*, 889–899.

Szapocznik, J., Kurtines, W. M., Foot, F., Perez-Vidal, A., & Hervis, O. (1986). Conjoint versus one-person family therapy: Further evidence for the effectiveness of conducting family through one person with drug-abusing adolescents. *Journal of Consulting and Clinical Psychology, 54*(3), 395–397.

Szapocznik, J., Kurtines, W.M., & contributors. (1989). *Breakthroughs in family therapy with drug-abusing and problem youth*. New York: Springer.

Szapocznik, J., Rio, A., Perez-Vidal, A., Santiseban, D., & Kurtines, W. (1989). Family effective-ness training: An intervention to prevent drug abuse and problem behavior in hispanic adoles-cents. *Hispanic Journal of Behavioral Sciences, 11*(4), 4–27.

Tarter, J. (1991). The effects of parental alcohol drinking patterns on adult children of alcoholics. Doctoral dissertation, United States International University.

Thornton, R., & Nardi, P. M. (1975). The dynamics of role acquisition. *American Journal of Sociology, 80*(4), 870–885.

Todd, T., & Selekman, M. (1991). *Family therapy with adolescent substance abusers*. Needham Heights, MA: Allyn & Bacon.

Treadway, D. (1989). *Before it's too late*. New York: Norton.

Usher, M. L. (1991). From identification to consolidation: A treatment model for couples and fami-lies complicated by alcoholism. *Family Dynamics of Addiction Quarterly, 1*(2), 45–58.

Usher, M. L., Jay, J., & Glass, D. R. (1982). Family therapy as a treatment modality for alcoholism. *Journal of Studies on Alcohol, 43*, 927–938.

Vaillant, G. S., & Milofsky, E. S. (1982). The etiology of alcoholism: A prospective viewpoint. *American Psychologist. 37* (5), 494–503.

Wegscheider, S. (1981a). *Another chance: Hope and help for the alcoholic family*. Palo Alto, CA: Science and Behavior Books.

Wegscheider, S. (1981b, January/February). From the family trap to family freedom. *Alcoholism*, pp. 36–39.

Whalen, T. (1953). Wives of alcoholics: Four types observed in a family service agency. *Quarterly Journal of Studies on Alcohol, 14*, 632–641.

Wilson, R. (1991). *A survey of family systems therapy of addiction in five inpatient treatment pro-grams in southern California*. Unpublished manuscript.

Wilson, C., & Orford, J. (1978). Children of alcoholics. *Journal of Studies on Alcohol, 39*, 121–142.

Winokur, G., & Clayton, P. J. (1968). Family history studies in comparison to male and female alcoholics. *Quarterly Journal of Studies on Alcohol, 29*, 885–891.

Wolin, S. J., & Bennett, L. A. (1984). Family rituals. *Family Process, 23*, 401–420.

Wolin, S. J., Bennett, L. A., & Noonan, D. L. (1979). Family rituals and recurrence of alcoholism over generations. *American Journal of Psychiatry, 136*, 589–593.

Wolin, S.J., Bennett, L., & Noonan, D. (1980). Disrupted family rituals: A factor in the intergenerational transmission of alcoholism. *Journal of Studies on Alcohol, 41*, 199–214.

Chapter 16

The "Taking Charge" Model of Recovery for Addictive Families

Stephen E. Schlesinger and Lawrence K. Horberg

This chapter describes a practical developmental formulation of family recovery. It is written for family counselors and therapists whose clientele includes addicts and their families. Its principal goal is to describe the developmental tasks of recovery in sufficient depth to equip therapists to use their own methods to help families accomplish the tasks.

This approach to family treatment and recovery grew out of work the authors have done with families of people addicted to a wide variety of substances and behaviors (for example, alcohol, drugs, gambling, sex, spending). These families spanned the range of social, economic, and cultural groups, and the settings in which they were treated included both public and private and both inpatient and outpatient programs. The model borrows elements from systems theory, as well as from cognitive-behavioral and psychodynamic approaches to family functioning, and it assembles these elements into a stepwise model that helps family members and therapists pursue an organized journey through the developmental tasks of recovery. It was conceived to help addicts and their loved ones repair damage done by (or in reaction to) addictive behavior, create more satisfying lives, and prevent long-lasting deleterious effects. The tasks of recovery are presented in logical sequences to facilitate the assessment of differences among families and among members of the same family. Once an assessment is complete, the clinician is equipped to focus the attention of the family on the next logical tasks.

The approach focuses on engaging all interested family members in a journey from chaos to integration, from sickness to family health. It differs sharply from those approaches that view the family as an instrument to coerce the addict into recovery, with those that ignore the addiction, with those that ignore the family's needs, and with those that require the entire family to participate. In our experience, it is often fruitful to begin with those family members who are ready to work on the problem and to invite others to participate as they become interested. For many families, the journey begins in "Region I," a state of exasperation, hopelessness and helplessness. It proceeds through "Region II," a period of experimentation and effort, and culminates in "Region III," a state in which family members feel hopeful about, in charge of, and competent to handle their lives.

Note: Correspondence concerning this chapter should be addressed to the authors at 333 East Ontario, Suite 3303B, Chicago, IL 60611.

The tasks that promote the development of successful recovery fall into four main groupings: Getting Started, Strengthening the Family, Confronting the Addiction, and Thriving as a Family. Schlesinger and Horberg (1988) present a series of exercises to help family members assess their progress, to guide them through these tasks, to prompt actions that help solve family problems, and to focus attention on issues that promote health.

Families begin treatment at varying points. Some have not yet identified the links between family problems and addictive behaviors; others seek help after having accomplished many of the tasks of recovery. Within each family, individual members differ from one another. Assessing the extent to which tasks have already been accomplished is extremely valuable in guiding treatment and bolstering hope and self-efficacy.

OVERVIEW OF RECOVERY

In the first task area, *Getting Started*, family members develop a realistic basis for hope that they can solve their problems. They learn to define problems in a manner that promotes action and to define their aspirations in terms that transform demoralization into hope and fresh effort.

Many families decide that they will take action on their problems—including coming for professional help—at a point at which they are emotionally depleted, physically exhausted, and overly focused on the addicted member. Family members need to refocus their attention on their *own* lives, *apart* from the addict, in order to fortify themselves and begin the process of psychological separation. Family members cannot confront problems associated with addiction either in an exhausted state or an enmeshed state. Therefore, in the second task area, *Strengthening the Family*, family members learn to take better care of themselves, live fuller lives, and develop the supportive relationships they will need in order to face the addiction once again.

Once they have begun to strengthen themselves, family members are better prepared to face the third task area, *Confronting the Addiction*. Family members may confront the addict, but they also need to accomplish other tasks, such as withdrawing from destructive experiences related to addiction, avoiding inadvertent support for addiction, and setting limits. Limits are set both to protect the family and to communicate the family's healthy resolve.

When family members have withdrawn from the destructive experiences so often associated with chaotic behavior, they are ready to focus their attention on the fourth area, *Flourishing as a Family*. This involves replacing a "survivor" mentality with a "flourishing" mentality. Among other things at this point in recovery, family members learn to let go of the lingering traumatic effects of living with an addict, navigate some common pitfalls in recovery, build healthy communication patterns, and move on to resume normal family development.

As we shift our focus now to a closer examination of the four developmental tasks and the therapeutic methods of facilitating their accomplishment, we acknowledge that the scope of this chapter does not permit us to be as detailed as the reader might like. For a more thorough description of this approach, see Schlesinger and Horberg (1988). For a discussion of other approaches to family treatment, please see Schlesinger (1988) and Schlesinger and Gillick (1989).

GETTING STARTED

Among other things, addictive families frequently feel hopeless and helpless in their situation. Many family members feel despair, blame themselves for the addict's behavior, ignore their own pain, and neglect their safety, comfort, and well-being. How does one engage such a family in treatment? This is a type of family in which there is a lot of motion—energy expended randomly in reaction to the chaos that an addiction creates—but little movement—energy expended *pro*actively in healthy and productive directions. One family reported,

> It's completely exhausting to devote so much attention to John. You know, is he using? Are we safe? Will he be violent? Will he trash the house? I think about that at home, on the way to work, all day, on the way home from work. I use up all my energy— and I feel helpless.

To help family members make sense of the pain they feel and to work past it, the approach teaches them to make use of a metaphor. This metaphor casts recovery as a journey, thereby helping to dispel the notion that recovery is an *event*. It suggests that family members who recover successfully move through three regions. The metaphor is useful in helping unmotivated or "resistant" families begin and sustain recovery over the long haul. As the student of karate learns to aim beyond the wooden target, so must the recovering family learn to focus on a point beyond merely surviving to a time in which members can flourish. Removal of pain is not a sufficiently credible or inspiring goal. We employ the journey metaphor to help families develop their shared dreams and aspirations and to measure their progress as they work toward their goals.

Recovery as a Journey

In Region I of the journey, chaos is a fact of everyday life. Family members frequently come for help in a state in which they feel confused, exhausted, scared, and extremely pessimistic about their ability to influence important events and share their experiences. It is a state of fragmentation in which family members feel *E*xasperated, with little idea of what they can do to end their pain.

A moment in Region I was recounted by Oscar:

> We had been at a banquet sponsored by our church. During the social hour after dinner, [my wife] Enid went around to all the tables and finished the leftover wine in all the glasses. I was completely humiliated. I cut off contact with all my church friends for several *years* after that. I just couldn't face them.

As Oscar's experience illustrates, one problem with being consumed with an addiction—either one's own or that of a loved one—is that the resultant chaos interferes with family health and well-being, with personal growth, and with maintenance of health, hygiene, safety, comfort, and property. In the process of diverting one's attention from growth to destructive behaviors, one misses many opportunities to grow. Time spent in the chaos of Region I is a time of emotional exhaustion and paralysis. It is not uncommon for adult addicts who have drug use histories dating to childhood or adolescence, and for family members emerging from Region I, to characterize recovery as "growing up."

Family members affected by addictions often need to undertake the challenge of personal growth in a very conscious and deliberate manner, and the first step after emerging from Region I often is a period of exploration and experimentation to make up for lost experiences. Region II is a period of unrelenting *E*ffort, often in what family members see as a grey world. They begin to do things that are different (or to do old things in new ways) without a clear idea of where they will lead. It is a period that can be taxing in that family members do not get a specific return for particular actions they take. It frequently strains the family's resolve to get better.

In Region III, family members develop a sense of purpose and become meaningfully involved in many aspects of their lives. They feel alive and lively, competent to face and solve problems that come up, and eager to make commitments to healthy activities and relationships. They feel a sense of *E*mpowerment. Whereas Region I was a period of fragmentation, Region III is one of integration.

An irony presents itself in the midst of this journey. Recovery really begins when family members decide, in Region I, that they will do *whatever it takes* to end their pain. It is in this way that they pass into Region II. However, in Region II family members find the required effort rather tedious. This results, in part, from the lack of direction people often feel in Region II. Although the anxiety in the recovering family is often far more intense and pervasive, it can be compared to the feelings of boredom and anxiety reported by couples in sex therapy after sensate focus exercises. There are frequent complaints about fumbling and awkwardness, with resentments and skepticism lurking just beneath the surface. Change seems to require too much work and forces a confrontation with emptiness and uncertainty. How, then, do family members continue to invest themselves in their recovery in Region II when a sense of direction, orientation, and accomplishment may not exist for them until Region III?

Movement from Region I (Exasperation) to Region II (Effort) to Region III (Empowerment) occurs as family members learn to answer four basic questions:

• Question 1: What kind of experience do I want *right now*?
• Question 2: What choices or actions would I admire in myself *in this situation*?
• Question 3: What strengths do I have that would be valuable *in this situation*?
• Question 4: What do I feel *right now*?

These four questions can be helpful in providing a temporary framework within which people can stop and make considered decisions in their journey to health. As these questions are answered *in each situation*, self-esteem and self-knowledge grow, and the individual gains awareness of his or her feelings, wants, standards, and strengths. Use of the four questions allows family members to see themselves taking charge of their lives, even if they do not know and cannot see the ultimate destinations of their journey. It inspires fresh hope and effort, and for some this may have followed a substantial period in which they felt helpless and paralyzed.

Learning to answer the four questions is an excellent way to overcome anxiety. It is much easier to face an uncertain future knowing one's wants, standards, feelings, and personal strengths. A positive vision of oneself in the future provides direction to hold onto at times of uncertainty.

To clarify the ways in which the four questions are answered at different stages of the journey, let's examine a specific situation. Genevieve is a 34-year-old advertising executive, married to Jim, a 42-year-old stockbroker who had once been addicted to cocaine. In Table 16–1, Genevieve's reactions to the prospect of spending a weekend with Jim are depicted at three different points in her recovery. Jim was drug and alcohol free throughout Genevieve's recovery.

From this point, family members are guided through a stepwise process of defining their problems in behavior-based terms. This is an accomplishment that, sometimes for the first time, allows them to construct the foundation of an action plan. Then family members turn their attention away from the addiction and to their own depleted state.

Table 16–1 Genevieve's Readiness for a Weekend Alone with Jim

(Recovery Reflected in the Four Questions)

Region	What do I want?	What would I admire?	What strengths do I have?	What do I feel?
Region III: Empowerment	I want to be away for a while so that I can visit my friend Joan, work out, and go to church. But I also want to see a play with Jim and have a sexual-romantic date with him.	Telling Jim what I want. Looking attractive and fit. Listening to my friend, praying with sincerity at church.	I can plan a great evening, push myself in a workout, listen to and support my friend, look attractive, show affection to my husband, and understand a good sermon.	I am excited about my plans for the weekend. I am a little annoyed that my friend Joan still holds a grudge against Jim. I am tired and need a nap before we go out.
Region II: Effort in a Grey World	I don't know. Maybe we will try something new. There's probably nothing we would both enjoy, and it's all too expensive. The plays are probably weird. I'll see what Jim wants to do.	Jim will want me to wash the floors and take care of the mound of bills and mail on our dresser. I suppose I should go to church.	I guess people think I'm nice. Jim thinks I'm loyal and dependable. I don't know.	I'm not looking forward to anything. It seems like so much work! I wish the weekend were over.
Region I: Exasperation	To binge on Haagen-Das, to run away, to have an affair with my boss, to join a convent and to kill Jim. It's all his fault.	Nothing! What do people want from me? I'm dumb for staying with Jim. But I'm disloyal for wanting to leave. There's no way to win.	I'm a lousy doormat! Maybe I'm a saint, who knows?	Like garbage. I'm scared and I feel sick. I'm completely lost.

Source: Reprinted with permission from *Taking charge: How families can climb out of the chaos of addiction . . . and flourish,* p. 26, by S. E. Schlesinger and L. K. Horberg. Copyright 1988 by S. E. Schlesinger and L. K. Horberg.
L. K. Horberg, 1988, New York: Fireside Books/Simon and Schuster. Copyright 1988 by S. E. Schlesinger and L. K. Horberg.

STRENGTHENING THE FAMILY

Once strengths and problems have been defined, the process of setting realistic goals begins by turning attention away from the addiction and focusing on the family members themselves and on their lives.

Helping family members focus on their wants, abilities, commitments, and good points will help them counteract the feelings of hopelessness that bog down the family. By acknowledging areas of strengths, the family equips itself to make use of them.

Until *self*-examination begins, despair increases, and the world appears to shrink. Eventually, it may seem that the only important events in the family have to do with the addiction: "Did he seem high when he came home?" "Will she overdose tonight?" "Will she even come home?"

In considering their depleted state, families focus on three areas: living a full life, taking better care of themselves, and developing supportive relationships.

Living a Full Life

Family members get stronger when they connect their desire for a full life with the need to stop participating in family pathology. Living a full life is at the core of recovery.

To the extent that family members know which experiences they want and which they detest, which of their choices and actions make them proud and which shame them, which situations stir feelings that enrich their lives and which detract from them, they will feel the motivation to take action and leave chaos behind. To the extent that they know and exercise their strengths, they will feel confident in their ability to live a full life. To the extent that members are unable to answer the four questions, they will be mired in confusion.

Families vary in their determination to live a full life and maintain their values. As a result, they also differ in the way they decide when enough is enough and when to take decisive action. Of interest to therapists are the general questions: When do families act? When do they become determined to fight their way out of the exasperation of Region I?

People in addictive families act at different points to tackle their problems. Decision points can be conceptualized on a continuum ranging from relatively untraumatic to life threatening, as follows:

1. distaste for the addict's behavior
2. public embarrassment; distaste for own behavior
3. threat to property/safety
4. endangered lives

Many factors influence how far on the continuum a given family can be pushed before taking action. McCubbin and McCubbin (1991) offer one useful model from which to generate predictions. Pragmatically, we find it very useful to help families that overfocus on "saving the addict" to understand the connection between tackling their problems at an earlier point along the continuum and their determination to live a full life.

Two tasks help family members approach living a fuller life. The first is for family members to clarify their wants, standards, strengths, and feelings. The second task guides family members through an examination of some of the cognitive components of recovery. It focuses on overcoming barriers to a full life and zeroes in on some opinions that obstruct recovery efforts and others that motivate healthy action. One useful approach to this task is cognitive-behavioral. We help families identify the dysfunctional philosophies that keep them isolated and block the development of personal and community resources. Table 16–2 is excerpted from Schlesinger and Horberg (1988).

Increasing Self-Care Activities

Whereas deteriorating self-care can damage the family further, habits of self-care, vigorously maintained, provide a family with strength and a sense of dignity and well-being. These habits fall into three important areas: general health and hygiene; maintenance of safety, well-being, and comfort; and management of stress. Each individual assumes some responsibility for himself in these areas, and the adults in the family assume additional responsibility to establish routines for the family. We will focus here on stress management.

Managing Stress in the Family

An important aspect of self-care that frequently is neglected in addictive families concerns their abilities to manage stress. In many cases, family members equate stress management with problem solving. Although problem solving is clearly an aspect of effective stress management, constantly trying to solve unsolvable problems (e.g., someone else's addiction) merely leads to repeated failure and a sense of helplessness. Even when problems can be solved, reliance on problem solving, to the exclusion of other forms of stress management, leads to frustration, depletion, and burnout.

An alternative to this unidimensional view of stress management is to view the management of stress from the broader perspective of an individual's lifestyle. This view follows from the work of Ayala Pines and Elliott Aronson (see, for example, Pines & Aronson, 1988).

Table 16–2 Overcoming Barriers to a Full Life

Opinions That Weaken	Opinions That Motivate
1. I failed myself and my family, and do not deserve to live a good life.	1. I did the best I knew how to do. I want to live the best life I can. Hurting myself, holding back, or being miserable will help no one. I am human and will make mistakes. For now, I'll "do the next right thing."
2. There is a blight on my family. We'd better not show our faces. We are pariahs.	2. All families endure pain, shame, or vulnerability at some point. There is dignity in accepting and coping with family problems. Some people may "throw stones," but others will respect what we are trying to do.
3. Our lives are awful because of the addiction; they will get better only when the addict learns how terrible he is and pays us back for our trouble. There is nothing I can do until then.	3. Our lives are what we make of them. If I am frustrated, I must want something. If I feel inadequate, there must be something I want to do better. If I feel unfulfilled, there must be something I want to accomplish. I cannot wait for the addict, I must live my life *now* (and help my children live their lives now!) My values, my satisfactions, my problems are my responsibility.
4. My satisfaction will come when I reform the addict. Then I will have done something really important. The addict has such potential, so much more than I do! If I could be the one to help him, he would take care of me and accept my weaknesses.	4. I cannot "save" anyone. I have to develop my own strengths, be the best person I can be.
5. The addict is only hurting me, and that does not really matter. If he were hurting others in our family, then I would have to do something. My welfare is unimportant.	5. I will no longer permit anyone to damage me or to stop me from living a full life. I am important, every bit as important as any other member of my family.
6. I am—for the addict—the patient and loving person I myself needed all of these years. To be firm right now would be harsh and cruel. It would create, for the addict, the same lousy condition I have had to live under my whole life.	6. I am different from the addict. I have not abused people who have been kind to me. I want support and will seek it. I want to give support, but I can only support health. I can no longer cater to abuse.

Activities to manage stress can be conceptualized along two dimensions: the type of activity (active vs. inactive) and the focus of attention (toward the stressor vs. away from the stressor). Assembling these dimensions in a 2 × 2 format defines four components of a stress management lifestyle (Exhibit 16–1).

Active methods that focus on the stressor reduce future stress by getting directly at the source. For example, when the family prohibits drunk driving among its members, it prevents worry and suffering. Successful stress reduction depends in part on effective problem solving. In this regard, it is helpful to review with family members seven necessary components of problem solving. They are as follows:

1. Quickly and naturally focus attention on problems as they arise.
2. Define and redefine problems clearly to promote problem solving.
3. Talk with others to get information, support, and help in organizing an approach to the problem.
4. Think of alternative solutions.
5. Take direct action by asserting self and making arrangements with others.
6. Take direct action by doing independent work.
7. Follow up and stick with routines designed to prevent problems in the future.

Inactive methods that focus attention on the stressor involve thinking, writing, and talking about problems. Family members often think of problems in a "mental shorthand" that does not lend itself to problem resolution. Putting thoughts into words requires that the problems be made concrete. In this way, the value of ventilating can be explained, and family members are encouraged to develop outlets.

Complaining is a highly underrated activity. It promotes ventilation of feelings, reorganization of thoughts, clarification of goals and wants, and identifica-

Exhibit 16–1 Components of a Stress Management Lifestyle

	Active	*Inactive*
Focus Attention on Stressor(s)	Problem Solving	Thinking Writing Talking
Focus Attention Away From Stressor(s)	Growing and Having Fun	Escaping

Source: Reprinted with permission from *Taking charge: How families can climb out of the chaos of addiction . . . and flourish,* p. 86, by S. E. Schlesinger and L. K. Horberg, 1988, New York: Fireside Books/Simon and Schuster. Copyright 1988 by S. E. Schlesinger and L. K. Horberg.

tion of stressors. To move forward, families must give themselves permission to complain. When complaining replaces suffering in silence, the family is getting better.

Active methods of focusing attention away from stressors refresh the spirit and enhance self-esteem away from the "field of battle." There is no way to help the addict if family members stop living, if they let themselves be consumed by the problem. They must include activities in their lives that help them have fun and grow. These may involve hobbies, exercise, and other active pursuits that family members enjoy, but that do not bear directly on the addict or the addiction.

Inactive methods of focusing attention away from stressors require the individual to set aside the compulsion to remain productive every waking moment. In fact, we all need time to "escape," to become absorbed in "idle" activities that help refresh us. These may include naps, meditation, reading a book, watching television, or anything else that allows a respite from the stress of one's life.

Balance is important in any lifestyle that is created to enhance the capacity to cope with stress. Those who spend most of their energies in one or another of the four categories of activities will be less successful in managing their stress than those who spread their activities among the four. For example, those who spend all of their time working will "burn out"; the "wheels will fall off the cart." And, those who complain excessively will alienate their friends, sink into despair, convince themselves of their impotence, and face an unchanging set of problems. Not only do all four activities fit nicely into a lifestyle approach to stress management, but also they work nicely as a set of guidelines for therapists to offer patients in crises. When an anxious client asks for direction in coping *tonight,* therapists can help the client draw out a balanced plan based on the 2 × 2 table.

Developing Supportive Relationships

Families grow stronger as their members develop relationships with people outside the family. In treatment, we focus family attention and behavioral experiments on four important benefits of involvement. First, involvement with friends, community groups, and task-oriented groups *strengthens personal identity.* Because addiction and social isolation go hand in hand, family members are often stripped of their roles and therefore stripped of their identities. When we perform our roles well, we think of ourselves as competent. Others help us maintain a stable sense of identity.

Second, involvement with others *enhances positive aspects of our lives.* Relationships and social contacts provide stimulation, variety, recognition, communication, closeness, attraction, intimacy, sense of purpose, useful activity, practical help, challenge, and structure.

Third, involvement with others *increases emotional support and challenge.* Addicts often command most of the attention in the family, interfering with the family's attempt to understand its everyday world and blinding family members to the possibility of finding support through involvement with others. Events in a chaotic family are difficult to think about and comprehend. In order to develop an understanding of their experiences, family members must first put those experiences into words and describe them to others, even though at first their descriptions may sound incomplete, disloyal, provocative, or offensive. Without access to supportive listeners, family members can never get past the numerous dead ends in their thinking. With support, however, experiences—no matter how painful—are accepted, discussed, and incorporated into the family's understanding of itself. Families can then describe their everyday lives in terms that remain stable over time and under different circumstances.

Fourth, involvement with others *increases informational support and challenge* by providing practical knowledge that helps in problem solving or in accomplishing tasks as they work toward their goals. Involvement with friends and groups naturally increases our access to expertise generally.

Developing supportive relationships is crucial to family recovery. However, there are many barriers to developing supportive relationships. This approach emphasizes four common ones: (a) outside contacts are viewed as extremely threatening; (b) outside relationships stir up feelings of inadequacy in people who suffer from low self-esteem; (c) family members may accept the idea that the addict has the right to limit their involvement in life; and (d) some of the family's beliefs may impede the effort to develop outside relationships. Table 16–3 gives examples of opinions that may either motivate or block action.

When family members feel stronger, they can turn their attention back to the addiction. Some family members are able to start the process of confronting the addiction soon after they start feeling stronger. As strength and confidence build, they are able to construct meaningful plans to separate themselves from the effects of another's destructive behavior. The crucial factor is that getting stronger must be incorporated into the process of confronting the addiction.

CONFRONTING THE ADDICTION

Once the family has begun to strengthen itself and to replenish its depleted emotional and physical stamina, it is time for members to focus once again on the addiction. The focus is not on how the family can manipulate a reluctant addict to stop his destructive behavior or force treatment upon him or her. Rather, the focus is on how the family can extricate itself from involvements with the addict that are unhealthy for the family and that may inadvertently support the addiction, and on how family members can invite the addict to join them in health and in flourishing.

Useful techniques at this stage resemble in some aspects the "intervention" strategies developed at the Johnson Institute (see, for example, Johnson, 1986). The major differences are that the Taking Charge approach focuses on family health rather than exclusively on the addict, and it views the process of intervening in the family's unhealthy behavior as a growth *process* rather than a coercive *event*.

The therapeutic goal at this point is to safely cut off support for destructive and other chaotic behaviors in the family, while selectively increasing the family's ability to support and participate in healthy patterns. The approach in this area is guided by a particular understanding of the construct of "enabling." This approach defines enabling as the degree to which family members support addictive behavior and/or the extent to which they fail to encourage healthy patterns that are incompatible with addictive behavior. Family actions support addictive behavior to the extent that they buffer negative consequences of addictive behavior, provide positive consequences for addictive behavior, or alter the addict's environment to make addictive behavior possible. Family

Table 16–3 Overcoming Barriers to Developing a Support System

Opinions That Block Action	*Opinions That Motivate*
1. Groups (churches, clubs, etc.) are open only to families. If I went alone, people would think I was weird. I'm angry that he won't go with me, and he's in no shape to go even if he were willing. I refuse to consider going alone.	1. I am very disappointed in the way our family has turned out, but I can't stop living. There must be room for me in the community. I'll find a group that will accept me and meet my needs, even though I may have to look for a while and even though I'll have to go out without him.
2. I became part of one group—my family—and it failed. I failed. I am afraid to meet other people only to be rejected again. Other people will see in me what my family sees and treat me just as poorly—because I deserve it.	2. The family has been distorted by addiction. I have to take the chance that others will respond to me in a healthier way. I will likely run into people who treat me poorly as I try to get involved in something better, but I *will* meet some nice people if I keep looking.
3. I owe all my time and energy to my family. Any time spent with others is a sign of disloyalty.	3. If I am getting support apart from my family, I will have more energy and purpose when I am with my family. No one owns my time. I am prepared to stand up for the way I spend it. I am entitled to enjoy relationships with people outside the family.

Source: Reprinted with permission from *Taking charge: How families can climb out of the chaos of addiction . . . and flourish*, p. 86, by S. E. Schlesinger and L. K. Horberg, 1988, New York: Fireside Books/Simon and Schuster. Copyright 1988 by S. E. Schlesinger and L. K. Horberg.

"support" can be in the form of material assistance, effort, companionship, or confirmation/approval to the addict. Enabling may continue despite family members' awareness that the behavior may be counterproductive.

Families encourage healthy patterns when—during times the addict is doing "well" and is committed to making progress—they respond warmly and supportively and help each other achieve their goals. When family members fail to acknowledge beneficial changes, they withhold support for healthy behavior (i.e., confirmation). When family members hold grudges and fail to work out their differences after recovery is well underway, they withhold "companionship." When they refuse to pitch in and participate in the recovering addict's life, they withhold effort and material assistance that helps support progress.

The structure of the overall effort to confront the addiction involves guiding the family through four decisions as they cut off support for chaotic or destructive behavior:

1. What *goals* are we setting out to accomplish?
2. *What* support should we withhold?
3. *When* should we withhold support?
4. *What should we say* to the addict about the changes in the family?

The process of withdrawing support for destructive behavior is similar in some ways to the classical intervention techniques practiced widely in addictions treatment centers. However, as practiced, intervention may have some drawbacks because it allows little room for flexibility of response. That is, it tends to evoke "all-or-none" reactions in the addict. So a first problem is that if it does not achieve the desired result, there may be no other options beyond the intervention. Second, it may inadvertently put the family in a position that they cannot maintain, so that the family is unable to follow through with its plan. The result is a continued inconsistency in their dealings with the addict. For example, a family that tells the addict, in effect, to "get well or get out" may provoke unnecessary resistance and then may have to decide whether they really want to stick to their threat to kick him or her out. If not, then once again "no means yes," and chaotic behavior is reinforced on an intermittent schedule.

With some crucial modifications, intervention can set the family in an important direction—to help the addict get help. The *Taking Charge* approach includes some differences in orientation and some ideas to make the work go more smoothly, with specific steps counselors and family members can take to move the process along. These methods are helpful for most addictive families, but they are particularly helpful with families who cannot yet respond to traditional intervention techniques, those who prefer cooperation to issuing coercive threats, and those who are not entirely alienated from their addicted significant other.

An alternative to the traditional techniques is for the family to take a less dramatic, more persistent approach in which it withholds only part of the support it provides the addict and escalates only if necessary. Family members approach their disengagement in a stepwise fashion. Limit setting is not approached as a method of controlling the addict. Loved ones learn when to limit their involvement with the addict so as to avoid unhealthy or harmful contact. They begin with an assessment of the resources they controlled that support addiction and proceed to create an action plan to withhold them when certain chaotic behaviors occur.

When asked to list the resources under their control, family members often draw a blank. In chaotic families, benefits are given in a way that buffers the negative consequences of addiction, rewards destructive behavior (e.g., making the addict the center of attention), or creates opportunities for destructive behavior (e.g., paying the gambler's bills, thereby allowing him to use his income to finance new wagers). To confront an addiction effectively is to harness the benefits of family membership to support health in order to help family members thrive together, or apart if separation is preferable.

Decision 1: What Goals Are We Setting Out To Accomplish?

It is important to discuss with family members ahead of time that the addict's drug use may continue even after the family withholds support for addiction. It is crucial that the family be very clear that their goal is to withhold support for destructive behavior. Many families can rally around the goal of disengaging themselves from complicity—intended or not—in the addictive process so *they* can get better and invite the addict to join them if they wish.

Decision 2: What Support Should We Withhold?

Family members frequently find it difficult to identify the things that they control and could potentially withhold from the addict when the addict engages in self-destructive behaviors. The most easily identified benefits typically are material. They include, for example, room and board, use of the car, money, and basic necessities. Nonmaterial support includes companionship, effort and attention, and personal acknowledgment or confirmation that the addict is a member of the family in good standing.

Decision 3: When Should We Withhold Support?

Once family members have an idea of what they have available to withhold, they are ready to consider the next question: when to withhold benefits from the addict. The answer to this question is twofold. First, family members need to identify the types of involvement with the addict that are poisonous for them and the ways in which they are painfully or self-destructively involved with the addict (e.g., handing the car keys to an adolescent who will drink).

The second part of the answer regarding when to withhold support is to consider the stance the addict has toward his or her addiction at the time. Stances range from the addict being in a life or death struggle as a result of his or her addiction through five other stances, ending with being abstinent and committed to a program of recovery. Family members may learn to vary their responses to otherwise unacceptable behavior depending on the stance in which they find the addict. If the addict is truly in a life or death situation, for example, the family may choose to respond in a manner to "rescue" the addict, even though at other times this may seem to support the very behavior they find unacceptable.

Family members are encouraged to think of limit setting in "if-then" (or contingent) terms. In other words, family members provide material and nonmaterial benefits only when they support health and when the family can do so with a good, free, clear feeling (i.e., the feeling one gets when one knows he is neither supporting illness nor participating in a humiliating or otherwise painful experience).

In the "if-then" formulation, family members create an action plan in which the "ifs" are specific behaviors and the "thens" are benefits to be withheld if the behaviors occur (or to be offered in the absence of those behaviors). The "if-then" chart that results from this process constitutes an action plan to guide the family's response to unacceptable behavior and to signal both its refusal to collude in illness and its resolve to live together in a healthy manner. We do *not* suggest that families assume the stance of the behavior analyst.

Having placed itself in a position to act, how then does the family talk to the addict about its decisions?

Decision 4: What Should We Say to the Addict?

Limits are incomplete unless they are communicated to the addict. Although counselors cannot tell their clients what to say, there are several guidelines to frame family members' thoughts about talking to the addict. First, make *simple statements* of facts, derived from the "if-then" chart, if necessary. Second, telling the addict *one thing at a time* is most effective. Third, being *brief and to the point* is crucial. Fourth, it is most helpful if family members place emphasis on the *positive reasons* the family is going to the trouble of communicating. This is not an invitation to a lynching party. It is an invitation to work toward a good life, either together or separately.

The fifth consideration is that of *safety*. Chaotic families are at higher risk for violence, and it is important that family members not expose themselves to potential danger in talking to the addict.

FLOURISHING

When family members have withdrawn themselves from unhealthy involvement with the addiction, they are ready to look ahead to creating satisfying lives for themselves. The goals in treatment at this point are to help families let go of trauma, overcome some common obstacles to progress, see images of recovery that can act as guides until they can formulate their own, and direct their energies to master the many arts of good living.

Letting Go of Trauma

Living with the impact of addictive behaviors can be traumatic for family members. They feel considerable pain, sometimes for extended periods of time. When they have removed themselves from the traumatic situation successfully, they must face the effects of the trauma so they can move on. For this, family members are introduced to a three-step process through which they can move past the impact of the trauma. It is called *the 3 Rs*. In Step 1, family members feel an acute need for *R*etribution, a longing for the addict to suffer in a manner commensurate with the pain they believe he or she has inflicted. Making concrete the means through which this suffering would occur usually is not possible, however. When the family sees the futility of revenge and when family members have been able to talk about traumatic events and empathize with each other, members move on to Step 2, in which they hope for *R*estitution from the addict for their suffering. When the currency of this repayment becomes hard to define and when current needs are gratified, family members typically move on to the third step. This involves seeking *R*efuge, or protection, from the possible recurrence of conditions that caused pain previously. The idea of refuge is an important one to reduce the feeling of vulnerability family members sometimes feel when they tackle the job of moving forward with their recovery. The action plan they develop in the "if-then" chart often provides a good measure of protection for family members. To rebuild deep trust, intimate communication is necessary.

Overcoming Obstacles to Progress

There are several obstacles to progress against which it is helpful to "inoculate" family members. Family members who expect "smooth sailing" sometimes interpret what are otherwise common obstacles as major complications in treatment and signs of the failure of their efforts. These obstacles are divided into eight categories, listed below.

1. Fear of uncertainty, change, and emptiness
2. Getting over the hump
3. Losing sight of the goal
4. Getting hung up on details
5. Embarrassment
6. Counterproductive or dysfunctional communication
7. Blaming
8. Inertia

At this point, family members have progressed through the stages of getting started, strengthening themselves, safely withdrawing their support for the addiction, formulating and communicating their healthy resolve, getting past the trauma that chaotic family life left in its wake, and preparing themselves to face the obstacles that may present themselves as they continue their recovery. Family members now need to learn to flourish.

The first step in understanding the concept of flourishing is to recognize that family recovery can have any of a variety of outcomes. Anticipating the possibilities is important if family members are to free themselves from the single-minded focus on healing the addict. If, for example, family members come to expect that "successful" family recovery can be achieved only if all members of the family get better at the same time and the family reconstitutes itself fully, many families may be disappointed and interpret their efforts as failures. Preparing families for the possibility that recovery may be represented in a variety of healthy outcomes is another way of "inoculating" them and helping them anticipate potential obstacles to a realistic view of their efforts.

Recovery at this point continues with the family's focus on creating healthy, satisfying lives. In our experience, family members who complete the steps in Getting Started, Strengthening the Family, and Confronting the Addiction emerge with fresh energy and confidence. Often the addict becomes involved in the recovery process; sometimes the family moves on without the addict. But in either case, family members are then ready for fresh challenges. If they avoid finding new challenges, their energy will leave them, and they may go through protracted periods of emptiness and dysphoria. The four questions, presented in connection with the journey metaphor, are helpful in focusing family attention on what to think about and do next. Feelings, wants, values, and strengths provide the best road map for the continuation of the journey. It is at this stage that the needs of families in recovery diverge markedly.

REFERENCES

Johnson, V. E. (1986). *Intervention: How to help someone who doesn't want help.* Minneapolis: Johnson Institute Books.

McCubbin, M. A., & McCubbin, H. I. (1991). Family stress theory and assessment: The Resiliency Model of Family Stress, Adjustment and Adaptation. In H. I. McCubbin & A. I. McCubbin (Eds.), *Family assessment inventories for research and practice* (pp. 3–32). Madison: University of Wisconsin at Madison, Family Stress Coping and Health Project.

Pines, A., & Aronson, E. (1988). *Career burnout: Causes and cures.* New York: Free Press.

Schlesinger, S. E. (1988). Cognitive-behavioral approaches to family treatment of addictions. In N. Epstein, S.E. Schlesinger, & W. Dryden (Eds.), *Cognitive-behavioral therapy with families* (pp. 254–291). New York: Brunner/Mazel.

Schlesinger, S. E., & Gillick, J. J. (1989). *Stop drinking and start living.* (2nd ed.) Blue Ridge Summit, PA: TAB Books.

Schlesinger, S. E., & Horberg, L. K. (1988). *Taking charge: How families climb out of the chaos of addiction . . . and flourish.* New York: Simon & Schuster.

Chapter 17

Couple-Focused Therapy for Substance-Abusing Women

*Joseph L. Wetchler, Thorana S. Nelson,
Eric E. McCollum, Terry S. Trepper, and
Robert A. Lewis*

This chapter presents a brief, couple-focused therapy model, Systemic Couples Therapy (SCT), currently being tested in the treatment of substance-abusing women. Although couple-based models have had success with male substance abusers (McCrady, 1990; O'Farrell, 1992), little is known about what works with women (Vanicelli, 1984). The project in which SCT is being utilized deals specifically with female substance abusers.

SCT is an integrated model utilizing aspects of structural (Minuchin, 1974), strategic (Haley, 1987; Watzlawick, Weakland, & Fisch, 1974), and transgenerational (Bowen, 1978) family therapies. It is an abstinence-based model designed to be used in conjunction with an individual substance abuse treatment program. It is suggested that a woman complete detox prior to the start of SCT.

Women eligible for treatment with the research project must have a sustained substance abuse problem and be involved in an ongoing dyadic relationship. A dyadic relationship is defined as a marital or a cohabiting relationship. The model is being utilized with both heterosexual and lesbian couples.

PHILOSOPHY OF THE MODEL

SCT is based on a family systems concept of substance abuse (e.g., Stanton & Todd, 1982; Steinglass, 1987; Todd & Selekman, 1991). Specifically, it asserts that a woman's ongoing substance abuse problem is maintained by the relational context in which it exists. Further, the woman's substance abuse serves to stabilize the couple's relationship. It is hypothesized that when a woman detoxifies from drugs, unresolved relationship issues that were previously not addressed spring to the forefront. Because the couple have relied on the substance abuse as a way of avoiding these problems, they often lack the coping mechanisms to deal with them. This often leads to greater stress than the couple are able to handle. A common outcome is the woman returning to substance abuse as a way of escaping these issues and stabilizing the relationship.

SCT is designed to be an adjunct to individual substance abuse treatment for women. It is not recommended for use on its own. The woman must deal with the personal issues of giving up her drug as well as the relationship issues that arise in its absence.

The Family Systems Concept As an Alternative to the Disease Concept

The authors suggest that the family systems model may be preferable to the disease concept in treating women substance abusers. The disease concept and 12-step model were initially designed to deal with male alcoholics who believed they should be able to control their drinking. Accepting one's powerlessness over a substance due to a disease counters the societally induced belief that it is manly to drink and that a strong man should be able to control his liquor (Bateson, 1972; Elkin, 1984).

The issue of power is central to the treatment of women substance abusers. Society supports the concept of the isolated, powerful male and the dependent, relationship-oriented, submissive female (Goodrich, Rampage, Ellman, & Halstead, 1988; Walters, Carter, Papp, & Silverstein, 1988). Bepko (1989) asserts that males drink to feel powerful whereas females drink to suppress the desire for power. Further, the issue of power cannot be overlooked in the relationships of substance-abusing women. Many male partners are themselves substance abusers and may actively or passively resist the woman's recovery (Beckman & Amaro, 1984; Wanberg & Horn, 1970).

Asking women substance abusers to claim their powerlessness over a specific drug may add to the general feeling of powerlessness they already experience (Haney, 1989; Johnson, 1990). On the other hand, a family systems model attempts to alter the interactional patterns that maintain the power imbalance in the relationship. The attempt is to create a more egalitarian relationship that supports mutual problem solving and supports a drug-free lifestyle.

Although SCT is nondisease oriented, it recognizes that most treatments are based on this concept. Because it is systems based, it works within the woman's belief system. SCT is contextually respectful. If a woman's orientation is toward a 12-step approach, her therapist should attempt to make treatment consistent with her beliefs. If a woman is not 12-step oriented, the therapist is advised to avoid this language. The important issue is that the SCT therapist is concerned with altering the interactional system that maintains a woman's substance abuse. This is the major theoretical issue within this model.

Theoretical Roots of Systemic Couples Therapy

As stated earlier, SCT combines aspects of present-centered and transgenerational family therapies. From the strategic school (Haley, 1987; Watzlawick et al., 1974) comes the idea that a woman's substance abuse problem is maintained by present-centered interactional behaviors. Therefore it is important that those behaviors a woman and her partner engage in around her substance abuse must change if she is to remain drug free.

Important structural family therapy (Minuchin, 1974; Minuchin & Fishman, 1981) concepts are hierarchy and power. Traditional gender role arrangements give men a disproportionate amount of power in relationships (Goldner, 1991; Goodrich et al., 1988). Is the hierarchy in the relationship such that the partner consistently has more influence over what happens in the relationship than the woman? Can the couple compromise without the woman giving in to avoid conflict (Hare-Mustin, 1980)? Is the woman faced with the threat of abuse or abandonment? These are important issues in the treatment of woman substance abusers.

The transgenerational schools (e.g., Boszormenyi-Nagy & Krasner, 1986; Bowen, 1978; Kerr & Bowen, 1988) provide the concept that relationship patterns are repeated across generations. SCT therapists help the couple understand how their relationship and the woman's substance abuse problem are part of a multigenerational pattern. Understanding their problem in a transgenerational context helps the couple to devise new strategies for improving their relationship and maintaining a drug-free lifestyle.

STAGES OF TREATMENT

SCT is designed as a 12-session model. Each session lasts approximately 1 hour. Of course, therapy may be shorter or longer depending on how fast issues are resolved or if new problems arise. SCT is conceptualized in three broad stages:

1. Creating a Context for Change
2. Challenging Behaviors and Expanding Alternatives
3. Consolidating Change

Stage 1 is concerned with assessing the couple and creating a treatment contract. Stage 2 focuses on altering those dysfunctional patterns that maintain the substance abuse. Stage 3 helps the couple solidify their changes and prepares them for termination. These stages, and all of their components, should be personalized to fit the needs of each specific couple. They are not intended to be followed in a rigid manner.

STAGE I: CREATING A CONTEXT FOR CHANGE

Joining

Developing a strong therapeutic relationship is crucial in treating the substance abuser (Burton & Kaplan, 1968; Stanton & Todd, 1982). This is especially true with women because they are highly reluctant to enter drug treatment (Beckman & Amaro, 1984). Male alcoholics enter treatment two and one-half times more frequently than females (Beckman & Amaro, 1984). Much of this is related to the fact that it is more socially acceptable for a man to have a substance abuse problem than a woman (Kane-Caviola & Rullo-Cooney, 1991). Further, many women do not seek treatment until they are coerced by the courts or child protective agencies (Beckman & Amaro, 1984).

Important issues deal with the accessibility of treatment for women. Adequate child care is a major issue for women in substance abuse therapy (Beckman & Amaro, 1984; Kane-Caviola & Rullo-Cooney, 1991). It is important that treatment sites either provide child care facilities or help women find appropriate support. Further, alternative financial considerations (Kane-Caviola & Rullo-Cooney, 1991) and transportation services (Beckman & Amaro, 1984) are important factors in helping women remain in therapy.

A further consideration is developing a relationship with the woman's partner. Because SCT takes a couple-focused approach to treatment, therapists must be sure that the partner does not feel blamed for the problem. Further, many partners of female substance abusers may be resistant to treatment because they too have a drug problem (Beckman & Amaro, 1984; Wanberg & Horn, 1970).

Assessment

Problem Definition

Therapists start the assessment by asking the couple to state their view of the problem. Each partner is asked his or her perception of the problem and what he or she wants out of therapy. It is important to help them define their problem in a specific behavioral manner (Haley, 1987; Watzlawick et al., 1974). Many couples will state more than just substance abuse problems. This is appropriate and workable in therapy. However, therapists should state that one goal of the treatment will be abstinence for those couples who do not perceive substance abuse as a problem.

Individual Assessment — Mental Status Exam

Therapists need to be aware of dual-diagnosis issues that may impact treatment. Part of the assessment should focus on the potential for violence, depression, and suicide. It also is important to assess whether a history of sexual abuse exists with either partner or if either is facing legal difficulties. Referral for further evaluation is in order if indications of psychiatric disturbance exist.

Identifying Interpersonal Sequences Surrounding Substance Abuse

An important assessment component involves identifying the interpersonal sequences that surround the substance abuse and other relationship problems. It is helpful for therapists to ask factual, sequential questions to better understand the pattern (Watzlawick et al., 1974). Therapists should focus on behaviors that occur both before and after the drug-abusing behavior.

A common pattern exists surrounding conflictual behavior. Although both partners may actively engage in the conflict, the male partner begins to dominate. The woman often gives in to the partner or escapes the situation to avoid a major escalation. She then engages in substance abuse to anesthetize her feelings of pain and anger. Afterward, the partner may continue to be dominant and intrusive by demanding that the woman discuss the incident. The woman refuses to discuss the issue, the situation becomes emotionally charged, and the pattern repeats itself.

Multigenerational Family System Assessment

The fourth component of the assessment involves the use of a genogram to examine transgenerational patterns that maintain the substance abuse problem. The first aspect of this procedure is to assess family relationship patterns as far back as the grandparents' generations. Identifying similar patterns of behavior and issues for other family members helps the couple place their problem in a broader context. This can relieve some of the stress and help the couple define new ways of relating to each other.

A second aspect of this assessment is to identify the occurrence and function of substance abuse in the family of origin (Steinglass, 1987). Of specific concern is the way substance abuse was a part of family rituals (Bennett & Wolin, 1990; Bennett, Wolin, Reiss, & Teitlebaum, 1987; Steinglass, 1987). For example, did family members typically get drunk and pass out during holiday celebrations? Was heavy drinking a normal part of the dinner routine? Only after the couple have identified how they have continued the ritualized pattern of substance abuse in their lives can they alter this behavior.

Finally, therapists should assess for incidents of childhood physical and sexual abuse because these have been linked to women's abuse of drugs and alcohol (Barrett & Trepper, 1991). Further, the therapist should ask who in the family knew about the abuse, what action was taken to protect the victim, and what emotional tone surrounded the discovery of the abuse (Trepper & Barrett, 1989).

Contracting

The final aspect of Stage 1 is to contract with the clients for the goals of therapy. During this phase, the therapist summarizes the findings of the assessment and links them to the substance-abusing behavior. This provides a rationale for the couple to work together on the problem.

It is important that the therapist secure the couple's agreement to work together. Any forward movement is dependent on their willingness to engage in the treatment process. Further, if they agree to work together, the problem begins to shift from the woman to the couple.

It is helpful for the therapist to discuss the negative consequences of change with the couple. This is not done in an attempt to paradoxically move the couple to change; rather, it is a statement of the therapist's knowledge of the problems that may occur. Helping the couple to become "informed consumers" lessens the negative effect of problems down the road and enhances the degree of trust toward the therapist.

STAGE II: CHALLENGING BEHAVIORS AND EXPANDING ALTERNATIVES

The main objective of Stage 2 is to change the process of the couple's relationship. The therapist attempts to alter the dysfunctional couple sequences surrounding the drug use and help the couple increase their problem-solving and communication skills. The focus is not necessarily on the content of the communication as much as it is on the process.

Couple Negotiation

A cornerstone of SCT involves helping the couple to negotiate in a new manner. Alcoholic couples report high levels of marital conflict (Leonard, 1990; McCrady, 1990), and those who relapse have more conflict than those who do not (Moos & Moos, 1984). It is important to have the couple negotiate in a new way. As the couple begin to work together on problem areas, they develop a mutuality in their relationship and improve their ability to handle differences of opinion. The process of couple negotiation enhances the couple's degree of intimacy. They develop a greater degree of trust and caring because they can share differences and work together to resolve them.

The therapist actively helps the couple develop a new negotiation process. The therapist blocks attacking behavior and has the partners state their wants and needs. Further, the therapist acts as a gatekeeper to allow each partner to talk and to block one from dominating the discussion. This is especially important when working with women. Because women tend to give in to their partners to preserve harmony, therapists must be vigilant in empowering them to state their needs.

Less emphasis is placed on the topic the couple chooses than on the process they engage in. However, it is usually helpful to discuss a topic that is related to the presenting problem. For example, the couple can negotiate alcohol-free activities that they mutually agree upon. Further discussion is needed as they plan and implement these behaviors. Many couples will begin to discuss marital issues. Relationship problems provide excellent topics for discussion.

Altering Dysfunctional Couple Sequences

Interventions within this phase involve the couple's identifying a problem-maintaining sequence and discovering a potential way to alter it. Sequences can be discovered through having the couple describe a situation or having them enact it in the room (Haley, 1987). After the sequence has been identified, the therapist has the couple discuss how they can alter it. This can be especially useful with problems that arise in the couple negotiation process. The therapist might point out how the couple always interrupts each other when they disagree. She then might have them negotiate a process in which each must first repeat back what the other has said before stating his or her position.

A second process involves the therapist's developing a homework assignment for the couple to do outside the session. For example, a therapist might assign a potentially violent couple to agree to separate for a few hours at the first sign of a major conflict. They can try to discuss the problem when they come back together or wait until the next therapy session.

It is important that each partner focus on how to alter his or her behavior as opposed to his or her partner's. A woman who feels pressured to explain herself to her husband may choose to say she needs time to relax and will talk to him later as opposed to her usual pattern of yelling at him or leaving the house to get high. He will then have to do something to keep himself busy while his wife relaxes instead of pressuring her to talk now.

Another important aspect of altering a substance-abusing sequence is to change the process as early in the pattern as possible. As the sequence progresses, it reaches a stage of inevitability where it is extremely difficult to stop.

It is easier to intervene at the point where the couple is in the early stages of negotiating a problem than to wait until the argument becomes abusive or the wife has begun drinking.

Neutralizing Family of Origin Themes and Patterns in the Present Context

Family of origin themes can be brought into the present in one of three ways. The first has the therapist discussing similar patterns between the couple and their families of origin and having them decide whether to change them. For example, the therapist might point out how the couple include liquor with dinner much as the woman's alcoholic father did. They would then be asked if they wished to continue the process of drinking with dinner or do something else.

A second intervention involves discussing transgenerational information to facilitate a stuck negotiation process. After noticing that a woman repeatedly gave in to her husband when negotiating an evening out, the therapist pointed out that she was responding to her husband much as her mother responded to her father. Recognizing that this was a learned response, the woman was able to become more assertive with her husband.

A third intervention involves actually having the couple respond differently with their families of origin. This should be attempted with much guidance from the therapist. One woman recognized that she always relapsed when she went home to her parents on holidays. The woman identified that she could not say no to her father when he offered her a drink. She did not want to hurt his feelings. Because her father was an alcoholic, she was offered several drinks throughout the night. The woman developed a plan in which she would reject the alcohol but ask for a soft drink instead. This way she could allow her father to give her something while still maintaining her sobriety.

STAGE III: CONSOLIDATION

The final stage of therapy focuses on consolidating the changes the couple have made. Specifically the therapist and couple discuss what they did to achieve their gains and plan how they will deal with future problems.

It is important that the couple have a clear understanding about what they did to bring about change. Discussing this is helpful in three ways. First, it helps them to see how far they have come and to feel that they have accomplished something important. Second, they recognize that they have control over their lives. Third, by identifying what they have done to solve their problems they realize that they have the tools to resolve similar problems in the future.

Discussing possible future problems with the couple provides them with a strong dose of reality. They realize that problems exist throughout life and their current change is not an all-encompassing panacea. As they discuss how they can deal with these problems, they further consolidate the idea that they can control their lives and that they have the tools to do this. Planning for the future may also include referrals for treatment for other problems such as sexual abuse or past traumas.

CONCLUSION

SCT provides a brief, couple-focused approach for the treatment of substance-abusing women. It is designed to be used in conjunction with an individual substance abuse program. It is hoped that the SCT study will provide more information on what is effective with women substance abusers.

REFERENCES

Barrett, M. J., & Trepper, T. S. (1991). Treating women drug abusers who were victims of childhood incestuous abuse. *Journal of Feminist Family Therapy 3*, 127–146.

Bateson, G. (1972). *Steps to an ecology of mind.* New York: Ballantine.

Beckman, L. J., & Amaro, H. (1984). Patterns of women's use of alcohol treatment agencies. In S. C. Wilsnack & L. J. Beckman (Eds.), *Alcohol problems in women* (pp. 319–348). New York: Guilford.

Bennett, L. A., & Wolin, S. J. (1990). Family culture and alcoholism transmission. In R. L. Collins, K. E. Leonard, & J. S. Searles (Eds.), *Alcohol and the family* (pp. 194–219). New York: Guilford.

Bennett, L. A., Wolin, S. J., Reiss, D., & Teitlebaum, M. A. (1987). Couples at risk for transmission of alcoholism: Protective influences. *Family Process, 26*, 111–129.

Bepko, C. (1989). Disorders of power: Women and addiction in the family. In M. McGoldrick, C. M. Anderson, & F. Walsh (Eds.), *Women in families* (pp. 406–426). New York: Norton.

Boszormenyi-Nagy, I., & Krasner, B. (1986). *Between give and take: A clinical guide to contextual therapy.* New York: Brunner/Mazel.

Bowen, M.(1978). *Family therapy in clinical practice.* New York:Aronson.

Burton, G., & Kaplan, H. (1968). Group counseling in conflicted marriages where alcoholism is present: Client's evaluation of effectiveness. *Journal of Marriage and the Family, 30*, 74–79.

Elkin, M. (1984). *Families under the influence.* New York: Norton.

Goldner, V. (1991). Sex, power, and gender: A feminist systemic analysis of the politics of passion. In T. J. Goodrich (Ed.), *Women and power: Perspectives for family therapy* (pp. 86–106). New York: Norton.

Goodrich, T. J., Rampage, C., Ellman, B., & Halstead, K. (1988). *Feminist family therapy.* New York: Norton.

Haley, J. (1987). *Problem-solving therapy.* San Francisco: Jossey-Bass.

Haney, E. (1989). *Vision and struggle: Meditations on feminist spirituality and politics.* Portland, ME: Astarte Shell Press.

Hare-Mustin, R. (1980). Family therapy may be dangerous for your health. *Professional Psychology, 11*, 935–938.

Johnson, S. (1990). *Wildfire: Igniting the she/volution.* Albuquerque, NM: Wildfire Books.

Kane-Caviola, C., & Rullo-Cooney, D. (1991). Addicted women: Their families' effect on treatment outcome. In E. B. Isaacson (Ed.), *Chemical dependency: Theoretical approaches and strategies working with individuals and families* (pp. 111–119). Binghamton, NY: Haworth.

Kerr, M. E., & Bowen, M. (1988). *Family evaluation.* New York: Norton.

Leonard, K. (1990). Marital functioning among episodic and steady alcoholics. In R. L. Collins, K. E. Leonard, & J. S. Searles (Eds.), *Alcohol and the family* (pp. 220–243). New York: Guilford.

McCrady, B.S. (1990). The marital relationship and alcoholism treatment. In R. L. Collins, K. E. Leonard, & J. S. Searles (Eds.), *Alcohol and the family* (pp. 338–355). New York: Guilford.

Minuchin, S. (1974). *Families and family therapy.* Cambridge, MA: Harvard.

Minuchin, S., & Fishman, H. C. (1981). *Family therapy techniques.* Cambridge, MA: Harvard University Press.

Moos, R. H., & Moos, B. S. (1984). The process of recovery from alcoholism, III. Comparing functioning of families of alcoholics and matched control families. *Journal of Studies on Alcohol, 45,* 111–118.

O'Farrell, T. J. (1992). Using couples therapy in the treatment of alcoholism. *Family Dynamics of Addiction Quarterly, 1*(4), 39–45.

Stanton, M. D., & Todd, T. C. (1982). *The family therapy of drug abuse and addiction.* New York: Guilford.

Steinglass, P. (1987). *The alcoholic family.* New York: Basic Books.

Todd, T. S., & Selekman, M. D. (Eds.). (1991). *Family therapy approaches with adolescent substance abusers.* New York: Norton.

Trepper, T. S., & Barrett, M. J. (1989). *Systemic treatment of incest.* New York: Brunner/Mazel.

Vanicelli, M. (1984). Treatment outcome of alcoholic women: The state of the art in relation to sex bias and expectancy in women. In S. C. Wilsnack & L. J. Beckman (Eds.), *Alcohol problems in women* (pp. 369–412). New York: Guilford.

Walters, M., Carter, B., Papp, P., & Silverstein, O. (1988). *The invisible web.* New York: Guilford.

Wanberg, K. W., & Horn, J. L. (1970). Alcoholism symptom patterns of men and women: A comparative study. *Quarterly Journal of Studies on Alcohol, 31,* 40–61.

Watzlawick, P., Weakland, J., & Fisch, R. (1974). *Change.* New York: Norton.

Chapter 18

The Use of Denial and Its Gender Implications in Alcoholic Marriages

Gail S. Lederer

Some degree of denial and invalidation of circumstances and feelings occurs in most marriages, whether or not alcoholism is present. What makes denial different when it occurs in alcoholic marriages is the overlay of dynamics attributable specifically to alcoholic systems. Typically, alcoholic systems exhibit an oscillation between reciprocal extremes of under- and overresponsibility along with issues of pride and shame (Bepko & Krestan, 1985). When these dynamics occur in conjunction with gender prescriptions for women related to issues of overresponsibility, entitlement, and power, the strength of denial in the marital system increases. If a therapist tries to deal solely with the alcoholic denial in the marital relationship without attending to the process of invalidation and the underlying gender issues, she may meet with considerable resistance. The therapist is asking her female client to make changes that conflict directly with society's defined expectations for women. Using gender concepts to examine denial of alcoholism addresses denial in a way that is understandable to the woman because it matches her experience of herself in the family and the world.

DENIAL AND INVALIDATION

It is an accepted tenet with both AA and those treating alcoholic families that denial is a major stumbling block to the recovery process (Bepko & Krestan, 1985; Bowen, 1978; Davis, Berenson, Steinglass, & Davis, 1974). One component of denial is its inherent invalidation of reality. In order to deny the existence of a problem, one must invalidate either one's own perceptions or those of others. *Invalidation* here refers to discounting or refusing completely to acknowledge the validity of what another person says, believes, or does. Alcoholic systems constantly use denial and so are continually invalidating each family member's perception of what is happening (Lederer & Brown, 1991).

When a woman's thoughts and feelings are routinely discounted or nullified by her spouse, she begins to doubt what she does perceive. Told often enough that she is wrong, that she does not know what she knows, whittles away at her self-esteem. When it is the woman who *denies her own* perceptions, she invalidates the circumstances of her life.

DENIAL AND OVERRESPONSIBILITY

Feminists have long pointed to how societal gender messages train a woman to feel responsible for her family's problems and emotional well-being (Bepko & Krestan, 1985; Chodorow, 1978; Goodrich,1991; Lederer & Brown, 1991; Walters, Carter, Papp, & Silverstein, 1988). The message that she is responsible for any problems that arise in the family gives her the belief that she can fix what supposedly she has caused. Such messages, heard since birth, become internalized, shaping her sense of herself (Bepko & Krestan, 1985; Chodorow, 1978; Goldner, 1989; Hare-Mustin, 1989; Walters et al., 1988). Once these gender role prescriptions form part of a woman's belief system, the groundwork for denial is laid. In fact, these traditional gender role prescriptions actually encourage the use of denial and make the therapist's job of shifting alcoholic relationships more difficult.

Feeling responsible for someone else's emotions leaves a woman susceptible to alcoholic denial. When alcoholism occurs in the family, she is quick to blame herself and feels shame at "falling down on the job" of caretaking. Asking a woman to admit that she has a drinking problem, an underresponsible position, is asking her to admit that she has failed in her prescribed gender role. Denial of alcoholism offers a way to avoid acknowledging this failure. Most likely, she is already feeling shame and guilt at being an alcoholic because society views women alcoholics with more stigma than it does men (Bepko, 1988; Bepko & Krestan, 1985; Fossum & Mason, 1989). If children are involved, a woman is stigmatized further because society gives motherhood top priority.

Asking a woman to admit that her husband has a drinking problem is also a clear breach of her perceived role because she holds herself responsible for his problem. If she denies his drinking, she can also deny any responsibility for it. In fact, her denial of his drinking actually allows her to take on even more responsibility as she compensates for his underresponsibility (Bepko, 1988; Bepko & Krestan, 1985). Either way, if she is to feel successful in adhering to societal prescriptions to be overresponsible, she has no choice other than to deny the existence of a drinking problem in the marriage.

DENIAL AND ENTITLEMENT

The overresponsibility of trying to take care of other people's needs first and putting her own needs last eventually erodes a woman's sense of entitlement

(Lederer & Brown, 1991). She comes to believe that her own thoughts and feelings don't matter. *Entitlement* here refers to a woman's right to her own thoughts and feelings, as well as the right to expect that these thoughts and feelings matter to her spouse. Over time, as a woman's self-esteem continues to decrease, she loses the ability to take action on her own behalf. She fears such action would be construed as selfish by her husband (Miller, 1982; Walters et al., 1988), a view she probably also holds (Miller, 1982).

If the woman's husband is the alcoholic, he adds to her feeling unentitled each time he denies his drinking problem. His denial invalidates her personal truth, robbing her of self. She goes along with her husband's denial because her overresponsibility for his drinking and her own low sense of entitlement prevent her from challenging him. If the woman is the alcoholic, her denial of a drinking problem further chisels away at her sense of entitlement (Bepko, 1988; Jordan, 1989). She is only too aware of societal gender messages that tell her how lucky she is that her husband stays with her despite her drinking. Her feelings of guilt and shame, coupled with her low self-worth, preclude her from admitting a problem or asking for help. Denial seems a better choice to her than acknowledging how needy she feels.

DENIAL AND VALIDATION

When a therapist validates a woman's right to get her needs met, the process of building entitlement begins. The strength of the therapist's belief in the legitimacy and worth of the woman's feelings supports this process. Over time, as the therapist continually validates a woman's right to her own thoughts and feelings, the woman begins to believe in herself. As the therapist points out gender messages and gives permission to disregard these messages, she helps shift her female client's belief system to a more entitled stance. When a woman's sense of entitlement increases, she starts to expect more for herself. The more she expects her opinions and needs to be heard, the easier it becomes to acknowledge drinking as a problem. However, when the woman is the alcoholic, a greater sense of entitlement does not take care of the problem alone. The woman's relationship with alcohol and its effect on her definition of herself must also be addressed . The greater sense of entitlement facilitates this process, but the addiction must also be treated (Bepko, 1989). When the woman is the nondrinking spouse, gaining a strong sense of entitlement will empower her to disengage from her husband's drinking and stick to it, no matter how he responds. It is putting this increased sense of entitlement into action that creates the personal power to lead her life as she chooses, making denial unnecessary.

DENIAL AND POWER

Men's sense of entitlement and power differs from women's by virtue of their different experience of a world that confers higher status and privilege to men than to women (Bepko & Krestan, 1985). This higher status gives a man a strong sense of entitlement to get his needs met by others. He knows from gender messages that women are supposed to accede to this entitlement. This is not the same entitlement as a woman's learning how to get her own needs met by taking responsibility for herself. What makes it so difficult for a woman to gain this type of entitlement is that she comes at it from a one-down position that parallels societal power arrangements. Unlike men, women do not have society's sanction to get their needs met. This lack of sanction gives a woman little power to negotiate a more equitable position in her marital relationship. Denial reinforces this power differential.

Gender prescriptions for men to be strong, to be the primary wage earner, to be reasonable and not emotional, and to have answers and come up with solutions to problems also support alcoholic denial. Like women, men use denial to avoid seeing the disparity between these male gender prescriptions and their personal reality. They fear that if they do not live up to society's expectations for men, they will lose their higher status and greater power that the culture has granted them. When a man invalidates a woman, his invalidation serves the purpose of maintaining power over her, a power that is culturally sanctioned. This inequitable power arrangement is conducive to a climate in which denial can flourish. When it is the husband who is alcoholic, his refusal to acknowledge the problem serves to keep the woman in a one-down position. The unstated message behind his denial is that his views count and hers do not. If he can get her to back off and not take any action that would challenge his denial and hold him accountable, he can maintain his power over her. He is using the force of his entitlement to continue the status quo that keeps him in a one-up position (Bepko & Krestan, 1985; Goodrich, 1991).

In some cases, the woman goes along with her husband's denial in an attempt to gain additional power through overfunctioning for him. The more he drinks, the more she can take on those functional responsibilities he no longer can manage. But she cannot acknowledge this power (Bepko, 1989; Bepko & Krestan, 1985) because it is dependent on his continuing to underfunction. Power gained in this conditional manner is not true power; it is merely the illusion of power. The reality is that it is just another instance of a woman overfunctioning and therefore still consistent with what her female gender role dictates. The illusion of power has merely served to prevent her from seeing how much of herself she sacrifices when she gains power through overfunctioning for her husband. Her low sense of entitlement prevents her from recognizing that far from gaining power, her husband's denial disempowers her even more. The inequity within the marriage still exists.

The imbalance of power in the marital relationship becomes even more skewed when the woman is the alcoholic. Her alcoholism lowers her status, disempowering her further. Although denial in this instance can protect her from seeing the inequity and powerlessness in her life (Bepko, 1988; Fossum & Mason, 1989), it also reinforces the existing power arrangement. She does not feel entitled to challenge this inequitable power arrangement because powerlessness breeds more powerlessness.

DENIAL AND RESPONSIBILITY FOR SELF

When a woman feels powerless, unentitled, and overresponsible, challenging alcoholic denial, either for herself or her spouse, seems too difficult. Until she is able to stop overfunctioning for her spouse or underfunctioning for herself, the power in the marital relationship cannot be shifted (Barrett, 1992). She will need to take more responsibility for herself and define her own needs (Bowen, 1978; Brown, 1991; Krestan & Bepko, 1988), which, by virtue of the complementarity in the relationship, will decrease her overresponsibility for her husband. As she gains a stronger sense of entitlement to her own needs, she can begin the process of gaining more personal power for herself in the marriage.

Power, or lack of it, is related to a person's sense of entitlement (Bepko & Krestan, 1985; Lederer & Brown, 1991), but a strong sense of entitlement in and of itself does not equal power. It is the combination of stating one's entitlement and then acting on that entitlement that creates power for a woman. The transition from entitlement to action is very difficult to make but crucial if a woman is to experience a sense of personal power to affect the quality and direction of her life. The feeling of power comes as she puts her new-found sense of entitlement into action *and* holds fast in the face of invalidation. The more she takes action, the more entitled she feels to continue to ask for and expect her needs to be recognized. Only then can she really begin to look at the areas of her life that previously she has had to deny.

As a woman's sense of entitlement grows and her personal power increases, the power imbalance in the marital relationship begins to shift. The more equity she feels in the marital relationship, the more she is able to take a stand for herself and challenge the denial in the system. As a woman is able to be truer to her authentic self, no longer denying who she is as a way to meet gender expectations, facing either her own or her husband's addiction becomes less daunting. The following case illustrates the need to address gender issues of overresponsibility, entitlement, and power as a way to challenge alcoholic denial.

THE PRESENTING PROBLEM

Claire, age 35, and Jim, age 36, came for marital counseling. She complained that she felt like a single parent with their two girls, age 5 and 2. She blamed

Jim's lack of participation in family life on his drinking. Jim denied that drinking was a problem. He said the reason he was not home more was because he was trying to make partner at his company and that required long hours. He said he had only come to this session at Claire's request. He did not plan to continue. Claire decided to continue therapy on her own. I had only been meeting with Claire for a few weeks when she told me about the following incident.

CLAIRE'S STORY

Saturday night we go to that stupid dinner and Jim drinks too much, and when I ask to drive, he doesn't let me. So he gets behind the wheel of the car, and he misses the right-hand turn that we're supposed to make and gets on a major artery, passes the divider, and turns into the oncoming traffic. I scream, "Just pull over, you're drunk. Just pull over, Jim," and I'm screaming at the top of my lungs, and he says, "No!" So then I don't insist. I've been a wreck for the last 2 days. I'm so upset that I didn't just get out of the car or do something so he wouldn't stay driving. I don't know what to do. I've been thinking of all the things that could have happened, the least of which is he'd get fired. I have all this in my head when I get a call about my dad. He had a car accident and was in the hospital. Thank God, it isn't anything life threatening, but he was drunk, too. He swears he wasn't, but they found an open bottle of Scotch in his car. I can't believe it. Jim has all the same issues as my father, even though they're completely different. I see me repeating my mother's life all over again. It's just amazing.

Jim used to drink Scotch like my dad, but since we moved here he's given up all hard liquor and only drinks wine and beer. But this Saturday night, because he was tense and these were new, important clients we were entertaining—you know I didn't even want to go—but he says, "Oh please go for me. You'll make such a good impression on them." He holds me responsible for his business meetings, and then *he* ends up drunk. Now what is that—that's like putting everything on me—not only do I have to be a great conversationalist, discussing world politics, but I don't realize, not only is he sitting over there and not talking, but he's drinking to boot.

And there's nothing I could say to him about Saturday night that would not end up somehow being my fault. Even if I wrote it down on a piece of paper and handed it to him so he would not accuse me of intonation, he would still blame me. How could he turn it around to be my fault, when he ended up drunk and almost killed us? Am I just crazy or is this a drinking problem?

EXPOSING DENIAL

The very first intervention a therapist can make with a woman is to validate her story. Often it is the first time a woman has experienced this kind of support. Claire ends her story asking the therapist for just this kind of corroboration. Certainly she has not gotten any validation from Jim, who refused to let her drive. By refusing, he denied his own drinking, and this denial invalidated Claire's very real concerns. If Jim were to acknowledge Claire's request to drive, he could not continue this denial. He could not both acknowledge and deny at the same time. Acknowledgment and denial are mutually exclusive. Therefore invalidating Claire's request is a necessary component of Jim's denial. As long as Claire allows herself to be invalidated, she and Jim will be caught in a repetitive loop in which Jim denies his drinking and Claire acquiesces to this denial. Claire is not yet able to challenge Jim's denial because his denial has caused her to doubt her own reality. It is clear from Claire's question at the end of her story that she still isn't sure Jim has a drinking problem. In fact, she is willing to consider that maybe it isn't Jim who has a problem; maybe *she is crazy.*

In order to connect alcoholic denial and traditional gender role prescriptions for women that support denial, it is necessary for the therapist to recognize the effect denial and invalidation have on reinforcing a woman's adherence to these prescriptions. If this connection is not recognized and acknowledged, the therapist is placed in the position of being one more person who invalidates Claire's experience. If the therapist only talks about how Jim is denying his alcoholism, she will by omission be colluding with Jim's invalidation of Claire because silence is "heard" by the system as agreement (Hare-Mustin, 1989). Unless the therapist first recognizes that Jim's denial invalidates Claire's belief and then actively comments on his invalidation, the therapist will miss how disempowered Claire feels in the face of Jim's alcoholism.

The other half of the equation is how Claire buys into this invalidation by doubting herself. The therapist needs to tell Claire in a straightforward manner that she is not crazy and that yes, this is a drinking problem. She might wonder aloud with Claire how his denial changes what she believes or question why Claire is willing to assume Jim knows better than she. It is important to foster Claire's belief in herself. By repeatedly validating Claire's own perceptions and feelings, the therapist helps her gain confidence in her own knowledge. Once Claire begins to trust herself, she will not have to deny her own experience.

RAISING GENDER ISSUES

For Claire to stop denying the degree to which alcohol is running her life, she will need to understand how gender messages have influenced her. The therapist can explain to Claire how men and women are socialized to follow certain prescribed roles, and point out how many of these gender scripts do not work well. One aspect of this socialization is that a man thinks that it is a wife's responsibility to entertain his business clients and that his success is dependent on getting this support (Hochschild,1989; Luepnitz,1988; Miller, 1982; Papp, 1988). Women buy into this same message. If Jim blames Claire for his being drunk, implying that it was because she did not do a good job of entertaining his clients, Claire worries that this might be true. After all, she is used to blaming herself when things go wrong between them.

The therapist gives Claire permission to break these gender rules and helps her make choices that work better for her. She can inform Claire that it is Jim's responsibility, not hers, for how his relationship goes with clients. She should tell Claire that Jim is the only one accountable for his getting drunk. The therapist helps Claire see that by taking responsibility for Jim, she is being underresponsible for herself. It is not responsible to get into a car with Jim after he has been drinking. The therapist uses the strength of her own entitlement to assure Claire that she has every right not to drive with Jim unless he is sober. The therapist models entitlement for Claire through her tone (Berg, & Miller, 1992) and her direct expression of horror at Claire's harrowing experience. By expressing empathy, the therapist can increase connection with Claire (Jordan, 1989) and empower her to have empathy for herself. This self-empathy is an important aspect of validation and a precursor to feeling entitled.

Another aspect of Claire's overresponsibility is her willingness to accept Jim's excuse that he was tense, as if that made getting drunk acceptable. Because relief of tension is a common misuse of alcohol, Claire is also at risk of drinking as a solution to the tension that comes from being overresponsible (Bepko, 1989). The therapist helps prevent this risk by helping Claire lay down her burden of overresponsibility in a self-responsible way. Telling Claire that being tense does not excuse Jim's drinking and driving relieves her of the responsibility for Jim's behavior and is one step toward lightening this burden.

Claire is ahead of the game because she recognizes that Jim is putting it all on her, but she is used to being overresponsible, so she doesn't know how to hand the responsibility back to Jim. She feels that nothing she says to Jim will have any effect. She knows Jim's drinking isn't really her fault, but she can't take any action yet because she feels so powerless. Claire's inability to hold Jim accountable for his behavior takes him "off the hook." The hope is that continued validation from the therapist will help build Claire's sense of entitlement to the point where she can bring up these issues with Jim in a way that holds him accountable for his own drinking.

DEFINING A SELF

Seeing similar patterns being repeated generationally also helps build entitlement (Bepko & Krestan, 1985; Bowen, 1978; Brown, 1991; Carter & Orfanidis, 1976). Initially, Claire goes along with the myth that defines her as the problem.

Seeing the connection between her own and her mother's life shows her that patterns are learned and not the result of some personal flaw in her personality. This makes the possibility of change seem more hopeful. When a client can say she does not want to participate in that pattern anymore and is willing to take responsibility for changing her part in the transaction, then she is taking responsibility for herself alone (Bowen, 1978; Brown, 1991; Lederer, 1991). This self-definition helps break the pattern of overresponsibility for others. As Claire's sense of entitlement grows, she will feel more empowered to put her entitlement into action and say to Jim, "I am not driving with you when you drink" or, "I am not responsible for your relationship with your clients." When Claire is able to take a position and maintain it, even if Jim tries to invalidate her position, she will no longer need to use denial. At that point, the repetitive loop between denial and invalidation will have been broken.

Claire's story is one that has a happy ending. Claire continued to come to therapy for 1 year and 9 months, during which time she learned to feel entitled to be taken seriously and to act on this entitlement by holding her ground and not participating in her husband's drinking. She stopped therapy, and I did not hear from her for over a year. The reason she called again was because her dad had a series of small strokes and had been convalescing at her house for the past 4 months. She said it had been a very stressful time for her, Jim, and the children. As a result, she felt caught in the "sandwich generation" between her kids and her dad. When I saw her again, she reported the following events.

THE SEQUEL TO CLAIRE'S STORY

Before we get into my dad, let me tell you the good news: Jim and I are great. I don't know what happened, but he's just been wonderful. I think it was partly the children, partly getting the partnership at work, partly me, and partly himself realizing he needed to get himself together. And his drinking is gone! He's had maybe 4 beers in the past 6 months.

Let me tell you what happened. I confronted him that his sister was an alcoholic. I told him his uncle was an alcoholic. I told him his grandfather, who ran out on his grandmother, was an alcoholic. I told him all this to his face. I made it an "I" message because I said, "I'm concerned about the kids, and they're linking alcoholism now to genetic traits, and I don't want them to grow up and be alcoholics. From now on, when your parents come to visit, I don't want them offering the kids sips and I don't want you to give them any sips either." Jim said I was overreacting. But I stood my ground. I told him, "If you drink that's fine with me, but I can't have you affecting my life and the kids." That hit him like a cold bucket of water. I told him, "I don't care, drink until you die because you will, but I can't have you do it around me and the kids." I don't know if that meant I was willing to leave him, but maybe there was a part of me that said that to him. I don't think he ever heard those words come out of my mouth. Before it was always, how can I help you. This time it was, I'm not going to help you. And the funny thing is that while we were on vacation in Hawaii, he thanked me for helping him take control of his life and get off drinking. I really think it startled him that I was no longer going to be the enabler for him. Also, it may have been that around the same time, his father had a quadruple bypass and his uncle Denny, who was the alcoholic, had an alcoholic fit and my mother-in-law had to kick him out of her house physically with the aid of her neighbor.

Everything came crashing in on Jim the night his mother told him that—facing that his uncle really was an alcoholic and I wasn't just talking off the top of my head. And that was the end of it. Now he's participating in family life. He's home at night with the kids and he doesn't go to work on weekends anymore. And he's very concerned about the kids' behavior and he's parenting with me. Remember how when he was here he said, "Oh there's nothing wrong"? Now he's facing problems and not being an ostrich. And would you believe it that when my dad got sick, Jim said, "What can I do to help you?" You could have bowled me over with a feather.

Four months later Claire had regained her sense of equilibrium from her dad's illness. She realized that his stroke had reactivated her overresponsibility and in the process she had depleted her own resources. It did not take long for her to pull back and call on her sisters to work out a plan of shared responsibility for their dad. She was on her way once again.

DILEMMA: PERSONAL OR POLITICAL?

My views on how to be with a client regarding denial and gender issues continue to evolve as I struggle with some of the following therapist dilemmas. Because gender issues lie behind denial, the question arises as to what degree a therapist initiates discussion of these gender issues. Does she point out power inequities in the relationship if the woman has not acknowledged power as a problem? If this isn't pointed out, how can denial be challenged? How can a therapist help her female client build a sense of self-esteem without showing her how the political arena has impacted on her gender socialization? What is a therapist's personal responsibility to raise her female client's awareness of how this socialization has influenced how she has led her life and tied her to a less than equal relationship in her marriage? Should we follow Pasick and White's (1991) suggestion that "a feminist informed stance means giving our opinions and direct feedback as well as asking questions. It means being collaborative as opposed to hierarchical, and being challenging instead of confrontive" (p. 101)?

The danger for the therapist if she challenges the status quo and points out inequities is that she may increase her female client's dissatisfaction with the marriage. Maybe all the client wanted was for her husband to stop drinking. Or maybe the client does not want to know how inequitable her relationship is because knowing might mean leaving or wanting to leave and not having the financial or inner resources to do so. Does a therapist take the risk that she may be seen as a "flaming feminist" because she is breaking all the female gender role restrictions by voicing opinions and being direct, forceful, unruffleable, strong, and angry at times on her client's behalf? If the therapist sees the couple conjointly, how direct should the therapist be about challenging the man's misuse of power, knowing that the risk of making the power arrangements in the marital relationship explicit is that the man may drop out of therapy?

Given these dilemmas, a therapist must continually decide with each client how far to go in raising gender awareness and pointing out power inequities. It is a continual struggle for a therapist to balance her own beliefs with what is best for the client. At this time, my thinking leads me to wonder—if we, as therapists, do not raise gender issues or point out power inequities with our women clients, does this not place us in the position of being just one more representative of our patriarchal society?

CONCLUSION

Deciding how to respond to a client in the face of denial depends on the therapist's perspective of what denial represents. From a feminist perspective, denial can be seen as a method of invalidating a woman's reality. Invalidation contributes to a woman's low sense of entitlement, giving her little power to effect change in her marital relationship. The lack of self-esteem is a by-product of gender role prescriptions for women. As women try to live up to societal expectations, they often find that they need to use denial to cover up their inability to fulfill those expectations. When this gender-based denial is active in the context of an alcoholic relationship, the denial of alcohol as a problem becomes more entrenched. Educating women about gender socialization validates their experience of themselves in the marital relationship. This validation raises a woman's sense of entitlement so she is less willing to meet all these gender expectations. As a woman begins to feel more authentic and acts accordingly, she gains more personal power. This shifts the marital balance, obviating the need for denial. As gender expectations that support denial change, alcoholic denial can be challenged more effectively.

REFERENCES

Barrett, K. (1992). Addiction treatment: Solution or problem? *Family Dynamics of Addiction Quarterly, 2*(1), 33–43.

Bepko, C. (1988). Female legacies: Intergenerational themes and their treatment for women in alcoholic families. In L. Braverman (Ed.), *A guide to feminist family therapy* (pp. 97–112). New York: Haworth.

Bepko, C. (1989). Disorders of power: Women and addiction in the family. In M. McGoldrick, C. M. Anderson, & F. Walsh, (Eds.), *Women in families: A framework for family therapy* (pp. 406–426). New York: Norton.

Bepko, C., & Krestan, J. A. (1985). *The responsibility trap.* New York: Free Press.

Berg, I. K., & Miller, S. D. (1992). *Working with the problem drinker: A solution focused approach.* New York: Norton.

Bowen, M. (1978). *Family therapy in clinical practice.* New York: Aronson.

Brown, F. H. (1991). Stage 2: Reweaving the tapestry. In F. H. Brown (Ed.), *Reweaving the family tapestry: A multigenerational approach to families* (pp. 53–66). New York: Norton.

Carter, E., & Orfanidis, M. M. (1976). Family therapy with one person and the family therapist's own family. In P. Guerin (Ed.), *Family therapy: Theory and practice* (pp. 193–219). New York: Gardner.

Chodorow, N. (1978). *The reproduction of mothering: Psychoanalysis and the sociology of gender.* Berkeley, CA: University of California Press.

Davis, D. I., Berenson, D., Steinglass, P., & Davis, S. (1974). The adaptive consequences of drinking. *Psychiatry, 37*, 209–215.

Fossum, M., & Mason, M. (1989). *Facing shame: Families in recovery.* New York: Norton.

Goldner, V. (1989). Generation and gender: Normative and covert hierarchies. In M. McGoldrick, C. M. Anderson, & F. Walsh, *Women in families: A framework for family therapy* (pp. 42–60). New York: Norton.

Goodrich, T. J. (1991). Women, power, and family therapy: What's wrong with this picture. In T. J. Goodrich (Ed.), *Women and power: Perspectives for therapy* (pp.3–35). New York: Norton.

Hare-Mustin, R. T. (1987). The problem of gender in family therapy. *Family Process, 26,* 15–27.

Hare-Mustin, R.T. (1989). The problem of gender in family therapy (rev.). In M. McGoldrick, C. M. Anderson, & F. Walsh, (Eds.), *Women in families: A framework for family therapy* (pp. 61–77). New York: Norton.

Hochschild, A. (1989). *Second shift.* New York: Viking Penguin.

Jordan, J. V. (1989). *Relational development: Therapeutic implications of empathy and shame. Work in progress.* Wellesley, MA: Stone Center for Developmental Services and Studies.

Krestan, J. A., & Bepko, C. (1988). Alcohol problems and the family life cycle. In B. Carter & M. McGoldrick, (Eds.), *The changing family life cycle.* (rev. ed.) (pp. 484–512). New York: Gardner.

Lederer, G. (1991). Alcohol in the family system. In F. H. Brown (Ed.), *Reweaving the family tapestry: A multigenerational approach to families* (pp. 219–241). New York: Norton.

Lederer, G., & Brown, F. (1991). The interlocking issues of gender and entitlement in alcoholic marriages. *Family Dynamics of Addiction Quarterly, 1*(3), 1–9.

Luepnitz, D. A. (1988). *The family interpreted: Feminist theory in clinical practice.* New York: Basic Books.

Miller, J. B. (1982). *Women and power. Work in progress.* Wellesley, MA: Stone Center for Developmental Services and Studies.

Papp, P. (1988). Couples. In M. Walters, B. Carter, P. Papp, & O. Silverstein (Eds.), *The invisible web: Gender patterns in family relationships* (pp. 200–221). New York: Guilford Press.

Pasick, P., & White, C. (1991). Challenging General Patton: A feminist stance in substance abuse treatment and training. *Journal of Feminist Family Therapy, 3*(3/4), 87–102.

Walters, M., Carter, B., Papp, P., & Silverstein, O. (1988). Toward a feminist perspective in family therapy. In M. Walters, B. Carter, P. Papp, & O. Silverstein (Eds.), *The invisible web: Gender patterns in family relationships* (pp.15–30). New York: Guilford.

BIBLIOGRAPHY

Sloven, J. (1991). Codependent or empathetically responsive? Two views of Betty. *Journal of Feminist Family Therapy, 3*(3/4), 195–210.

Chapter 19

Adult Children of Addicted Parents: Family Counseling Strategies

F. James Hoffmann

There is ever-increasing alarm and concern being expressed in both the popular media and the clinical research literature regarding the special issues frequently encountered by adults who have grown up in an alcoholic or substance-abusing family system. It has been estimated that there are 30 to 40 million adults in America today who have grown up in such a family environment (Rivinus, 1991). Corazzini, Williams, and Harris (1987) indicated that adults who have grown up in a home where alcohol or substance abuse was a central issue often develop roles that, though adaptive for them as children, frequently become maladaptive later in adult life. A number of writers have identified and described the primary characteristics, roles, and behavioral markers adopted by adult children of alcoholics/adult children of substance-abusing parents (ACA/ACSAs) (Brown & Cermack, 1980; Gravitz & Bowden, 1985; Seixas & Youcha, 1985; Woititz, 1983). Kress (1989) further suggested that such characteristics frequently produce family dysfunction when these individuals marry and develop families of their own. More recently, Logue, Sher, and Frensch (1992) have pointed out the necessity to exercise caution when applying such descriptor characteristics in clinical practice or applied research, given the apparent "Barnum Effect" (i.e., characteristics ascribed to the ACA/ACSA label often lack descriptive specificity and prognostic predictability). Their work does, however, suggest the validity of applying ACA/ACSA personality characteristics in clinical practice when the client identifies such characteristics as both present and problematic in some important aspect of his or her life.

Established literature also supports the concept that the dysfunctional addictive characteristics of alcoholic and substance-abusing families are often re-enacted from one generation to the next (Royce, 1989; Stanton & Todd, 1982). As Treadway (1991) so vividly pointed out, most adult children will encounter problems in their roles as intimate partners and parents. Although the efficacy of family therapy with families having one or more alcoholic or substance-abusing members has long been recognized (Stanton & Todd, 1979, 1982; Steinglass, 1979; Ziegler-Driscoll, 1979), and various forms of group counseling/therapy have proven helpful (Cermack & Brown, 1982; Corazzini et al., 1987; Delaney, Phillips, & Chandler, 1989; Downing & Walker, 1987; Roush & DeBlassie, 1989), little has been written concerning the use of family counseling/therapy as an intervention of choice with families where one or both parents are ACA/ACSAs. It seems only logical and appropriate to consider family therapy as a legitimate treatment modality for such individuals and their families. Kress (1989), though supporting the use of family therapy with families where one or both parents are ACA/ACSA, added an important perspective by stating that if the characterological deficits of the ACA/ACSA involve severely rigid defenses, marital or individual therapy may be indicated as an adjunct to family therapy.

Given the potential appropriateness of family therapy with this population, this chapter will focus on delineating the prominent characteristics commonly identified by married adults who have grown up in an alcoholic or substance-abusing family system, describe the impact of these characteristics on the individual's own spouse and children, and offer an integrative family intervention model based on family systems theory, Treadway's (1991) five-stage ACA/ACSA treatment model, and Miller and Rollnick's (1991) principles of "motivational interviewing."

CHARACTERISTICS AND BEHAVIORAL MARKERS OF ACA/ACSAs

Growing up in an alcoholic or substance-abusing family frequently results in the development of rigid and often dysfunctional patterns of behavior during adult life. As Treadway (1991) pointed out, "Although the tendency to overgeneralize about ACA/ACSAs is clearly one that has to be guarded against, there are specific issues that almost all adult children will share in common regardless of differences in family-of-origin roles and personality variations" (p. 228).

Brown and Cermack (1980) described a constellation of five characteristic behavior patterns worthy of note. The first and most central is the issue of control. Denial, suppression, and repression are typically used by the ACA/ACSA in an attempt to control the outward expression and inner awareness of thoughts, feelings, and behavior. Strong feelings are experienced as being out of control. The second characteristic identified by Brown and Cermack and supported by Treadway (1991) is trust, or more accurately, distrust—of others as well as of self. Repeatedly told in their family of origin to ignore the obvious, ACA/ACSAs learn to distrust their own perceptions. Such distrust leads naturally to a third characteristic, the avoidance of feelings. Interestingly, the findings of Berkowitz and Perkins (1988) suggest some degree of gender difference relative to this issue, in that women may tend to resort to greater self-deprecia- tion as a means of blunting affect, whereas males tend to create emotional dis- tance in their efforts to achieve the same effect. Learning how not to feel the emotional aspect of their experience was one of the most successful survival techniques employed by children who grew up in such families. Clearly, this state of being out of touch with one's feelings can create significant difficulties for adult children because they frequently are unaware of some of the motivat- ing affect and cognition underlying much of their behavior and often have little understanding of the responses they receive from others. This "affective numb- ness" frequently plays a significant role in the development and maintenance of interpersonal problems between the adult child and his or her spouse and chil- dren. This phenomenon will be discussed in more detail in the next section.

A fourth commonly occurring characteristic of the ACA/ACSA observed by Brown and Cermack (1980) is that of being "over-responsible." As children, ACA/ACSAs came to believe they were responsible for what was happening in their family of origin. Consequently many of them grew up believing that they were responsible for others' emotions and actions. For example, a middle-aged ACA/ACSA man in one of our therapy groups was utterly convinced that the absence of another group member during a session was due to something the ACA/ACSA had said during a previous session.

The fifth characteristic identified by Brown and Cermack (1980) is the tend- ency of adult children to ignore their own needs. They frequently have a sense that if they ask for something from family or friends, the other person then knows something dangerously important about them. To have needs is to be vulnerable, and if they allow themselves that feeling of vulnerability they may feel dependent on or obligated to the person who met their needs. These are all emotions that run counter to feeling in control. Therefore the adult child fre- quently operates from the belief that personal needs are best avoided or denied.

In addition to the five characteristic patterns identified by Brown and Cermack, Gravitz and Bowden (1985) reported four additional characteristics that they have regularly observed in ACA/ACSAs they see in counseling and those attending their public lectures and workshops. The most prominent of these is what Gravitz and Bowden refer to as "all-or-none functioning" or, more specifically, a tendency to think, feel, and behave as though every experience is either right or wrong. Those familiar with the defense mechanisms will recog- nize this pattern as essentially similar to the dysfunctional defense of splitting. For example, adult children will typically approach the issue of trust from a black-and-white perspective. They will either trust another person totally or distrust so fully that they will not share anything personal. Obviously, neither strategy is effective.

Another characteristic consistently observed by Gravitz and Bowden is dis- sociation, or the separation of the emotional aspects of an experience from the self. The outward manifestation of this characteristic might best be described as "flattened affect" and naturally functions as a form of self-protection. The author observed an example of this during a family therapy session when the ACA/ACSA father described a childhood experience of sexual abuse in an absolutely calm voice accompanied by no apparent nonverbal affect.

Still another commonly observed characteristic reported by Gravitz and Bowden is the tendency of adult children to behave like "adrenaline junkies." Because much of their growing-up life was laced with frequent crises and emergencies, they will often unconsciously stir things up whenever their lives are seemingly calm. As Gravitz and Bowden point out, a prominent result of this pattern is that they spend most of their energy coping with daily crises and are left with little energy to build for the future. Again, the impact on their relationships with spouse and children is reasonably apparent.

When all the characteristic patterns of thinking, feeling, and behaving outlined above are considered in their various combinations, it is easy to understand the relevance of the final characteristic observed by Gravitz and Bowden, namely low self-esteem. As Kress (1989) pointed out, ACA/ACSAs' ability to change their projected image in response to the family or relationship at hand is only possible with the existence of a denied, vulnerable, insecure self. Their frustrations are typically dealt with as narcissistic injuries, and this experience further increases low self-esteem. Because they were unable to get their needs met in a chaotic family of origin, they enter adulthood unable to recognize or meet such needs in themselves or in others.

In addition to the common occurrence of such characteristic patterns, ACA/ACSAs tend to separate into two rather distinct subgroups, those who exhibit some form of addictive behavior themselves (i.e., alcohol abuse, drug abuse, obesity/overeating, compulsive gambling, or other compulsive behaviors), and those relatively free of such addictive styles.

IMPACT OF ACA/ACSA CHARACTERISTICS ON FAMILY RELATIONSHIPS

Whether consciously or unconsciously, ACA/ACSAs tend to seek some kind of resolution of this past pain in their current marital and family relationships. Although this is normal to some extent for all people, it is frequently more traumatic for ACA/ACSAs because of the more intense pain and sense of deprivation they bring with them into these relationships.

ACA/ACSAs As Partners

It is not uncommon for adults from alcoholic or substance-abusing families to develop a differentially dysfunctional relationship with their spouse, considering the characteristics identified by Brown and Cermack (1980) and Gravitz and Bowden (1985). An exploratory study recently conducted by Kerr and Hill (1992) suggests that marital adjustment and level of satisfaction appear more problematic for adult children than for their non-ACA/ACSA counterparts. In addition, ACA/ACSAs evaluated the quality of their relationship with their spouses significantly lower than the non-ACA/ACSAs. It is not surprising, then, that Kerr and Hill found much higher rates of divorce in families where one or both partners were ACA/ACSA.

A strong fear of vulnerability coupled with a desire for intimacy and nurturance are frequently major motivating forces for ACA/ACSAs in their relationships with their spouses. However, the needs for intimacy and safety are, in some rather important respects, mutually exclusive. Successful intimacy is, in large part, a function of an individual's being trusting, affectively available, and interdependent. For an ACA/ACSA this is a precarious and unsafe position destined to evoke the old childhood sense of danger, dread, and ultimately rejection.

ACA/ACSAs employ differing behavioral strategies in their attempt to find intimacy with their partners without sacrificing safety. According to Treadway (1991), some will engage in a kind of self-protective partial intimacy in which they are able to be close without being too endangered. For example, one of the author's ACA/ACSA clients chose to marry a chronically depressed, underfunctioning man, thereby avoiding her own anxiety about being in the dependent role. Others will enact the opposite strategy, choosing to marry an individual who not only is affectively limited but also takes on the controlling position in the marital relationship, thereby relieving the ACA/ACSA of most all interpersonal responsibilities required for the development and maintenance of an intimate relationship.

ACA/ACSAs As Parents

Adults who have grown up in an alcoholic or substance-abusing family will often feel uncomfortable and insecure in their parental role. Treadway (1991) pointed out that these adult children are both more intense and more insecure as parents. The feelings of intensity typically come from wanting to give their own children all that was missing from their own childhood, and the feelings of insecurity are created from their experience of having had negative role models in their own parents. The net result is that they often do not have a sense of what is normal and therefore do not know how to parent in a healthy and appropriate way.

Although it is quite difficult to summarize the characteristics of these adults in their role as parents, there are themes that reflect some of the cognitive and affective reactions many ACA/ACSAs have in their parental role. Not surprisingly, many such adults tend to have an unnecessarily high need to be protective and in control of their own children, which frequently leads to unrealistic expectations that their children will look right, feel right, and act right at all times. In a related manner, many ACA/ACSA parents who work very hard to ensure that their children grow up in stable, nurturing, and protective homes often find themselves resentful and even a bit jealous of their children because they take such a family atmosphere for granted.

Because of their insecurity, ACA/ACSAs also frequently look to their children for affirmation of their parenting. For example, the father of a family the author recently worked with in family therapy commented to his children during a session, "Wasn't our Disney World trip wonderful? Aren't I a great Dad for taking you on that vacation?"

Adult children also tend to be hypervigilant about substance abuse. Thus, for example, it does not take the normal adolescent struggling for autonomy very long to become entangled in conflict with his or her parents around the issue of substance use or abuse. It is also altogether too common for ACA/ACSA parents to experience significant difficulty in allowing their children to become independent and leave home. Treadway (1991) pointed out that a high percentage of ACA/ACSA clients come for treatment at the time their children are getting ready to leave home.

FAMILY INTERVENTION METHODS AND STRATEGIES

The vast majority of ACA/ACSAs who seek assistance from a mental health professional do not describe the nature of their presenting concerns as emanating from their having grown up in an alcoholic or substance-abusing family. It is normal for adult children to enter treatment presenting a variety of symptoms that are seemingly unrelated in their minds to their childhood experiences. When their presenting concerns focus in any way on interpersonal difficulty with their spouse and/or children, the choice of a family-focused intervention may be particularly appropriate.

This section will outline and describe an integrative family counseling model for working with ACA/ACSAs presenting problems that involve members of their current family. This integrative model links Treadway's five-stage model for treating ACA/ACSAs (Treadway, 1991) with the use of intervention techniques drawn from the work of Satir (1967, 1982), Miller and Rollnick (1991), Prochaska (1984), and Prochaska, DiClemente, and Norcross (1992). The model provides a conceptually relevant avenue for helping both adult children and their current family increase their understanding of ACA/ACSA family-of-origin issues, as well as resolve the family-focused issues that precipitated their seeking treatment. When employing this approach, the therapist is encouraged to conceptualize the ACA/ACSAs presenting problem as having its roots in the family-of-origin system and having its "maintenance qualities" in the client's current family system.

Stage 1. Identification

The initial step in the treatment process involves the identification of the client as an adult who has grown up in an alcoholic or substance-abusing family, and some discussion regarding the rationale and appropriateness of working with both the client and his or her family. During the assessment interview, the counselor can pose sensitive questions designed to uncover or rule out the presence of alcohol or substance abuse by the one or both of the client's parents. Questions such as the following can inform the ACA/ACSA identification process: "How is your marriage better or worse than your parent's marriage? What did you want to make certain your children experience differently than you did when you were growing up? With which of your parents did you experience the same kind of frustration that you currently experience with your spouse?" The *Children of Alcoholics Screening Test* (CAST) developed by Jones (1982) can also be useful at this stage. Consistent with Treadway's (1991) recommendation, it is not usually prudent to use the ACA/ACSA label with clients prematurely because many adult children will likely find it threatening if the counselor emphasizes their childhood experiences as an explanation for their current interpersonal difficulties with their spouse or children. Treadway has stated,

> The value of this ACA/ACSA identification of the adult child's problem is not at all obvious to most clients, therefore, the counselor will need to proceed in small steps while overtly placing the primary focus of therapy on resolving the presenting problem. (p. 236)

A helpful strategy for bringing the client's spouse and children into the treatment process is to indicate to the client that problem resolution typically occurs most quickly when family counseling is used. Clinical experience suggests that once the client and his or her family have agreed to family counseling, it becomes more palatable to make explicit the linkage between family-of-origin issues and the client's presenting problems related to current family member(s).

Stage 2. Reframing and Restraint for Change

By the time the client has sought counseling, the intensity of the interpersonal conflict with his or her spouse and/or children is often rather intense and dysfunctional. Even though the counselor provides information to the family that is designed to help them better understand the impact of ACA/ACSA family-of-origin systemic dynamics, this seldom acts as an adequate mechanism to free them from their dysfunctional style of interaction. As Treadway (1991) suggests, it is at this juncture in the counseling process that the family counselor can "reframe the meaning of the problem in terms of how it serves a protective and useful function in the life of the ACA/ACSA's current family system" (p. 237). For example, if the presenting problem is the ACA/ACSA parent's distant and disengaged pattern of interacting with his or her children, the counselor might reframe this for the family. The counselor might suggest that too much intimacy and emotional availability on the part of the ACA/ACSA would most likely produce anxiety and stir old painful memories on the part of the adult child, thereby bringing up all his or her unresolved loss issues that have been long dammed up. However the counselor chooses to verbalize the reframe, it has to make sense to the ACA/ACSA and his or her family. Treadway (1991) further indicated:

> Since people are torn between the need to change and fear of the destabilization such change creates, a logical reframing that essentially appreciates why and how people need to be doing what they are doing serves as a foundation for later risk taking in the therapy. (p. 238)

When the family seems to be "intractably stuck" in their current attempts at resolving their interpersonal difficulty, it can also be useful to add a restraining statement to the reframe. For example, the counselor might suggest to the family that they purposefully stop from their current attempts to resolve their problems with one another. This strategy then allows the counselor time to work with the family on other issues that have been masked by the presenting complaint, as well as reducing the family's frustration about their unsuccessful attempts to successfully deal with the presenting complaint. For example, it is typical during this stage in the therapeutic process that the spouse and children of the ACA/ACSA are most likely to voice their requests for greater levels of emotional risk taking by the adult child. Given the ACA/ACSAs ambivalence and feelings of vulnerability about this issue, use of the above-mentioned restraining intervention is in order until some additional education concerning this issue can be addressed.

Stage 3. Supportive Exploration of Affect

Once ACA/ACSAs give up some of their well-ingrained defenses (denial, projection, addictive patterns of behavior), they can be expected to experience intense emotional reactions such as anxiety attacks and periods of depression.

Treadway (1991) suggests that before a therapist opens up the repressed feelings many ACA/ACSAs have about their own family of origin, it is both necessary and helpful to provide some education to the entire family about the natural history of growing up in an alcoholic or substance-abusing family, the roles people play, and the healthy ways such children survive. Discussing the characteristics identified by Brown and Cermack (1980) and Gravitz and Bowden (1985) in a family session frequently provides ACA/ACSAs and their families with important information that can have a "freeing-up effect" on the family's stereotyped method of communicating. This educational process typically helps the ACA/ACSA's spouse and children come to understand how they can be empathic without feeling they have to make up for the past.

At this point in the family counseling process, the counselor can suggest the use of ACA/ACSA literature and/or the many types of support groups available as additional support for the adult child or the entire family. If the family has begun to make some positive changes in their way of communicating with one another, the counselor might also suggest that they conduct weekly family discussion groups as a means of sharing their reactions to the ACA/ACSA literature they have been reading. The primary purpose of this educational/bibliotherapy process is to provide the family with still another way to view the ACA/ACSA and themselves. Clinical experience seems to indicate that such educationally based interventions often have a profound and freeing influence on the entire family system.

Stage 4. Coming to Terms with the Past

As adult children become more able to open up emotionally with their spouse and children, they frequently find that the unrealistic expectations they have typically held of their family dissipate. As a result, the pressure the family members have felt to fill the ACA/ACSAs emotional void lessens and they too are more responsive and forthcoming. In essence, as Treadway (1991) points out, everyone who has expected less gets more.

Once the adult child and his or her spouse and children begin interacting with one another in less stereotyped, dysfunctional ways, the family counseling "stage" can become a supportive setting in which the ACA/ACSA can explore and better understand the range of feelings (i.e., anger and sadness) that have been repressed. The task of therapy now becomes helping the ACA/ACSA experience how such feelings inform and direct present behavior with his or her current family. It is at this juncture that such family intervention strategies such as Satir's "family reconstruction" procedures can be employed to assist the adult child in making peace with his or her family of origin (Nerin, 1986). Involving the adult child's current family in family reconstruction processes such as guided fantasy and role playing offers a powerful method for helping the adult child reclaim his or her roots, and in the process view old perceptions in a new light. Involving current family members in the family reconstruction often allows them a powerful and moving experiential opportunity to better understand the adult child's early life experience. This setting also provides the therapist an opportunity to model more appropriate family communication styles.

Stage 5. Acceptance

The final stage of Treadway's treatment model is frequently the most difficult for the ACA/ACSA and his or her spouse and children. For the adult child, it means giving up the hope that one's family and friends can make up for the years of deprivation and abuse. During this stage of treatment, it is useful for the counselor to encourage the adult child to openly discuss with his or her family the disappointment that naturally flows from gaining such an awareness. Because the task before the adult child, and in some respects his or her family, is similar to coping with the loss of a loved one, the therapist might choose to offer the metaphor of the memorial ceremony as a way for the family to facilitate the "letting go" process. One particular ACA/ACSA and her family chose to plan and carry out a symbolic burial ceremony as a means of helping her actualize her sense of loss.

CONCLUSION

The experience of growing up in an alcoholic or substance-abusing family often proves to be debilitating when one enters the adult phase of the life cycle. The coping and adaptation mechanisms developed during one's childhood and adolescence frequently become a burden during the challenges of adulthood. When interpersonal and communications problems develop between the adult child and the members of his or her own family, the application of an integrated family intervention based on Treadway's (1991) five-stage treatment model for use with ACA/ACSAs, the family systems work of Satir, and the motivational interviewing procedures developed by Miller and Rollnick provide another effective method of working with this type of client-presenting complaint.

REFERENCES

Berkowitz, A., & Perkins, H.W. (1988). Personality characteristics of children of alcoholics. *Journal of Consulting and Clinical Psychology, 56,* 206–209.

Brown, S., & Cermack, T. (1980). Group therapy with the adult children of alcoholics. *Newsletter From the California Society for the Treatment of Alcoholism and Other Drug Dependencies, 7,* 1–6.

Cermack, T. L., & Brown, S. (1982). Interactional group therapy with the adult children of alcoholics. *International Journal of Group Psychotherapy, 32,* 375–389.

Corazzini, J. G., Williams, K., & Harris, S. (1987). Group therapy for adult children of alcoholics: Case studies. *Journal for Specialists in Group Work, 12,* 156–161.

Delaney, E. S., Phillips, P., & Chandler, C. K. (1989). Leading an Adlerian group for adult children of alcoholics. *Individual Psychology, 45,* 490–499.

Downing, N. E., & Walker, M. E. (1987). A psychoeducational group for adult children of alcoholics. *Journal of Counseling and Development, 65,* 440–442.

Gravitz, H. L., & Bowden, J. D. (1985). *A guide for adult children of alcoholics.* New York: Simon & Schuster.

Jones, J. J. (1982). Children of alcoholics screening test. In C. Black, *It will never happen to me.* Denver: Medical Administration Corp.

Kerr, A. S., & Hill, E. W. (1992). An exploratory study comparing ACOAs to Non-ACOAs on current family relationships. *Alcoholism Treatment Quarterly, 9,* 23–38.

Kress, Y. (1989). Special issues of adult children of alcoholics. In G. W. Lawson & A. W. Lawson (Eds.), *Alcoholism and substance abuse in special populations* (pp. 139–164). Rockville, MD: Aspen.

Logue, M. B., Sher, K.J., & Frensch, P. A. (1992). Purported characteristics of adult children of alcoholics: A possible "Barnum Effect." *Professional Psychology: Research and Practice, 23,* 226–232.

Miller, W. R. & Rollnick, S. (1991). *Motivational interviewing: Preparing people to change addictive behavior.* New York: Guilford.

Nerin, W. F. (1986). *Family reconstruction: Long day's journey into light.* New York: Norton.

Prochaska, J. O. (1984). *Systems of psychotherapy: A transtheoretical approach* (2nd ed.). Homewood, IL: Dorsey Press.

Prochaska, J. O., DiClemente, C. C., & Norcross, J. C. (1992). In search of how people change: Applications to addictive behaviors. *American Psychologist, 47,* 9, 1102–1114.

Rivinus, T. M. (Ed.). (1991). *Children of chemically dependent parents: Multiperspectives from the cutting edge.* New York: Brunner/Mazel.

Roush, K. L., & DeBlassie, R. R. (1989). Structured group counseling for college students of alcoholic parents. *Journal of College Student Development, 30,* 276–277.

Royce, J. E. (1989). *Alcoholism problems and alcoholism: A comprehensive survey* (rev. ed.). New York: Collier Macmillan.

Satir, V. M. (1967). *Conjoint family therapy* (rev. ed.). Palo Alto, CA: Science and Behavior Books.

Satir, V. M. (1982). The therapist and family therapy: Process model. In A. M. Horne & M. M. Ohlsen (Eds.), *Family counseling and therapy.* Itasca, IL: F. E. Peacock.

Seixas, J., & Youcha, G. (1985). *Children of alcoholism: Survivors' manual.* New York: Harper & Row.

Stanton, M. D. & Todd, T. C. (1979). Structural family therapy with drug addicts. In E. Kaufman & P. Kaufman (Eds.), *Family therapy of drug and alcohol abuse* (pp. 55–69). New York: Gardner.

Stanton, M. D., & Todd, T. C. (Eds.). (1982). *The family therapy of drug abuse and addiction.* New York: Guilford.

Steinglass, P. (1979). Family therapy with alcoholics: A review. In E. Kaufman & P. Kaufman (Eds.), *Family therapy of drug and alcohol abuse* (pp. 147–186). New York: Gardner.

Treadway, D. C. (1991). Breaking the cycle: Treating adult children of alcoholics. In T. M. Rivinus (Ed.), *Children of chemically dependent parents: Multiperspectives from the cutting edge* (pp. 226–250). New York: Brunner/Mazel.

Woititz. J. G. (1983). *Adult children of alcoholics*. Pompano Beach, FL: Health Communications.

Ziegler-Driscoll, G. (1979). The similarities in families of drug dependents and alcoholics. In E. Kaufman & P. Kaufman (Eds.), *Family therapy of drug and alcohol abuse* (pp. 19–39). New York: Gardner.

Chapter **20**

The CAST:
Penetrating Wet Systems

David A. O'Donnell

THE PROBLEM

Until recently, traditional alcohol treatment settings have opted to view family therapy as a more or less didactic tool to educate families about the disease concept of alcoholism. In these settings, the focus of family therapy did not lend itself to the structural issues surrounding the family system, such as hierarchy, dyads, family roles, and boundaries.

In social service youth agencies, a different problem occurred. According to Ackerman (1983), 25% of children of alcoholics in this country are in counseling. However, only 4% are there for the primary issue of parental alcoholism; the remainder are there because of their own dysfunctional behavior. It is well documented that denial is a common symptom of alcoholism, not only in the alcoholic but frequently in the entire "wet" family system as well. In many alcoholic families, the alcoholic's problem drinking and associated behaviors are a well-guarded secret that is not discussed in counseling. Therefore many of the specific issues indigenous to the alcoholic family are not addressed simply because parental alcoholism is never identified.

This is compounded by the fact that the alcoholic parent is seldom available for family counseling. All too frequently, the only problem behaviors addressed are those of the offspring. Ackerman (1983) notes that only 20% of all alcoholics ever get help and that "while we wait around for the other 80% to do something, families will continue to fall apart." Even worse, the cycle repeats itself in the offspring. It is crucial that this cycle be interrupted and that the needs of children of alcoholics (COAs) be addressed. To do so Ackerman indicates a primary need for a means of early identification either prior to or at the point of entry into counseling.

THE CAST: HOPE FOR EARLY IDENTIFICATION

In 1981, Dr. John Jones and Joanne Pilat developed "The Children of Alcoholics Screening Test" (CAST), a 30-question survey formulated from

289

"real-life experiences . . . shared by clinically diagnosed children of alcoholics." The survey was designed to measure "children's feelings, attitudes, perceptions, and experiences related to their parents' drinking behavior" (Pilat & Jones, 1984-1985). The CAST is a quick, self-administered tool geared toward children 9 years of age and up. (It can be used with younger children if the items are read to the child and explained.) Most important, it can be administered without the presence of the alcoholic parent.

The CAST was field tested on a group of 99 children of known alcoholics (either clinically diagnosed or self-identified). Their responses were then compared with those of a randomly selected control group (Pilat & Jones, 1984-1985).

All of the children in the group known to have an alcoholic parent scored 6 or above on the CAST, compared to 25% of the children in the control group. Therefore, 6 was designated as the cut-off that indicated a high probability of parental alcoholism, and the following scoring scale was adopted for use with the CAST:

0–2	No problem
3–5	Parental alcohol abuse
6 & over	Parental alcoholism

AUNT MARTHA'S AND THE CAST

At Aunt Martha's Youth Service Center, the CAST has been utilized since 1988. Aunt Martha's is a full-service youth agency serving the far south suburbs of Chicago. The agency offers 35 programs, including crisis intervention, several counseling programs, a health clinic, foster and group homes, and substance abuse treatment. The agency was precisely the type of setting Ackerman referred to when noting the large numbers of unidentified COAs in counseling because of their own problem behaviors.

Initially the CAST was used only in our substance abuse program. However, after observing the high percentages of COAs and the effects parental alcoholism has on these youth, the CAST was made available to our other programs, and agency staff were trained in administering the CAST, interpreting and utilizing the results, and addressing COA issues. Although the CAST is used most consistently in the substance abuse program, other programs have continued to utilize it and to have greater awareness of COA issues as a result of the availability of this tool.

Through our experience at Aunt Martha's, we have found CAST results to be highly accurate. We have also been able to make additional observations to supplement Jones's original findings. For example, his initial field testing did not address the issue of false positives and negatives. Because we administer the

CAST at assessment and then follow the client through treatment, we have been able to collect anecdotal data regarding this issue.

False Positives

It has been our observation that the CAST rarely falsely identifies clients as COAs when in fact they are not. It is particularly unlikely to identify youth from nondrinking or social drinking homes as COAs. We have encountered only two such cases, and neither client had answered the questions accurately. In one instance, the youth was later diagnosed manic depressive; in the other instance, the youth eventually disclosed that he was extremely angry with his father at the time and thought that by scoring high he would get his father in trouble.

Although still rare, false positives are somewhat more likely to occur when alcohol has been an issue in the family for some reason. For example, one young man scored 12 a week after his father had been brought home drunk by the police, who had found him passed out in his car. This man's subsequent behavior was completely inconsistent with alcoholism. He was disturbed by the incident, requested an evaluation for alcoholism, and immediately stopped drinking. In fact, the son was asked to indicate which of the 12 items he would have marked positive prior to this incident, and he indicated none of them. Although false positives are rare, it is important when evaluating any given family to keep in mind that extenuating circumstances can impact upon a youth's responses.

A new issue surrounding false positives has surfaced at Aunt Martha's within the last year or so. We have been seeing a large number of screenings (approximately 5%) with scores of 3-4 where there is little or no evidence of any kind of problem drinking. These screenings never indicate any specific incidents surrounding parental alcohol use; instead the positive responses indicate that the child has thought the parent had a drinking problem, has wished the parent would stop, and has worried about the parent's health. In one of these cases, the youth indicated on an accompanying form that his father only has one or two drinks on holidays. It appears that these false indications of problem drinking are an inadvertent side effect of prevention. Apparently some youth have overinterpreted substance abuse preventive education efforts and are worrying needlessly about small amounts of alcohol consumption.

False Negatives

It is our experience that approximately 15% of those scoring below 6 on the CAST are in fact living with an alcoholic parent. As our staff began to look more closely at the high percentage of false negatives, an interesting correlation surfaced between the child's "role" in the family and his or her CAST scores, with certain roles consistently scoring higher than others. What we have found is that when there are larger families with clearly defined roles, there is a tendency toward a wide disparity among scores, even when there is proximity in age among the siblings.

There has been extensive literature in the field of alcoholism describing and examining the family roles played by children of alcoholics and the issues each individual has as a result of his or her specific roles. Although there is some variation in the names and descriptions, the most commonly recognized roles are the hero, caretaker, lost child, and scapegoat. The *scapegoat* clearly displays the effects of parental alcoholism through acting-out behavior, whereas children in other roles exhibit behaviors that give the impression the family is okay. The *hero*, for example, is super-responsible, is always in charge, and always does the right thing. The *caretaker* fixes problems for others and in so doing becomes the emotional "band-aid" of the family. The *lost child* attempts to emotionally insulate through dissociation and withdrawal.

In small families roles may overlap, whereas in larger ones they tend to be more clearly defined. It is not uncommon for adult children of alcoholics to recall maneuvering from one role to another while adapting to the constantly changing behavior of the alcoholic.

The roles children play appear to influence how many questions they mark affirmatively. We found that "heroes" and "lost children" tend to score significantly lower on the CAST than do "scapegoats" and "caretakers." This may result from the coping mechanisms characteristic of each role. "Caretakers" and "scapegoats" tend to be sensitive to pain and in touch with feelings, whereas "lost children" and "heroes" tend to suppress feelings by withdrawing from the family or by developing "looking perfect" behaviors. On the surface, the "lost child" appears independent and self-sufficient, and the "hero" excels and appears mature. This suppression of feelings could result in lower scores or even false negatives on the CAST. Another factor may impact the "hero's" lower scores. In an attempt to look perfect, the "hero" often has an insatiable need for approval from authority figures. This can translate into what Greenleaf (1981) refers to as "people-pleasing" behaviors. Because much of the child's self-esteem stems from the positive strokes received from parents for excelling, the child in return develops a misguided sense of loyalty, which, when coupled with suppressed feelings, exacerbates his or her denial system. The result can be inaccurate perceptions of how the parent's drinking affects him or her.

On the other hand, when a child scores lower on the CAST than his or her siblings, it is important that clinicians not automatically assume that the child is in denial and center clinical goals on penetrating his or her defenses. Ackerman (1983) has concluded that not all children are damaged by parental alcoholism, although all are in some way affected. He further notes that one of the most important factors that determines how a child is affected by an alcoholic parent is the child's perception of the parent as a person. Some children live in constant fear or worry of the alcoholic's behavior. Others remain optimistic, choosing to see the good in the parent. It is entirely possible that the child does not perceive the alcoholic's drinking and associated behaviors as threatening. Although many COAs survive by denying any impact of the parent's drinking on them, it should not be assumed that this is the cause of the lower scores. It is also conceivable that the child has a strong genetic tolerance for pain or has developed effective skills that may also influence his or her perceptions.

USING THE CAST CLINICALLY

Aunt Martha's has found the CAST to be valuable to agency program planning as well as to individual assessment, treatment planning, and intervention.

Program Planning and Development

Initially we screened all 300 youth who entered Aunt Martha's programs over a 2-month period. Sixty-five percent scored 6 or more, with a mean of 11. As a result of these numbers, we conducted more training dealing with the issues and needs of COAs. We also established educational/processing groups open to COAs from any of Aunt Martha's programs.

We also successfully used CAST statistics as a key in the needs assessment portion of grant proposals to obtain additional funding for expanded programming for COAs.

Initial Assessment

The CAST can be used to determine whether clients are living with parental alcohol abuse and are in need of intervention for this issue. For use in assessment of COA issues, administration of the CAST should be accompanied by a review of the affirmative responses to confirm the answers and to establish pertinent details: the identity of the alcohol abuser, whether this person is living in the home, and whether the person is currently drinking.

It should be noted that the purpose of the CAST is to identify children who are dealing with issues commonly seen in children of alcoholics; the purpose is *not* to "diagnose" the parent as alcoholic. Although this screening distinguishes, with a high degree of reliability, children living with parental alcoholism from those who are not, it measures the effect parental drinking is having on the child, not the degree or severity of problem the parent is experiencing. When actually labeling or diagnosing the parent as alcoholic, the CAST is not a substitute for traditional diagnostic procedures.

Assessment of Specific Treatment Needs/Treatment Planning

An evaluation of the specific items marked affirmatively can shed light on the specific problems the child is experiencing as a result of parental alcohol abuse. Jones designed the CAST so that it

> measures children's emotional distress associated with a parent's alcohol use/misuse; perception of drinking-related marital discord between their parents; attempts to control a parent's drinking; efforts to escape from alcoholism; exposure to drinking-related family violence; tendencies to perceive their parent as being alcoholic; and desire for help. (Pilat & Jones, 1984-1985)

Assessment of specific CAST responses may also aid in identifying the child's family role. The family "hero" may view him or herself as the family protector and provider. It is not uncommon for "heroes" to answer "yes" to such questions as:

> Did you ever protect another family member from a parent who was drinking?

> Did you ever take over any chores and duties at home that were usually done by a parent before he/she developed a drinking problem?

"Scapegoats" may be the focus of abuse and blame in the family. Typical "yes" responses by the "scapegoat" are:

> Did you ever argue or fight with a parent when he or she was drinking?

> Did you ever threaten to run away from home because of a parent's drinking?

> Has a parent ever yelled at or hit you or other family members when drinking?

> Have you ever been blamed for a parent's drinking?

> Have you ever felt a problem drinking parent did not really love you?

"Caretakers" act as the emotional "band-aid" for the family. They tend to worry excessively about things they can't control and to take responsibility for other's behaviors. Because they are so concerned, they are more likely to reach out. "Caretakers" frequently have high CAST scores. Most probable "yes" answers reflect the stress caused by excessive worry. They are:

Have you ever thought that one of your parents had a drinking problem?

Did you ever feel alone, scared, nervous, angry, or frustrated because a parent was not able to stop drinking?

Do many of your thoughts revolve around a problem drinking parent because of difficulties that arise because of his/her drinking?

Did you ever feel responsible for and guilty about a parent's drinking?

Did you ever feel that you made a parent drink alcohol?

Have you ever worried about a parent's health because of his/her alcohol use?

Did you ever wish you could talk to someone who could understand and help the alcohol-related problems in your family?

Have you ever felt sick, cried, or had a "knot" in your stomach after worrying about a parent's drinking?

It is crucial to treatment planning that these kinds of issues be accurately identified. The CAST provides a simple, accurate means of accomplishing this. As treatment progresses, the CAST can be referred to periodically to stimulate discussion and processing.

Penetrating the System/Intervention

As previously established, denial is a primary symptom in the alcoholic syndrome, and it frequently occurs in the family as well as in the alcoholic. Some children deny that they are affected by their parent's drinking even though their CAST scores indicate otherwise. The CAST can be a powerful tool to help penetrate the child's denial system as it is related to alcoholism.

Denial by the codependent spouse may also be penetrated as the counselor facilitates discussion of affirmative responses. Frequently children respond to this process by recalling exact times, dates, and details of experiences identified by their responses to CAST questions such as, "Have you ever been blamed for a parent's drinking?" or " Did a parent ever make promises to you that he/she did not keep because of drinking?" With the counselor acting as facilitator, confrontation is direct, child to parent. Healthy, direct communication between family members regarding the role of alcohol may be new for many alcoholic families and can provide the impetus for change.

When a family wishes to attempt an intervention with the alcoholic, the CAST responses can be used as the basis for intervention planning. The child is asked to list specific incidents to substantiate each affirmative response. When the actual intervention occurs, the CAST can be shown to the alcoholic. Along with the specific examples, the CAST itself provides clear-cut, hard evidence that the drinking is affecting the child.

SUMMARY AND CONCLUSIONS

Aunt Martha's experience with the CAST has been positive. Staff members continue to examine client scores in search of trends that may expand the usefulness of the instrument. We have attempted to broaden the scope of the CAST beyond parental alcoholism to parental chemical dependency by substituting identified substances for alcohol in the questions. Results have been mixed. The CAST questions were designed to identify children of alcoholics, not children of substance abusers in general. Some youth with drug-abusing parents, particularly those whose parents are cocaine dependent, identify with many of the same responses as do COAs. Others, however, have not. The specific pathology of drug abuse is not identical to that of alcohol abuse. For instance, although volatile, abusive behavior is frequently associated with chronic alcohol and cocaine abuse, it is less likely to result from marijuana abuse. Other questions would not apply due to the secrecy connected with parental use of illicit substances.

Another approach we have used is to include an additional form with the CAST. The purpose of the form is to obtain information regarding the specific alcohol abuser and the child's experiences with other alcohol/substance abusers and to give the child the opportunity to comment on any of the answers. One of the questions on this form is, "If the word 'drugs' were substituted for alcohol in the questions on the previous page, would you have answered 'yes' to any of them?" Although this gives us no information about which questions would have been answered affirmatively or how many, it does red flag the individual as a possible child of a drug abuser so that the subject can be further explored. In this regard, this approach has been effective.

Our experience with the CAST indicates that Jones's concept is an excellent one. With it, counselors are afforded the opportunity to penetrate "wet" systems without a diagnostic interview with the alcohol abuser, who is seldom available. For many COAs identified by the CAST, the few minutes taken to administer this simple test results in their having the opportunity, perhaps for the first time in their lives, to talk with someone who understands and can help them deal with the problems of living in an alcoholic family. For many, it may also result in the codependent spouse's taking more appropriate responsibility in the family and perhaps even taking steps to protect the children from the drinker. Although realistically neither the CAST nor any other tool will cause the alcoholic parent to enter treatment, it can result in some improvement in the family system and substantial improvement in the child's ability to deal with the situation.

REFERENCES

Ackerman, R. J. (1983). *Children of alcoholics.* New York: Simon and Schuster.

Greenleaf, J. (1981). *Co-alcoholic, para-alcoholic: Who's who and what's the difference?* Denver: MAC Publishing.

Jones, J., & Pilat, J. (1981). *The Children of Alcoholics Screening Test (CAST).* Test and manual available from Camelot Unlimited, 5 N. Wabash, Suite 1409, Chicago, IL 60602.

Pilat, J., & Jones, J. (1984–1985). Identification of children of alcoholics: Two empirical studies. *Alcohol Health and Research World,* 27–36.

BIBLIOGRAPHY

Ackerman, R. J. (1982). (Video). Indiana, PA: Addiction Research and Counseling Services.

Part V
Innovations in Thought and Practice

Chapter 21

Approaches to Case Management with Substance-Abusing Populations

Cheryl L. Mejta, Peter J. Bokos, Judith H. Mickenberg,
E. Michael Maslar, Albert L. Hasson, Virginia Gil, Zane O'Keefe,
Steven S. Martin, Howard Isenberg, James A. Inciardi,
Dorothy Lockwood, Richard C. Rapp, Harvey A. Siegal,
James H. Fisher, and Joseph H. Wagner

Case management has its historical origins in the traditional social work and mental health fields. As originally conceived, case management sought to deliver social services in a more integrated and comprehensive manner to client populations with chronic, complex, and multiple problems and needs (especially the mentally ill and developmentally disabled). In recent years, we have seen a resurgence in the use of case management approaches with these and other client populations. This renewed interest in case management partially is an attempt to more effectively utilize the increasingly limited social services available to all client populations. Therefore those endorsing the case management approach are challenged with demonstrating its effectiveness for diverse populations.

Case management is a process designed to mobilize resources for clients and to deliver social services in a systematic, coordinated, efficient, and cost-effective manner (Dybal, 1980). At a minimum, case management involves the following basic activities: (a) assessment—determining clients' strengths and needs; (b) planning—establishing priority areas and defining clients' goals/objectives; (c) linking—identifying resources, referring to appropriate agencies, and facilitating the intake process; (d) monitoring—assuring that clients are receiving the needed services; and (e) advocacy—working on clients' behalf to acquire needed services (Bagarozzi & Pollane, 1984; Sullivan, 1981; Weil, 1985a).

There is no consensus regarding how best to achieve the case management goals or to perform the basic case management activities. Weil (1985b) identified and described four commonly used case management models:

This chapter was prepared with support from the National Institute on Drug Abuse research grants numbers DA-06086, DA-06944, DA-06124, DA-06948, and DA-06250.

The authors would like to acknowledge the support of Dr. Arthur M. Horton, NIDA Project Officer, who encouraged us to share our research findings and experiences with each other.

1. Generalist Service Broker Model—the case manager orchestrates the entire case management process, performing all case management functions.
2. Primary Therapist Model—the primary therapist is the client's case manager.
3. Interdisciplinary Team Model—case managers work on a team in which each worker specializes in a case management function.
4. Comprehensive Service Center Model—centers provide comprehensive services to clients coordinated by staff members.

The appropriate case management model is partially determined by the client population's needs and the organization's and the service network's capabilities (Weil, 1985b).

To date, case management approaches have not been widely applied to substance-abusing populations. Several characteristics of substance abuse, substance abusers, and the substance abuse treatment delivery system suggest that case management may be an appropriate and effective approach with substance-abusing populations. Substance abuse is typically characterized as a chronic, relapsing condition, with 60% to 70% of substance abusers relapsing within 90 days after treatment discharge (Hunt, Barnett, & Branch, 1971). Because substance abuse often has adverse effects in many areas of the abuser's life, effective treatment requires comprehensive and diverse services. Although the substance abuse treatment system recognizes the multiple problems and needs of substance abusers, budgetary constraints and large counselor caseloads make it difficult for the substance abuse treatment system to adequately meet these needs. Pickens and Fletcher (1991) note that there have been significant reductions in the quantity and quality of services provided to substance-abusing clients in some programs.

The National Institute on Drug Abuse (NIDA) has funded several projects through its Research Demonstration Program to Enhance Drug Abuse Treatment. Four of these have as their focus the development, implementation, and evaluation of case management approaches for substance abusers. Interventions, a substance abuse treatment, education, and research organization located in Chicago, is investigating the effectiveness of a case management approach with intravenous drug users. The University of California at Los Angeles is exploring the effectiveness of a case management approach with chronic opiate abusers at high risk for HIV infection or reinfection. This project targets men who are gay or bisexual, persons who are HIV positive, people exchanging sex for money or drugs, and sexual partners of these groups. The University of Delaware, in conjunction with NorthEast Treatment Centers, is examining the effectiveness of assertive community treatment with a parolee population. Wright State University School of Medicine in Dayton, Ohio, is testing the effectiveness of a strengths-based model of case management and advocacy with veterans who have substance abuse problems. This chapter describes each of these models with specific reference to the following areas:

client population served, underlying philosophy or assumptions of the model, role of the case manager, case management functions emphasized, client life domains addressed, and strengths/weaknesses of the model.

INTERVENTIONS CASE MANAGEMENT PROJECT

The Interventions Case Management Study was funded to develop a case management approach for intravenous drug users (IDUs) and to examine the approach's effectiveness in improving treatment access, retention, and outcome. A total of 300 IDUs seeking treatment through Interventions' Central Intake facility[1] were recruited for participation in the study. Clients who agreed to participate in the study were matched according to gender, race, and age and were randomly assigned to either a case-managed group (*n* = 150) or a comparison group (*n* = 150). Clients in the case-managed group were assigned to a case manager who assisted the client with identifying needs, establishing goals, and acquiring services. Clients in the comparison group received "treatment as usual": that is, they received minimal assistance (three clinic referrals based on proximity to the client's residence) in entering the substance abuse treatment system.

Underlying Assumptions and Philosophy of Model

In designing the Interventions Case Management Model, the characteristics of the client population, the substance abuse treatment system, and the human services delivery network were considered along with current understanding and knowledge about addiction and its treatment. Clients served by the project are a predominantly minority client population with multiple and chronic problems, extensive addiction careers, and a history of multigenerational poverty. Most are opiate-dependent IDUs. The vast majority have been abusing multiple substances for 10 years or more and have had at least one unsuccessful prior treatment episode. Problems that plague this client population include unemployment, homelessness, lack of adequate food, untreated medical and psychological disorders, unresolved legal situations, financial problems, and dysfunctional family and social support systems. This is a constellation of problems that encourages continued drug use and antisocial behavior and impedes progress in treatment.

Recent budgetary cuts of substance abuse treatment programs have resulted in reductions in the numbers and types of services available, longer waiting periods to receive services, reductions in staff, and higher client-counselor ratios. A similar situation exists within other human service systems. IDUs seeking substance abuse treatment in the Chicago area may encounter waiting periods as long as 3 months (W. Watkins, personal communication, September 1992). Once a client makes the decision to change, he or she has a limited period of time to initiate action before the motivation to change dissipates (Prochaska & DiClemente, 1982). Preliminary data indicate that IDUs in the comparison group are likely to stop seeking treatment as a result of the long delays in treatment admission (Mejta & Bokos, 1992).

Key assumptions consistent with current knowledge about addiction and its treatment guided the development of the Interventions Case Management Model. These assumptions included the following:

1. Because substance abusers are a heterogeneous population, case management plans must be individualized.
2. Because addiction is a chronic, relapsing condition, case management services should be available to the client during treatment and after treatment discharge.
3. Because recovery from addiction is a process that occurs across stages with differing needs emerging, the case management plan must be reviewed and altered periodically.
4. Because different treatment systems and approaches may be more effective with different types of clients, the case manager must have referral relationships established with a variety of substance abuse and other human service delivery programs.

General Description of the Model

The case management model selected is a broad-spectrum model that addresses the multiple problems and needs of substance-abusing clients. Within this model, the case manager acts in the capacity of a generalist: he or she orchestrates the entire case management process, performs each of the five traditional case management functions, and interfaces with a multitude of substance abuse treatment and other human service providers (e.g., general assistance, public housing, social security, legal aid, public health, community mental health) in order to address the multiple needs of clients.

The goal of the case management process is to facilitate opportunities for clients to effect changes in their functioning and life circumstances necessary to eliminate health-compromising drug use by linking clients to appropriate and effective services. Similar to the goals of many substance abuse interventions, areas targeted for change include sustained abstinence from drug abuse; stabilized living situation; stabilized interpersonal relationships; adequate and regular source of legal income; resolved legal issues; positive view of self; and involvement in activities that support physical and mental health. Specific goals and behavioral measures of success are individualized for each client. Motivational counseling (Miller & Rollnick, 1991) is coupled with the five traditional case management functions in order to develop, implement, monitor, and revise a comprehensive, coordinated, flexible service plan that promotes movement toward the client's goals.

To effectively perform case management activities, the case manager needs sufficient time. The size of a case manager's caseload therefore becomes an important concern. The cost of the program also needs to be reasonable. To address the issues of case manager efficacy and cost effectiveness, clients are categorized according to their utilization of available case management services. More of the case manager's time and energy is required during certain stages of treatment and recovery, and with certain clients. Although a case manager's total caseload size may approach 30 clients, the total number of active clients (clients requiring ongoing contact) is about 15 clients per case manager. The case manager provides case management services to clients for 3 years. This enables the case manager to monitor clients' progress through the treatment process as well as after treatment completion. The case manager can intervene as needed in order to facilitate clients' retention in treatment, successful completion of treatment, and maintenance of behavior change after treatment discharge.

To promote a case management approach that was client focused and client driven rather than system focused and system driven, the case management project was organized as an entity separate from other direct service delivery programs. It was assumed that positioning the project as a separate unit would encourage the case managers to interface with a variety of substance abuse and other human service delivery systems rather than only those service systems easily accessed because of proximity to the project. It was also assumed that interfacing with many service systems would increase the likelihood that the client's needs would be addressed through referral to the most appropriate and effective service provider. This is predicated on the belief that recognizing clients' individualized needs and matching clients to appropriate substance abuse and human service systems facilitates recovery from substance abuse.

Application of the Case Management Model

Under the Interventions Case Management Model, the case manager performs the traditional case management activities with each client. These activities are repeated across three stages: (a) treatment initiation, admission, and engagement; (b) treatment retention and completion; and (c) recovery maintenance.

Initially, the case manager conducts a broad-based needs assessment with the client to identify presenting needs and problems, to ascertain services that the client is receiving currently, and to identify barriers to the client's accessing treatment. Some barriers to treatment include lack of transportation, lack of child care, inadequate financial resources to purchase care, missing prerequisite client documentation (e.g., ID, laboratory results, previous treatment records), comorbidity (coexistence of alcoholism, medical problems, or psychiatric issues precluding acceptance into a treatment program), poor reputation in the substance abuse treatment network, and personal ambivalence about entering treatment.

Based upon the results of the assessment, an individualized case management plan is developed that specifies the client's goals, plans to attain these goals, and methods to reduce or eliminate treatment barriers. The client is then linked with a variety of treatment providers and other services selected to meet the client's needs and matched on several variables including location, fees, hours of operation, degree of program structure, flexibility of program structure, comprehensiveness of services, and ease of entry into program. Linking is aided by preparing the client for the system by providing advance orientation to the program admission procedures, rules, policies, expectations, criteria for success, response to problematic relations, and other pertinent factors. Systems are also informed of client history, current needs, response style, patterns of success and crisis, and issues important to initial joining with the system. The client, provider, and services are then monitored with the purpose of recommending revisions in goals and/or services as appropriate. Efforts are made to reduce treatment attrition and interruption by identifying and addressing the client's patterns of relapse and potential client-system conflicts.

The assessment, planning, linking, and monitoring process is repeated as some problems are resolved, some goals are attained, and new needs emerge. To facilitate the maintenance of clients' changes, these case management services are available to the client for 3 years.

Potential Weakness of the Model

A major issue in the delivery of case management services to this particular client population is the development of a methodology supportive of health-enhancing behaviors and appropriate personal responsibility that does not shield individuals from the consequences of their own behavior and further facilitate health-compromising and other antisocial behavior patterns. Case managers need to strive continuously to define a role for themselves as change agents facilitating opportunities for the client's recovery. They must be alert to the danger of functioning as another enabler in the client's continuing process of addictive behavior patterns.

UNIVERSITY OF CALIFORNIA AT LOS ANGELES—ENHANCED METHADONE MAINTENANCE CASE MANAGEMENT

The development and implementation of the case management approach within the Enhanced Methadone Maintenance Project (EMM) has been a difficult process. During its first 2 1/2 years, EMM was housed within a preexisting methadone maintenance treatment program. In this setting, the EMM case management team functioned independently from the program's clinical team. The attempt to accomplish common treatment goals with two independent teams was inefficient and frequently unsuccessful.

Consequently, the University of California at Los Angeles (UCLA) Drug Abuse Research Center and the Matrix Institute on Addictions collaborated to create a clinic committed to research and treatment of opiate addiction, utilizing a case management approach. The process of locating a new facility, moving patients, and hiring and training new staff set the implementation of the case management approach behind schedule. Once the move was accomplished, patients began receiving counseling and supportive services from a single case manager.

The most appropriate way to describe the population served by the EMM project is to review the eligibility criteria for patient selection. Applicants must meet requirements set by state and federal regulations governing methadone programs and be a member of one of four target groups: (a) persons who are HIV positive; (b) males who are gay or bisexual; (c) persons who are sex workers; and (d) sex partners of any person belonging to one of those three groups.

To date, 440 patients have been enrolled in the EMM project. The population breakdown is as follows: 57% sex workers; 38% sex partners, with 20% being gay or bisexual males; and 19% HIV positive. Note that patients can be members of several target groups simultaneously. The ethnicity of the sample is 41% African-American, 27% Caucasian, 29% Hispanic, and 3% classified as other. Fifty-two percent of the sample are males and 48% females. Upon admission only 10% of the patients were employed, and 35% held valid driver's licenses. The mean age is 39.5 years, with a mean age of first heroin use of 19.9 years. A further illustration of the extent of disability within this population is that 37% have been prescribed psychiatric medications at some point in time. Nineteen and one-half percent have been hospitalized for psychiatric reasons. The decision to utilize a case management approach was made in consideration of the severity and extent of needs of the patient population served, and because case management optimized the quality and quantity of services delivered to patients in a methadone maintenance program.

The EMM model of case management is not sophisticated. Problem areas are identified and prioritized, possible solutions discussed, referrals made, and follow-up completed—simple, yet effective in working to support a client population with a myriad of needs. As a matter of economics and indirect public policy, methadone counselors have traditionally functioned as quasi-case managers. Programs applying for licensure through the State of California Department of Alcohol and Drug Programs (ADP) are required either to provide a wide variety of social services or to act as service brokers. These services are to be provided in addition to addressing issues of recovery. The majority of programs within

California do not have the budgetary allowances to provide a cursory, let alone an optimal, level of direct services.

IDUs are the fastest growing group of seroconverters, accounting for 32% of all HIV-positive cases (Centers for Disease Control, 1991). Given the HIV epidemic among IDUs, the issue of retention in treatment is critical from both the public health and the rehabilitation perspectives. Methadone treatment appears to lower the frequency of injection and needle sharing and provides an opportunity to educate IDUs about HIV disease and safe sex (Ball, Lange, Myers, & Friedman, 1988). Studies also show that the longer patients remain in treatment, the less likely they are to return to illicit drug use (Ball et al., 1988; Des Jarlais, Joseph, & Dole, 1981; Hubbard et al., 1989; Watters, 1986). Two other factors appear to positively influence patient retention: higher average doses of methadone (D'Aunno & Vaughn, 1992) and a patient's participation in decisions about dose level (Watters, 1986). The EMM project designs procedures in consideration of these research findings.

Studies about long-term retention in methadone maintenance programs have suggested that the majority of dropouts occur during the first 90 days of treatment (Hubbard et al., 1989). A transportation contingency program was implemented to increase attendance during this critical period. During the first 30 days in the program, patients are given bus tickets for the next day's transportation to the clinic. If a patient's attendance is greater than or equal to 75% during the first and second months, he or she receives a voucher for the following month's unlimited, free transportation. Bus tokens and monthly bus vouchers have increased attendance of many patients. Patients missing more than one consecutive day of clinic are contacted by their case managers, who encourage them to attend daily.

During admission to the EMM project, patients are given an orientation to the program that includes (a) the clinic's responsibilities, rules for patient behavior, services, and policies and procedures; and (b) the patients' responsibilities to the research project. Assessment begins during the admission process. Patients complete questionnaires regarding their history of opiate and other drug use, and their medical and psychiatric conditions. New patients receive a physical examination in which pressing medical issues are identified. Data gathered during admission and a needs assessment provide information critical to the formulation of the patient's treatment plan.

Treatment plans are developed by the patient and his or her case manager and reviewed at 90-day intervals, and updates are completed as needed. These treatment plans are detailed, time-sensitive blueprints of desired behavioral changes. The application of contingency programs to facilitate treatment plan compliance and behavioral change constitutes an important aspect of the EMM case management approach.

Referrals addressing specific patient needs are generally made upon completion of the needs assessment and treatment plan. Priority is given to medical and psychiatric referrals. Dual-diagnosis patients requiring psychopharmacological intervention are referred for evaluation and treatment to a staff psychiatrist.

Medical staff have become an integral component of EMM case management. Patients in need of medical treatment are given referral letters describing in detail symptoms, onset, and other relevant information. Even with referrals and support, patients frequently report being intimidated and overwhelmed by obstacles encountered in attempting to access medical services. Existing public health services are severely overburdened.

Health care professionals outside the substance abuse field often treat IDUs with intolerance and insensitivity. Patients' physical symptoms that would be indicative of common medical problems in a non-drug-using population are frequently attributed to withdrawal, and the patient is not appropriately diagnosed or treated. On occasion, an attending physician will refuse to administer methadone to a hospitalized patient and/or consult with the EMM program's medical director. Patients must choose between the pain of withdrawal or medical treatment for a potentially life-threatening condition. In spite of these obstacles, assertive follow-up by both medical and clinical staff has resulted in improved compliance by patients.

At the present time, caseload size varies from 1:30/35 patients per case manager. Case managers have indicated a caseload size toward the lower end of this range to be optimal. Even the lower ratio is considerably larger than other non-methadone treatment case management paradigms.

EMM case managers have been inundated by the number of patients in need of basic necessities. It has been relatively easy to provide sources of food and clothing; however, many shelters have excluded patients on methadone and are frequently located in drug-ridden sections of town. The shelter issue will only worsen as winter approaches.

Time demands on case managers as patient advocates and brokers of services often supersede the "therapist" aspects of the case manager's job description. Patients entering treatment are primarily interested in being medicated and acquiring transportation vouchers, food, clothing, and shelter. A case manager's attention to a patient's survival or other pressing personal issues is often the basis for an ongoing therapeutic relationship. Once these issues are addressed, behavioral interventions targeting drug use can be effectively implemented.

UNIVERSITY OF DELAWARE—ASSERTIVE COMMUNITY TREATMENT (ACT)

The drug-involved criminal justice client faces additional problems from contact with the criminal justice system, including the stigma of a criminal record, possible prison experience, and the disruptions caused in work, school, and family activities. The likelihood of relapse and recidivism from the failure of these clients to find support for their dual problems of recovery and reentry into society creates a more complex, problematic, and costly treatment situation than what most drug users face.

Given the diverse and complex needs of criminal justice clients and the correctional mandate to monitor and supervise offenders in community settings, the use of case management has great promise. Criminal justice treatment is recognizing the need to incorporate other services in community-based programs, part of a general movement in corrections toward community-oriented programs. The most visible and enduring of these programs is the Treatment Alternatives to Street Crime (TASC) program. Under TASC, community-based supervision is made available to drug-involved individuals who would otherwise burden the system with repeated drug-associated criminality (Inciardi & McBride, 1991).

The TASC model incorporates elements of assessment, planning, linking, and monitoring but not the advocacy function of case management. Under sponsorship of the NIDA Projects, a new program seeks to apply and evaluate an assertive community treatment (ACT) model for clients paroled from the Delaware prison system. The program was developed by NorthEast Treatment Centers (NET) and the University of Delaware and is administered by NET.[2] The program design integrates an intensive-outpatient biopsychosocial model of drug treatment with the community support system approach to assertive case management.

The program is based on a continuity of care model for the community treatment of the chronically mentally ill that originated in Wisconsin during the early 1970s (Test, Knoedler, & Allness, 1985). Often referred to as "assertive case management," the program's focus is proactive: counselors and case managers help the client reenter the community by providing "*in vivo* treatment" with small client staff ratios.

Clients are randomly selected from inmates released via parole from the Delaware correctional system who (a) have a previous drug-using history that puts them at increased risk for HIV infection, and (b) volunteer to participate in the program. By the time the program is finished, 200 inmates (about 150 men and 50 women) will be selected into the ACT program. Currently, clients represent the population of prison parolees; most are male (73%) and Black (74%). By definition, all are past drug users and have been in prison at least once. Most have extensive criminal histories; 62% have a violent crime on their record. The mean age is 29, and a majority (53%) have less than a high school education.

After classification to parole status and selection for the program, each ACT client ideally proceeds through treatment and case management in five stages:

1. *Intake* evaluation and assessment
2. *Intensive drug treatment*, which includes group counseling, drug and AIDS education and discussion groups, individual counseling, family assessment, and therapy
3. *Moderate treatment*, in which educational/vocational sessions come more to the forefront in group counseling and life skills planning, and treatment takes on a more supportive posture
4. *Relapse prevention*, in which group sessions, education, vocational counseling, and individual and family counseling all focus on support of relapse prevention
5. *Case management*, in which clients who have completed their active involvement in the treatment-oriented parts of ACT transfer completely into a case management phase, designed to support their transition into normal community life with instrumental support from case managers

The program emphasizes the graduation process through the stages; however, content often overlaps. For example, vocational issues may be discussed in the intensive treatment phase, and intensive drug counseling may occur when a case management client is returned to a previous treatment phase as a result of a relapse incident. More detail on the treatment stages is in Inciardi, Isenberg, Lockwood, Martin, and Scarpitti (1992).

The ACT program is designed to be highly individualized because each person has a different addiction history and therefore experiences different needs. Although the initial treatment phases are similar for all participants, individual differences are taken into account during the third and later stages of the program. As case management services are introduced, each treatment plan becomes increasingly more tailored to the needs of the individual.

Client-specific needs dictate much of the pattern. This is particularly true in relapse prevention. Skill development emphasizes the efficacy of lifestyle changes that produce increased self-esteem, including, but not limited to, developing healthy, supportive friendships; coping with social needs and services; and avoiding situations that risk relapse. Continued urinalysis monitoring confirms abstinence or identifies clients experiencing difficulty meeting goals toward sustained abstinence. Clients who need more treatment return to a previous treatment phase.

Success in treatment leads to increasing emphasis on case management issues. Providing case management is open-ended and emphasizes the relationship between client and counselor built into the earlier stages of treatment. Case management can include continued active participation in the supportive elements of the treatment program. The counselor, now case manager, is accessible to the client and prepared to provide individualized attention in the continuity of care (Bachrach, 1981). The overall goal for the integration of the assertive case management component with the clinical treatment program is to assist clients to become more active in their own treatment and eventually function as case managers for themselves. Giving clients a sense of instrumental empowerment permits them to transcend their typical role of dependency and prepares them for more participation in and responsibility for achieving their own goals.

Case managers act as advocates for the clients with other treatment and service providers in the local social service network, including parole officers. This requires linking and networking in order to maintain an active resource pool. Regularly scheduled case management contacts are initiated for each client to continually assess if the client (a) has remained alcohol and drug free, (b) has complied with vocational training/job placement plans, (c) is in a stable family and employment situation, and/or (d) is in need of further service or referral. Effective case management during the follow-up period has increased the likelihood of client involvement in recommended services as well as prevented relapse by intensifying direct involvement with the client in the event of a crisis.

Discharge is contingent on a client's progress rather than on time spent in the program. Because treatment is individualized, time in treatment and in case management varies depending on the specific services required and the time needed to benefit from them. The discharge and continuing care planning is the responsibility of the individual counselor, with input from the client and the treatment team. The treatment team includes a senior clinician, licensed case managers/counselors, and an intake coordinator with addiction treatment experience and excellent diagnostic skills. The client-to-staff ratio is 12:1 for caseloads. Direct clinical staff are supported by administrative personnel.

The treatment team meets weekly to discuss each client's progress and service needs, both in-house and with other providers. During the team meeting, staff evaluate the progress of the clients in the planned services on an ongoing basis and adjust services in response to each client's ability to benefit from them. Each case manager benefits from the input and support of other staff involvement with their client.

Despite the ACT program's promise, a practical limitation is the inability to require participation, which precludes a real test of the intervention. This points to the need to retain criminal justice clients in treatment. One consensual finding from treatment research is that the longer a client stays in treatment, the better the outcome in terms of decline in drug use and criminality (Anglin & Hser, 1990). One of the few advantages of dealing with criminal justice clients is the potential to compel treatment for drug offenders. Studies show that success in treatment is a function of length of stay and that those coerced into treatment do at least as well as voluntary commitments and may do better if they remain longer in treatment than voluntary commitments (Hubbard et al., 1989; Leukefeld & Tims, 1990).

Case management can encourage substance abusers to stay in treatment and reach treatment goals (Kofoed, Tolson, Atkinson, Toth, & Turner, 1986). If case management is combined with legal sanctions to enforce participation and monitoring (parole and probation stipulations), the potential for retention in treatment and getting services will be greatly increased. Collins and Allison (1983) found that legal coercion works well to retain clients in treatment. Case management with correctional clients has a positive side as well. It facilitates the relationship building and trust crucial in helping the client develop skills, become empowered, and assume his or her own case management duties (Rapp & Chamberlain, 1985).

Despite the limitations of being unable to mandate or encourage participation by clients in the full program, the Delaware ACT project is helping reduce client drug use and the risk of rearrest, recidivism, and HIV infection among a particularly difficult treatment population—drug-involved offenders under parole supervision.

WRIGHT STATE UNIVERSITY—ENHANCED TREATMENT PROJECT

The *Enhanced Treatment Through Induction and Case Management Project,* administered through the Wright State University School of Medicine in Dayton, Ohio, is testing two complementary techniques designed to enhance the outcome of substance abuse treatment. Veterans who apply for substance abuse treatment at the Polysubstance Rehabilitation Program (PRP), located at the Department of Veterans Affairs Medical Center (DVAMC), Dayton, Ohio, represent the pool of participants for the project. A complete description of the *Enhanced Treatment Project* can be found elsewhere (Cole et al., 1992).

Case management/advocacy was adopted as one of two enhancement techniques (pretreatment induction being the other) based on works that suggest that substance abusers who seek treatment have a broader range of problems than just the actual use of psychoactive substances (McLellan, Luborsky, O'Brien, Woody, & Druley, 1982; Oppenheimer, Sheehan, & Taylor, 1988; Westermeyer, 1989). These problems—homelessness, unemployment, lack of basic living skills—are perhaps related to substance use/abuse but nonetheless require interventions beyond core substance abuse treatment. In other words, an intervention is needed that is designed to assist substance abusers in identifying these collateral problems and in accessing the specific resources necessary to resolve them. Case management and advocacy (a distinct constituent of case management in many descriptions of the intervention) have long been used with other populations to accomplish the goals of identifying, accessing, and acquiring such resources. More recently, case management/advocacy has been suggested as a tool that might be used with substance abusers (Graham & Birchmore Timney,

1990; Kofoed et al., 1986; Rapp, Siegal, & Fisher, 1992). A strengths-based model of case management/advocacy has been selected as the model to be used in the *Enhanced Treatment Project.*

The Strengths Perspective of Case Management/Advocacy was used to assist a population of persons with mental illness make the transition from institutionalized care to independent living (Rapp, 1988; Rapp & Chamberlain, 1985). Since its development, the model has been adapted for work with other populations (Saleebey, 1992). Five key principles serve as the cornerstone of the model. The foremost two principles include providing disenfranchised populations with support for: (a) *asserting direct control over their search for resources,* such as housing and employment, and (b) *examining their own strengths and assets* as the vehicle for resource acquisition. The three remaining principles further clarify the premises of self-determination and a focus on strengths by (a) encouraging use of informal *helping networks* (as opposed to institutional networks); (b) promoting the *primacy of the client-case manager/advocate relationship,* and, (c) providing an *active, aggressive form of outreach* to clients (Rapp, 1988).

Project staff have precisely defined the conceptual basis and practice interventions used in implementing the Strengths Perspective. These points can be thought of as occupying a pyramid. The five key principles of the Strengths Perspective occupy the base of the pyramid. Moving up the pyramid, an operational definition, "essential elements," and specific practice interventions occupy successively higher levels. The effect of these conceptual and practice issues is to insure that the philosophy of the Strengths Perspective is integrated into all case management/advocacy activities. Although a detailed description of these points is beyond the scope of this work, a brief discussion is in order.

Creation of the project's operational definition of case management/advocacy was influenced heavily by the work of Intagliata (1982), as well as by the key principles underlying the Strengths Perspective. In the *Enhanced Treatment Project* case management/advocacy is defined as techniques used to assist the client in re-establishing an awareness of their internal resources such as intelligence, competence, and problem solving; establish and negotiate a referral path between the client and external resources; and advocate with those external resources in order to enhance the continuity, accessibility, accountability, and efficiency of those resources. This definition serves to remind case manager/advocates of the strengths-based nature of the model and of the nature of their work with clients, that is, acquiring needed resources.

Essential elements are statements that were created early in the project to serve as reminders of the intent of each Strengths Perspective principle. "Have client identify own goals" is an example of an essential element that supports the principle of client self-determination. Although these statements are relatively specific, they still lack the precision needed to guide specific practice interventions. Practice interventions, keyed to one or more of the five basic principles of the strengths perspective, are built into the engagement, assessment, and goal-setting stages of the process. These interventions are specific techniques that case manager/advocates use in assisting clients.

Case manager/advocates use several instruments created for the project to gather clinical information in a standardized format: these instruments include a strengths assessment, progress evaluation scales, and a case management plan. During the first several contacts with clients, case manager/advocates will complete the *Enhanced Treatment Project Strengths Assessment*. The focus of the semistructured interview is to obtain information pertaining to the veteran's healthy functioning in each of the nine life domains (life skills, finances, leisure, relationships, living arrangements, occupation/education, health, internal resources, and recovery). The Strengths Assessment may be completed as a structured interview but is more generally conducted in an open-ended, discussion format.

Clients are asked to complete the *Enhanced Treatment Project Progress Evaluation Scale (PES)* at several intervals during their involvement in the project. The *PES* is a nine-point ordinal scale used to measure healthy, productive functioning in each of the nine life domains. Modeled after the work of others (Ihilevich & Gleser, 1982; Martin, Isenberg, & Inciardi, 1993), the project's version of the *PES* was developed from client and staff focus groups.

One technique case manager/advocates will use to assist veterans in goal setting is the *Enhanced Treatment Project Case Management Plan (CMP)*. The *CMP* provides both veteran and case manager/advocate with a structured format for identifying goals, setting objectives, and creating strategies. Goals statements are conceptualized and written as broad, general, and perhaps never fully attainable. Objectives are always measurable, specific steps that lead the veteran toward his goal. Strategies are specific activities that lead to accomplishment of an objective. In addition to their information-gathering value, these instruments are all designed to serve as practice interventions in and of themselves and at the same time provide research and supervisory utility.

In addition to expected issues (role clarification and territorial concerns, among others) involved in implementing a research project in an existing service delivery system, three categories of independent and yet overlapping issues are potential impediments to implementation of the Strengths Perspective. These implementation issues could be characterized as (a) intrinsic to case management/advocacy, (b) inherent to the field of substance abuse treatment, and (c) specific to a strengths perspective of case management/advocacy. One of the implementation issues specific to a strengths-based perspective required that a decision be made regarding the model's place in the overall treatment system.

It was understood very early in the project that using a strengths approach to case management/advocacy interventions could create conflict in the treatment environment. PRP is oriented to a disease concept or medical model approach to treating substance abuse problems, and one aspect of this model—the focus on pathology, problems, and what is diseased—has major significance for a strengths-based model of case management/advocacy. Simply put, this approach to substance abuse treatment is the antithesis of a strengths perspective on working with clients.

Project staff integrated the strengths approach into the larger system and thereby defined a parallel track to that of the core treatment regimen. As might be expected, these parallel interventions—disease-based primary treatment and strengths-based case management/advocacy—will occasionally come into conflict. It is at the point of conflict that the need for advocacy and service coordination is most acutely felt.

The Strengths Perspective of Case Management/Advocacy, as it is being implemented in the *Enhanced Treatment Project*, offers an opportunity to systematically deliver and evaluate case management/advocacy interventions with substance abusers. The substance abuse field is also presented with an alternative method of assisting substance abusers through an approach that focuses on strengths and assets. Preliminary outcome data and anecdotal evidence suggest that this strengths-based approach to case management/advocacy holds promise as an effective and accepted approach to assisting substance abusers. Continued positive results may require the substance abuse field to rethink its longstanding preoccupation with approaches that focus on narrow conceptualizations of disease and illness.

CONCLUSION

Although case management approaches have been aptly described and discussed in the literature, there is a lack of empirical evidence demonstrating their effectiveness (Fisher, Landis, & Clark, 1988). The four NIDA-supported research demonstration projects described in this chapter are empirically testing several different case management approaches with different substance-abusing populations. Preliminary data from these projects suggest that case management is effective in improving treatment access and retention. Treatment retention, completion, and other outcome data will be available in the future.

In applying or translating case management approaches to substance-abusing populations, several important considerations were noted. Case managers, in delivering case management services, need to be cautious about further reducing clients' self-efficacy and self-esteem. Although case managers assist clients in securing needed services, case managers should help clients use existing skills or develop skills where deficiencies exist in order to successfully negotiate systems independently in the future.

A second implementation consideration is the difficulty of getting staff who are familiar with the substance abuse system to assume the case manager role. The more traditional "passive" convention of waiting for clients to visit counselors in treatment programs is in sharp contrast to the more proactive and even assertive procedures of delivering treatment and support to clients directly in the community. This was a difficult barrier to overcome in dealing with drug users where there is the perception by service providers that clients are responsible to a great degree for their life circumstances. Thus there is some evidence that substance abusers are less likely to receive the array of rehabilitation services available to other client populations (Solomon, 1986).

Case management offers the possibility of delivering services to clients in a more integrated, coordinated, and cost-effective manner. Alternatives to the traditional substance abuse treatment system are particularly critical now as continued reductions in funding threaten the quantity and quality of services available to substance-abusing populations. The severity of clients' problems has increased, and the potential health consequences (e.g., AIDS) of continued substance use has worsened.

NOTES

1. Interventions' Central Intake Facility provides substance abuse treatment referrals and performs initial and follow-up medical examinations and laboratory tests for substance abusers entering publicly funded substance abuse treatment programs.
2. NorthEast Treatment Centers is a nonprofit social service organization headquartered in Philadelphia, which operates over 25 programs in the Delaware Valley. NET provides a continuum of care for both substance abusers and troubled adolescents, including short- and long-term residential treatment, outpatient and intensive inpatient treatment, case management services, group homes, foster care, and in-home detention. NET also offers a variety of specialized programming for women, adult and juvenile criminal justice clients, and other high-risk populations.

REFERENCES

Anglin, M. D., & Hser, Y. (1990). Treatment of drug abuse. In M. Tonry & J. Q. Wilson (Eds.), *Drugs and crime* (pp. 393–460). Chicago: University of Chicago Press.

Bachrach, L. L. (1981). Continuity of care for chronic mental patients: A conceptual analysis. *American Journal of Psychiatry, 138*, 1449–1456.

Bagarozzi, D., & Pollane, L. (1984). Case management in mental health. *Health and Social Work, 9*, 201–211.

Ball, J. C., Lange, W. R., Myers, C. P., & Friedman, S. R. (1988). Reducing the risk of AIDS through methadone maintenance treatment. *Journal of Health and Social Behavior, 29*, 214–226.

Centers for Disease Control. (1991, January 31). *Aids Weekly Surveillance Report*.

Cole, P., Siegal, H., Forney, M., Rapp, R., Fisher, J., & Callejo, V. (1992, March/April). The Enhanced Treatment Project. *Addiction and Recovery*, pp. 72–74.

Collins, J. J., & Allison, M. (1983). Legal coercion and retention in drug abuse treatment. *Hospital and Community Psychiatry, 34*, 1145–1149.

D'Aunno, T., & Vaughn, T. E. (1992). Variation in methadone treatment practices: Results from a national study. *Journal of the American Medical Association, 267,* 253–258.

Des Jarlais, D. C., Joseph, H., & Dole, V. P. (1981). Long term outcomes after termination from methadone maintenance treatment. *Annals of the New York Academy of Science, 362,* 231–238.

Dybal, L. (1980). Human services development series—Case management in selected Wisconsin counties. *Wisconsin Department of Health and Social Services Report.* Madison, WI: Department of Health and Social Services.

Fisher, G., Landis, D., & Clark, K. (1988). Case management service provision and client change. *Community Mental Health Journal, 24,* 134–142.

Graham, K., & Birchmore Timney, C. (1990). Case management in addictions treatment. *Journal of Substance Abuse Treatment, 7,* 181–188.

Hubbard, R. L., Marsden, M. E., Rachal, J. V., Harwood, H. J., Cavanaugh, E. R., & Ginzburg, H. M. (1989). *Drug abuse treatment: A national study of effectiveness.* Chapel Hill, NC: University of North Carolina Press.

Hunt, W. A., Barnett, L. W., & Branch, L. G. (1971). Relapse rates in addiction programs. *Journal of Clinical Psychology, 27,* 455–456.

Ihilevich, D., & Gleser, G. (1982). *Evaluating mental health programs: The Progress Evaluation Scale.* Lexington, MA: Lexington.

Inciardi, J. A., & McBride, D. C. (1991). *Treatment alternatives to street crime (TASC): History, experiences, and issues.* Rockville, MD: National Institute on Drug Abuse.

Inciardi, J. A., Isenberg, H., Lockwood, D., Martin, S. S., & Scarpitti, F. R. (1992). Assertive community treatment with a parolee population: An extension of case management. In R. Ashery (Ed.), *Progress and issues in case management* (Research Monograph No. 127, pp. 350–367). Rockville, MD: National Institute on Drug Abuse.

Intagliata, J. (1982). Improving the quality of community care for the chronically mentally disabled: The role of case management. *Schizophrenia Bulletin, 8* (4), 655–674.

Kofoed, L., Tolson, R., Atkinson, R., Toth, R., & Turner, J. (1986). Outpatient treatment of patients with substance abuse and coexisting psychiatric disorders. *American Journal of Psychiatry, 143*(7), 867–872.

Leukefeld, C. G., & Tims, F. M. (1990). Compulsory treatment for drug abuse. *International Journal of the Addictions, 25,* 621–640.

Martin, S. S., Isenberg, H., & Inciardi, J.A. (1993). Assertive Community Treatment (ACT): Integrating intensive drug treatment with aggressive case management for hard to reach populations. In J. Inciardi, F. Tims, & B. Fletcher (Eds.), *Innovative approaches into the treatment of drug abuse: Program models and strategies* (pp. 97–108). Westport, CT: Greenwood.

McLellan, A., Luborsky, L., O'Brien, C., Woody, G., & Druley, K. (1982). Is treatment for substance abuse effective? *Journal of the American Medical Association, 247*(10), 1423–1428.

Mejta, C., & Bokos, P. (1992, February). *The effectiveness of a case management approach with intravenous drug users: Preliminary results.* Paper presented at the National Institute on Drug Abuse Technical Review Meeting, *Progress in Case Management.* Bethesda, MD.

Miller, W. R., & Rollnick, S. (1991). *Motivational interviewing: Preparing people to change addictive behavior.* New York: Guilford.

Oppenheimer, E., Sheehan, M., & Taylor, C. (1988). Letting the client speak: Drug misusers and the process of help seeking. *British Journal of Addiction, 83,* 635–647.

Pickens, R. W., & Fletcher, B. W. (1991). Overview of treatment issues. In R. Pickens, C. Leukefeld, and C. Schuster (Eds.), *Improving drug abuse treatment* (Research Monograph No. 91-1754, pp. 1–19).Rockville, MD: National Institute on Drug Abuse.

Prochaska, J. O., & DiClemente, C. C. (1982). Transtheoretical Therapy: Toward a more integrative model of change. *Psychotherapy Theory, Research and Practice, 19*, 276–278.

Rapp, C. (1988). The Strengths Perspective of Case Management with persons suffering from severe mental illness. Lawrence, KS: University of Kansas School of Social Welfare.

Rapp, C., & Chamberlain, R. (1985). Case management services for the chronically mentally ill. *Social Work, 30*, 417–422.

Rapp, R., Siegal, H., & Fisher, J. (1992). A strengths-based model of case management/advocacy: Adapting a mental health model to practice work with persons who have substance abuse problems. In R. Ashery (Ed.), *Progress and issues in case management* (Research Monograph No. 127, pp. 79–91). Rockville, MD: National Institute of Drug Abuse.

Saleebey, D. (1992). *The Strengths Perspective in social work practice.* New York: Longman.

Solomon, P. (1986). Receipt of aftercare services by problem types: Psychiatric, psychiatric/substance abuse and substance abuse. *Psychiatric Quarterly 58*(3), 180–188.

Sullivan, J. P. (1981). Case management. In J. A. Talbott (Ed.), *The chronically mentally ill* (pp. 121–133). New York: Human Sciences Press.

Test, M. A., Knoedler, W. H., & Allness, D. J. (1985). The long-term treatment of young schizophrenics in a community support program. In L. I. Stein & M. A. Test (Eds.), *Training in community living—Ten years later* (pp. 17–27). San Francisco: Jossey-Bass.

Watters, J. K. (1986). *Treatment environment and client outcome in methadone maintenance clinics.* Doctoral dissertation, University of Michigan, Ann Arbor.

Weil, M. (1985a). Adapting case management to specific programs and needs. In M. Weil & J. M. Karls (Eds.), *Case management in human service practice* (pp. 317–356). San Francisco: Jossey-Bass.

Weil, M. (1985b). Key components in providing efficient and effective services. In M. Weil & J. M. Karls (Eds.), *Case management in human service practice* (pp. 29–71). San Francisco: Jossey-Bass.

Westermeyer, J. (1989). Nontreatment factors affecting treatment outcome in substance abuse. *American Journal of Drug and Alcohol Abuse, 15*(1), 13–29.

Chapter 22
Substance-Abuse Counseling: A Developmental Approach

Judy Daniels and Michael D'Andrea

Regardless of their particular work settings, counselors can expect to be confronted with clients whose personal problems are complicated by the misuse and/or abuse of alcohol and other drugs. With this in mind, it is important that all professional counselors consider how they would go about working with persons who manifest substance abuse problems.

Upon reviewing the literature related to substance abuse counseling, some practitioners might be surprised to find that many of the basic techniques and strategies recommended for use with clients who are experiencing substance abuse problems are the same as those they are currently using with other types of clients. In this regard, George (1990) discusses a variety of counseling skills typically used by substance abuse counselors that are very similar to those used by most professional counselors in a variety of clinical work settings. These include the effective use of attending skills, empathic communication, and the appropriate application of confrontation and self-disclosure.

Although there are specific interventions that are unique to substance abuse counseling, such as aversion therapy (Forrest, 1978), most therapeutic interventions attempt to help clients gain control over negative and disturbing emotions, learn to substitute rational attitudes and beliefs for irrational ones, and/or eliminate self-defeating behaviors. To accomplish these goals, substance abuse counselors rely on a host of traditional counseling approaches and strategies when working with clients whose personal problems are directly related to the misuse and/or abuse of alcohol and other types of drugs. These divergent approaches include the use of various techniques associated with Adlerian, Behavioral, Existential, Gestalt, Person-Centered, Transactional Analysis, Rational Emotive, and other types of cognitive restructuring counseling models.

Collectively, these theoretical approaches represent a rich foundation from which practitioners can choose to assist clients who are experiencing substance abuse problems. However, despite the wide array of counseling approaches from which practitioners can choose when working with different clients who are experiencing substance abuse problems, two fundamental questions must always be answered for each person a counselor works with:"Which counseling

Note: Correspondence regarding this chapter should be sent to Dr. Judy Daniels, Department of Counselor Education, University of Hawaii, 1776 University Avenue, Honolulu, Hawaii 96822, (808) 956-7904.

approach should I use with this client?" and "Why would I select one approach with one client and a different approach with another client?"

Upon reviewing the professional literature related to substance abuse counseling, the authors were unable to find much information that adequately addressed the two fundamental questions mentioned above. Yet for those practitioners who have done substance abuse counseling for any length of time, it is clear that different clients abuse drugs and alcohol for different reasons. Counselors are also likely to note that the factors that motivate individuals to refrain from such behavior in the future often differs depending on each client's unique psychological disposition. The following case studies have been presented to clarify some of the different types of clients practitioners are likely to encounter in providing substance abuse counseling.

THREE CASE STUDIES

The Case of Thomas

Thomas, a single, unemployed, 20-year-old male, was referred to counseling through the court system. This client had a history of drug and alcohol abuse problems beginning in his early high school years. During the initial interview with the substance abuse counselor, Thomas appeared very nervous and agitated. He stated that it was hard for him to "keep still" for any length of time. As he spoke to the counselor, Thomas smoked several cigarettes, lighting one up as soon as he had finished another. In responding to the counselor's comment that he appeared nervous, the client stated that "I just can not help myself" and acknowledged that he was a "chain smoker."

The notion of not being able to control various behaviors was a theme that was repeated in different ways throughout the initial counseling session, especially in reference to his drug and alcohol problems. As Thomas explained, he would get high and/or drunk with or without the company of his friends. In fact, he described himself as being a "loner" who had a hard time controlling his temper whether he was "sober or drunk." This lack of control resulted in frequent fist fights with others over "little things." Further evidence of Thomas' lack of personal control was noted when he mentioned that "I had to get high before coming here this afternoon, so I smoked a joint before I left home."

In summarizing some of the outstanding impressions emerging from this initial counseling contact, the counselor stated that Thomas appeared to lack much insight into his personal problems, was unable to suggest reasonable alternatives to his current condition, and generally lacked impulse control.

The Case of Ira

Ira, a 20-year-old college student, was a self-referral for substance abuse counseling. During the initial counseling session, he indicated that although he was quite reluctant to receive counseling himself, his girlfriend and a couple of buddies in his dormitory had convinced him to get help because of his escalating abuse of drugs and alcohol.

Ira explained that he did not use any sort of illicit drugs or drink alcohol while he was in high school. As he pointed out, "I used to hang out with a group of guys who weren't into those things, so it wasn't a real big deal not to use drugs while I was in high school." He also expressed the positive relationship he had with both of his parents and how he didn't want to let them down by getting involved in using drugs and alcohol.

However, upon leaving home to go to college, Ira admitted that the social pressure to use alcohol and drugs increased substantially. He stated that he got tired of being what other students referred to as the "straightest guy on campus" and began using alcohol at weekend parties during his freshman year. During his sophomore year he experimented with marijuana and had a couple of opportunities to try cocaine with his friends.

He indicated that when he returned home for semester breaks and summer vacation, his parents joked about his alcohol use but were not aware of his experimentation with marijuana and cocaine. Although his use of drugs and alcohol was a genuine source of guilt and shame for Ira, he stated "it was not that big of a deal" because he limited use of these substances to "partying on the weekends."

However, during his junior year, Ira's friends (and especially his girlfriend) expressed concern about his drug use. Although he continued to generally refrain from using drugs and drinking alcohol during the week, Ira was consistently getting "smashed" during the weekends. These "weekend drunks," as he referred to them, involved "partying with friends from Friday afternoon until late Sunday night." This included not only routine and excessive use of alcohol and marijuana during the weekends but an increasing use of cocaine and other types of drugs.

As a result of this escalating use of alcohol and other drugs, Ira began to be less interested in his school work. Consequently, he began getting lower grades in all of his courses. Several of his friends also pointed out that he was becoming increasingly irritable with them and not as actively involved in keeping in good physical shape as he had been in the past.

In summarizing the first session, the counselor noted that peer pressure was an important factor that affected the way Ira acted and made decisions. His girlfriend and college friends were especially influential in this regard. For example, it was their consistent encouragement that had led Ira to seek professional help. However, the counselor was also aware that his drinking and drug use was directly linked to social situations in which he felt "more a part of the crowd" when he partied with his friends. As Ira said, "It was hard not to socialize with his friends without doing what is normally expected in those kind of situations." Unlike Thomas, Ira neither continued to abuse drugs and alcohol during the week nor used these substances unless he was around friends.

The Case of Donald

Donald was a 20-year-old male who had dropped out of college 2 months earlier. A review of his high school and college records indicated that he was rated in the top 5% of his classes in terms of his academic achievement. Donald's intelligence was complemented by his ability to express himself in a very mature manner.

In explaining his personal story, Donald stressed that he felt "personally lost." He stated, "I simply don't know where I am going with my life." Although he received very good grades in his first 2 years of college, Donald expressed increasing frustration over the types of "games people played at college." When the counselor asked for clarification about this statement, he talked about "how there seemed to be so many problems in today's world and that few people my age seem very concerned about making a difference to help improve things." He acknowledged that he was genuinely concerned about various problems confronting our society but was confused as to the best way to make a positive contribution to help improve some of the current conditions with which he was concerned.

Feeling increasingly upset with what he referred to as the "hypocrisy of college life," Donald decided "to drop out of school for a while" to work as a full-time volunteer at a local hospice where he provided various support services for AIDS patients. He also worked as a security guard during the evenings to help pay for his rent and daily needs.

Upon explaining why he had sought counseling, he discussed two major areas of concern. First, he admitted that he was concerned about the amount of alcohol he was consuming on a daily basis. Although he stressed that he never drank alcohol before going to work as a volunteer at the hospice or when working as a security guard, he indicated that he found himself "coming home in the late evenings, watching some television, and drinking myself to sleep several times a week."

Given his commitment to his work as a hospice volunteer and the need to maintain the income from the security job, Donald noted that he did not have much time or interest to socialize with his old friends and that this sense of isolation was a contributing factor in his increasing use of alcohol. In addition to his lack of contact with friends, and perhaps more importantly, Donald stated that he realized that he would frequently get drunk to escape the persistent feelings he had about the general lack of direction and purpose his life had taken. As he indicated during the first counseling session, he was looking for professional help both because of his immediate concern over what he thought was an "alcohol problem" and because he wanted someone to help him "figure out where I am going with my life."

***

A review of these three case studies suggests several important considerations in providing effective substance abuse counseling with these and other clients. First, although all of these clients are of the same gender and age, it is apparent that they operate at very different levels of psychological functioning. One might reasonably suggest that these three clients are likely to be distinguished by the way they view themselves and their personal capabilities (self-concept/personal identity), the manner in which they make sense of their environment (world view), and the factors that are likely to motivate them to make personal changes, especially in terms of their misuse/abuse of drugs and alcohol.

A second important point to consider when working with these clients is related to the types of counseling approaches and techniques the practitioner will utilize with them. In this regard, counselors would do well to tailor counseling interventions that effectively match the different psychological needs and dispositions of the clients with whom they work.

Although these issues represent important considerations in the provision of effective substance abuse counseling, little has been written about matching specific types of counseling approaches with clients exhibiting different psychological characteristics. Despite the lack of attention that has been directed to this clinical issue, substance abuse counselors are urged to develop a sound theoretical framework within which various counseling approaches can be integrated and applied when working with persons experiencing substance abuse problems.

By striving to develop a sound rationale for matching various counseling approaches with clients who are operating from different psychological perspectives, substance abuse counselors would avoid a major problem that plagues the profession today: that is, they would replace the often haphazard and nontheoretical manner of selecting different counseling approaches with a more systematic and intentional professional approach.

With this in mind, the authors present a new model for substance abuse counseling that is both theory driven and a reflection of clinical work with individuals experiencing a range of alcohol and/or drug problems. This model is based upon the dramatic increase in the knowledge base related to human development that has emerged over the past two decades.

HUMAN DEVELOPMENT THEORY AND COUNSELING PRACTICE

Advancements in human development theory have enabled counselors to more accurately understand their clients in two important ways. First, the new knowledge that has been generated in this area helps practitioners understand the different ways children, adolescents, and adults think about and react to various life events and problems. Developmental theories that describe the unique ways in which individuals of different ages think, feel, and behave about themselves and their environment at different points across the lifespan are referred to as "maturational theories" (Erikson, 1963; Havighurst, 1972; Levinson, 1986).

"Structural-developmental theories" (Gilligan, 1982; Heath, 1977; Kegan, 1982; Kohlberg, 1980; Loevinger, 1976; Selman, 1980) help to explain not only the specific psychological traits that typically characterize persons at different ages but also elucidate why persons of the same general age range are frequently noted to think, feel, and react to their environment in very different ways. The information associated with structural-developmental theories is particularly useful for substance abuse counseling in a couple of ways.

First, by becoming familiar with structural-developmental theories, counselors can gain more insights into the reasons why similar-aged persons (such as Thomas, Ira, and Donald) demonstrate such qualitatively different ways of thinking, feeling, and behaving. From this perspective, such differences suggest that Thomas, Ira, and Donald are operating at very different levels of psychological maturity.

Second, the fact that clients may frequently be noted to operate at different levels or stages of psychological development has profound implications for counseling. If substance abuse counselors work with clients who are functioning at different levels or stages of development and if these levels or stages represent qualitatively different ways of conceptualizing and responding to personal problems, it is unlikely that the same counseling approach will be equally effective with a developmentally diverse client population (Corey, 1990; Diamond, Havens, & Jones, 1978; Loew, 1975; Swensen, 1980).

Taking these points into consideration, a new framework for substance abuse counseling called "developmental eclecticism" (D'Andrea & Daniels, in press) is presented. In developing this model, we have incorporated numerous premises associated with Jane Loevinger's (1976) theory of ego development in such a way as to provide counselors with a new conceptual framework that can be used to assess and interact with clients who are experiencing substance abuse problems.

LOEVINGER'S THEORY OF EGO DEVELOPMENT

As one of the leading developmental psychologists during the past 25 years, Jane Loevinger devoted her research to understanding how individuals construct a sense of self and give meaning to their life experiences. She labeled this global psychological process "ego development" (Loevinger, 1976). The ego represents the master personality trait that describes an individual's self-system and organizes all other aspects of a person's life experiences (Swensen, 1980). Loevinger's framework comprises seven developmental stages that progress from a simple, undifferentiated, and unintegrated personality to a complex, highly differentiated, and well-integrated personality. An overview of the seven stages and some of the dominant characteristics of each stage are presented in Table 22–1.

In discussing the relationship of a person's level of ego development to other variables, Sprinthall and Collins (1984) indicated that there is a consistent correlation between an individual's stage of ego development and one's behavior, although the relationship is not exact. This is an important consideration for substance abuse counseling in that it suggests that the reasons a person operating at one ego development stage is noted to abuse drugs and alcohol may be very different from those of another person who is functioning at a different developmental stage.

USING DEVELOPMENTAL ECLECTICISM IN SUBSTANCE ABUSE COUNSELING

Assessing Clients' Level of Development

The first step in using the developmental eclectic model in substance abuse counseling requires that practitioners accurately assess the particular stage of psychological maturity at which a client is generally thought to be operating. This is important because persons functioning at the Impulsive, Self-Protective, Conformist, Conscientious, and Autonomous Stages are psychologically very different from one another (see Table 22–1).

Counselors might go about assessing clients' ego development in two ways: administering the standardized test designed to measure ego development (Loevinger, Wessler, & Redmore, 1978) and/or using information gained from clinical observations to formulate a typological profile of a client's level of personality development (D'Andrea & Daniels, in press).

Upon using both of these assessment techniques with the three clients described earlier in this chapter, it was noted that Thomas scored at the Self-Protective Stage, Ira scored at the Conformist Stage, and Donald scored at the Autonomous Stage of Loevinger's model of personality development. With this information in mind, the counselor was able to gain a clearer understanding of a number of psychological factors that characterized their personal development and contributed to their ongoing substance abuse problems. For instance, given Thomas' ego development rating, the counselor was better able to appreciate how his lack of impulse control, limited understanding of the inappropriateness

Table 22–1 Description of Ego Development Stages

Ego Stage	Descriptive Characteristics
Symbiotic Stage	At birth, infants do not differentiate themselves from their surroundings. Major task at this stage is to learn to identify oneself as different and distinct from one's surrounding environment. A person who fails to accomplish this task often exhibits autistic characteristics.
Impulsive Stage	Modal stage for children around 2-5 years of age, although adolescents and adults may have their development arrested here under certain conditions. Preoccupied with responding to impulses (e.g., the persistent felt need to have a drink or use drugs). Personality characterized by aggressive tendencies. Limited verbal abilities. Generally lacking in terms of fully understanding the short- and/or long-term consequences of their behavior.
Self-Protective Stage	Individuals have developed greater impulse control, a better understanding of socially appropriate norms and expectations, and an increased capacity to verbally express their thoughts and feelings. Persons at this stage are very manipulative in attempting to satisfy personal interests. Life viewed primarily as a matter of reward and punishment contingencies. External locus of control orientation. They work best within a highly structured environment.
Conformist Stage	Persons at this stage identify their welfare with a particular group of people (e.g., peers, school, church members, family members, co-workers). Emergence of a strong sense of group obligation and trust. Motivated by fear of group disapproval. Behaviors are generally evaluated in external terms, with much emphasis on appearances and concern about "the right way of doing things." Increasing one's capacity for self-evaluation and self-discovery are critical components for movement beyond this developmental stage.
Conscientious Stage	An increasing sense of self-awareness and social consciousness emerges here. This is manifested by an increasing ability for accurate self-criticism and taking the perspective of others in an empathic manner. Rather than "internalizing" group values and having them be the primary basis of their behavior, persons at this stage more consistently determine what they should do for themselves as a result of evaluating choices and options available to them. As a result, they measure personal achievement and fulfillment in self-evaluative terms. Expanded cognitive capacities provide greater flexibility to discuss inter- and intrapersonal experiences. Relationships at this stage are very important and are based on values reflecting concern with mutuality and reciprocity.
Autonomous Stage	To the characteristics mentioned above, add: persons at this stage struggle with the internal conflict to be dutiful and respond to the expectations of others and strive to realize one's own interests and potential. Issues related to personal identity and the meaning of one's life (existential concerns) become highlighted at this stage. A heightening cognitive capacity reinforces a person's ability to understand oneself and see how family patterns become relived in one's own life. Due to a person's level of psychological maturity at this stage, one often feels "disconnected" and/or "isolated" from others in a personal sense.
Integrated Stage	To the characteristics listed at the preceding stage add: increased tolerance for ambiguity and contradictions in life, tolerance for limitations/failings in oneself and others, and a strong desire to live a life that is personally integrated.

of his constant abuse of drugs and alcohol, and lack of cognitive awareness of the short- and long-term consequences of this sort of behavior all contributed to a highly complex and challenging clinical case.

In contrast, Ira's Conformist Stage score was consistent with several themes reported in his case study. Specifically, the high value Conformist Stage persons place on being accepted by their peers was noted to be a major factor contributing to Ira's initial experimentation with drugs and alcohol as well as the increased use of these substances during the parties he regularly attended during the weekends. Paradoxically, the strong sense of trust and the need to be accepted by one's friends (which are hallmarks of the Conformist Stage) were also clearly motivating factors that led Ira to seek professional counseling despite his own personal reservations about doing so.

Finally, Donald's ego development score not only helped the counselor better understand some of the motivational factors that contributed to his substance abuse problems but also provided guidelines regarding some of the issues to be addressed during their counseling sessions.

By using a developmental eclectic approach in this way, the counselor was able to gain important insights into the different psychological issues that contributed to the problems facing his clients. Once developmental assessment has been conducted, the next step in the model involves selecting a counseling approach that "best fits" each client's level of psychological maturity.

Selecting Counseling Strategies That Complement Clients' Psychological Maturity

Using the developmental assessment method mentioned above has proved to be helpful in establishing appropriate goals and selecting effective counseling techniques with clients experiencing substance abuse problems. For instance, establishing short-term goals, using various behavioral techniques, and teaching self-management strategies (Kanfer & Goldstein, 1986) were noted to be particularly well suited for clients functioning at the Impulsive and Self-Protective Stages of Loevinger's ego development framework.

Also, although there has been a general decrease in the use of various types of aversion-therapy approaches with persons experiencing substance abuse problems (George, 1990), these therapeutic techniques are thought to be a particularly useful complement to a comprehensive counseling intervention with persons at the Impulsive and Self-Protective Stages. From our counseling experiences we have found that these sorts of behavioral and self-management counseling strategies were not as appealing or effective when used with persons assessed to be functioning at or above the Conformist or Conscientious Stages of Loevinger's model.

Table 22–2 Matching Developmental Stages with Specific Tasks and Approaches in Substance Abuse Counseling

Developmental Stage	Counseling Tasks	Suggested Counseling Approaches
Impulsive Stage	—Teach delayed gratification. —Promote increased impulse control. —Teach appropriate social skills. —Increase verbal skills for describing events and skills.	—Aversion therapy —Behavioral therapy — Environmental conditioning —Self-management training
Self-Protective Stage	—Reward conforming behavior. —Help client discriminate between own and others' thoughts and feelings. —Teach value of trust and cooperation.	—Aversion therapy —Behavior modification —Reality therapy —Focus on current behavior
Conformist Stage	—Promote more sophisticated decision-making skills. —Facilitate the development of more effective interpersonal skills. —Help clients learn to differentiate own needs and wants from those of family and/or friends. —Assist clients to identify and express thoughts and feelings in more differentiated ways.	—Rational Emotive therapy —Transactional Analysis —Assertiveness training —Supportive counseling —Explore life scripts
Conscientious Stage	—Promote more in-depth self-exploration. —Help clients accept responsibility for drinking and drug abuse. —Support clients to balance a sense of duty and obligation to achieve with time for recreational activities.	—Gestalt counseling —Rational Emotive therapy —Person-Centered counseling
Autonomous Stage	—Facilitate client's capacity for self-understanding and acceptance. —Analyze strategies that will promote self-actualization. —Provide support as client attempts to make sense of and cope with life's paradoxes.	—Existential therapy —Gestalt counseling —Supportive counseling
Integrated Stage	Note: When interacting with persons operating at the Integrated Stage, ask for advice as how to best provide substance abuse counseling services to others.	

Counseling strategies that emphasize the importance of establishing long-term goals, promote personal behaviors rooted in self-evaluated standards, and explore various affective issues underlying a person's alcohol and drug abuse problems are helpful when used among clients operating at the Conformist Stage. Specific counseling approaches that incorporate these strategies include Transactional Analysis (Berne, 1961), Rational Emotive Therapy (Ellis, 1989), and Reality Therapy (Glasser, 1986).

Like other developmental counselors (Ivey, 1986; Young-Eisendrath, 1988), we recommend the use of Person-Centered and Gestalt Counseling techniques with clients at the Conscientious Stage. These approaches were noted to be particularly useful with clients operating at this stage in that they encouraged them to explore and express various thoughts and feelings they had about their substance abuse problems in vivid and personal terms.

Clients like Donald, who scored at the Autonomous Stage of Loevinger's framework, were often very receptive to an Existential Counseling approach (Bugental, 1986). In the past, we have noted that these highly developed persons could be more effectively engaged in the therapeutic process when the counselor fostered discussions related to their ability to cope with inner conflicts associated with issues concerning their personal identity. A further delineation of the types of counseling approaches and techniques that we noted to be useful among clients' operating at different stages of Loevinger's paradigm is provided in Table 22–2.

In summary, we have presented a new framework for substance abuse counseling that integrates Loevinger's theory of ego development with a variety of counseling approaches that are typically used by practitioners in the field. The developmental eclectic model includes a description of those counseling techniques we have found useful when working with persons manifesting differing levels of psychological maturity.

It is important to point out that this framework is not offered as a prescriptive model, nor are we encouraging other practitioners to use the counseling approaches outlined with clients assessed at different levels of psychological development in a rigid or dogmatic manner. One of the most important lessons our clients have taught us is that counselors must remain sensitive, respectful, and flexible in addressing the complex dynamics associated with substance abuse counseling. However, we do hope that other professionals will find this model useful in considering a systematic approach to working with different types of persons who are manifesting alcohol and/or drug-related problems.

REFERENCES

Berne, E. (1961). *Transactional analysis in psychotherapy.* New York: Grove.

Bugental, J. F. T. (1986). Existential-humanistic psychotherapy. In I. L. Kutash & A. Wolfe (Eds.), *Psychotherapist's casebook* (pp. 222–236). San Francisco: Jossey-Bass.

Corey, G. (1990). *Theory and practice of group counseling* (3rd ed.). Pacific Grove, CA: Brooks/Cole.

D'Andrea, M., & Daniels, J. (in press). Group pacing: A developmental eclectic approach to group work. *Journal of Counseling and Development.*

Diamond, R. E., Havens, R. A., & Jones, A. C. (1978). A conceptual framework for the practice of prescriptive eclectism in psychotherapy. *American Psychologist, 33,* 239–248.

Ellis, A. (1989). Rational emotive therapy. In R. J. Corsini & D. Wedding (Eds.), *Current psychotherapies* (4th ed.) (pp. 197–238). Itasca, IL: Peacock.

Erikson, E. (1963). *Childhood and society* (2nd ed.). New York: Norton.

Forrest, G. G. (1978). *The diagnosis and treatment of alcoholism* (2nd ed.). Springfield, IL: C. Thomas.

George, R. L. (1990). *Counseling the chemically dependent: Theory and practice.* Englewood Cliffs, NJ: Prentice Hall.

Gilligan, C. (1982). *In a different voice: Psychological theory and women's development.* Cambridge, MA: Harvard University Press.

Glasser, W. (1986). *The basic concepts of reality therapy.* Canoga Park, CA: Institute for Reality Therapy.

Havighurst, R. J. (1972). *Developmental tasks and education* (3rd ed.). New York: McKay.

Heath, D. (1977). *Maturity and competence.* New York: Gardner.

Ivey, A. E. (1986). *Developmental therapy.* San Francisco: Jossey-Bass.

Kanfer, F. H., & Goldstein, A. P. (1986). *Helping people change: A textbook of methods* (3rd ed.). New York: Pergamon.

Kegan, R. (1982). *The evolving self: Problem and process in human development.* Cambridge, MA: Harvard University Press.

Kohlberg, L. (1980). The cognitive-developmental approach to moral education. In V. L. Erikson & J. M. Whitle, *Developmental counseling and teaching* (pp. 16–38). Monterey, CA: Brooks/Cole.

Levinson, D. (1986). A conception of adult development. *American Psychologist, 41,* 3–13.

Loevinger, J. (1976). *Ego development.* San Francisco: Jossey-Bass.

Loevinger, J., Wessler, R., & Redmore, C. (1978). *Measuring ego development.* San Francisco: Jossey-Bass.

Loew, C. A. (1975). Remarks on integrating psychotherapeutic techniques. *Psychotherapy: Theory, research, and practice, 12,* 241–242.

Selman, R. (1980). *The growth of interpersonal understanding: Developmental and clinical analysis.* New York: Academic Press.

Sprinthall, N. A., & Collins, W. A. (1984). *Adolescent psychology: A developmental view.* New York: Random House.

Swensen, C. H. (1980). Ego development and a general model for counseling and psychotherapy. *Personnel and Guidance Journal, 58*(5), 382–388.

Young-Eisendrath, P. (1988). Making use of human development theories in counseling. In R. Hayes & R. Aubrey (Eds.), *New directions for counseling and human development* (pp. 66–84). Denver: Love Publishing.

Chapter 23

Oxford House: Community Living Is Community Healing

Leonard A. Jason, Margaret E. Pechota, Blake S. Bowden,
with Katherine Kohner, Steven B. Pokorny, Peter Bishop,
Elena Quintana, Cindy Sangerman, Doreen Salina, Stephanie
Taylor, Linda Lesondak, and Gwen Grams

Ninety percent of Americans endorse the notion that alcoholism is a disease and that medically related treatment, in conjunction with strict adherence to an Alcoholics Anonymous (AA) program, is the only effective means of combatting this disorder (Peele, 1988). If anyone deserves credit for the overwhelming consensus this notion enjoys, it would be the 1944 founder of the National Council on Alcoholism (NCA), Marty Mann. Integrating the traditions of AA and the Yale School of Alcohol Studies, she managed to irrevocably shape America's view of alcoholism and substance dependence. Prior to Mann's involvement, the AA approach was strongly antimedical. Indeed, Mann may be credited with what has been called the "alcoholism movement" that has swept our country. Treatment modalities consistent with this movement advocate detoxification, brief hospitalization (as needed), and strict adherence to an AA program.

The impact of the alcoholism movement has been bolstered by the remarkable successes reported by treatment programs that endorse this model. Founded in 1935 by William (Bill) and Dr. Robert Smith, AA emphasizes the value of self-help, spirituality, and total abstinence from alcohol, as well as the notion that only alcoholics can help fellow alcoholics (Robertson, 1988). Snyder (1980) estimates that 40% of those who join AA become totally abstinent immediately, 25% after 1 year, and another 20% after 2 years. These figures are encouraging for psychotherapists, who often agree that psychotherapy alone is an ineffective treatment choice for most alcoholics (Kaufman, 1990–1991; Miller & Hester, 1980).

Some academic researchers have been skeptical about success rates of the current approaches to alcoholism (Brandsma, Maultsby, & Welsh, 1980; Vaillant, 1983). For example, Edwards, Hensman, Hawker, and Williamson (1967) suggest that many people who join AA programs drop out. Snyder (1980) maintains that only 10% of identified problem drinkers in America are actually involved in an AA program. Research aimed at verifying the outcome results of alcoholism movement programs has been rather controversial (Davison & Neale, 1986). Most adherents agree with Wallace's (1985, 1987) implied notion that it is best not to tamper with what "works."

Note: Correspondence regarding this chapter should be sent to Leonard A. Jason, Professor of Psychology, DePaul University, 2219 North Kenmore, Chicago, Illinois 60614-3504, 312/362-8277.

Despite some claims to the contrary, evidence would suggest that nontreatment (or post-treatment) variables are better predictors of successful recovery than the treatment modalities themselves (Westermeyer, 1989). Vaillant (1983) found that recovering clients found changed life circumstances rather than clinical interventions to be crucial to their abstinence. Maddux and Desmond (1982) found that abstinence rates of opiate addicts were three times higher for individuals who residentially relocated. Moreover, living with supportive others has been found to increase the likelihood of abstinence and continued recovery (Hoffman & Noem, 1976; Zimberg, 1974).

The therapeutic community (TC) has recently enjoyed great success in the field of alcoholism and substance dependence treatment. Recognizing the social factors that impact upon the recovery of addicts, these residential communities seek to bridge the gap between the rigorously controlled environment of inpatient hospitalization and the sometimes chaotic and unstructured world beyond institutional walls (De Leon, 1989). Although psychiatric and substance dependence TCs evolved concurrently, their development is often viewed as separate and unrelated (De Leon, 1989). Despite this independent development, it is essential to note that both TC models rely heavily upon professional and paraprofessional staff members who are often called upon to institute and enforce community rules and regulations (De Leon, 1989).

TCs seek to integrate the conduct, feelings, values, and attitudes associated with a drug-free lifestyle into the safe and supportive environment of a surrogate family (De Leon, 1985). Individuals who incorporate the ideals of fellowship, responsibility, and community contact advocated by TCs into their daily living report that the experience is extremely helpful in overcoming addictive behavior (Mackay & Marlatt, 1990–1991; Stead, Rozynko, & Berman, 1990). Unfortunately, despite the fact that a strong relationship has been found between the length of time in a TC and reduced recidivism (McLellan, Luborsky, O'Brien, Woody, & Druly, 1982; Wexler, Falkin, & Lipton, 1990), most TCs require residents to leave after a 6-month maximum stay. It is unclear how successful TCs are in the maintenance of nonalcoholic behavior. De Leon (1984) claims positive results in a 5-year follow-up evaluation of Phoenix House, a finding that is supported by Wexler, Falkin, and Lipton (1990), among others. And although some "cure rates" are claimed to be as high as 90% (Casriel & Amen, 1971), it is suggested that methodological constraints limit the conclusive power of these results (Smart, 1976). It does appear likely, however, that the issue of non-self-direction or hierarchical interference from professional staff members may contribute to the lack of effectiveness of some of these programs (Brill, 1971).

Oxford House, which combines the traditions of the alcoholism movement with the nontraditional ideas of a self-directed community (that goes beyond the traditional TC), allowed our researchers to explore this unique therapeutic environment. What follows is a brief history of the Oxford House Model and the research relationship that we developed with a local chapter in Illinois.

THE OXFORD HOUSE MODEL

An alternative solution to the traditional therapeutic community was developed by Paul Malloy. A recovering alcoholic living in a halfway house on the verge of collapse, Malloy and five other residents were concerned about maintaining their sobriety. Realizing a substance-free community environment was essential to their recovery, and having no other options, Malloy and the other residents formed a self-run, self-supported recovery house.

Named after the Oxford Group, a religious organization that influenced the founders of AA, Malloy started the first Oxford House in 1975. Members adopted a democratic form of government due to necessity and formed a less structured, less regimented environment than the halfway house, with the belief that peer pressure would be more effective in promoting successful rehabilitation. Members voted to repeal the 6-month time limit (advocated by more traditional TCs), abolished curfews, and implemented two mandatory requirements for residency— maintaining sobriety and paying rent. Cost to individual members was low due to pooling of resources, and within 6 months of operation the house accumulated $1,200 in its treasury. Members voted to start another house with the funds. The Oxford House concept was born, and expanded to 13 houses in 12 years without outside funding.

Malloy escalated the proliferation of houses when he used his political connections to provide funding. Initially unwilling to relinquish their independence, members of Oxford House resisted accepting government funding but soon realized that some type of funding was needed to start new houses. In 1988, the House of Representatives was drafting an anti-drug bill, and Malloy worked with Rep. Edward Madigan, his close friend, in adding a provision mandating each state to provide a revolving $100,000 fund to loan start-up costs to "self-run and self-supported recovery houses." The law was enacted by the fall of that year, with funds monitored by the Illinois Department of Drug and Alcohol Abuse (DASA). Due to the revolving fund, Oxford House quickly expanded to a network of over 400 recovery houses throughout the United States.

To ensure adherence to the Oxford House principles of fellowship, self-reliance, self-respect, and commitment to recovery, Oxford House formed a nonprofit corporation and developed a hierarchy of recovering addicts to assist with the start-up of new houses. Field representatives locate rental housing, recruit initial members, and provide guidance in the development of a supportive group environment. When several houses are formed within a geographical area, chapters are formed and monthly meetings conducted with representatives from each house. The board of directors of Oxford House, Inc., is made up of nine current and past presidents, who are selected by and from the presidents of the individual houses.

Each house is financially independent and democratically governed, and elects officers to ensure smooth operation and facilitate personal growth through responsibility. Houses are located in "good neighborhoods" to help minimize the possibility of relapse. Unlike therapeutic communities, Oxford House does not impose a restriction on length of stay. In addition, no professionals or paraprofessionals are recruited by Oxford House, but members are encouraged to participate in 12-step programs, and Oxford House has nine traditions similar to AA's 12 steps and 12 traditions.

THE DEPAUL STUDY

A team of researchers at DePaul University led by Leonard A. Jason, Ph.D., was interested in studying the process of community living. Oxford House offered the opportunity to observe the evolution of a "sense of community" within a healing environment and its effect upon recovery. This research team believed that validating the Oxford House model as an effective recovery environment would have strong implications for adapting the model to other unempowered populations. They contacted Paul Malloy and expressed interest in conducting a study. Administrators at DASA, monitoring the funding for Oxford Houses in Illinois, agreed to allow researchers at DePaul University to document the expansion of Oxford House within the state and evaluate the impact of the Oxford House model on recovery. Evaluation was requested at three levels—client, community, and system, with particular emphasis on systems issues due to impending budget cuts; Oxford House could offer a low-cost alternative to some traditional services.

The literature on self-help and alternative services emphasizes the importance of autonomy, respect, and mutual support as essential factors in the healing process. The Oxford House model seems to facilitate these values while providing a safe environment during recovery. DePaul's researchers theorized that positive social interactions would increase an individual's sense of community, increase perceptions of social support and hope, and reduce stress.

The research team chose to collect both quantitative and qualitative forms of data in order to obtain comprehensive information on all residents entering the Oxford Houses and at a 6-month follow-up. A shortened version of The Interpersonal Support Evaluation List (ISEL) (Cohen, Mermelstein, Karmarck, & Hoberman, 1985), which measures appraisal, belonging, tangible (perceived availability of material aid), and self-esteem, was chosen to determine subjects' perception of social support. A shortened version of the Perceived Stress Scale

(PSS) (Cohen, Kamarck, & Mermelstein, 1983), was used to measure the degree to which individuals perceived their life situation as stressful. Hope, or expectations about the future, was measured by the Expected Balance Scale (EBS) (Staats, 1989). A shortened version of the Perceived Sense of Community Scale (PSCS) (Bishop, Chertok, & Jason, 1994) was used to measure an individual's perceptions of connection, mission, and reciprocal responsibility.

Open-ended questions were included for qualitative analysis and theory generation, to determine measures needed for a more comprehensive study. In keeping with the nontraditional approach to research most community psychologists adopt, DePaul's research team has worked extensively to develop collaborative and cooperative relationships with Oxford House and DASA representatives. Due to the innovative and ever-changing nature of the Oxford House model and the unpredictability of individual and group behavior, the researchers have encountered many situations not found in more controlled community studies. Consequently, creative strategies are occasionally employed to collect data. Given the evolving nature of the study thus far, concepts for continued evaluation continue to develop, including leadership roles; group dynamics; power issues; stages of community development; values; and verbal, action, and material symbols.

Information gathered to date seems to indicate that each house has a unique set of challenges endemic to factors such as finances, support of the local therapeutic community, commitment to recovery, adherence to Oxford House principles, and relationship with Oxford House and its representatives.

We are presently in the process of collecting data, but our initial impressions are positive. We believe that Oxford House might represent a cost-effective approach for helping those individuals who fail to benefit from more traditional therapeutic settings. We feel that the sense of community, belonging, and hope found in the Oxford House model provide the supportive and nurturing environment crucial to healing and health.

REFERENCES

Bishop, P., Chertok, F., & Jason, L. A. (1994). A factor analysis of the perceived sense of community scale. Manuscript submitted for publication.

Brandsma, J. M., Maultsby, M. C., & Welsh, R. J. (1980). *The outpatient treatment of alcoholism: A review and comparative study.* Baltimore: University Park Press.

Brill, J. (1971). Some comments on the paper "Social control in therapeutic communities." *International Journal of the Addictions, 6,* 45–50.

Casriel, D., & Amen, G. (1971). *Daytop: Three addicts and their cure.* New York: Hill & Wang.

Cohen, S., Karmarck, T., & Mermelstein, R. (1983). A global measure of perceived stress. *Journal of Health and Social Behavior, 24,* 385–396.

Cohen, S., Mermelstein, R., Karmarck, T., & Hoberman, H. M. (1985). Measuring the functional components of social support. In I. G. Sarason & B. R. Sarason (Eds.), *Social support: Theory, research, and applications* (pp. 73–94). Dordrecht, the Netherlands: Martinus Nijhoff.

Davison, G. C., & Neale, J. M. (1986). *Abnormal psychology: An experimental clinical approach*. New York: John Wiley.

De Leon, G. (1984). *The therapeutic community: Study of effectiveness*. (Treatment Research Monograph Series). Washington, DC: National Institute on Drug Abuse.

De Leon, G. (1985). The therapeutic community: Status and evolution. *International Journal of the Addictions, 20*(6 & 7), 823–844.

De Leon, G. (1989). Therapeutic communities for substance abuse: Overview of approach and effectiveness. *Journal of the Society of Psychologists in Addictive Behaviors, 3*(3), 140–147.

Edwards, G., Hensman, C., Hawker, A., & Williamson, V. (1967). Alcoholics Anonymous: The anatomy of a self-help group. *Social Psychiatry, 1*, 195–204.

Hoffman, H., & Noem, A. A. (1976). Criteria for the differentiation of success and failure in alcoholism treatment outcome. *Psychological Reports, 39*, 887–893.

Kauffman, E. (1990–1991). Critical aspects of the psychodynamics of substance abuse and the evaluation of their application to a psychotherapeutic approach. *International Journal of the Addictions, 25*, 97–116.

Maddux, J. F., & Desmond, D. P. (1982). Residence relocation inhibits opioid dependence. *Archives of General Psychiatry, 39*, 1313–1317.

Mackay, P. W., & Marlatt, G. A. (1990–1991). Maintaining sobriety: Stopping is starting. *The International Journal of the Addictions, 25*, (9A & 10A), 1257–1276.

McLellan, A., Luborsky, L., O'Brien, C. P., Woody, G.E., & Druley, K. A. (1982). Is treatment for substance abuse effective? *Journal of the American Medical Association, 247*, 1423–1428.

Miller, W. R., & Hester, R. K. (1980). Treating the problem drinker: Modern approaches. In W. R. Miller (Ed.), *The addictive behaviors: Treatment of alcoholism, drug abuse, smoking and obesity* (pp. 3–13). Oxford: Pergamon.

Peele, S. (1988). Can alcoholism and other drug addiction problems be treated away or is the current treatment binge doing more harm than good? *Journal of Psychoactive Drugs, 20*(4), 375–383.

Robertson, N. (1988). *Getting better: Inside Alcoholics Anonymous*. New York: Morrow.

Smart, R. G. (1976). Outcome studies of therapeutic community and halfway house treatment for addicts. *International Journal for the Addictions, 11*(1), 143–159.

Snyder, S. H. (1980). *Biological aspects of mental disorder*. New York: Oxford University Press.

Staats, S. (1989). Hope: A comparison of two self-report measures for adults. *Journal of Personality Assessment, 53*(2), 366–375.

Stead, P., Rozynko, V., & Berman, S. (1990). The SHARP Carwash: A community-oriented work program for substance abuse patients. *Social Work, 35*, 79–80.

Vaillant, G. E. (1983). *The natural history of alcoholism*. Cambridge, MA: Harvard University Press.

Wallace, J. (1985). *Alcoholism: New light on the disease*. Newport, RI: Edgehill.

Wallace, J. (1987). Waging the war for wellness: I. The attack of the "anti-traditionalist" lobby. *Professional Counselor*, January–February, 21–39.

Westermeyer, J. (1989). Nontreatment factors affecting treatment outcomes in substance abuse. *American Journal of Drug and Alcohol Abuse, 15*(1), 13–29.

Wexler, H. K., Falkin, G. P., & Lipton, D. S. (1990). Outcome-evaluation of a prison therapeutic community for substance abuse treatment. *Criminal Justice and Behavior, 17*(1), 71–92.

Zimberg, S. (1974). Evaluation of alcoholism treatment in Harlem. *Quantitative Journal of the Study of Alcohol, 38*, 550–557.

Chapter 24

Working with Substance-Abusing Adolescents through Project Adventure

H. L. "Lee" Gillis and Cindy A. Simpson

Mental health professionals conducting drug and alcohol recovery groups use various methods to teach concepts such as (a) how to ask for help, (b) how to get support from one's sponsor, (c) how to positively use support groups, and (d) how to prevent relapse. Adventure-based counseling, a mixture of experiential learning, outdoor education, and group counseling techniques (Schoel, Prouty, & Radcliffe, 1988), is one unique way of making concepts of addiction and recovery active and more easily understandable. It makes use of carefully designed activities such as trust exercises, cooperative games, problem-solving initiatives, and challenge ropes course elements to promote the improvement of clients' self-concepts (Schoel et al., 1988). The goal of this chapter is to show the power of an adventure-based approach to group counseling when activities are sequenced around the concept of recovery from addiction.

The ultimate objective of adventure-based counseling is to transfer lessons learned into changed behavior patterns. The belief is that participants learn these lessons best when they

1. experience an activity which shares some elements of the concept,
2. reflect upon the activity or listen to others reflect on their experience during a discussion or debriefing,
3. abstract some practical insights about themselves or others, and
4. apply the learned results to changing their behavior.

The belief in this format is grounded in Project Adventure's experience with client populations for more than 20 years. The activities presented in this chapter are currently being used successfully within a variety of programs, including those in schools, prisons, psychiatric hospitals, residential treatment centers, youth detention centers, and those run by independent mental health practitioners. Participants in groups using this approach report they are better able to understand the concepts they are being taught following a carefully designed adventure experience. Perhaps the concrete nature and shared experience of the activity followed by a discussion of the meaning and application of the experience makes the increased understanding possible (Gillis, Williams, & Hollis, 1992).

A meta-analysis of drug prevention programs (Tobler, 1986) appeared to agree that adventure programming is effective for working with substance abuse when it noted that alternative programs focused on physical adventure (e.g., camping and wilderness activities) were most effective for drug-abusing adolescents. Gass and McPhee (1990) have specifically addressed the use of adventure-based programming for substance abusers. They conducted a survey of existing treatment programs and found that the majority responding to their survey only used adventure-based programming in conjunction with an existing drug and alcohol treatment program. The most frequent use of such programming was only 1 day (although multiple 1-day use was not accounted for in the survey). The 1-day use of adventure programming is perhaps indicative of substance abuse treatment programs responding to the survey, but not normative for all adventure programming with adolescents. Project Adventure's cooperative drug treatment program uses a 16-week approach based on principles of Alcoholics Anonymous (1981) and adventure-based counseling. Outcome findings on the initial clients in the program show a decrease in self-reports of depression and an increase in self-esteem following the initial 8-week intensive treatment program (Gillis & Simpson, 1991).

Having a clearer understanding of Project Adventure and adventure-based counseling may help the reader understand how experiencing a recovery concept and challenging clients to literally "walk the talk" of recovery may lead to greater success helping clients free themselves from addiction. The remainder of this chapter will explain some of the basic principles of adventure-based counseling and describe several activities that the reader may use immediately in his or her group counseling program.

PROJECT ADVENTURE

Project Adventure, Inc. began in 1971 as an attempt to put Outward Bound concepts into traditional school formats. They offer action-oriented experiences through games, initiatives, and "challenge ropes course" activities (Rohnke, 1984, 1989). An adventure activity involves physical challenges that are both individually and group focused. The activities generally require cooperation, problem solving, trust, and communication among group members for completion.

School counselors began to work with special needs populations using Project Adventure's games, initiatives, and activities. These same activities also began being used in corrections, psychiatric hospitals, and youth detention centers because they were found to be more successful than previous treatments (Maizell, 1988; Witman, 1989). Therapeutic concepts and counseling techniques began to be incorporated into the recreational atmosphere of the experiences. The challenges of cooperative games, problem-solving initiatives, and stressful high ropes course events enabled clients to achieve specific educational or therapeutic goals (Gass, 1991).

Gass (1993) believes the following seven points account for how counseling from an adventure base works:

1. It is *action-oriented*. Traditional approaches are expanded by a focus on a concrete, physical activity that is usually shared by all group members.
2. The *unfamiliar environment* of an initiative game or a ropes course is usually involved.
3. The positive use of stress (eustress) is used to provide a healthy *climate of change*.
4. The use of activities provides leaders with observable *assessment information* as participants spontaneously project their behaviors into the activity (Gillis & Bonney, 1989).
5. The use of a *small group format* with activities perceived as risky or stressful can create conflict that allows for opportunities to balance individual and group needs.
6. This approach typically focuses on *solutions and successful behavior* instead of patterns that lead to further failure.
7. The *role of the counselor* becomes active as strategies of change (activities) are designed to target specific client behaviors.

Adventure-Based Counseling

Adventure-based counseling experiences often begin with structured exercises that allow a group to encounter one another, to feel more comfortable interacting as a group, and to begin to experience the spontaneity of the adventure process (Gillis & Bonney, 1986, 1989). Ethically, the choice to participate when encountering adventure activities rests with the client. Adventure-based counselors generally follow Rohnke's (1989) attitude of "challenge by choice." Challenge by choices offers participants

- the opportunity to "back off" when performance pressure or self-doubt becomes too strong
- an opportunity to find a different level of participation that is comfortable and safe
- a chance to try a potentially difficult activity in a supportive atmosphere
- respect for the ability to take care of oneself (Schoel et al.,1988, p. 131)

A concept related to challenge by choice is the "full value" contract (Schoel et al., 1988). With the full value contract, all clients in the group are asked to make a commitment to

- work together as a group and work toward individual and group goals
- adhere to certain safety and group behavior guidelines
- give and receive feedback, both positive and negative
- work toward changing behavior when it is appropriate (p. 95)

The Adventure Wave

The adventure-based counseling experience has been compared to an ocean wave (Schoel et al., 1988). This wave incorporates the peaks, valleys, turbulence, excitement, calm, and activity that take place in an adventure-based counseling experience. The wave involves the following three components.

First is the *briefing* or preparation of the participants for the adventure experience. This briefing may involve telling the group a story or drawing some similarities of the adventure activity to the targeted concept. The briefing is also the time when the leader discusses any safety considerations the group must adhere to while completing the activity.

Second is the *leading* or implementing of the adventure experience (see Exhibit 24–1). A difficult part of this component for many beginning facilitators is not interfering with the group process by offering suggestions to aid the group in completing the activity. The group leader monitors the safety considerations of the group while trusting in the power of group dynamics.

Project Adventure believes strongly in a multicultural co-leading team for groups, especially groups for persons who are addicted or in recovery. These "cultures" from which the leaders come can include race, ethnicity, formal education, personal addiction and recovery, urban and rural backgrounds, and functional and dysfunctional families. This multicultural "tag-team" approach to co-facilitation allows for staff to utilize their backgrounds for effective treatment.

Finally, the *debriefing* or processing of the adventure experience is a time when participants are offered a chance to reflect on their own experience and benefit from any personal insight or other group member's perception about how the activity relates to issues in their own lives.

One useful debriefing technique for many adventure-based counselors is *"The What, So What, Now What"* (Rohnke, 1989; Schoel et al., 1988). *"The What"* is used to describe the group interaction and what happened to the individuals during the experience. The *"So What"* asks the group to describe the difference the experience made to them—the consequences and the meaning. The

"*Now What*" provides structure for planning the next activity or relating the activity to behavior change in the future.

A series of waves is created when activities are sequenced together to concentrate on particular goals or on a particular theme such as recovery. In order to adjust the adventure wave to meet various group needs and goals, facilitators can make use of a scanning checklist. One helpful checklist flows from the acronym GRABBS (Schoel et al., 1988).

The *G* in GRABBS stands for *goals:* How does the activity relate to the individual or group goals that have been set? Group goals for an addiction recovery group can include the ability to more accurately understand the following four concepts: (a) how to ask for help, (b) how to get support from one's sponsor, (c) how to positively use support groups, and (d) how to prevent relapse.

The *R* stands for *readiness*: Is the group mentally, physically, and emotionally capable of handling this activity safely? Using warm-up activities, the leader can assess how physically able the group is to participate in more challenging activities. From observation of how the group handles touching or other forms of close physical contact, the leader can assess the group's readiness for emotionally handling more difficult challenges. Finally, by presenting several simple problem-solving tasks, the leader can assess the group's readiness for more difficult cognitive tasks.

The *A* is for *affect:* What level of feeling do group members have for one another? Similar to the assessment of readiness, an assessment of how group members feel toward one another must be conducted. During the debriefing of an activity, do group members demonstrate the full value contract?

B stands for *behavior:* How does the group act toward one another? Because many of the activities are physical, the leader can adjust the adventure wave when group members are not showing respect for each other. Such disrespect might be shown through making assumptions that only the males can handle the physically challenging activities or by sending all the small people in the group through an activity first.

The second B is for *body:* Are the activities appropriate for the physical ability of the group? Can the group appropriately touch one another? In assessing for readiness, the physical nature of the group is also assessed. Many times with recovering persons in various stages of withdrawal, the leader must make a special effort to know the physical capacity of the group. Such an effort can be made by having medical releases signed by a physician or at least by giving the group a chance to disclose any particular physical ailments that may prevent them from participating in a given activity. This opportunity to share can easily be framed as part of challenge by choice and the full value contract.

The *S* is for *stage* of group development. Depending on which group development theory the leader finds most useful, he or she should evaluate how particular activities fit within the formation, transition, experimentation, or termination stage of group process. The leader would also evaluate a one-shot group experience differently than an ongoing group process and would also treat an open membership group differently from a closed group.

Assumptions

The following four assumptions are made in sharing activities in this chapter that can be easily put into practice in an addiction recovery group: (a) you are

---

Exhibit 24–1 Activities for Recovery and Addiction

---

1. **Activity**: Quail Shooters Delight,or Phones & Faxes
   Source: Rohnke (1984, p. 63)
   Concept: Too much too fast coming in all at once; losing control; unmanageability.
   Goal: All group members throw their (soft) object to the pair in the middle to see how many of the items they can catch.
   Materials: Enough soft frisbees, nerf balls, or combination for all group members to have one.
   Safety Considerations: Minimal; be careful not to use materials that could hurt if/when they hit the people in the middle.
   Description: Have two group members stand back to back in the center of the circle of group members. Try several pairs and see who can catch the most.
   Debriefing: The feeling of having all the items coming at you at once and trying to retain any of them can be used to discuss the addiction concepts of feeling helpless over the world when things looked so simple. Also the issue of trying to manage an unmanageable situation has implications for many persons wrestling with Step 1 (Alcoholics Anonymous, 1981).

2. **Activity:** Balloon Frantic
   Source: Rohnke (1984, p.19)
   Concept: Unmanageability.
   Goal: To keep all balloons aloft for as long as possible; this activity works best indoors.
   Materials: One 12" balloon per person plus 5–10 additional balloons.
   Safety Considerations: Minimal; be careful that participants do not bump into one another as they try to keep balloons aloft.
   Description: At the start, ask each member to throw/hit their balloon into the air. After 15 seconds, and for each additional 15 seconds, add another balloon to the frantic. If/when a balloon hits the floor, designate it a HECTIC by issuing a BERSERK (screaming at it loudly) or counting it off ("1, 2," etc.). When 6 BERSERKS are reached, you have a FRENZY.
   Debriefing: A focus on how one can manage numerous issues, one's own and others', when more are being placed upon the individual and the group.

3. **Activity**: Marshmallows/Stepping Stones
   Source: Rohnke (1994, p. 105)
   Concept: 12 steps to recovery and need to have others' help.
   Goal: To cross a designated area using only blocks or "steps" provided. There must be human contact with the blocks while they are in the designated area.
   Materials: Various sizes of wooden blocks (12) that one person can stand on.
   Safety Considerations: Minimal.

Exhibit 24–1 *continued*

Description: Participants are asked to cross a designated area (25–100 ft.) using only the blocks provided. If anyone steps off a block or the group loses human contact with a block, they lose that block for the duration of the activity. If someone "falls off" a block, he or she, along with anyone touching him or her must start the activity over.

Debriefing: Focus on how the group needs all 12 steps to recover; look at the impact of losing a particular block (Step 4, for instance); look at the importance of keeping human contact with each block.

4. **Activity:** Blindfold Line-Up

   Source: Rohnke (1994, p. 98)

   Concept: Feelings of powerlessness and powerfulness when not finding one's place in line/finding one's proper place.

   Goal: The object is to have the group line up in an order you have given them.

   Materials: Blindfolds if the group is unable to close their eyes for the duration of the activity.

   Safety Considerations: Minimal.

   Description: Split the group in half (if larger than 12 people) for this activity. Number the group from "1" to however many people are in that half of the group. Have unnumbered persons wander around blindly with hands in front of them (bumpers up) while you or a cotherapist number them (by whispering in their ear) quietly. Tell the group they must communicate their number to the rest of the group without speaking in this activity. Their goal is to form a line based on their given number.

   After the group has successfully lined up, you can attempt the activity again with a "twist." Tell the group one member will be designated as a liar/fooler and that that person's job will be to confuse the group members by giving them false information and by generally mixing them up. The group member's job is to determine when they are being lied to and when they are being told the truth. If they believe they are being lied to, they can point their finger in the direction of the liar and say "liar" (or "fooler"). If they are successful in pointing out the liar/fooler, the liar/fooler is out of the game for 30 seconds. If they are unsuccessful, that individual has blown his or her (one) chance, and some other group member will have to call the liar's bluff.

   Debriefing: It is very useful to focus on the feelings of group members when they *first* participated in the activity. What was it like to not know where you belonged in the group? What are other times in your life when you have felt similar? What was the feeling when you found your proper place in the group? What are other times in your life when you have felt similar? How might this experience relate to feelings of helplessness? How did you as a group member gain power to find your place? Did you do it alone or were others involved?

   The experience of being lied to is also very useful to discuss here. How do you know when you are being lied to and when you are being told the truth? How can you tell the difference? When are you not sure? What can you do about it? How might these feelings be similar to how you felt in the past (or how you might feel in the future) if/when someone offers you a chance to use (drugs/alcohol) again?

5. **Activity:** Willow in the Wind

   Source: Rohnke (1991, pp. 12–13)

   Concept: Asking the group for help when trying to stay straight.

   Goal: To pass a blindfolded or eyes-closed participant around in a shoulder-to-shoulder circle of participants.

   Materials: None, unless blindfolds are used.

   Safety Considerations: Participants need to have "bumpers up" in that they will have their hands out in front of them and stand with one foot ahead of the other in order to support the participant in the center of the circle. Participants should have participated in other "trust activities" prior to doing this activity. With younger/immature groups, be careful the group slowly passes and does not push the participant around the circle.

Exhibit 24–1 *continued*

Description: One by one participants will stand in the center of a circle composed of participants standing shoulder-to-shoulder.

Debriefing: Focus on how the group can support the individual to "stay straight" in recovery.

6. Activity: Mine Field

Source: Rohnke (1994, p. 52)

Concept: Support needed from others since you can't make it alone.

Goal: To traverse, with eyes closed or blindfolded, a designated area full of obstacles without
touching any obstacle or any person.

Materials: Blindfolds (if used), objects to "litter" the mine field, and some way to designate
the boundaries of the area.

Safety Considerations: Minimal; be careful about blindfolded participants running into one
another.

Description: Participants can begin by trying to cross the field by themselves. In a second
round, they ask someone to help them traverse the field by "talking" them through the field
without touching them.

Debriefing: Focus on differences between going alone and being guided by another (sponsor).

---

familiar with basic concepts of adventure-based counseling or group counseling; (b) you will ethically conduct only those activities with which you are competent; (c) you will focus on both the physical and emotional safety of participants while conducting each activity and debriefing; (d) you realize this chapter
is presenting *a* way to introduce and debrief activities that Project Adventure
has found to be successful, but that it is not the only way.

These six activities have been found useful when presented in a 1- to 2-day
workshop sequence or as part of an ongoing group. For the most part, it is helpful to use the sequence of activities as presented here and not to put a higher
numbered one earlier in the activity sequence. As noted earlier, safety considerations, both physical and psychological, are of utmost importance. However, the
leader's competence to ethically conduct these activities in a group counseling
session is by far the most important element of leadership behavior and responsible group counseling behavior that can be stressed here.

CONCLUSION

It is often difficult to present in narration an adequate description of adventure-
based counseling activities such that the reader can get a picture of the action.
But it is hoped that the reader will be able to try these activities from the
description here and will adapt them or other activities from any of the sources
listed below to help achieve the goals for participants in addiction and recovery
groups. The purpose of this chapter has been to provide readers with a rationale
and sampling of activities that can stimulate curiosity about further applications

of adventure-based counseling and enhance creativity in designing effective therapeutic activities for dealing with addiction and recovery. Any feedback as to the effectiveness readers find when using them will be greatly appreciated.

REFERENCES

Alcoholics Anonymous World Service, Inc. (1981). *Twelve steps and twelve traditions.* NY: Author.

Gass, M. A. (1991). Enhancing metaphor development in adventure therapy programs. *Journal of Experiential Education, 14*(2), 8–13.

Gass, M. A. (1993). *Adventure therapy: Therapeutic applications of adventure programming.* Boulder, CO: Association for Experiential Education.

Gass, M. A., & McPhee, P. J. (1990). Emerging for recovery: A descriptive analysis of adventure therapy for substance abusers. *Journal of Experiential Education, 13* (2), 29–35.

Gillis, H. L., & Bonney, W. C. (1986). Group counseling with couples or families: Adding adventure activities. *Journal for Specialists in Group Work, 11*(4), 213–219.

Gillis, H. L., & Bonney, W. C. (1989). Utilizing adventure activities with intact groups: A sociodramatic systems approach to consultation. *Journal of Mental Health Counseling, 11*(4), 345–358.

Gillis, H. L., & Simpson, C. (1991). Project choices: Adventure-based residential drug treatment for court-referred youth. *Journal of Addictions and Offender Counseling, 12,* 12–27.

Gillis, H. L., Williams, A., & Hollis, H. (1992). A psychological rationale for adventure therapy with hospitalized adolescents. In Karla A. Henderson (Ed.), *Coalition for Education in the Outdoors Research Symposium Proceedings.* (Bradford Woods, IN, January 17-19, 1992 ERIC Document Reproduction Service RC 018876.

Maizell, R. S. (1988). Adventure-based counseling as a therapeutic intervention with court-involved adolescents. *Dissertation Abstracts International,* 50/06B, 2628. (University Microfilms No. AAD8921901).

Rohnke, K. E. (1984). *Silver bullets.* Hamilton, MA: Project Adventure, Inc.

Rohnke, K. E. (1989). *Cowstails and cobras II.* Hamilton, MA: Project Adventure, Inc.

Rohnke, K. E. (1991). *The bottomless baggie.* Dubuque, IA: Kendall Hunt.

Rohnke, K. E. (1994) The bottomless bag again. Second edition. Dubuque, IA: Kendall Hunt.

Schoel, J., Prouty, D., & Radcliffe, P. (1988). *Islands of healing: A guide to adventure-based counseling.* Hamilton, MA: Project Adventure, Inc.

Tobler, N. S. (1986). Meta-analysis of 143 drug prevention programs: Quantitative outcome results of program participants compared to a control or comparison group. *Journal of Drug Issues, 16,* 537–568.

Witman, J. P. (1989). Outcomes of adventure program participation by adolescents involved in psychiatric treatment. *Dissertation Abstracts International,* 50/01B, 121. (University Microfilms No. AAD8907355).

Chapter 25
Adolescents, Self-Esteem, and Substance Use

Lynn D. Miller

The changing structure of our American society will demand changes in efforts to deal with adolescent drug and alcohol use/abuse. The leading researchers are concentrating their efforts on successful prevention programs. This trend is a result of recent developments in the field of substance research. In the last two decades, the American public has shown increasing awareness and concern over the use and experimentation with alcohol and other drugs by its youth. The alarming statistics and the high profile the media accords this subject have contributed to this awareness. In the late 1970s, many states responded to this increased interest by mandating drug and alcohol information in curriculum (Pipher & Rivers, 1982).

Lacking clearly defined goals other than to comply with the mandate, schools bought packaged programs or hastily put together their own health education and drug information courses. This approach, assuming that the student used drugs and alcohol because of a lack of information regarding negative health consequences, did not work (Bell & Battjes, 1986; Finn, 1979; Ketchel & Bieger, 1989; Pickens, 1985). Indeed, the trends in drug use grew to a frightening level. In Johnston's 1986 study, nine out of every 10 high school seniors had used alcohol within the previous 30 days, 50% had smoked marijuana, one in six had used cocaine, and one in eight had used hallucinogens. One in five seniors were daily smokers, and more than 37% of the respondents reported at least one occasion of heavy drinking (five or more drinks in a row) in the 2 weeks prior to the survey (Onestak, 1989). Recent figures place the average beginning age for an American youth drinking alcohol at 12.5 years (McCurdy, 1986).

REACTIVE PROGRAMMING

Drug education program designers, after seeing the failure of purely informational programming, theorized that students with a higher level of self-esteem might exhibit lower levels of drug and alcohol use (Swisher, 1989). Programs took on an affective approach. Encouragingly enough, the latest research by the National Commission on Drug-Free Schools indicates decreased use (1990):

- Illegal drug use decreased from a high of 66% of seniors having ever used an illicit drug in 1981 to 51% in 1989.
- Marijuana use within the previous 30 days among high school seniors declined from a high of 37% in 1978 to 17% in 1989.
- Cocaine use within the previous 30 days among high school seniors declined from 67% in 1985 to a low of 2.8% in 1989.
- Alcohol use within the previous 30 days among high school seniors declined from a high of 72% in 1978 to 60% in 1989.
- 34% of high school seniors engage in binge drinking (5 or more drinks in a row) at least once every 2 weeks.

It would be tempting to conclude that this affective programming approach can directly be traced to the reduced use reported by the National Commission. However, the reduction in use obviously could have been a result of any number of social changes. Perhaps it is more important to ask to what extent does self-esteem predispose a teenager to channel "normal" adolescent rebellion either toward acceptable behaviors or toward deviance? Although current literature that explicitly correlates measures of self-esteem and substance abuse is sparse, research suggests that teens who believe themselves unable to live up to societal (familial and peer) pressures to succeed will compensate by acting out in negative ways, specifically by abusing substances.

What distinguishes between the occasional user and the teen who becomes addicted? Where should prevention efforts be concentrated? Does it hold true that a child with poorly developed self-esteem will grow into an adolescent who will adopt dangerous avenues of adolescent rebellion such as the use of substances as a means to medicate or nurture a flagging self-image? This is an imperative area of study, especially since the mid-1980s popular theory of combatting drug use by "just saying no" has failed. This is not a strong enough defense; the problem is infinitely more complex and requires a more comprehensive approach.

WHAT IS SELF-ESTEEM?

Much controversy exists over the definition of self-esteem. Nathaniel Branden (1992), the "father of the self-esteem movement," defines self-esteem as the disposition to experience oneself as competent to cope with the challenges of life and deserving of happiness. Self-esteem is a difficult construct to establish because of numerous factors. Juhasz (1985) claims that evaluations of self often include aspects of self on which esteem does not rest. Measurement instruments, especially when used with an adolescent population, may include values and traits that reflect adult assumptions. Different factors may carry more weight with a person and may compensate for other areas that register low on testing instruments.

A related problem is that of selectivity. All people can have higher self-esteem by concentrating on areas in which they excel (Rosenberg, 1979). The things that people cannot change generally assume less importance. Sometimes, however, some of these biological, familial, societal, or individual aspects of one's social identity may garner more attention and contribute to negative self-esteem. The person then will ignore, accept, or try to change these particular traits. Self-esteem is a product (Branden, 1992). It is acquired over time. It is dynamic.

An adolescent may not have the verbal maturity to express a complex and difficult concept such as self-worth. The adolescent may have trouble not only identifying but also valuing self-esteem types of qualities. Furthermore, physical, mental, relationship, school, and family concerns may all affect self-esteem differently.

Although a definitive concept of self-esteem and its measurement is lacking, there are general inferences to its meaning (Bell & Battjes, 1986).

FACTORS AFFECTING SELF-ESTEEM

What, then, influences or shapes this construct? Obviously, family relationships play a crucial role. Amato (1986) found no difference in self-esteem of children in cohesive one-parent families and cohesive two-parent families. However, parent-parent conflict and parent-child conflict are associated with low self-esteem.

Research suggests that parents who have good self-esteem and model it engenders self-esteem in children (Branden, 1992). But no research has ever found this result to be inevitable (Coopersmith, 1981).

Differences in parenting may lead to varying degrees of self-esteem. Aristotle first defined effective parenting, emphasizing that children must be "habituated to desirable behavior—attending to tasks, sharing, honesty—before they can understand theoretically the benefit of doing so" (Hawley, 1987, p. 25). Rewards naturally follow and reinforce the desired behavior. Without this structure, children do not receive approval for their behavior from their parents, which in turn reinforces a negative sense of self.

Family cohesiveness and communication patterns have been studied in families with adolescent substance abuse (Barnes, 1984; Jurich, Polson, Jurich, & Bates, 1985). "Drug abusing adolescents report having little impact on family processes and feeling little closeness with their parents. These families are characterized by a lack of love and minimal support for their members, and as a result, the drug user's needs for recognition, love, and trust go chronically unfulfilled" (Onestak, 1989, p. 3). This family interaction is bound to affect one's self-esteem. If a child is not well attended on a consistent basis, this shapes the child's appraisal of self-worth. The discounting by one's own family is a forceful blow.

Other researchers have placed drug users on a continuum, from nonusers on one end to the opposite extreme of abusers. The differences in behaviors of nonusing and using adolescents have been associated with self-esteem levels. Users have a tendency to get lower grades, less likely to be involved extracurricularly (clubs, sports), and more likely to lie, steal, and cheat. They are characteristically aggressive, rebellious, impulsive, and more depressed (Botvin & Tortu, 1988). These users typically are profiled as having low self-esteem, needing greater social approval, exhibiting higher anxiety, displaying low assertiveness, and having an external locus of control. Additionally, the students who used multiple drugs had "high values for independence, peer conformity, and risk; high social alienation, tolerance of deviance, and drug use; low delay of gratification, time perspective [and] expectancies for interpersonal trust" (Capuzzi & Lecoq, 1983, p. 202).

An interesting project conducted 25 years ago by Blum (1969) studied the medicating habits of parents with their young children. He believed the most important finding for subsequent users of all classes of drugs is the consistent recollection that there were advantages of being sick as a child. Several conclusions may be drawn from this finding. One may be that the parents did not care for the child's physical well-being, thus the child was more often sick and remembered being sick more often than healthy children. Another could be that the child enjoyed the drugged state induced by the medication. The appeal of extra attention during sickness from busy parents is obvious. The project brings attention to a fairly desperate child seeking parental attention or approval at any cost. The project has not been repeated. It would be interesting to study if, based on Blum's work, medicating habits of small children increase in the frantic pace of 1990s and, therefore, drug use increases for the teenagers of the early 21st century.

ADOLESCENCE

Adolescence is a particularly crucial stage in human growth and development for maintaining elevated levels of self-esteem. People at this stage of development, by virtue of attending school, have a higher and more active level of interaction with others and the environment. Independent thinking, part of the process that contributes to healthy self-esteem, can be especially difficult and even frightening for teens (Branden, 1992). Peer acceptance is imperative. An event that may seem trivial from an adult perspective can impair an adolescent's basic sense of well-being. Teens have not developed a complex understanding of time like an adult's. Experiencing love or intimacy, finding oneself adequate—all these can be confusing for anyone, regardless of age, but they are made more confounding for the teen due to the lack of social experience. Erickson's fifth stage (identity achievement vs. role confusion) in his psychosocial model of developmental tasks provides explanation of this process. Erickson argued that the adolescent must make important decisions but is unable and therefore unwilling to do so (1968). One adapts and learns to manage these crises through the maturation process. As Hawley (1987, p. 24) perceptively writes, "the only way out of adolescence is through it." When a teen uses substances to dull the pain of his problems or situation, he or she feels more able to cope with tension and anxiety (Ketchel & Bieger, 1989).

A child needs encouragement, just as a plant needs water.

Rudolph Dreikurs

How are levels of self-esteem related to frequency of substance abuse? If the premise is correct, as self-esteem drops, frequency of substance abuse should increase. Conversely, individuals with high levels of self-esteem would be less likely to become substance abusers. A corollary also is that substance abuse is blind to socioeconomic status; a better predictor in all social classes of drug dependency should be strength of self-worth. Lowell Horton concurs, adding that fewer than 3% of adult alcoholics are jobless, homeless, and without families (1988).

Association with alcohol- and other drug-using peers is consistently cited as the strongest predictor of adolescent alcohol and other drug use (Goperud, 1991; Hawkins & Catalano, 1989; Office for Substance Abuse Prevention, 1991).

Individuals with impaired self-esteem feel inadequate to cope with their environment (Kandel, 1979). They perceive troublesome events as posing a further threat to their self-esteem. They react with feelings of fear, inadequacy, and depression, and thus their adaptive behavior becomes distorted. At this point they value the drug for its perceived ability to lessen the pain and to give them greater confidence.

Other arguments bolster the belief that abuse depends greatly on level of self-esteem. Whether an individual first chooses to try a drug and then continues depends more on the personality than on the factor of availability (Onestak, 1989; OSAP, 1991; Pransky, 1991). Blum concurs, stating that "for the majority, initiation into tobacco and illicit-exotic drug use is not in response to felt social pressures—that is, no strain or compulsion is admitted" (Blum, 1969, p. 348). There is a definite difference between the adolescent user who indulges because the need to belong overpowers other considerations and because he or she is reacting to peer pressure, and the abuser who indulges repeatedly due to overwhelming internal considerations. The user is called a *reactive addict*, responding to transitory developmental pressures of adolescence and seeing drugs as a means for acceptance and a vehicle to defy traditional norms. He or she feels impotent and lacking in status, and is looking for support and approval. The abuser, or primary addict, looks to drugs for their specific adjustive value for particular personality defects (Scherer, Ettinger, & Mudrich, 1972).

Sakell says the two traits common in substance abusers are low self-esteem and an external locus of control (1985). Ketchel and Bieger (1989) found statistical significance between adolescent low self-esteem as measured by Coopersmith Self-Esteem Inventory and increased substance use. Lewis, Dana, and Blevins (1988) state that health behaviors are determined most by self-concept and self-esteem. Thus current research is highly supportive of the correlative aspect of substance use and the variable of low self-esteem, low self-efficacy, and depression (Ketchel & Bieger, 1989).

CULTURE

Another interesting aspect to examine around the issues of teen use and abuse is that of today's culture. Although drug and alcohol use levels are lower today than in the 1970s and mid-1980s, the fact remains that there is widespread use, especially of alcohol and tobacco. Self-esteem cannot be the only variable that should be scrutinized.

Drug use, especially alcohol and tobacco, is seen as a "rite of passage" in our country. The teenage peer group apparently views use of alcohol as an initiation into adulthood—as is shown by the fact that over 90% of seniors have used alcohol, and nearly 73% of seniors have been drunk (American Drug and Alcohol Survey, RMBSI, Inc., 1991). This pattern persists even though in 1988 the purchase age for alcohol was raised in all 50 states to 21 years. Does the value of being like peers, subscribing to adolescent cultural mores, contribute to the decision to use drugs and alcohol? Would a teen's self-concept be enhanced by using and being more like the peer culture?

If change is to occur, if use needs to decline, if the message should be that drug and alcohol use is not an appropriate rite of passage, then the culture needs to adapt to this change. Bonnie Benard is leading this movement by beginning to identify "protective" factors, or "those traits, conditions, situations, and episodes that appear to alter—or even reverse—predictions of [negative outcome]" (Benard, 1991, p. 2). She goes on to point out that "if we can determine the personal and environmental sources of social competence and wellness, we can better plan preventive interventions." Some of the protective factors are:

- The individual's close bond with at least one person who has provided him or her with stable care and from whom he or she receives adequate and appropriate attention
- High parental expectations
- Valuable childhood participation (i.e., chores)
- Effective peer programs in schools
- Schools that show an academic emphasis, teachers' clear expectations and regulations, high student participation, and many alternative resources
- Competent communities (i.e., supportive of their families and schools) that provide access to basic necessities of health care, child care, housing, education, job training, employment, and recreation (Benard, 1991)

CONCLUSION

Substance abuse among adolescents depends on a number of factors, but lack of self-esteem predisposes a teenager to become a victim of substance abuse. The term *victim* is appropriate because this deviant behavior really reflects a society and media advertising that glamorizes abusive drinking and drunkenness. If adolescent chemical use is to be reduced, then communities must also demand that adults reflect on their own patterns of use. Society is the foundation that has to encourage change (Pransky, 1991).

Substances are seen as the magical cure for adolescent pain, feelings of worthlessness, and feelings of inadequacy, and as a mechanism for coping with either overwhelming high parental expectations and aspirations or parental neglect.

The approach to drug and alcohol prevention must be comprehensive and multifaceted. It must begin early. It should include the community, the family, and the school. It should offer interpersonal and intrapersonal skill development. The myth that alcohol and drug use is a rite of passage must be shattered. Zero tolerance should be the mass message. And finally, it must be understood that a child's mental health and well-being, his or her self-esteem, is a crucial target in this campaign against substance use.

REFERENCES

Amato, P. R. (1986). Marital conflict, the parent-child relationship and child self-esteem. *Family Relations, 35,* 403–410.

American Drug and Alcohol Survey. (1991). RMBSI, Inc.

Ausubel, D. P. (1958). *Drug addiction: Physiological, psychological, and sociological aspects.* New York: Random House.

Barnes, G. M. (1984). Adolescent alcohol abuse and common parental influences. *Journal of Youth and Adolescence, 13,* 329–348.

Bell, C. S., & Battjes, R. (1986). *Prevention research: Deterring drug abuse among children and adolescents.* National Institute on Drug Abuse Research Monograph No. 63 (DHHS Publication No. ADM 87-1334). Washington, DC: U.S. Government Printing Office.

Benard, B. (1991, August). *Fostering resiliency in kids: Protective factors in the family, school and community.* (Available from [Western Regional Center for Drug-Free Schools and Communities, 101 SW Main Street, Suite 500, Portland, OR, 97204]).

Blum, R. H. (1969). *Students and drugs.* San Francisco: Jossey-Bass.

Botvin, G., & Tortu, S. (1988). Preventing adolescent substance abuse through life skills training. In R. H. Price, E. L. Cowen, R. P. Lorion, & J. Ramos-McKay (Eds.), *14 ounces of prevention* (pp. 98–110). Washington, DC: American Psychological Association.

Branden, N. (1992). *The power of self-esteem.* Deerfield Beach, FL: Health Communications.

Capuzzi, D., & Lecoq, L. (1983, December). Social and personal determinants of adolescent use and abuse of alcohol and marijuana. *Personnel and Guidance Journal, 62*(4), 199–205.

Coopersmith, S. (1981). *The antecedents of self-esteem.* Palo Alto, CA: Counseling Psychologist Press.

Erickson, E. (1968). *Identity: Youth and crisis.* New York: Norton.

Finn, P. (1979). Alcohol education in the school curriculum: The single discipline vs. the interdisciplinary approach. *Journal of Alcohol and Drug Education, 24*(2), 41–57.

Goperud, E. N. (Ed.). (1991). *Preventing adolescent drug use: From theory to practice* (OSAP Prevention Monograph No.8). Rockville, MD: U.S. Dept. of Health and Human Services.

Hawkins, J. D., & Catalano, R. F. (1989, April). Risk-focused prevention: From research to practical strategies. *High risk youth update.*

Hawley, R. A. (1987). Schoolchildren and drugs: The fancy that has not passed. *Phi Delta Kappan, 68*(9), 23–28.

Horton, L. (1988). The education of most worth: Preventing drug and alcohol abuse. *Educational Leadership, 45* (6), 4–8.

Johnston, L. D., O'Malley, P., & Bachman, J.G. (1986). National trends in drug use in high school and college. *Education Digest, 52*(4), 23–25.

Juhasz, A. M. (1985). Measuring self-esteem in early adolescents. *Adolescence, 20*(80), 877–887.

Jurich, A. P., Polson, C. J., Jurich, J. A., & Bates, R. A. (1985). Family factors in the lives of drug users and abusers. *Adolescence, 20*, 143–159.

Kandel, D. B. (1979). *Longitudinal research on drug use: Empirical findings and methodological issues.* New York: John Wiley.

Ketchel, J. A., & Bieger, G. R. (1989, April). *The efficacy of a psychosocially based drug prevention program for young adolescents.* Paper presented at the Annual Meeting of the New England Educational Research Organization, Portsmouth, NH.

Lewis, J. A., Dana, R. O., & Blevins, G. A. (1988). *Substance abuse counseling: An individualized approach.* Pacific Grove, CA: Brooks/Cole.

McCurdy, J. (Ed.). (1986). *The drug free school: What executives can do.* Arlington, VA: National School Public Relations Association. (ERIC Document Reproduction Service No. ED 276936).

National Commission on Drug-Free Schools (1990, September). *Towards a drug-free generation: A nation's responsibility.* Final Report. Washington, DC: U.S. Department of Education.

Office for Substance Abuse Prevention. (1991, October). *Too many young people drink and know too little about the consequences.* (DHHS Publication). Rockville, MD: Office for Substance Abuse Prevention.

Onestak, D. M. and others. (1989, August). *Family variables and alcohol use in high risk adolescents.* Paper presented to American Psychological Association, New Orleans.

Pickens, K. (1985). Drug education: The effects of giving information. *Journal of Alcohol and Drug Education, 30*(3), 32–44.

Pipher, J., & Rivers, C. (1982). The differential effects of alcohol education on junior high school students. *Journal of Alcohol and Drug Education, 27*(3), 73–89.

Pransky, J. (1991). *Prevention: The critical need.* Springfield, MO: Burrell Foundation.

Rosenberg, M. (1979). *Conceiving the self.* New York: Basic Books.

Sakell, T. (1985, April 14). Substance abuse: Addicted must want to change. *Guidepost*, 4–5.

Scherer, S. E., Ettinger, R. F., & Mudrich, N. J. (1972). *Need for social approval and drug use. Journal of Consulting and Clinical Psychology, 38* (1), 118–121.

Swisher, J. D. (1989). Educational factors influencing adolescent decision making regarding use of alcohol and drugs. *Journal of Alcohol and Drug Education, 35*(1), 1–15.

BIBLIOGRAPHY

Hawkins, J.D., & Catalano, R.F. (1992). *Communities that care: Action for drugs and alcohol prevention.* San Francisco: Jossey Bass Publishers.

Chapter 26
The D.A.R.E. (Drug Abuse Resistance Education) Program

Karen A. Koch

Prevention strategies are an important component of our societal efforts to address the problems associated with substance abuse and misuse. Past prevention efforts have yielded marginal success, yet the widespread use of psychoactive substances continues to demand a better response. Educators have been keenly aware of the impact of drug use on young people. Subsequently, they have taken an active role in developing primary prevention programs. These programs have been initiated in an attempt to keep young people from ruining their lives with drugs.

In order for a drug education program to be effective, it is essential that the design and implementation of the curriculum meet the needs of the intended population. Educationally based programs have therefore expanded beyond providing factual information on the problems associated with drug use. The new generation of prevention programs attempts to prevent a number of self-destructive behaviors related to drug use, such as juvenile crime, vandalism, running away, and gang affiliation. In addition, the more comprehensive approaches attempt to enhance social skills and self-esteem, develop an awareness of peer and social pressures to use drugs, utilize effective coping skills to resist pressures, and suggest healthy alternatives to drug-using behaviors, thereby developing a proactive approach to drug-free lifestyles and ultimately reducing the demand for drugs.

Utilizing the resources inherent within the community can positively impact on the effectiveness of comprehensive prevention programs. The law enforcement sector is a community component that has had an active role in combating the negative influences of substance abuse. The role of law enforcement involves eradicating the supply of drugs, punishing offenders, and deterring use through enforcement endeavors.

In an effort to better address the needs of young people as they face choices about drug use and gangs, a group of educators and law enforcement officers combined talents to initiate an innovative educational endeavor. The efforts of the Los Angeles Unified School District and the Los Angeles Police Department emerged as the D.A.R.E. (Drug Abuse Resistance Education) Program. Since 1983, thousands of young people have been educated regarding the dangers of using drugs. The D.A.R.E. curriculum helps to instill in young children the knowledge about how to deal with the pressures of peers, gangs, and media as they relate to drug usage.

D.A.R.E. is a drug abuse prevention program that targets young people at formative ages. It attempts to inform them about the negative aspects of substance abuse and also the positive aspects of a healthy lifestyle. Since its 1983 beginning in the Los Angeles Unified Schools, the D.A.R.E. Program has spread nationally to all 50 states and the Virgin Islands. In addition, personnel from the United States Air Force have been trained and are currently teaching the D.A.R.E. curriculum to children on military bases. The unique aspect of the D.A.R.E. Program, what distinguishes this prevention program from other drug abuse prevention programs, is the fact that the instructor is a specially trained, uniformed police officer.

The comprehensive curriculum is designed to meet the long-term goals of the D.A.R.E. Program, which include:

- Reducing the supply of controlled substances by reducing the demand
- Developing a more positive image of police officers by children through interaction
- Improving decision-making skills in children for a variety of life situations
- Initiating an overall reduction in criminality

To achieve these goals, the D.A.R.E. program has established curricula designed to meet the educational and social needs of students at various ages. The core curriculum is targeted toward fifth- and sixth-grade students and is delivered in 1-hour sessions by a uniformed police officer for 17 consecutive weeks. While the D.A.R.E. officer presents the lesson and manages classroom behavior, the certified teacher remains in the room and acts as a support system for the officer.

Each lesson is designed to address a specific life skill area. The lessons in the core curriculum are:

1. *Practices for personal safety:* This lesson will review practices for student safety and the need for laws to protect citizens.
2. *Drug use and misuse:* Lesson 2 presents an overview of drugs, legal and illegal, and hazards when used and misused.
3. *Consequences:* This lesson will help students understand that both positive and negative consequences result from their choice to use or not use drugs.

4. *Resisting pressure to use drugs:* Students are provided with examples of the types of peer pressure they may experience when faced with drug offers and how they can refuse.

5. *Resistance techniques:* This lesson features the "8 Ways to Say No," where students role play ways to resist the various types of peer pressure to use drugs.

6. *Building self-esteem:* The concept assists the students to understand that a healthy self-image will empower them and that self-image results from positive and negative experiences.

7. *Assertiveness:* The object is to enable the students to stand up for his or her rights without loss of self-esteem.

8. *Managing stress without taking drugs:* Students learn to recognize stress and manage it without using drugs.

9. *Media influences on drug use:* Students will develop skills to understand and resist media presentations on alcohol and drug products.

10. *Decision making and risk taking:* Students learn to use decision-making process and apply it to risk-taking behaviors, including drug taking.

11. *Alternatives to drug use:* The lesson helps students identify activities that are fun, rewarding, and drug free.

12. *Role modeling:* Positive, drug-free, high school student leaders are invited to speak to students about choosing not to use drugs and to clarify misconceptions that drug users are in the majority.

13. *Forming a support system:* Students learn to identify and develop positive relationships with different people and utilize these people as a support system.

14. *Resisting gang pressure:* Students learn to recognize and resist pressure to join a gang.

15. *D.A.R.E. Summary:* This lesson reviews essential points made in previous lessons.

16. *Taking a stand:* Students write out their own commitments not to use drugs and read these aloud to their class.

17. *Culmination:* A commencement exercise is held to present students with a certificate of achievement and other recognitions, and family members are invited to attend.

In order for the students to follow the lessons and digest the material, each student receives a workbook that is used each class. At the conclusion of Lesson 16, the students take their workbook home to share with their family. Throughout the 17 lessons, the police officer brings a mascot, commonly referred to as "DARE Bear," for the students to hold, as part of the responsibility of caring for oneself and role modeling appropriate behavior. In order to answer questions that students may have or to handle disclosures students often make to the officer, a "DARE Question Box" is available for students to leave messages for the D.A.R.E. officer. All disclosures are handled confidentially, following child protection laws and policies of each jurisdiction.

In addition to the original D.A.R.E. core curriculum, other components have been developed to enhance the process of reducing the demand for drugs through prevention education. The following curricula are also taught by specially trained D.A.R.E. officers:

- *Kindergarten—Grade 4:* The primary focus in the five sessions is drug safety. Students are alerted to potential dangers of misuse of drugs, medicine, and other household products, as well as an awareness that alcohol and tobacco are drugs.
- *Special Education Adaptation:* This curriculum was created to meet the needs of learning-disabled/behavior-disordered children. The 17 lessons maintain the same concept, purpose, and objectives as the core curriculum. The lessons have been adapted to meet the special needs of the students in terms of teaching modalities and strategies. The workbook has also been adapted to enhance learning and understanding of materials. Specialized training of the officer is required for the presentation of this curriculum.
- *Junior High Curriculum:* This curriculum targets seventh- and eight-grade students in an effort to reinforce information and resistance skills. Ten lessons cover the following topics:

1. *Drug use and abuse:* Students learn how psychoactive substances alter the way their minds and body work.
2. *Drugs, violence, and the law:* This lesson is to help students understand how laws governing the use of drugs work and their role in adhering to these laws.
3. *Consequences:* To assist students in understanding how the results of drug use affects their environment.
4. *Assertive resistance:* Students learn assertiveness as a response style for resisting pressures to use drugs.
5. *Forming positive friendships:* The needs for affection, belonging, and recognition are important to young people and, to fulfill these needs, students to learn ways to develop positive relationships.
6. *Resolving conflicts without violence:* This lesson is designed to assist students to learn appropriate conflict resolution.
7. *Destructive ecology:* Students learn how vandalism affects everyone in their community.
8. *Pressure from gangs and gang violence:* This lesson acquaints students with how gangs may pressure youths and choices they may be expected to make.

9. *D.A.R.E. Review:* Students are provided with an opportunity to review material learned in D.A.R.E.
10. *D.A.R.E. to be*: Students are challenged to plan their personal strategy for how they will react under pressure.

• *D.A.R.E. Senior High Program:* To further accomplish the initial goals of the D.A.R.E. Program, a secondary prevention program was developed for the high school student. This program is taught jointly by a certified high school teacher and the D.A.R.E. officer over an 11-day period. It is designed to reinforce the information and skills students need to enable them to act in their own best interest when faced with risk-taking situations. Students also learn how to deal appropriately with anger and their responses to feelings of anger. An overview of the lesson schedule is as follows:

1. *Introduction:* The teaching team is introduced and a pretest to measure current knowledge about drug abuse is administered.
2. *Reducing the demand for drugs:* The officer teaches this section, which focuses on drug abuse in the community and the negative impact.
3. *Follow-up:* The teacher reinforces the concept of negative consequences of drug abuse on the individual and community.
4. *Communicating choices assertively:* The officer teaches the skills for stating choices assertively in situations involving drug use. Students have opportunities to role play the different skills.
5. *Drug-related behaviors and the law:* The officer instructs students on how drug-related behaviors affect the balance between rights of the individual and rights of society.
6. *Follow-up:* The teacher utilizes this lesson to address blood alcohol levels and risks involved. Cooperative learning groups are a part of this lesson.
7. *Drugs, media, and violence:* The officer teaches the lesson, which focuses on how drug use and the media can affect violent behavior.
8. *Managing anger and resolving conflicts without drugs:* The officer instructs the students in positive ways to express and manage anger without resorting to drugs.
9. *Conflict resolution continuation*
10. *Follow-up:* This lesson emphasizes the use of effective communication skills such as "I message" statements.
11. *Evaluation and posttest:* A posttest is administered by the teacher to measure students' knowledge of all related skills.

• *D.A.R.E. Parent Program:* In response to interest expressed by parents of D.A.R.E. students and their desire to learn more about drug abuse, an informational program was developed entitled *D.A.R.E. Parent Program*. The intent was to provide parents of D.A.R.E. students with basic information about drug use and abuse. The focus of the parent program is to develop better communication skills and to strengthen family communication as a prevention tool. The program also provides parents with an awareness of current drug trends and strategies, as well as an understanding of life skills needed by young people to resist peer pressure. The conclusion of the parent program involves a panel discussion with community resource personnel from a variety of disciplines, who interact with the parents and exchange ideas.

Over the past decade, the D.A.R.E. Program has prospered as a nationally known school prevention program. It has gained recognition and acceptance among law enforcement agencies. The marriage of educators and law enforcement, for the application of this program, appears to be a workable alliance. School districts are able to apply for federal funds to implement the D.A.R.E. Program through grants available under the Drug Free Schools and Communities Act. Certification and training of the D.A.R.E. officers are the responsibility of the five Regional Training Centers. Longitudinal studies of the D.A.R.E. Program are being conducted across the nation. Publication of the results are forthcoming as the students are being tracked from fifth grade through high school.

Information on implementing the D.A.R.E. Program or regarding qualifications for any of the specialized programs is available by contacting:

> Midwest Regional Training Center
> D.A.R.E. Bureau
> Illinois State Police Academy
> 3700 East Lake Shore Drive
> Springfield, Illinois 62707
> (217) 786-7057 (voice)
> (800) 255-3323 (TDD)

Chapter 27
Entry of Women of Diverse Backgrounds Into Alcoholism Treatment

Linda J. Beckman

Before addicted women can receive help for their alcohol and drug abuse problems they must be able and willing to seek and accept help. This review examines factors that affect entry into treatment for women who abuse alcohol and other drugs. Although the primary focus is on alcoholism in women, many women who abuse alcohol are poly-substance abusers (Ferrence & Whitehead, 1980; Mulford, 1977). For instance, Mays, Beckman, Oranchak, and Harper (1993) found that 78% of their sample of African-American women in alcoholism treatment centers had frequently used marijuana and 45% had frequently used cocaine.

In this review I emphasize interpersonal and environmental variables rather than personal traits, values, or attitudes because the interpersonal and environmental realms present many opportunities for treatment providers to enhance help seeking by women and promote appropriate substance abuse services for women. A second emphasis is on diversity. Women who abuse alcohol are heterogeneous in cultural background, age, socioeconomic status, and many other ways. We cannot continue to assume that barriers and facilitators to alcoholism treatment are at equal levels for women with diverse cultural backgrounds, nor can we assume that interpersonal and environmental influences have identical effects on treatment entry for all groups. Although my own work primarily has involved comparisons of African-American and white women, there is a great need for research on treatment entry that concentrates on other racial and ethnic groups.

The conceptual model (Beckman & Kocel, 1982) that guides much of my work is adapted from the more general model of medical services utilization of Aday and Andersen (1974). This model provides a framework for viewing influences on treatment entry, considering both systemic and intrapersonal factors. Characteristics that affect a person's ability to obtain and propensity to use services include: (a) *individual predisposing factors,* such as age, socioeconomic status, ethnicity, religion or gender; (b) *perceptions and beliefs* about alcohol, treatment, and health; (c) *personal enabling traits,* including personality characteristics such as personal efficacy and depression, drinking history, and previous treatment history; and (d) *social enabling characteristics*, that is, interpersonal and situational variables such as child care responsibilities and geographic proximity to treatment. *Social enabling characteristics* are further subdivided into (a) *social/interpersonal variables,* such as social support from family and child care responsibilities; and (b) *other environmental/situational variables,* such as insurance coverage, geographic proximity to treatment, and types of treatment services available. Individual predisposing factors such as gender and racial/ethnic group affect social enabling characteristics, for example, social support patterns and insurance coverage, that in turn influence treatment utilization patterns.

DIFFERENCES BETWEEN WOMEN AND MEN ALCOHOLICS

The question of whether women have special circumstances that must be considered when developing appropriate treatment services is at present unanswered and controversial. There are some who believe that feminist therapy is the solution (e.g., Bekpo, 1991) that will prove most effective in treating addicted women and enticing them to enter and remain in treatment. There are others who deny the need for separate treatment for women or outreach techniques focused toward women's needs. The reality is that scant research addresses such issues. This is as equally true now as it was in 1984, when Vannicelli noted that methodologically sound research had not yet compared the relative effectiveness of various treatment techniques for women or compared specific techniques for women and men. We know little about gender differences in treatment entry, but what we do know suggests that the costs associated with treatment entry, social support for help seeking, and environmental/situational obstacles vary by gender, *at least for whites.*

Costs of Entering Treatment

Research suggests that white women perceive more costs associated with treatment entry than do white men (Beckman, 1984; Beckman & Amaro, 1986). In one sample of alcoholics undergoing treatment, almost half of the women but only 28% of the men reported a cost associated with entering treatment. The types of perceived costs that women generally reported were social and interpersonal. Women in this sample were more likely to report experiencing family problems and problems involving friends than were men. The costs included disruptions in family relations, feelings of loneliness and discomfort, lack of financial resources, loss of employment, avoidance by friends and co-workers, loss of friends, and anger of spouse (Beckman, 1984). Sometimes a drinking spouse or live-in boyfriend objected to the woman's sobriety.

These findings are congruent with many of the self-in-relationship theories of female identity development that suggest a greater emphasis on connection and social relationships for women than for men (Chodorow, 1978; Miller, 1984). It is interesting to speculate about the effects of women's greater attention to connection rather than dominance in relationships. Do women *perceive* greater costs associated with treatment entry on their relationships than men do, that is, are they are more sensitive to indicators of disruption or conflict in relationships, or are women's relationships *actually* more severely disrupted by entry into alcohol treatment?

Social Support and Treatment Entry

Social networks have been shown to influence help-seeking behavior (Birkel & Reppucci, 1983; McKinlay, 1972). Research suggests that the family and friends of white women alcoholics are more likely to oppose their entry into treatment than are the families and friends of white men alcoholics (Beckman, 1984; Beckman, & Amaro, 1986). Approximately one-quarter of women in this sample reported such opposition, whereas opposition to treatment was extremely rare for men alcoholics. Different members of one's social network also may recommend treatment for each gender. Although there were no differences in overall support for entering treatment (about 70% of both groups reported that someone such as a family member, friend, coworker, health professional, or employer urged or helped them to enter treatment), encouragement for treatment entry came from somewhat different sources. Parents and children were more likely to encourage treatment for women, whereas spouses were more likely to encourage treatment for men.

Situational/Environmental Factors

Other important factors likely to influence treatment entry are insurance coverage, employment status, and the appropriateness of services provided. Research has shown that insurance coverage affects continuation in treatment (Beckman & Bardsley, 1986). Women with drinking problems are less likely to be employed (Beckman & Amaro, 1986) than men alcoholics. Subsequently, they may be less likely to have insurance coverage for alcoholism treatment. Beckman and Kocel (1982) found that women alcoholics more frequently use treatment agencies that hire more professionals, have more women on their treatment staff, provide treatment for children, and provide after-care services. It is hypothesized that the availability of specific types of treatment services, such as residential treatment with live-in facilities for children, will increase women's utilization of alcoholism treatment services.

RACIAL/ETHNIC GROUP AND TREATMENT ENTRY

Culture is an important variable in help seeking for many types of mental health problems. Prior research has shown that some cultural groups are more likely to utilize services than others (Clark & Midanik, 1981). However, there is little research focusing on women of color who abuse alcohol and other drugs. As yet we do not know if findings of gender differences among white alcoholics also apply to people of color. Members of a racial/ethnic group may view alcoholism and define appropriate treatments differently than do Anglo men and women. For instance, Brisbane and Wells (1989) suggest that African Americans are more likely to view the alcoholic as "crazy," have negative responses to the disease concept of alcoholism, and believe that an alcoholic's treatment should involve some form of punishment. In the African-American community, the church appears very important in the treatment of women's alcohol problems. Rather than seek advice or treatment from mental health professionals, many African-American women alcoholics seek sobriety through their relationship with God and the African-American church (Brisbane & Wells, 1989).

Despite lack of gender comparisons in ethnic samples, there is valuable research focusing on African-American women. One study compares a small sample of African-American and white women, and another examines subgroups of African-American women. Differences between African-American and white women entering alcoholism treatment were found in access to alcoholism insurance, contact with important others, and degree of opposition to treatment from others (Amaro, Beckman, & Mays, 1987).

Social/Interpersonal Variables

The two interpersonal variables that best discriminate between African-American and white women are frequency of contact with important others and degree of opposition/support from others. In general, African-American women have more social support and more close friends than white women. When income and age differences are controlled, they have more frequent social contact with important others than do white women. There are no differences in the costs of entering treatment for women in the two ethnic groups, but African Americans report more support for treatment entry from family members or friends (68% versus 49%) and less overall opposition to seeking treatment (8% versus 25%). These findings conflict with the view (Brisbane & Wells, 1989) that many African-American alcoholics may have families that hold hostile attitudes about alcoholism treatment because of their beliefs about the nature of alcoholism itself.

Situational/Environmental Variables

African-American women have lower incomes and much less access to insurance coverage for alcoholism treatment than white women. They also are younger and have more children under the age of 18 living at home. Thus they are likely to have greater financial needs, although they have less income. The situational variable that most clearly discriminates between the two groups is insurance coverage for alcoholism—10 times as many whites as African-American women reported such coverage.

Other Enabling Factors

It is noteworthy that when age and income are controlled, African-American women attribute greater importance to the role of health care providers in the maintenance of their health than do white women. They also perceive fewer negative consequences of drinking and have both higher social isolation and higher self-esteem than do white women (Amaro et al., 1987). They also are more likely to be poly-substance abusers (Beckman, 1984).

Sexual Preference

A second study sampled 70 African-American women in alcoholism treatment facilities in Los Angeles county (Mays et al., 1993). The major variables examined were emotional and tangible social support for seeking help for one's alcoholism. Emotional support was defined as "feeling helped, cared for or understood in attempts to get treatment for one's alcohol problems." The sample differed from many earlier samples of African-American women alcoholics in that it was younger and relatively well educated (the median level of education was "some college"). Over 70% of the women indicated use of drugs other than alcohol, and 36% were lesbians or bisexuals. Overall the women reported relatively high levels of support for treatment entry.

There were no significant differences in social support by relationship status (married or living with someone versus other) or age. On the other hand, clear differences in sources of social support emerged based on sexual preference. Although quality of support did not differ, heterosexual women perceived more sources of and a greater amount of family (as traditionally defined), casual (acquaintance), and male support and more total support than did lesbian and bisexual African-American women. This study emphasizes the important caveat that there are many background characteristics that define culture, not only racial/ethnic group. Even within a particular gender and racial ethnic group, there are characteristics, such as sexual preference and social class status, that may lead to important lifestyle variations and varying levels of social support from family of origin. Sexual preference is one of many variables that influences the sources, levels, and types of support for treatment seeking that women experience. All these variables need to be considered by those providing treatment services to alcoholics and poly-substance abusers.

IMPLICATIONS FOR CLINICIANS

On one hand, it is dangerous to extrapolate from the limited data presented, and many caveats should be applied. On the other, it is essential to use the knowledge that does exist. Failure to do so results in the perpetuation of stereotypes, assumptions, and suppositions about alcoholic women that most likely are unwarranted, untrue, and unsupportive of women's needs. Therefore I will discuss the implications that reasonably can be drawn from my research and that of others.

The Definition of Family

The term *family* must be broadly defined if we are to adequately consider cultural variations that affect entry and continuation in treatment. For instance, African-American women may have larger extended families that are important sources of emotional and tangible support, and lesbian/bisexual women may have replaced more traditional definitions of family, such as spouse and family of origin, with a different concept of family that better suits them (for instance, female partner and close friends who share a lesbian lifestyle). The client's definition of family is of utmost importance, and it is her support network, however self-defined, that must be engaged in the treatment process.

Outreach to Family and Friends

However social support network is defined by the alcoholic woman, these persons must be considered when developing outreach programs and engaging the alcoholic woman in treatment. If these persons oppose treatment, the woman is more likely not to enter or to abandon treatment quickly. Therefore programs to educate a broad range of persons considered as family and to involve them in the treatment process are important. Moreover, the greater disruption in relationship with family and friends found for white women versus white men suggests that these costs must be acknowledged and dealt with early in the women's treatment.

Family/Friend Opposition to Treatment

Findings suggest that clinicians must take into account differences in the situational circumstances of women and men alcohol abusers and carefully evaluate attitudes toward treatment held by various members of a person's social network. My work largely has been limited to those who have entered treatment. Even lower support for treatment entry probably occurs for women with similar levels of alcohol problems who are not in treatment. When a woman seeks and secures help, family or friend opposition to treatment does not cease. Such opposition may cause her to quickly abandon treatment. If the opposition of significant others is recognized, it can be considered in developing a treatment plan. The importance of an adequate case history that includes information on culturally relevant factors and all significant sources of social support is underscored.

Racial/Ethnic Differences In Treatment

Women from different racial/ethnic or sexual preference groups experience different levels of social support or opposition for alcoholism treatment. Although others suggest that African-American women may be less likely to seek treatment (King, 1985) and it may be difficult to involve African-American families in the treatment process (Brisbane & Wells, 1989), our data show that African-American women who enter treatment may have stronger support than Anglo women. The more extensive social networks, more frequent social contacts, and greater support for treatment suggest the importance of integrating persons close to the African-American women into treatment and of providing education to further strengthen the support African-American women receive for maintaining sobriety. Sources of support must be further educated about alcoholism and its treatment and how to cope with and support an alcoholic. Residential programs should be designed so that families are able to visit the alcoholic women and attend educational programs and, if appropriate, family therapy sessions at convenient times.

Other differences between African-American and white women suggest variation in the importance and timing of certain issues for women of these two ethnic groups. The often mentioned low self-esteem of alcoholic women may not apply as strongly to African-American alcoholic women. Yet African-American women alcoholics may experience a sense of social isolation, in part due to African Americans' marginal and oppressed status in American society for 200 years.

Environmental/Situational Influences

Women of different cultural groups in the United States do not have equal access to alcoholism services. In part, this occurs because treatment services have not been sensitive to the needs of various groups; in addition, it is due to environmental conditions—to a lack of economic resources that limit access. Sensitivity to the needs of different cultural groups requires a treatment staff that is culturally knowledgeable about and, whenever possible, representative of those cultural groups. Unfortunately, ethnic minorities are underrepresented among mental health professionals. Both knowledge and cultural sensitivity are necessary if the outreach and services provided are to meet the needs of culturally diverse groups of women.

Among the service delivery characteristics that may limit treatment access for minority women are the financial costs of treatment, indirect opportunity costs, a lack of linguistically and culturally relevant services, a lower proportion of professionals in treatment centers available to ethnic women, and a lack of child care (Amaro, 1993; Beckman & Kocel, 1982). Characteristics more typical of ethnic than Anglo women may interact with the delivery system to limit treatment access. For instance, lack of child care is a problem for women, but this lack may be a more serious obstacle for African-American than white women because African-American women are more likely to have young children living at home.

Certain racial/ethnic groups may be less likely to enter inpatient therapy because of strong beliefs that it is improper to leave children in the care of others even for a limited time period. Yet few treatment services provide residential facilities for children. Another example might be that visiting hours or family therapy are primarily scheduled only during usual working hours (9–5 Monday through Friday), but members of some ethnic groups are unlikely to have the flexible work schedules that allow them to visit or attend therapy during these hours.

The environmental conditions that clearly result in unequal access to treatment are disturbing. Some people are privileged relative to others in our society. Males are privileged compared to females, and whites are privileged compared to people of color (McIntosh, 1988). Whereas the characteristics of individual treatment programs presumably can be changed by concerned providers, the environmental factors that limit treatment access are much more resistant to such change. Prime among these is unequal access to services because of socioeconomic conditions and access to insurance coverage. Mental health professionals have an ethical obligation to try to change this situation—to equalize access to treatment by improving the free and low-cost services offered and by providing universal insurance coverage for alcoholism and drug abuse treatment. All types of Americans, men and women, African-American and white, heterosexual and homosexual, rich and poor, are afflicted by substance abuse problems, and all should have a wide range of options available to deal with these problems. Such a range of options also necessitates a better knowledge of what works and for whom it works so that women can be matched with the treatment that is likely to be most beneficial for them.

In summary, barriers to treatment for women, particularly for ethnic women, arise primarily because of characteristics of the alcoholism service delivery system and the unequal access to power and resources for ethnic minorities. Women also may be limited by the greater opposition and enhanced costs of treatment seeking and treatment entry that they experience compared to men.

REFERENCES

Aday, L., & Andersen, R. (1974). A framework for the study of access to medical care. *Health Services Research, 9,* 208–220.

Amaro, H. (1993). *Women's health research.* Testimony presented before the U.S. Senate Committee on Labor and Human Resources. Boston: Boston University Medical Center.

Amaro, H., Beckman, L. J., & Mays, V. (1987). A comparison of black and white women entering alcoholism treatment. *Journal of Studies on Alcohol, 48,* 220–228.

Beckman, L. J. (1984). Analysis of the suitability of alcohol treatment resources for women. *Substance and Alcohol Actions/Misuse, 5,* 21–27.

Beckman, L. J., & Amaro, H. (1986). Personal and social difficulties faced by women and men entering alcoholism treatment. *Journal of Studies on Alcohol, 47*(2), 135–145.

Beckman, L. J., & Bardsley, P. B. (1986). Individual characteristics, gender differences and dropout from alcoholism treatment. *Alcohol and Alcoholism, 21,* 213–224.

Beckman, L. J., & Kocel, K. M. (1982). The treatment-delivery system and alcohol abuse in women: Social policy implications. *Journal of Social Issues, 38*(2), 139–151.

Bepko, C. (1991). *Feminism and addiction.* New York: Haworth.

Birkel, R. C., & Reppucci, N. D. (1983). Social networks, information-seeking, and utilization of services. *American Journal of Community Psychology, 11,* 185–205.

Brisbane, F. L., & Wells, R. C. (1989). In T. D. Watts & R. Wright, Jr. (Eds.), *Alcoholism in minority populations.* Springfield, IL: C. Thomas.

Chodorow, N. (1978). *The reproduction of mothering.* Berkeley: University of California Press.

Clark, W., & Midanik, L. (1981). Alcohol use and alcohol problems among U.S. adults: Results of the 1979 survey. In W. Clark, L. Midanik, & G. Knupfer (Eds.), *Report of the 1979 National Survey.* Berkeley: Alcohol Research Group.

Ferrence, R. G., & Whitehead, P. C. (1980). Sex differences in psychoactive drug use: Recent epidemiology. In O. J. Kalant (Ed.), *Research advances in alcohol and drug problems: Vol. 5. Alcohol and drug problems in women.* New York: Plenum.

King, S. W. (1985). Black females and alcoholism: Prevention strategies. In R. Wright, Jr., & T. D. Watts (Eds.), *Prevention of black alcoholism.* Springfield, IL: C. Thomas.

Mays, V., Beckman, L. J., Oranchak, E., & Harper, B. (1993). *Characteristics of social support in the help-seeking behaviors of black heterosexual and homosexual women alcoholics.* Unpublished manuscript.

McIntosh, P. (1988). *White privilege and male privilege.* Unpublished manuscript. Wellesley College.

McKinlay , J.B. (1974). Social networks, lay consultation and help-seeking behavior. *Social Forces, 9,* 275–292.

Miller, J. B. (1984). *Toward a new psychology of women* (2nd ed.). Boston: Beacon.

Mulford, H. A. (1977). Women and men problem drinkers: Sex differences in patients served by Iowa's community alcoholism centers. *Journal of Studies on Alcohol, 38*, 1624–1639.

Vannicelli, M. (1984). Treatment outcome of alcoholic women: The state of the art in relation to sex bias and expectancy effects. In S. C. Wilsnack & L. J. Beckman (Eds.), *Alcohol problems in women: Antecedents, consequences and intervention* (pp. 369–412). New York: Guilford.

Part VI

Additional Resources

Recent Books about Treatment

Berg, I. K., & Miller, S. D. (1992). *Working with the problem drinker: A solution-focused approach*. New York: Norton.

The solution-focused approach, which was pioneered at the Brief Family Therapy Center in Milwaukee, is applied here for the first time to alcohol-related issues. The solution-focused model attempts to help the individual find his or her unique solution. Clients work toward achieving well-formed treatment goals based, in part, on identifying what works and doing more of it.

Bireda, M. R. (1990). *Love addiction: A guide to emotional independence.* Oakland, CA: New Harbinger.

Bireda identifies "love addiction" as a learned response and suggests a number of cognitive-behavioral strategies for overcoming the problem. The book, which includes inventories, step-by-step procedures, and practical exercises, is suitable for use as a self-help volume.

Chiauzzi, E. J. (1991). *Preventing relapse in the addictions: A biopsychosocial approach*. New York: Pergamon.

After reviewing several models of relapse, Chiauzzi introduces the biopsychosocial model, which takes into account biological, psychological, and social risk factors. The model is used as the basis for Chiauzzi's discussions of techniques for assessing and preventing relapses. Practical materials for use with clients are included as appendixes.

Donovan, D. M., & Marlatt, G. A. (Eds.). (1988). *Assessment of addictive behaviors*. New York: Guilford.

After introducing the biopsychosocial model for understanding addictions, the editors provide detailed information concerning the assessment of a variety of addictive behaviors. Behavioral, physiological, and cognitive assessments are among the methods describing for examining alcohol use. Other chapters describe assessment strategies for eating disorders, cannabis abuse, cocaine abuse, and heroin addiction.

Hsu, L. K. G. (1990). *Eating disorders*. New York: Guilford.

This book begins with a conceptualization of eating disorders, with Hsu highlighting the differences between "normal dieting" and eating disorders and between anorexia nervosa and bulimia nervosa. The pros and cons of a number of alternative treatment methods are presented. Among the treatments discussed are cognitive-behavioral approaches, nutritional treatments, individual psychotherapy, group therapy, support groups, psychoeducational treatments, and pharmacotherapy.

Institute of Medicine (1990). *Broadening the base of treatment for alcohol problems: Report of a study by a committee of the Institute of Medicine.* Washington, DC: National Academy Press.

This important publication represents the outcome of an Institute of Medicine study of alcoholism treatment. The committee asked such basic questions as the following: What is being treated? What is treatment? Who provides treatment? Does treatment work? Is treatment necessary? Is treatment available? Who pays for treatment? The committee's final recommendations involve the creation of systematic mechanisms that would allow people with mild or moderate problems to be treated through brief interventions by nonspecialized community agencies. People with more severe problems would be matched with appropriate specialized interventions after completion of a comprehensive assessment process.

Institute of Medicine (1990). *Treating drug problems.* Washington, DC: National Academy Press.

This book provides the results of the institute's study of the evolution, effectiveness, and financing of public and private drug treatment systems. The committee that carried out the study examined the goals and effectiveness of treatment and also reviewed financing structures. Among the specific treatment strategies reviewed were methadone maintenance, therapeutic communities, outpatient nonmethadone treatment, chemical dependency programs, detoxification, and correctional treatment.

Khantzian, E. J., Halliday, K. S., & McAuliffe, W. E. (1990). *Addiction and the vulnerable self: Modified dynamic group therapy for substance abusers.* New York: Guilford.

Khantzian, Halliday, and McAuliffe present a detailed description of the group therapy they developed for use with cocaine-addicted clients. Their approach represents a modification of dynamic group therapy adapted to address the "psychological vulnerability" of drug users. Supportive and expressive group experiences are used to place focus on affect, self-esteem, relationship, and self-care problems.

L'Abate, L., Farrar, J. E., & Serritella, D. A. (Eds.). (1992). *Handbook of differential treatments for addictions.* Boston: Allyn & Bacon.

L'Abate and his coeditors offer a broad view of the therapeutic issues involved in addictions. Chapters address "socially destructive addictions," including alcohol and drug abuse, tobacco addiction, domestic violence, and sexual abuses; "socially unacceptable addictions," including interpersonal and love relationships and eating disorders; and "socially acceptable addictions," including gambling, workaholism, excessive exercise, excessive spending, religious fanaticism, and codependence. Focus is placed on prevention as well as treatment.

Lewis, J. A., Dana, R. Q., & Blevins, G. A. (1993). *Substance abuse counseling: An individualized approach (2nd ed.)*. Pacific Grove, CA: Brooks/Cole.

This book, which was first published in 1988, emphasizes approaches that meet the varying needs of individual clients. The authors suggest that counseling should proceed on the basis of treatment plans that are individualized, multidimensional, and based on careful assessment. The second edition expands on the first by providing new case examples as well as expanded sections on family counseling and group work.

Marlatt, G. A., & Gordon, J. R. (1985). *Relapse prevention: Maintenance strategies in the treatment of addictive behaviors*. New York: Guilford.

This frequently cited classic presents the results of years of research on relapse and its prevention. The Marlatt and Gordon model is applied to a number of addictive behaviors, including alcohol and drug abuse, eating disorders, smoking, and compulsive gambling. The book combines creative theoretical work with practical applications.

McAuliffe, W. E., & Albert, J. (1992). *Clean start: An outpatient program for initiating cocaine recovery*. New York: Guilford.

"Clean Start" is a program offered at the Harvard Cocaine Recovery Project. This book describes the program, first discussing the rationale and design of the program and then reviewing the content of the program's group and individual sessions. Copies of client handouts are also included.

McGurrin, M. C. (1992). *Pathological gambling: Conceptual, diagnostic, and treatment issues*. Sarasota, FL: Professional Resource Press.

McGurrin presents an overview of the history and epidemiology of pathological gambling before addressing the specifics of treatment. His discussion of the treatment needs of pathological gamblers focuses both on theoretical issues and on practical intervention strategies. Several case studies are included.

Milkman, H. B., & Sederer, L. I. (Eds.). (1991). *Treatment choices for alcoholism and substance abuse*. Indianapolis, IN: Lexington.

This book brings together chapters addressing a number of issues related to treatment. Among the topics addressed are biological factors affecting substance abuse, methods for prevention and early intervention, and ways to work with multiproblem patients. A number of treatment alternatives are discussed.

Miller, W. R., & Rollnick, S. (1991). *Motivational interviewing: Preparing people to change addictive behavior*. New York: Guilford.

Motivational interviewing provides an important alternative to the direct "confrontation-of-denial" that is often assumed to be appropriate for substance-abusing clients. In this book, Miller and Rollnick describe an approach that is characterized by a deemphasis on labels and an emphasis on the client's personal choice and responsibility. When motivational interviewing is used, treatment goals and strategies are negotiated between the client and the therapist. A number of additional authors describe the application of this model in various settings.

Monti, P. M., Abrams, D. B., Kadden, R. M., & Cooney, N. L. (1989). *Treating alcohol dependence: A coping skills training guide*. New York: Guilford.

Monti and his colleagues report on their use of coping skills training for the treatment of alcohol problems. The authors describe in detail their methods for enhancing clients' interpersonal and intrapersonal skills. Each skill-training session, as recounted in the book, includes skill guidelines, modeling, behavior rehearsal role plays, and practice exercises.

Moos, R. H., Finney, J. W., & Cronkite, R. C. (1990). *Alcoholism treatment: Context, process, and outcome*. New York: Oxford University Press.

The authors of this book have developed an expanded view of alcoholism treatment and evaluative research. Moos and his colleagues recognize that treatment outcomes are affected by a variety of factors, including the client's life context prior to treatment, the client's pretreatment level of functioning, the components of the treatment program, and the client's life context after treatment. This book is unique in its attention to the effects of stress and contextual factors on the formation and resolution of alcohol problems.

Shaffer, H. J., & Jones, S. B. (1989). *Quitting cocaine: The struggle against impulse*. Indianapolis, IN: Lexington.

Shaffer and Jones use a number of examples to shed light on the processes through which people addicted to cocaine have achieved abstinence on their own. The authors begin by discussing addiction and its manifestation in cocaine use, going on to describe the natural recovery process, from using to quitting to "staying quit."

Shaffer, H. J., Stein, S., Gambino, B., & Cummings, T. M. (1990). *Compulsive gambling: Theory, research, and practice*. Indianapolis, IN: Lexington Books.

In this book, Shaffer and his coauthors explore the problem of pathological gambling from a number of perspectives. Sections of the book are devoted to theories of compulsive gambling, models of treatment, public policy implications, and current research.

Straussner, S. L. A. (Ed.). (1992). *Clinical work with substance-abusing clients.* New York: Guilford.

A number of clinicians contributed to this overview of approaches for working with substance abuse clients and their families. The authors discuss assessment and treatment methods used with a variety of clients in a number of treatment settings.

Vannicelli, M. (1992). *Removing the roadblocks: Group psychotherapy with substance abusers and family members.* New York: Guilford.

Vanicelli uses dynamically oriented group psychotherapy to help substance abusers and their family members. In addition to discussing the rationale and procedures for her groups, Vanicelli provides specific examples of strategies for working with substance-abuse-affected populations. Identifying a number of "roadblocks" that need to be removed before effective help can be given and received, the author suggests techniques for removing roadblocks in the group, within the individual patient, and within the therapist.

Washton, A. M. (1989). *Cocaine addiction: Treatment, recovery, and relapse prevention.* New York: Norton.

Washton's years of experience in the outpatient treatment of cocaine addiction make this book an important contribution to the literature. The author discusses the issues and strategies relevant to four stages of treatment: stabilization and crisis intervention, early abstinence, relapse prevention, and advanced recovery. He suggests that a structured program, preferably provided on an outpatient basis, should include family involvement, urine testing, group and individual therapy, self-help groups, alternative activities, and appropriate nutritional and medical care.

Recent Books about Families and Addictions

Collins, R. L., Leonard, K. E., & Searles, J. S. (Eds.). (1990). *Alcohol and the family: Research and clinical perspectives.* New York: Guilford.

This book presents a multidisciplinary approach to the study of alcohol-affected families. Several contributions discuss the role of genetics, with one chapter discussing the contribution of genetic factors to alcoholism and another spelling out the biological markers for vulnerability to alcoholism. A section on family processes includes consideration of the mutual effects of alcohol and family functioning on adolescent drinking patterns, marital relationships, and general family processes. A section on family-oriented treatment perspectives includes discussions of behavioral and systems perspectives, the stress-and-coping perspective, and other approaches.

Friedman, A. S., & Granick, S. (1990). *Family therapy for adolescent drug abuse.* Indianapolis, IN: Lexington.

Friedman and Granick begin with an overview of the interactions between adolescent substance abuse and family life. The second section of their book moves from theory into practice. Verbatim transcripts of family therapy sessions are followed by critiques based on varying points of view.

Schlesinger, S. E., & Horberg, L. K. (1988). *Taking charge: How families can climb out of the chaos of addiction.* New York: Simon & Schuster.

Schlesinger and Horberg provide a step-by-step model that families affected by addictions can use to address issues and move in the direction of health. The authors suggest that the "journey" of recovery takes families from exasperation through effort and, finally, to empowerment. Clients are helped to move through this process by asking themselves what kinds of experiences they want, what choices or actions they would admire in themselves, and what strengths and feelings they bring to the situation.

Todd, T. C., & Selekman, M. D. (Eds.). (1991). *Family therapy approaches with adolescent substance abusers.* Boston: Allyn & Bacon.

Included in this book are a myriad of innovative ideas for working with the families of substance-abusing adolescents. A number of theoretical approaches have been adapted for use with this population. Among the family therapy models discussed here are the Purdue Brief Family Therapy Model, contextual family therapy, solution-focused therapy, systems therapies, strategic therapy, and network therapy. Each of these approaches is described by an experienced clinician, resulting in a good blend of theory and examples.

Woodside, D. B., & Shekter-Wolfson, L. (Eds.). (1991). *Family approaches in the treatment of eating disorders*. Washington, DC: American Psychiatric Press. The authors suggest that because multiple factors affect anorexia nervosa and bulimia nervosa, multifaceted treatments are needed. It has long been recognized that family dynamics affect and are affected by eating disorders, making family interventions especially important. This book describes several specific programs, including outpatient family therapy for bulimia, family therapy of early-onset anorexia, family treatment in a day hospital, a family relationships group, and a mutual support group for families. The book also addresses specific issues, such as methods for overcoming impasses in family treatment.

Recent Books about Meeting the Needs of Specific Populations

Argeriou, M., & McCarty, D. (1990). *Treating alcoholism and drug abuse among homeless men and women: Nine community demonstration grants.* Binghamton, NY: Haworth.

Also published as Volume 7, Number 1, of the *Alcoholism Treatment Quarterly*, this monograph describes nine approaches for working with homeless individuals. Included among the projects described are a program for homeless and mentally ill substance abusers, a strategy for transitional housing and employment, an outreach effort for homeless women, a treatment program for homeless women and their preschool children, and several comprehensive programs designed for this special population.

Bell, P. (1990). *Chemical dependency and the African-American.* Center City, MN: Hazelden.

Bell emphasizes the importance of recognizing the cultural factors affecting addictions, pointing out that adherents of the disease theory must find ways to bring racial and cultural issues into treatment. His overview of the impact of substance abuse on the black community includes discussions of health problems, crime, family stability, employment, and education. The author suggests that important roles can be played by the church, civil rights organizations, and human service organizations in the African-American community. Within specialized chemical dependency treatment, race and culture need to be discussed and addressed.

Heinemann, A. (Ed.). (1993). *Substance abuse and physical disability.* Binghamton, NY: Haworth.

This book provides a rare overview of the dual problem of substance abuse and physical disability. Substance abuse can act both as a contributing factor to disabling injuries and as a special threat to the health of the physically disabled. Authors with expertise in working with affected clients discuss here such issues as the consequences of substance abuse following spinal cord injury, the relevance of prescription medication in pain management and rehabilitation, and the importance of matching clients with treatment. Controversies regarding chemical dependence treatment for persons with physical disabilities are also addressed.

Lawson, G. W., & Lawson, A. W. (Eds.). (1992). *Adolescent substance abuse: Etiology, treatment, and prevention.* Gaithersburg, MD: Aspen.

This book uses a broad, multidisciplinary perspective to examine the phenomenon of adolescent substance abuse. The first chapter lays the groundwork for this exploration by placing drug use in the adolescent developmental context and by introducing the biological, psychological, and sociological factors affecting this behavior. Subsequent chapters discuss the implications of varying theories for etiology, treatment, and prevention.

Schinke, S. P., Botvin, G. J., & Orlandi, M. A. (1991). *Substance abuse in children and adolescents: Evaluation and intervention.* Newbury Park, CA: Sage.

This book presents a useful overview of the alternatives for preventing substance abuse among adolescents. The authors contrast traditional approaches with more promising current strategies such as resistance-skills training, social-skills training, and community-based approaches. Research findings and evaluation methods are discussed.

Shernoff, M. (Ed.). (1992). *Counseling chemically dependent people with HIV illness.* Binghamton, NY: Haworth.

Shernoff has brought together a number of readings that describe practical approaches for working with HIV-affected clients. The monograph, which was also published as Volume 4, Number 2, of the *Journal of Chemical Dependency Treatment*, reviews what substance abuse specialists need to know about HIV illness. In addition, authors describe approaches for working with specific groups, including HIV-positive adolescents; HIV-infected clients in inpatient, methadone maintenance, residential, and criminal justice settings; and HIV-infected Native Americans. Both prevention and treatment are discussed.

Weinstein, D. L. (Ed.). (1993). *Lesbians and gay men: Chemical dependency treatment issues.* Binghamton, NY: Haworth.

This monograph was published simultaneously as Volume 5, Number 1, of the *Journal of Chemical Dependency Treatment*. The authors provide concrete information concerning the treatment needs of gay and lesbian clients with substance abuse problems. Among the issues discussed are the effects of homophobia, the experiences of gay men in Alcoholics Anonymous, the effects of alcoholic families, and the applications of family therapy concepts for this population.

Recent Books about Prevention

Goldstein, A. P., Reagles, K. W., & Amann, L. L. (1990). *Refusal skills: Preventing drug use in adolescents.* Champaign, IL: Research Press.

> The authors provide a fine overview of the role of refusal skills in substance abuse prevention. The refusal skills curriculum they describe is used in the context of a more general "skillstreaming" approach for adolescents. Here, they identify 20 core refusal skills and describe the training procedures they use to build these skills. The procedures used to teach each skill include modeling, role playing, performance feedback, and transfer training.

Lorion, R. P., & Ross, J. G. (1992). *Programs for change: Office for Substance Abuse Prevention demonstration models.* Special issue, *Journal of Community Psychology.*

> This publication describes eight of the 130 demonstration programs funded during the first cycle of of OSAP's high-risk youth initiative. The editors state that the interventions described here point up the importance of targeting combinations of risk factors and, at the same time, demonstrate the complications in delivering and evaluating preventive programs. The projects described here include the following: (a) The SUPER II Program (an early intervention program), (b) an after-school program for latchkey children, (c) a prevention program for kindergarten-aged children and their mothers, (d) CODA (a creative therapy program for children in substance-abuse-affected families), (e) a psycho-educational intervention for children of substance abusers, (f) a collaborative effort focused on juvenile delinquents, (g) a program for adolescent substance abusers, and (h) a project for Boys' and Girls' Clubs in public housing developments. Research findings are presented for each program.

Rhodes, J. E., & Jason, L. A. (1988). *Preventing substance abuse among children and adolescents.* New York: Pergamon.

> The authors review psychosocial and social stress models of substance abuse and describe the impact of these theories on prevention. This book also provides concrete descriptions of preventive interventions, as well as a set of prevention program guidelines. Several exemplary programs are described.

Recent Books about Pharmacology and Addiction

Erickson, C. K., Javors, M. A., Morgan, W. W. & Stimmel, B. (Eds.). *Addiction potential of abused drugs and drug classes*. Binghamton, NY: Haworth.

After discussing the concept of addiction and distinguishing it from abuse in the opening chapter, the authors of the remaining nine chapters discuss the addiction potential of separate drugs or drug classes. Each chapter is written by a different author and focuses on pharmacological, physiological, and biological research findings, with some discussion of the social implications of this research also included.

Hamilton, L. W., & Timmons, C. R. (1990). *Principles of behavioral pharmacology*. Englewood Cliffs, NJ: Prentice Hall.

This book focuses on various classes of behavior and then discusses how different drugs affect each of the categories described. The classes of behaviors include the following: specific fears and vague anxieties; pain and other stressors; depression; schizophrenia; arousal; and tolerance, drug abuse, and habitual behavior.

Jacobs, M. R., & Fehr, K. O. (1987). *Drugs and drug abuse: A reference text* (2nd ed.). Toronto: Addiction Research Foundation.

This is an encyclopedic handbook of abused drugs that is a classic reference text. Section 1 provides a general overview of biopsychosocial aspects of drug use. Section 2 focuses on five major classes of drugs: depressants, hallucinogens, mood modifiers, narcotic analgesics, and stimulants. Section 3 provides a synopsis of major abused drugs (e.g., cocaine). Section 4 summarizes many of the less frequently encountered substances (e.g., trimethoxyamphetamine), and Section 5 very briefly identifies some addictional drugs. Section 6 provides information on trade names, medical/scientific terms, and street drug language.

Schuckit, M. A. (1989). *Drug and alcohol abuse: A clinical guide to diagnosis and treatment* (3rd ed.). New York: Plenum.

Developed as part of a series for psychiatric residents and clinicians, this book offers a unique scheme for classifying adverse reactions to drugs. The classification scheme involves panic reactions, flashbacks, toxic reactions, psychosis, organic brain syndrome, and withdrawal or abstinence syndrome.

387

United States Department of Health and Human Services (1991). *Drug abuse and drug abuse research: The third triennial report to Congress*. Rockville, MD: United States Government Printing Office.

This report from the Secretary of Health and Human Services is mandated by federal law. Each report attempts to summarize biological and social research on illegal and legal drugs. The purpose of the reports is to lay the groundwork for improving prevention and treatment efforts.

United States Department of Health and Human Services (1990). *Seventh special report to the U.S. Congress on alcohol and health*. Rockville, MD: U.S. Government Printing Office.

This report focuses on alcohol abuse and alcoholism research since 1987. It addresses etiology, epidemiology, genetics, neuroscience, medical consequences, fetal effects, social consequence, diagnosis and assessment, prevention, intervention, and treatment of alcohol abuse and alcoholism.

Winger, G., Hofmann, F. G., & Woods, J. H. (1992). *A handbook on drug and alcohol abuse: The biomedical aspects* (3rd ed.). New York: Oxford University Press.

Since its introduction in 1975, this has become a standard and often-cited text on the pharmacology of abused substances. Typically, patterns of use, effects, mechanisms of action, and pharmacokinetics of the drugs are discussed. The chapters on "The Medical Diagnosis of Drug Abuse" and "Management of Selected Clinical Problems: Pharmacologic Aspects" may be particularly helpful to clinicians.

Index